Praise for

GUNSLINGER

"Jeff Pearlman's deeply reported book is an unprecedented picture of an unprecedented athlete. Brett Favre emerges as at once incorrigibly childish and a magnetic leader of men. Perhaps never in sports history has a star so big inhabited a market so small. *Gunslinger* leaves an impression of Favre that is neither simply good nor bad, but rather something nearly nonexistent in sportswriting today: a full portrait of a human being." **—David Epstein, author of *The Sports Gene***

"Terrific . . . It's not only a page-turner, but it's built on a foundation of solid journalism by an author who has a background as a newspaper reporter . . . Many [stories] are new and draw back the curtain on Favre's life in a way that hadn't been done."

—Gary D'Amato, *Milwaukee Journal Sentinel*

"Here's a story as iconic as 'The Gunslinger' himself, Brett Favre. Like Favre, Jeff Pearlman goes deep—and scores."

—Adam Schefter, coauthor of
Romo: My Life on the Edge* and *Think Like a Champion

"Jeff Pearlman writing about Brett Favre is a perfect match of author and subject, making *Gunslinger* as rollicking and raucous and joyous as Favre was improvising at Lambeau Field."

—David Maraniss, author of
When Pride Still Mattered* and *Once in a Great City

"What does *Gunslinger* offer the Wisconsinite who has read a gazillion words about Favre over the past decades? A perspective outside the Packerland bubble, for one. He also delivers detailed reporting on aspects of Favre's life that we tend to dismiss in a line of background . . . Compelling." **—Jim Higgins, *Milwaukee Journal Sentinel***

GUNSLINGER

The Remarkable, Improbable,
Iconic Life of
BRETT FAVRE

Jeff Pearlman

Mariner Books
Houghton Mifflin Harcourt
BOSTON   NEW YORK

First Mariner Books edition 2017

Copyright © 2016 by Jeff Pearlman

For information about permission to reproduce selections from this book,
write to trade.permissions@hmhco.com or to Permissions, Houghton Mifflin Harcourt
Publishing Company, 3 Park Avenue, 19th Floor, New York, New York 10016.

hmhco.com

Library of Congress Cataloging-in-Publication Data is available.
LIBRARY OF CONGRESS CONTROL NUMBER: 2016287244
ISBN 978-0-544-45437-8 (hardcover)   ISBN 978-1-328-74568-2 (pbk.)

Printed in the United States of America
DOC 10 9 8 7 6 5 4 3 2 1

To Michael J. Lewis

The Jo-Jo Townsell of writers, the Jerald Sowell of proofreaders,
the Ryan Yarborough of fathers, the Paul Frase of husbands.
And a remarkable friend.

(Moment of silence for Dennis Bligen.)

We were up north in Wisconsin, deer hunting, and we went to this bar called Hilltop. And every bar had strippers. So we walked in — seven of us — and Brett had a hat pulled on low. It's just packed inside, and all of a sudden somebody picked up that Brett Favre was in there. All these people started coming up, asking him for autographs. I was like, "You know what? He's not here to do fucking autographs. Get lost." We had our own little corner and the people just wouldn't leave us alone. So I go, "Brett, fuck it. Let's let the guy get on the fucking PA and say you're signing autographs for $50. Anyone who wants an autograph, it's $50. And he's gonna sign until all your shit is done, then leave us alone." So the guy gets on the fucking microphone — $50, Brett's signing autographs! It was all guys. No women at all — except the strippers. It wasn't a strip club, it was a normal bar. But during deer-hunting opening weekend all the bars had strippers. So Brett signs, probably, Christ, he had to sign over 100 items, easily. And you know what he did? He took the fucking money, rolled it up in a ball, and he threw it at the bartenders. Every fucking dime. Seriously. Every penny. It was the coolest thing I've ever seen, and it was total Brett Favre.

— KEVIN BURKEL,
owner, Burkel's One Block Over sports bar,
Green Bay, Wisconsin

CONTENTS

PROLOGUE

BRETT FAVRE has a Superman shield tattooed on his left biceps. He has hairy arms and crooked knees. Brett Favre is a lousy texter. His grammar is awful. He's probably the worst tipper known to humanity. It's not because he's overwhelmingly cheap. He just doesn't like carrying money.

Brett Favre is a bad dancer and an even worse basketball player. Brett Favre used to know all the words to "Rapper's Delight" — the 14-minute, 35-second version. One of his favorite lines is, "If the chicken had lips, he'd whistle." He also used to say someone was sweating "like Shaq at the line."

His favorite hat color was, for many years, red. Now it's beige. His favorite beer was Miller Lite; his favorite dip was Copenhagen. He likes eating crushed pineapple from a can. Brett Favre is mediocre with names, fantastic with nicknames. Mark Chmura was Chewey, Cary Brabham was Catfish, Patrick Ivey was Poison. For nearly a year he thought Rob Davis, the Packers long snapper, was named Ron. One day he wondered why Ron Davis never responded when he asked him a question.

"Because," a teammate told him, "you're saying the wrong fucking name."

Brett Favre is missing 30 inches of his small intestine. It's the by-product of a car accident that happened before his senior year of college, and as a result, he produces the worst-smelling gas in the history of civilization. The scent has been described as "skunk," "crushed worm," "rotten milk mixed with squid," and, best of all, "death."

Brett Favre loved LeRoy Butler, tolerated Sterling Sharpe, had little use for Aaron Rodgers. His all-time favorite coach is Mike Holmgren, his all-time least favorite coach is Brad Childress. He threw the football so insanely hard that Derrick Mayes, a Packers wide receiver, has mangled pieces of fleshy barbed wire doubling as fingers. "Can't even tell you how many he broke," Mayes said. Favre used to be able to drive a golf ball in excess of 300 yards. His short game was awful. He once went hunting and finished off a deer that refused to die by submerging Bambi's head in a pond.

These are the kinds of things a biographer knows, because when you speak with enough people (in this case, 573), you learn stuff. I can tell you every mailing address from Brett Favre's life. I can tell you what the bushes outside his Green Bay house smell like. I can tell you how he spit, what cars he drove, what he ordered to eat the first time he visited Boston. There are facts upon facts upon facts.

They are interesting.

They are intriguing.

They mean little.

There's this weird thing most of us do with celebrities. We meet them, we shake their hands, maybe we even exchange a few words — and, therefore, we presume to know them. We assign adjectives to their person-hoods based upon six minutes of interaction. *Ice Cube is a jerk. Eddie Vedder is awesome. Kate Upton is an asshole. Peyton Manning is amazing.* On and on and on, until we start to believe one can be wholly surmised in the 140-character Twitter allotment.

It's nonsense.

In many ways, a biography is a search for definition of character. You can't possibly re-create every moment, or enter the brain of a subject matter, or know precisely what someone was thinking at any particular moment. (This is something that has forever bothered me about sports media: "Joey, what was going through your mind as you dunked that basketball?" is a near-impossible question to actually answer.) What you *can* do is understand what causes a person to tick, and how he became who he ultimately became, and what he did to make the world a better, or worse, or more interesting place.

Which leads to two of my favorite Brett Favre stories . . .

First: In 2003 the Green Bay Packers hired a young coach named John Bonamego to serve as the special teams coordinator. He and his family moved down the street from the Favre household, on a cul-de-sac filled with kids who always looked for the quarterback. Bonamego's oldest son, Javi, was five, and easily impressionable.

One day Favre pulled the boy aside. "Hey, Javi, you and I are buddies, right?" he asked.

"Yes!" Javi said.

"Great," Favre said. "So there's this special hand signal, but it's just for really close buddies to use to say hello to one another. I want to teach it to you, and any time I drive by you can do it to me. How does that sound?"

"Great!" Javi said. "Just for us buddies!"

"Right," Brett said. "You have to keep it a secret, OK?"

"Yeah," Javi said. "I won't tell anyone!"

"You promise?" Favre said.

"I promise!" Javi replied.

"Perfect," Favre said. "So what you do is you hold your hand in a fist, like this, and then you just lift the middle finger so it's all alone, and . . ."

Second: When Favre was late in his time with the Packers, he learned of a Wisconsin boy named Anderson Butzine, who in February 2006 was diagnosed with ependymoma, a rare tumor of the brain and spinal cord. The quarterback wrote the child a letter, which — while cherished in the Butzine household — was merely one of hundreds of notes Favre penned to the ill and infirm. "I never saw Brett not respond to a person in need," says David Thomason, who handled much of the quarterback's fan mail. "He was amazing when it came to that."

As the years passed and his health worsened, the one thing Anderson clung to was his football hero. "By the time he was five, he was not do- ing well," said Michelle Butzine, his mother. "Anderson was bedridden, he couldn't move his arms, he couldn't speak, he was on a ventilator, he couldn't hold up his head." Thomason was updated on Anderson's con- dition, and reminded Favre that there was a boy in Oconomowoc, Wis- consin, who needed him. One day, out of the blue, Michelle was told that the quarterback (now a Viking) and his wife would like to fly in from Minnesota and visit their home. The year was 2010. "The doorbell rings," she said, "and there's this big guy, big smile on his face." When Anderson saw Favre, he excitedly lifted his right leg into the air. He was wearing a purple-and-yellow Vikings sock. "It took such an effort," said Michelle, "but he always loved the stinky-toes game, where we'd pretend his feet smelled." She explained this to the Favres, and Brett bent to one knee, gently held Anderson's right foot, took a whiff, and said, "Aw, they're not so bad." Favre spent three hours with Anderson, at one point sitting by his side and stroking the hair atop his head, whispering warm words into his ear. He complimented the different pictures Anderson had drawn — many featuring Favre in a Minnesota uniform, wearing a backward No. 4 (as the tumor progressed, Anderson struggled to write numbers correctly). "It was the sweetest thing," said Michelle. "Lots of people have heroes. Lots of people are fans. But to know your hero loves you as much as you love him . . . that's special."

Later that season, the Vikings hosted the Bears in what turned out to be Favre's final NFL appearance. After the 40–14 loss, he was hit with questions from the press about a rough season and a potential concussion and whether he was, at long last, done with football. When all the pertinent material was supplied, and the media session wrapped, a reporter posed a seemingly meaningless inquiry about the white towel that had dangled from his waist throughout the game.

"Brett," he said, "this might be a dumb question, but why was there a backward No. 4 written on it?"

Anderson Butzine died less than a year later.

GUNSLINGER

1

BEGINNING

T HE HOUSE was white and small. Two bedrooms, a kitchen, a bathroom with a dinky tub, a tiny common area. It was located in Gulfport, Mississippi, at 1412 37th Avenue, one block from Milner Stadium, where many of the youth teams in the state's second-largest city (after Jackson) held their football games.

This is where Alvin and Mary Spikes Favre raised their five children.

This is where the modern Brett Favre story slowly comes into focus.

Alvin was a smallish man — only five feet nine and 160 pounds. He worked as a welder at the nearby shipyard, and when that position was eliminated he was hired by the local wholesale company Wigley and Culp, where he managed a warehouse overloaded with cigarettes and candy. "He'd get there at 5:00 a.m.," said Janet Peterson, a daughter. "Dad would make sure all the trucks were loaded, make sure the orders were right. Then they'd be sent on their way." Based upon his gruff facial expressions and calloused hands, one might have presumed Alvin Favre to be a hardened tough guy; a belt-wielding terror; a man you didn't want to mess with. "He was actually very easygoing," said Karen Favre, the youngest of the children. "In our house, he wasn't the parent you feared."

If the Favre children ran toward Alvin when he entered the front door, they tiptoed hesitantly around Mary, a homemaker who Karen believes, in hindsight, was likely bipolar. "Mom tore our tails up," said Karen. "She'd hit us with anything she could find — brooms, lamps, belts, whatever. In today's world, she'd be abusive. Back then, she was just disciplining. But she was not a nice person."

The oldest child, Jim, was born in 1941. Four years later, on January

5, 1945, a second son arrived. The boy was big and burly, weighing eight pounds, one ounce when he first appeared at Memorial Hospital. He was named Irvin — Irvin Ernest Favre. And, from a very young age, he was the obvious possessor of both serious athletic ability and an indefatigable competitiveness. "If you gave Irv a ball," said Jim, "he knew what to do with it."

Back in the 1940s and '50s, well before specialty sports camps and cable television and Xbox 360s and iPhones, the boys and girls of Gulfport spent their free time outside, running through fields, hiking through woods, fishing, hunting, throwing, kicking. The Favre family was enormous (more than 60 relatives lived in Gulfport alone), and just a stone's throw down 37th Avenue was the home belonging to Mallett and Nora Spikes, the kids' maternal grandparents. "We had aunts and uncles, cousins — all nearby," said Jim. "You were never alone. And we didn't take vacations. We were home, playing." Family was everything. Mary made elaborate homemade cakes for birthdays and Christmas, and on Thanksgiving she would bake five scrumptious sweet potato pies, one for each child. "It wasn't like today, where people move far away," said Jim. "Being a Favre meant being together. I probably didn't appreciate it back then as I do now."

All of the children were bequeathed nicknames by their father. The sisters, Janet and Karen, were Sister and Kay Kay, respectively. Jim was Jimbo; Alvin Jr. was Rock. And Irvin, tightly wound and built like a miniature refrigerator, was Butch. Although Alvin Sr. had played football at Gulfport High, he all but swore off sports after breaking his ribs in a game as a junior flanker. That role-model void, however, was filled for Irvin by Richard, Cecil, Archie, and Lou Cospelich, his older cousins who lived across the street. "When the Cospelich boys played," said Janet, "they played *to win*." Irvin regularly sat on the porch, tattered blue jeans, hand-me-down T-shirt, a wad of chewing gum pinched between his lip and gums, and watched, mesmerized, as the kids threw a baseball back and forth, making it whistle through the air. By the time he was eight, Irv could cross 37th Avenue, glove in hand, and join in. He was strong-armed and hard-headed and — as a kid nicknamed Butch would be — vicious. Few peers remember Irvin crying from a ball to the ribs or a bat to the head, but he was known to storm off in anger after a blown call. Irvin Favre didn't merely take losing badly. He didn't take losing at all.

By the time he reached Gulfport High, Irv was a blossoming two-sport star. In football, he played split end and linebacker, using his physicality and fearlessness to excel. His first love, however, was baseball. Irv was one of the best right-handed pitchers in the area; as a senior he tossed a 13-inning no-hitter. He was a serious kid and an average student, with little time for girls or trouble. The closest he came to mischief was when he accidentally shattered a taillight on the family car by throwing a misguided pair of pliers.

Shortly before graduating from high school in the summer of 1963, Irvin Favre chose to matriculate at Perkinston Junior College, one of the region's finest (and only) community colleges. Located 30 miles north of Gulfport in Perkinston, the school was best known for its vast stretches of nothingness. It was home to a creek, a couple of stores, a radio station, a hamburger joint.

Irv Favre knew he needed a college degree, but came to Perkinston because the coaches offered a chance to continue his two-sport path. He would pitch for the Bulldogs baseball team and play end in football (until a broken ankle ended his career during his sophomore season). It was also here, in the middle of nowhere, that his life would forever change.

One night, while attending a beach party in Henderson Point, Irvin was speaking with Jimmy Benigno, the Perkinston quarterback, when he was introduced to a college classmate named Bonita French. Although she was 10 months younger than he, Bonita had graduated from high school at age 16 and was midway through her sophomore year of college. The two chatted for a while, and Irv was smitten. Bonita had a warm smile, defined cheekbones, and chocolate-brown eyes, and smoked cigarettes as if they were two days from extinction. Like Irv, she was straightforward and took no guff. The stereotypical Southern belle of the era was genteel and soft. Save for her accent, Bonita was more New York sass. As for her early impression of the man standing before her? "Nothing special," she said. "We hung out at the Perk but it wasn't any big deal. There was nothing to do. So you hung out with people."

Over the next year, Irvin came to appreciate the improbable story of an improbable woman. The Perkinston Junior College campus was filled with young coeds whose biographies were somewhat standard-issue: two-parent home, raised on the Gulf Coast, here for a couple of years of study with the hope of landing a husband.

And then there was Bonita . . .

Her father, Bennie Lorenzo French, was a character. With his first wife, Hazel, he had six children. His second marriage, to Jessie, was childless. Bennie's third wife, Izella Garriga, was 18 years his junior, and attended the Bay St. Louis High School senior prom with his son, Bennie French II. Based out of Henderson Point, the elder Bennie French was a man of many trades and talents. He was a womanizer, a gambler, a bar owner, and a rumrunner. He kept a .45-caliber pistol in his pocket and owned a pair of side-by-side taverns — Bennie French's and the Beachcomber. Both smelled of tobacco and gin and served as a second home to the region's most notorious gamblers. Every few months Bennie would pack a bag, catch a boat to Cuba, and return with huge quantities of alcohol to bootleg. "We're not talking about old stump juice that they made out here in the stills," said Bonita. "This was some good whiskey." During Prohibition, local moonshine stills were hidden beneath mounds of sawdust.

Bennie French was well regarded by a certain underground element, but was as warm and affable as a brick. He once took Izella to New Orleans for some shopping, and instructed her to meet him at a particular corner at 2:00 p.m. When she failed to arrive on time, he drove home without her — one and a half hours away. "She had to take the bus," said Bonita. "But she told me it was OK — she was the one with the credit card."

Shortly after their wedding in 1943, Izella made it clear she desperately wanted a child. Bennie, knowing he would have minimal involvement with his seventh (at least) offspring, begrudgingly acquiesced, and when his young bride was unable to become pregnant, they agreed to adopt. On September 27, 1945, a woman named Audrey Sears — 20 years old, married, impregnated during an extramarital fling in Portland, Maine — gave birth to an eight-pound, six-ounce girl and surrendered her to the French family. Izella named her Bonita Ann, after an aunt. Before Audrey returned home, Bennie sat her down and said, "Are you sure this is what you want to do?"

She nodded and left — never to be heard from again.

"The best thing that happened to me was being given up for adoption," said Bonita. "My mother wanted a baby badly, and she was the greatest. Everything I did and everything she did, it was always me and Mama, me and Mama. I had a wonderful childhood because of her."

Not that she was easy. Bonita wasn't one to sit still. As a teenager she brought home boyfriends for her parents to meet, only to hear Bennie snarl, "Ain't no way you're dating that McDonald boy again!" Bonita would be out with him the next night. She attended St. Joseph's Academy in Bay St. Louis, an all-girl prep school with high academic and moral standards. "I remember we had this one teacher, a nun," Bonita said. "She'd sometimes fall asleep during classes and we'd sneak into her book and read all the answers. I had a mischievous side to me."

And now, here she was in Perkinston, hanging around with the ball-player. They were an item for two years — the surly jock who was all about winning and the petite health and physical education major whose goal was to become a teacher. "Irvin's the only boy Daddy ever liked," she said. "He didn't like anybody. But something about Irvin worked for him." Maybe it was the young man's utter disinterest in affection. Irv was an attentive and interesting boyfriend, but a fan of neither holding hands nor public kisses. Bennie and Izella never saw their daughter in any sort of lovey-dovey moment with Irv, and they were perfectly fine with that. Why, his proposal was vintage Butch Favre: he took Bonita to the Perkinston baseball field, stood by her side in the parking lot, and grunted, "Eh, let's get married."

Did Irvin Favre at least get down on a knee?

"Down on a knee?" said Bonita, laughing. "Irvin? *Noooo*, honey."

Both Irvin and Bonita had school to complete. After her sophomore year at Perkinston, Bonita transferred to the University of Southern Mississippi in Hattiesburg. Irvin arrived a year later, joining the baseball team and majoring in education.

The wedding was held on November 27, 1965, at St. Paul United Methodist Church in Pass Christian. A reception followed at the Gulfport Community Center. About 200 people attended. There were no overly emotional or sentimental speeches. Schmaltz and Favre don't mix. "I was happy," Bonita said. "But if you're looking for the cliché, it's not here." Both ultimately graduated from Southern Miss — Bonita with a degree in health and physical education, Irvin as an education major. After the wedding, they moved briefly into — of all places — Bennie French's, the family bar in Henderson Point. Izella hung a curtain to divide the saloon from Irvin and Bonita's bedroom. "You could have had some drunks fall through," Bonita said, laughing. "Aw, not really. But a lot of times we helped with the bar at night. You do what you can to assist your family."

• • •

A couple of months after her wedding, Bonita Favre — now a 20-year-old physical education teacher and girls' basketball coach at all-black North Gulfport High — was pregnant. Was she excited? "My biggest goal in life at that time was to marry and have a large family," she recalled. "I actually wanted eight kids."

Her colleagues soon found out, and then her bosses learned the news. She was quickly out of a job. "It was a different time," she said. "Old folks wouldn't say 'pregnant,' they'd say 'When you lookin'?' or 'You're PG.' If a job found out you were expecting, they wouldn't hire you back. And it was allowed."

Her first son, Scott Earnest Favre, was born on December 22, 1966, while Irv and Bonita were living in Southern Miss student housing (Bonita had already graduated; Irv was finishing up and playing baseball). When Irv graduated in 1967, they relocated to Hancock County, to a piece of property wedged between two small towns (Kiln and Diamondhead) near the Gulf of Mexico. In the early 1940s, Bennie French had purchased just over 52 secluded acres of land in the area, with the intention of one day retiring there. He built a couple of houses on the property, including the one his daughter and son-in-law moved into. It was small, with two bedrooms and one bathroom. The land was tucked in between Mill Creek and Rotten Bayou — a mile-long stretch of the Jourdan River, which passed in front of the house. The waters were so close, Brett Favre later recalled, "that we could spit into it off our deck." The property was overrun by pine trees and fields, with enough lingering alligators that one needed to keep pets on a very short leash. The actual location of the property is somewhat confusing. It is closest to the tiny village of Fenton, but the mailing address is Pass Christian. And yet, the Favres consider their hometown to be Kiln, which runs parallel to Fenton. Locals refer to it as the Kill, just as they call Pass Christian the Pass. When people asked, Brett Favre would say he's from the Kill.

"You have to say something," Bonita said. "So that's the answer."

Irv Favre kicked off his teaching career at Long Beach High, where he handled physical education classes and worked as an assistant baseball and football coach. He then went to St. John High, and in 1970 guided the school to the state baseball championship. It was during this span, on October 10, 1969, that the couple's second son was born. The delivery — like all four of Bonita's eventual deliveries — was not easy. For Scott, she spent 42 hours in labor. For the second, a painful 10. "[Gulfport] Memorial Hospital back then was not like Memorial Hospital now," she said. "They had two labor rooms. I was there so long they put me in a hallway with some curtains around it. There was this little black doctor, and he'd come, deliver one baby, leave, come back, deliver another baby."

One might think the arrival of a son would render Irvin Favre somewhat emotional. And, indeed, it did. As his wife suffered through labor, he paced the hallways. "Please hurry this up!" he bellowed repeatedly. "Please . . . please." That evening, St. John had a game scheduled against Hancock North Central, and Irv needed to be there. "He was serious," Bonita said. "He would have left me if I didn't have Brett in time for the game."

At 2:35 p.m., Brett Lorenzo Favre entered the world. He weighed eight pounds, nine ounces, measured 21 inches long, and shared a middle name with Bonita's father. "He's a big one, Bonita," the doctor told her with a smile. "Right now he's back in the nursery doing push-ups. He'll be ready for a hamburger in a few minutes."

Before long, Irvin was out the door. He made the game with time to spare.

2
CHILDHOOD

MEAN."

The word is uttered by the youngest of the four Favre children. Her name is Brandi. She is sitting at a kitchen counter, 38 years old and far removed from a childhood of snakes and alligators and her three older brothers ripping the heads off her dolls, then using them as baseballs.

"Brett," she said with a slight Southern drawl and great emphasis, "was *mean.*"

When someone speaks like this of a relative, it is often either a joke or intentional exaggeration. One look at Brandi's facial expression makes it clear this is serious. She is asked for an example, and between sips from a can of Coca-Cola quickly offers one. The third Favre child, Jeff, was a quiet kid, seven years younger than Scott, four years younger than Brett. He was shy and awkward, and struggled to stand up for himself. When Brett was nine, he concocted a drink made from tobacco goop, Worcestershire sauce, and cow manure. Then he urinated in it, and forced Jeff to drink. "I'm not saying Brett's mean now," said Brandi, who was born three years after Jeff in 1976. "But long ago . . . *God.*"

A pause follows, one that suggests Brandi is asking herself, *Am I revealing too much?* Then, more words . . .

"Brett ran over Jeff with his motorbike," she said. "Like, completely ran over him. He'd beat us until he knocked us out. Knocked us out cold — no exaggeration. He would grab us by the throat, throw us across the room. He hit me one time in the eye with a shaved block of wood. I don't know why. Maybe he was searching for something . . . I don't know."

Another pause.

"I just don't know."

Before he was mean, Brett Favre was terrified. Of this. Of that. Of shadows. Of noises. Of spiders. Of ghosts and wasps and ants and tall people. Whereas Scott seemed to emerge from the womb with the confidence of a five-star general, Brett looked around — then checked twice. Creaks in the floor freaked him out. Wind made his hands shake. "When he got the ESPY Award [in 2004] and they talked about him being tough and courageous, we all laughed," said Bonita. "If they only knew how, when we'd come home when he was little, he'd turn every light in the house on. If we'd go to a haunted house for Halloween, he'd lock himself in the car. Courageous? Honey, not even close." Perhaps the nervousness had to do with an incident from the toddler days, when Brett — decked out in an overcoat and cowboy boots — ran from the front yard to the bayou and into the cold water. Bonita's mother, affectionately nicknamed Mee-Maw by her grandkids, was fishing nearby, and she caught the boy by his boot — "his head still in the water," recalled Bonita. "We had forbidden the kids from going down to the bayou without an adult but that didn't stop Brett from doing it."

Although neither Bonita nor Irv could know that baby Brett Favre would turn into *the* Brett Favre, there was an expectation that he would toughen up. Little Brett's nervousness? Not tolerated. In the world of Irv, boys were hard and men were harder. You didn't cry. You didn't complain. A 101-degree fever was no excuse. Neither were chicken pox, measles, cuts, bruises, or dents. If there was a game to play, you played. If there was work to do, you did it. Water breaks? What the hell was a water break? Coddling? Hell, no. "Irv was up on the roof one day doing some stuff at the house," said Clark Henegan, one of Brett's longtime friends. "He fell off and landed on his head on the concrete. He got up, dazed, blood running down his face, and wouldn't go to the hospital."

"When Mom went into town to go shopping, we'd beg her to take us with her because the second she left, Dad would work our tails off," Brett recalled. "It was like being in the military. Dad would grab the rakes and say, 'Let's get after it.'"

When Brett and his siblings speak of their childhoods, there's often a fuzzy romanticism lifted straight from a *Wonder Years* marathon. If you listen closely, you can hear Joe Cocker singing as the color fades to sepia. It was, the narrative goes, a simpler time. Because they lived in relative isolation in Kiln, there was an emphasis on togetherness, right down to their address: 1213 Irvin Farve Road — strange even before one realizes the town accidentally misspelled the name on the street sign. "The roads used to have numbers down there, but the police wanted to give them names so they could find people in case of emergencies," Irvin Favre once explained. "It just so happens that I'm the one living on the road, so they named it Irvin Farve Road in the 1970s." You were unlikely to find a solitary Favre there. No, it was always 2, 3, 4, 5 . . . 10, 15. Cousins and aunts and uncles and grandparents. Birthday parties were excuses for deep-into-the-night crawfish boils accompanied by large coolers of iced beer and Irv and Bonita's smoldering cigarettes. Debates could get heated and last for hours. Favre vs. Favre. "We called where we lived the Compound," said Brandi. "Because it really is a Favre compound."

At the end of the long gravel road sat the house. "There was always someone there, eating food, taking a nap, talking, whatever," said Bonita. "That, you could count on." Without fail, Bonita would wake at 6:00 a.m. to prepare breakfast. And not merely bowls of Corn Flakes. Nope, pancakes, waffles, eggs, biscuits.

The family owned four dogs — a collie named Fluffy, a Saint Bernard named Whiskey, a German shepherd, Bullet, and Lucky, the chocolate Lab. All were beloved and cherished. All were consumed by alligators. ("Alligators don't eat a dog right away," Brett once said. "First they roll around and let it writhe awhile before they take it down.") Or, perhaps, done in by a cottonmouth. It's hard to say with 100 percent certainty.

The boys — Scott, Brett, and Jeff — shared a room. Brett had his own sofa bed against one wall, Scott and Jeff were together in an adjacent king bed against another wall. The walls and ceiling were covered with sports posters. T-shirts and pants were passed down from kid to kid to kid. Trophies — plastic, topped with the ubiquitous gilded figurines — sat atop a shelf. "It got so dark [in the house] you couldn't see the brother next to you," Brett recalled. "We'd lie there and talk about the home run we were going to hit or the football game we were going to have. There was a little weight set by the bed, and I would pump weights in the dark. Scott and Jeff laughed at me." The brawls were legendary. "We'd tear shit up and move shit around," Jeff said. "The beds were on cinder blocks, and you'd slam into them, bleed, get cut up. We'd play football right there, in the room. Hard tackle."

When Brett was two or three, Irvin's grandparents celebrated their 50th wedding anniversary with a large party. While preparing to leave the house, Bonita noticed little Brett sitting on the floor, holding her purse and acting funny. "He took some sort of medicine, which doesn't seem like a great idea," Bonita said. "I called the doctor, who told me to bring him in. So I put him in the car, and we have meatballs in the back of the station wagon, because I made them for the party. Well, Irvin is driving and he hits a German shepherd with the car. The meatballs go flying, Brett is high on medicine, the dog can't be doing so good, what with the bumper in his head and all. We finally get to the doctor, and Brett throws up, and the doctor said I need to watch him, and not to let him sleep for more than an hour. Now we're at the party, I'm watching him. And he's fine, but the meatballs never really make it."

Hunting is a major pastime in Hancock County. One of Brett's first experiences with a gun and the woods came when he was seven. "He went out one morning, all bundled up because it was kind of cold, and he was going deer hunting," Bonita said. "On the other side of the creek he came right up on a deer and it scared both of them to death. You know, one of those things where Brett ran one way and the deer ran the other."

"Our family was always familiar with alligators," Brett said. "One time three of them were in the backyard. My brother Scott and I got a pack of Oreo cookies. We threw it in the river and watched them tear it up . . . if we didn't have Oreos we'd throw hot dogs and bread. Then one day Daddy comes home and the alligators are up on the bank by the house, waiting for their cookies. My dad went berserk. He shot all three of them."

Because the Favre kids grew up in geographic isolation, they did not ride bicycles to town (there really was no town) or catch double features at the local movie theater (there was no local movie theater). No, 95 percent of boyhood activities took place on the property. Blood was often unapologetically spilled. Trash talk was encouraged. "Brett didn't have many close pals," said Scott. "We were sort of it."

"There were no friends around, and that was great," said Jeff. "All we did was play together. We played ball together. We made our own basketball goal. We'd go cut down trees and make our backboards best we could. We did everything ourselves. We made do with what we had. And it was wonderful. Wiffle ball. We made a ball out of anything. Duct tape, electrical tape, socks, paper. Anything that we could creatively come up with our minds.

"People wonder why the state of Mississippi produces so many athletes. It's because, here, you make use of what you have. And that brings out the creativity. That's what allows you to overcome things. You don't have a ball, don't say we can't play ball. Make a ball. Take a piece of paper, crumple it up. Take another piece of paper. Or take a sock, wrap it up with electrical tape, with duct tape. Whatever you have to do. If you want to play, you'll find a way to make it happen."

On weekends, the Favre kids would chow down their breakfast, watch an hour or so of cartoons—then exit. Irv's standard line was, "Inside or out?" and he meant it. "You didn't go back and forth," Jeff said. "You picked inside, you stayed inside. You picked outside, you stayed outside. He had some simple ways, but they were mostly good. He'd say to us, 'Look, you don't wanna work around the house? Get a ball in your hand, get a bat in your hand, get a glove in your hand.' Of course, he'd still eventually get the work out of us."

There were 101 methods to pass the time. Swim in the bayou. Fish for crawfish. Scale trees. Set things on fire. Unload pellets at squirrels and groundhogs. "I wish I had a nickel," Irvin once said, "for every window that got shot out." An old barn sat adjacent to the house, and the boys would climb its splintered beams and launch rocks at one another. "We'd see if we could knock each other out," said David Peterson, a cousin. "See, there wasn't nothing to do—but we didn't know there was nothing to do. We did everything we could to stay busy, and it helped that we knew nothing else."

Once, Brett accidentally shot Scott in the face with a Red Rider BB gun. "I was sure there weren't any BBs left," Brett recalled, so he approached his brother, placed the cylinder beneath his chin, and asked, "You want to feel the compression of my gun on your face?"

"Go ahead," Scott replied. "I dare you."

With a BB lodged in his chin, Scott ran off to tell his father. "I got whipped good for that one," Brett said.

Another time, with Scott chasing him around the yard, Brett dashed up to the loft in the barn. He threatened to throw a brick at his older brother's head if he approached. "You couldn't hit me if you tried," Scott replied.

That was all Brett needed to hear. He wound up, let loose . . . and missed. A chunk of the brick broke off, however, and caught Scott beneath the left eye. He was rushed to the hospital, and once again Irv let Brett have it.

When asked which of the parents was softer, all of the Favre children cite their mom. Bonita, said Peterson, was "the mother hen — she would hug you, advise you, take you in, pray with you. She's a real down-to-earth woman. A saint." But, even were Bonita a strict disciplinarian, it's not a hard battle to win. Compared to Irvin Favre, Suge Knight seems cuddly. Which, again, might explain young Brett's propensity toward cruelty. Although it has often been said that Irvin "refused" to tell his children he loved them, the characterization is misleading. The words "I love you" were not deliberately avoided. They simply never entered his cranium. Not toward his parents, not toward his wife, not toward his offspring. "He was probably a little different with me because I was a girl," said Brandi. "But it'd be hard for my brothers to know Dad loved them. That's just fact." Love and affection were emotions never designed to be verbally expressed. One loved by giving maximum effort. One loved by molding his soft kids into stones. One loved by arriving on time, by putting in nine hours of work, by making certain the bills were paid. To Irvin, Brandi was of little worth. Girls, in his mind, weren't athletes. And without athletics, what was the value of a person? "My mom went to every dance recital, every event, everything I had," she said. "But my dad had no interest in my activities, even if they were sports. He would come, but not really by first choice. Looking back, it killed me. You want love. You're a kid. You need love. And he didn't offer it in a way a child needed it."

Irvin ruled the household with a stern voice and a tendency toward violent resolution, and would beat the boys (and, on occasion, his daughter) with whatever appropriate item was closest. It could be a stick from the yard. Or a belt or black rubber hose. Sometimes they'd be offered a choice — a thrashing with an inanimate object, or kneeling for a prolonged period on a rock pile.

"You'd take the rocks," said Brandi. "Dad had this blue belt. And he would pop it before he'd hit us, just so we knew."

That.

Whop!

Was.

Whop!

Love.

Whop!

"One time we were on the back of my dad's truck, and I was fighting with one of my cousins and Dad told us to stop," said Brandi. "Well, we flipped off the back of the truck while it was moving. I kept beating my cousin up on the ground, and Dad beat me from out there all the way until we were inside. He wasn't wearing a belt, so he used his hands and knees."

"My favorite moment has to be the bike story," said Scott. "We were riding bikes down our road, which was gravel." Brett was 10, and the cuff on one of the legs of his blue jeans wound up caught in the chain of his Huffy. He pulled to the side of the road, bent down, and repeatedly tried to yank the pants loose. Irv approached in his pickup truck, and Brett yelled out for help. "Dad! Dad!" he said. "Get us home!"

"Nope," Irv hollered, "gotta go."

He drove off, and Brett flipped the middle finger. "All of a sudden, here comes the truck in reverse," said Scott. "Brett's trying to run through the woods with the bike attached to his leg. I mean, he's limping along and it's really pathetic. He had no chance." Irv stopped the truck, jumped out, grabbed his son's middle finger and bent it backward. "You think that was funny?" Irv yelled.

"No, Daddy! I'm sorry . . ."

"You're what?" Irv said.

"I'm sorry! I'm sorry!"

"You wanna do that again?" Irv said. "You ever gonna do that again?"

"No!" Brett whimpered. "No."

Irv released the finger and stormed off back to his truck, leaving Brett and his bicycle attached at the leg.

Of all the outdoor activities embraced by the Favre children, nothing trumped sports.

In 1972 Big Irv, as he was increasingly referred to, took over as the head baseball and football coach at Hancock North Central High, and Bonita was later hired as a special education teacher. When Irv wasn't at the school, coaching or teaching physical education and driver's ed, he was working with his sons on baseball and football, or talking to his sons about baseball and football, or lecturing his sons about baseball and football. Scratch that — not lecturing. Barking. Demanding. Blaming. "You could go out there and say it was just a game; that second place was OK sometimes, but that's not really true," Irvin once said. "You don't go out there to come in second. Heck, you go out there to win." The idea that his boys would perhaps forgo athletics for, say, drama or music wasn't an idea at all. They would be jocks, just like their father.

Scott, the oldest of the four children, was prodigious from the very beginning. He started playing Little League baseball at age seven, and also excelled in Pop Warner football. Every town has a child who does what the others cannot, and in Kiln that was Scott Favre. He was the fastest, the strongest, the most confident. "If you picked one guy from back then who you thought could be a pro at something, it was Scott," said Charles Burton, a childhood classmate of the Favre boys. "He knew the games better than any of us."

By comparison, Brett was merely good. Because he was three years behind his big brother, Brett could seem small, slow, undistinguished. He was an average-looking kid — floppy, sandy hair, crooked teeth, scabbed knees and elbows. When they played games around the house, Scott ordered Brett around — *run this route, throw this pass, play this position.* He wasn't as quick as Scott, or as charismatic. But the one thing he clearly inherited from Big Irv was the snarl. Peterson vividly recalled a backyard game of two-on-two tackle football, when he and Brett teamed up against Scott and another boy. After Peterson surrendered a deep touchdown pass, Brett reamed him out, demanding he use what they referred to as the Mississippi Bulldog method of tackling. "So the next time the kid caught a pass, I Mississippi Bulldogged him just like Brett said," Peterson recalled. "I jumped on top of his head and brought him down by his head." The boy rose from the ground, bloodied and lacking his two front teeth. After scanning the ground, Peterson noticed two rectangular white objects embedded in the skin of his right arm.

Brett laughed and laughed, until the boys sought out Big Irv inside the house. He grabbed a pair of pliers, yanked the teeth from Peterson's body, and covered the wound with duct tape. "Now get the hell out of here," Irvin said. "Go do something."

Another time, Bonita took Brett and Peterson to a local Punt, Pass & Kick contest. "I didn't even want to go," Peterson said. "But Brett insisted." The two went station to station, and to everyone's surprise, Peterson won. "Brett was so mad, I thought we were going to fight," Peterson said. "He was just that way with everything. He didn't know how to lose."

To most American parents, this would be a source of disappointment. Irvin loved it. In his world, losers accept losing. That's why, in his job as the Hancock North Central High football coach, he didn't merely browbeat players who disappointed. He removed a wood stick from his desk, ordered teenage boys (many bigger than he was) to bend over, and paddled them. He also cursed kids out, threatened their happiness, worked them to the brink of exhaustion.

This same methodology took place at home. For years, one of the staples of the Favre boys' entertainment was a game called goal line. Scott and Brett would place a football five yards from an imaginary goal line, then give Jeff—little, understated Jeff—four plays to run for a score. Sweeps were not permitted. "Jeff had to run through us," Brett recalled. "We beat the shit out of him . . . noses got smashed, fingers got mangled. There'd be blood."

Irv approved.

When Brett Favre was a year old, he received a full football uniform—helmet and pads included—as a Christmas gift from his parents. The little boy wore the duds everywhere, and shortly thereafter was presented with an equally sweet gift—a baseball uniform. Both outfits became regular parts of the Brett Favre wardrobe, and would have never left his body were it not for Bonita's insistences.

A couple of years later, Irvin Favre started taking his sons to football and baseball practices. Along with coaching the teams at Hancock North Central, Big Irv served as the manager of Joe Graham Post 119, Gulfport's entry into the summer American Legion baseball circuit, as well as the Gulf Coast Stars of the Connie Mack league. Much of Brett's time at the fields was spent goofing around with his brothers and the other young children in attendance. When he wasn't causing mischief, however, the boy paid attention. He loved seeing his father berate the teenaged players. It was fine entertainment. He also liked trying to grasp the strategies that came so easily to his old man. At 5 feet 10 and 220 pounds, with broad shoulders, an anvil-shaped jaw, and a rectangular head, Irvin Favre was physically imposing. But through his boys' eyes, his stature went beyond mere physique. "God, it was incredible to watch my dad coach," Brett recalled. "I remember going out to watch the high school football practice thinking, 'Someday I want to be just like those guys.'" Favre saw the players as gladiators, if not gods. They were skyscrapers, and his father owned them all. "Nobody messed with him," Brett recalled. "I remember standing on the sidelines thinking, 'My dad has got some nuts.'"

The games were little Brett's slices of heaven. That the players knew him — *talked to him!* — was a $100 million bonus. He was enlisted as a team batboy, so he'd dash back and forth, fetching gloves, chasing down equipment. Before American Legion contests, Irv's players loved having Brett and his brothers slide across the dirt in their spotless white mascot uniforms. "Who do you think had to get them clean for the next game?" said Bonita. "It wasn't my husband." The kids on the teams were usually 16 and 17. They would spit and curse and stick pinches of chewing tobacco between their gums and lips. The lessons were not lost upon the children. "Jeff came to me at the age of three," Bonita recalled, "wanting to buy Red Man."

"I saw the catcher adjusting his cup," Brett said, "so I'd reach down and play with my balls, too."

Before a state championship game in the summer of 1974, members of the Joe Graham Post 119 squad were goofing around when Brett walked into the practice swing of a slugger named Leon Farmer. The resulting knot on his forehead was the size of a cantaloupe, and Bonita rushed her son to the emergency room. When the attending physician asked Bonita how long her son was out for, she shrugged and said, "He wasn't."

"Surely it knocked him down, no?" he said.

"Nope," replied Bonita.

If the sporting events were intended to motivate the Favre boys toward athletic excellence, mission accomplished. But they also served another purpose. The state of Mississippi's long and ugly struggles with racism are no secret, and Hancock County is hardly an exception. When, in 1954, the United States Supreme Court decreed via *Brown v. Board of Education of Topeka* that America's public schools had to be desegregated, most of Mississippi delayed and hoped the ruling could be ignored. Were there riots in Kiln? No. But many white families greeted the inevitability of desegregation by having their children enroll in Annunciation Catholic School, which opened in 1960 as a rebuke to the *Brown* ruling.

Unlike many of her contemporaries, Bonita Favre was raised with a surprising open-mindedness about race. Could she have dated someone black as a teenager? "No," she said. "My daddy would not have that. There were lines you didn't cross." But come three o'clock every afternoon, Bennie French would drive to the black part of Pass Christian and pick up his cooks and busboys for work at the bar. There was a black dishwasher, Kenneth Youngblood, who was so little he had to stand atop crates of Coca-Cola to reach the sink. "Kenneth and I would cut up and play together, and I never thought about him being black, or like there was supposed to be a separation," she said. "He was a friend." Later, when Bonita taught at all-black North Gulfport High, she coached the girls' basketball team. "When we'd go to games people would say, 'Here comes that white woman with all them niggers,'" she said. "To me, they were my kids."

When Brett and his brothers watched Irvin coach, it wasn't merely a lesson on hitting and throwing and tackling. No, they witnessed a rainbow coalition in action. The teams were black and white, and Irvin refused to play favorites based on race. If you could do the job, you were given the job. Players of all colors would come to the Favre household for dinner. Later, when the boys played varsity sports, their teammates — black, white, whatever — were regularly invited inside the home for meals, for games, for TV. "I can't speak for my friends, but we never thought about race," said Scott Favre. "It was about who you were as a person, as an athlete. I looked at blacks as teammates and friends. My brothers were the same way."

Brett Favre's organized athletic career began at age six, when Irv and Bonita signed him up for the local Harrison-Hancock Baseball League. Although he was technically too young, Brett was assigned to a team of eight-year-olds. He played third base, shortstop, and pitched, the first official inkling that his arm was particularly strong. "He could really bring it," said Drew Malley, a childhood friend who played for an opposing team. "He didn't have the best control, and that made you a little nervous when you stepped in the box. But he had a lot more talent than most of us."

A standard Brett Favre mound appearance would go something like this: strike out, walk, walk, walk, strike out, hit by pitch, hit by pitch, strike out. "Brett's thing," said Bonita, "was strike them out or knock them out." Some opposing coaches questioned his age, wondering if the 6-year-old with the lightning bolt extending from his right shoulder was, perhaps, 9 or 10. Nobody enjoyed stepping to the plate against him. Favre had Nolan Ryan's velocity and a blind drunkard's control. In one game, he struck out 15 hitters while hitting 3 — *in a row.* "I thought that was great," he recalled. "It just made me want to throw it harder."

His organized football career began as a fifth grader, when he joined the local Hancock Hawks Pee Wee squad. It was an experimental experience both for prepubescent Brett and the town, which had never before

fielded its own youth teams. As the high school coach, Irv always wondered why Hancock wasn't developing his future players. So he asked
Paul Cuevas, a former Hancock North Central halfback who had graduated in 1966, to kick-start a program. Cuevas agreed, and one thing he
noticed early on in practices was that Irv's son could *really* throw a football.

The Hawks' 17-man roster was comprised of fifth and sixth graders. They wore red jerseys with white pants, practiced on a ragtag field,
and traveled the region, oftentimes competing in multiteam jamborees
that would require playing three or four games on a single day. On the
high school level, Irv's offensive philosophy was run, run, and run. "You
turned and you gave it to the halfback," said Scott Favre. "That was a
quarterback's job."

Cuevas felt no fealty toward the system. "We saw right off the bat we
had a kid who could throw and we also saw we had a bunch of kids who
could catch," he said. "We would shock the other teams."

The Hawks were loaded with athletically gifted children destined to
one day excel for Irv. There was a tall, fast boy named Tommy Bond,
who slammed into opposing ball carriers like the door of a bank vault.
There was Delano Lewis, the nifty tailback. Receiver Corey Blaze ran as
his name suggests, and Vincent Cuevas, the coach's son, would spend
much of the decade catching Brett's balls across the middle of football
fields. "It was awesome," Vincent Cuevas said. "I can't say we knew Brett
would turn into a pro. But he had this talent, and leadership, very early
on. He was in charge, even as a young guy."

Brett's debut was neither noteworthy nor charmed. The Hawks were
scheduled to participate in a jamboree in nearby Bay Saint Louis, but that
morning Irv decided he first needed a trim at his favorite barbershop in
Gulfport. "I'm sitting there in full uniform waiting for my dad to have
the finishing touches put on his flattop," Brett recalled. "I was not a happy
fifth grader."

By the time they arrived, the game was underway. Paul Cuevas inserted Brett at split end, and on one of his first plays he caught a pass for
a short gain, fell on the ball, and had the wind knocked from his gut. He
rolled around the grass, unable to breathe, tears streaming from his eyes.
"You're in the fifth grade," he recalled, "and you're sure you're going to
die." Upon reaching the sideline, Brett begged his coach for a position
switch. "I hate playing split end," he said. "I want to play quarterback."

Cuevas acquiesced, and the next game began with Brett Favre under center. For years, people would refer to his debuts as his first games at Hancock North Central, at Southern Miss, in the National Football League. But here, on a small field with 30 or so spectators spread out along the rotted wooden bleachers, was Brett Favre's legitimate quarterback debut. He wore uniform No. 10. His teeth were crooked, lips thin and fruit-punch red. His helmet had two white bars — one vertical, one horizontally splitting his sight line. Cuevas loved the way Brett walked toward the line of scrimmage. Not like a boy figuring things out, but as a man in charge. "He had a feel for it," said Cuevas. "Maybe having a coach for a dad does that."

Brett ran for two touchdowns, threw for one. Memory of the final score has vanished with time. Did the Hawks win? Lose? No one seems to know. But a seed was planted. "I thought to myself, 'Hey, quarterback is a cool position,'" Favre recalled. 'It sure would be nice to play this for a long time.'"

The Hawks competed in eight games that first season, winning six. Though no official statistics were maintained, Brett threw between 10 and 12 touchdown passes, with a small handful of interceptions. He also played linebacker, and was allowed to roam the field seeking out hits. "If we needed a big stop on defense, Brett was usually the one," Vincent Cuevas said. "We all wanted to win, but he wanted to be the best. Even way back then."

3

HIGH SCHOOL

THE WING-T OFFENSE haunts Brett Favre's dreams.

OK, this is something of a guess. Perhaps Brett Favre hasn't given the Wing-T a second thought for decades; perhaps it's nothing more than a distant memory and a life hiccup, not unlike the aftereffects of eating week-old sushi.

In the fall of 1981, however, as he began his seventh-grade year at Hancock North Central High, 11-year-old Brett was first asked to direct a relative of the wishbone offense his father utilized at the varsity level. Joe Shaw, a teacher at Hancock North Central, served as the junior high head coach, and he was under strict instructions to teach kids to play the game as they would once they reached the Friday-night varsity lights of Hawks Stadium. "So we didn't throw it," said Shaw. "Hardly ever."

This was fun for pretty much nobody. Shaw, a University of Southern Mississippi graduate who had been hired by the school district in 1976, loved high-flying football. Brett, a fan of quarterbacks like Roger Staubach and Archie Manning, loved high-flying football. Irvin Favre, however, believed the game was won via stout defense and ball control. So he devoted the Hancock program to following the offense made famous by Coach Tubby Raymond and the University of Delaware Blue Hens — multiple backs, misdirections, 95 percent running. "We sat down with the Delaware coaches, got their numbering system, took their concepts, and tried to use them effectively," said Shaw. "When you watched Hancock, you were watching a high school version of Delaware." According to Irv, there would be no deviating from the system. Whatever the Blue

Hens did, the young Hawks would do. "Irv's thing was, 'We're gonna run over people,'" said Shaw. "And his teams did."

Which was great. Only most people hated it. The Hancock football program was blessed with marvelous athletes and a coaching philosophy that shunned that very athleticism. Through the years, as his son emerged as an icon, Irvin Favre was repeatedly hailed as a genius, a guru, a football coach for the ages, a developer of legends. In reality, his offensive approach was simplistic and stale, quietly criticized by peers and assistants too intimidated to suggest upgrades. At the same time men like Bill Walsh and Don Coryell were revolutionizing passing in the NFL, Hancock's coach was living in a philosophical cave. "Irv was tough and hard-nosed," said Rocky Gaudin, his longtime assistant. "He was also unyielding." Were the Hawks successful, perhaps the steadfastness would make sense. Between 1979 and 1984, though, Hancock's varsity was a model of mediocrity, posting only two winning seasons and drawing so-so crowds. Everyone, from opposing coaches to opposing players, knew the Hawks' limited playbook.

The junior high team was composed of seventh and eighth graders, and while Shaw initially positioned Brett Favre at split end ("He was big and could run"), he was permanently moved behind center midway through the second game. "He had a great arm," said Shaw. "But since we never threw, that didn't matter so much. The reason I put Brett at quarterback was because he just had this way about him. The other kids would play better with him out there barking out things."

There was also the Irv Favre factor. The varsity coach was adamant about his boys playing quarterback. Not because he aspired for them to be stars, but because he knew they would always show up and show up on time. A team could survive without a defensive lineman or a fullback. But the quarterback had to be there.

Irv Favre's kids were always there.

In Brett's two years as a junior high quarterback, his teams went 14-1, often playing before 12 people and a couple of squirrels at Hawks Field. He averaged, by one teammate's estimation, three throws per game — usually screens to the halfback or short outs. Joy for the boy came primarily on defense, where he excelled as a hard-hitting linebacker/safety hybrid. Although Brett didn't love being tackled as a quarterback, he relished popping receivers and halfbacks as they crossed the middle of the field. In practices, when his balls were intercepted, he went out of his way to show his displeasure. "You'd pick him off, he'd try spearing you," said Drew Malley, a teammate. "He wanted you to know how he felt."

"At Hancock we'd refer to players as either milk drinkers or whiskey drinkers," said Gaudin. "Whiskey drinkers are full of piss and vinegar and drive you crazy. Brett was all whiskey."

Off the field, Brett Favre was as memorable as a brown leaf. He attended school, earned ordinary grades (he was a dependable B student). "In the classroom, I was a follower," he once told ESPN's Jeff Bradley. "But on the field, I was always a leader." His clothes were often hand-me-downs from Scott: plaid shirts and jeans. Browns, grays, blacks. Peers began to experiment with alcohol and marijuana, but Brett abstained. First, he knew of the paternal beating that would accompany a slipup. Second, he wasn't *that* guy. "I remember Brett telling me he was disappointed in me because a bunch of us were out having a good time, and we were drinking," said Jesse Dupree, a classmate. "He showed up at a dance, saw us drunk, and let us have it." A Friday night for Brett Favre involved lifting weights in the garage and dreaming of the 50-yard spirals he wasn't allowed to throw. He wanted greatness, but wasn't entirely sure what the stuff looked like. "Everybody else was going out, hanging out with their friends, and Brett would be doing a full workout at home," recalled Brandi. "And I used to think, 'What is wrong with him?' I'd say that all the time — '*What is wrong with you?*'"

Brett's springs were consumed by baseball, the high and wild pitches consistently high and wild. He gave winter basketball a quick try, but displayed a precise inability to dribble and shoot. "He once took the ball out at the end of the gym and hit the fire extinguisher on the wall on the back side of the gym," recalled Bonita. "He didn't like the sport." He noticed girls, but rarely mustered up the courage to approach. He cracked jokes and pulled pranks with teammates and friends, some of them mildly funny. At home, he feared his father, loved his mother, idolized his older brother (Scott joined the Hawks' varsity in 10th grade, and started at quarterback for three years), and continued to torment his younger siblings, Jeff and Brandi. If there were parties going on in Hancock County, Mississippi, Brett Favre either didn't know about them or wasn't invited. Which was fine with him. "We had a pretty simple life," said Scott. "The way we liked it."

Then, toward the end of his eighth-grade year, Shaw pulled his quarterback aside. "Brett," he said, "I've got you a running back coming."

"Is he fast?" Favre said.

"Yeah," Shaw replied. "Charles Burton is fast."

His first-ever football team was named the Rockets. Although Charles Burton was but a fourth grader at the time, his school — Charles B. Murphy Elementary in Pearlington, Mississippi — was willing to make an exception and add the 8-year-old to the squad. Even though rules stated one had to be 11 or 12 to play. Even though he was as tiny as a peanut, with the skinny legs and pipe cleaner arms to match. Even though there was no precedent.

"They took me," Burton said, "because I could fly."

Indeed, from the time he was walking, Charles Burton was sprinting. Up the stairs. Through the yard. Down the block. Often with a football tucked beneath his arm. His mother, Diane Burton, worked as a janitor at the Stennis Space Center on the banks of the Pearl River. His father, Charles Burton, was a construction grunt. As was the case with Irvin and Bonita, the Burtons insisted their three children (Charles has an older sister, Angela, and a younger sister, Dietra) devote as much time as possible to being outdoors. So after school, Charles bounded from his family's small shotgun house and joined the neighborhood kids in spirited games of tackle. "They were all older and bigger," he said. "It caused me to grow up quickly."

In Hancock County, Irvin Favre was working to create a family football dynasty. Only, one already existed. Throughout the 1970s and '80s, a string of Burton relatives not only played for the Hawks' varsity, but excelled. There was Don Lee, the uncle halfback who wore No. 30. There was Andrew Willis, the cousin halfback who wore No. 30. And now, entering Hancock Central High School along with Brett Favre, was a new No. 30.

"The first time I met Brett, I was struck by how big he was," said Burton. "I was like, God dang, they grow these boys big here!"

To Brett's delight, the affable Shaw coached the Hancock North Central freshman team, a job that included the tricky task of merging large numbers of players who had never before competed alongside one another. "They had their stars, we had our stars," said Burton. "So how do you decide who plays and who sits?" Before any of the Hawks' squads began practices, Irv Favre held his annual Meet the Football Team night inside the school auditorium. Parents of the players were required to attend, and when Irv took to the stage, the small talk and chatter died off. "When your son is out here with me on the field, and with my coaches, he's ours," he said. "If you need help with him at home, I'll help. That's what I try to do. But if you're raising a baby, take your baby home. Out here your sons are expected to be men." The days that followed were brutal — two-a-day practices designed to test mettle and manhood. Water breaks were kept to a minimum; vomiting was greeted scornfully. "If you survived two-a-days, you had a chance of playing," said Burton. "But if you quit, it was over." According to Burton and several other black Hancock players, the social wedges one might expect from Mississippi didn't arise. Some of this was a product of the intense workouts — the team that sweated together bonded together. The freshman Hawks' roster included but five blacks, including Burton. "Race just wasn't a problem at the school," said Burton. "I guess it'd be a better story had it been. But . . . we all got along really well." From the earliest practices, Shaw knew he had a spring-loaded weapon in the new halfback. So did Brett Favre. Even though he fantasized of throwing 30 passes per game, the quarterback marveled at Burton's burst and precision. On the varsity, Scott Favre handed off to Lydell Curry, a dazzling six-foot-one, 190-pound whirlwind of a runner who would go on to play at Mississippi State. "Charles Burton," said Shaw, "was even better."

At the same time Scott Favre was guiding the varsity Hawks to a 6-4 mark, Brett Favre was leading the freshman team to an undefeated record and Deep South Conference title. Well, not leading. But he did flip the ball to Charles Burton left, Charles Burton right. Burton became a master of the 38 Sweep, which involved him taking the ball from Favre and bursting around the right tackle. "Our offensive line was just amazing, even in ninth grade," Burton said. "When I ran inside, I would go through the line laughing. Not in my head — laughing aloud. I wasn't a trash talker, but it was just too easy. It seemed funny."

Before it was common for Mississippi blacks and whites to socially mingle, Brett Favre and Charles Burton were tight. On occasion Burton slept over at the Favre house, waking up to the bountiful breakfast served up by Bonita. "She's like my other mother," said Burton. "If I have any problems, I call her." If Burton didn't feel like enduring the 45-minute bus ride home after school, he'd spend the afternoon with the Favres, playing sports in the yard, watching TV. In between seasons, Brett sometimes traveled to Pearlington to hang with the Burtons. "My parents loved Brett," Burton said. "He was family."

Across Hancock County, few people knew a freshman named Brett Favre existed. There was no hype for the rising young quarterback, no talk of future greatness. People didn't flock to see him play. Brenda Heathcock, prep-football writer for the local *Sea Coast Echo,* wasn't pitching profiles of the kid. "Scott was a big deal," Heathcock said. "Brett was not."

Burton, however, knew the truth. When practice ended and teammates walked off to the locker room, quarterback and halfback often stuck around. At the time Brett's favorite quarterback was Miami Dolphins phenom Dan Marino. He mimicked his cadences — "Blue 50! Blue 50!" — and sent Burton out for deep passes. "He would launch that thing," Burton said. "Not 20, 30 yards like most kids. I'm talking 50 yards easy, without much effort. We were a running team. I understood that. But, dang, you couldn't watch Brett throw the ball and not think it kind of special."

The physicality remained a secret. Shaw's offense ran often and effectively, and Favre dutifully handed off the ball. Then, in the last game of the season, the Hawks squared off against Pearl River Central, the conference's power team. The Blue Devils successfully stymied Burton, loading the line with seven and eight players. Burton ran the ball on a sweep — *Bam!* Up the middle — *Thwap!* With 12 seconds remaining in the game, the Hawks trailed 12–7. Hopes of the conference title were dwindling away. "It was against our nature," said Shaw, "but I said, 'The only way we're gonna win this game is if Brett throws it and Charles catches it.'" The play call was simple — Burton, lined up wide, ran a go route straight down the field. Favre, out of the shotgun, dropped back and threw it far.

Very . . .

Very . . .

Very . . .

Far.

Despite standing only five feet seven and weighing but 160 pounds, Burton split two defenders, glanced over his right shoulder, and hauled in the pass. "We used a Wilson football for freshmen, which was a little bit smaller than the regulation ball," said Shaw. "But Brett threw that thing 50 yards in the air — 50 yards! Easily!" As soon as Burton crossed the end zone, Shaw charged the field, smothering his quarterback in a bear hug.

"Amazing," he screamed in the 14-year-old's ear. "Just amazing!"

"Son, do you know what mononucleosis is?"

The words hung there like a speech bubble in an *Archie* comic. Did

14-year-old Brett Favre know what mononucleosis was? *Did 14-year-old Brett Favre know what mononucleosis was?* How would he know what mononucleosis was, what with sports and a million other things to worry about? No, he didn't know what mononucleosis was.

What he did know, sitting in the office of Dr. Jare Barkley on that August day, staring at bland walls and the bland floor, was that something didn't feel quite right. A boy usually overloaded with energy suddenly lacked energy. A kid who typically leapt from the couch now found himself glued to the couch. Still, the doctor's visit was all his mother's idea. Favre men don't do physician appointments. "Irvin hated those medical places," said Bonita.

So did Brett. Especially when Barkley explained to him that a blood test had confirmed his diagnosis: his symptoms were a result of infection with the Epstein-Barr virus. Were it not taken seriously, mono could lead to a rupturing of the spleen, which often becomes enlarged as a result of the illness. Until he recovered, contact sports would not be a good idea. When Brett exited the room, Barkley told his mother, "Bonita, if he were mine, I wouldn't let him play football. But obviously it's your decision."

She brought the news home to Irvin, who was devastated. With Scott having graduated, the Hawks' starting varsity quarterback position was wide open, and Brett stood as the natural heir apparent. Only two days of practice had passed. It wasn't simply that Irv needed a signal caller. Hell, most any schlub could turn around and place the ball in Burton's chest. And it wasn't merely that Brett knew the plays — even though he did, by heart. No, Irvin Favre simply cherished (a word he would *never* use) having his sons play quarterback under his tutelage. Scott had been the Hawks' hardest worker for his three seasons on varsity, and Brett was, if possible, even more driven. He knew his sons would keep their teammates in line, and he also knew he could make an example of Brett without having the kid crumble. The Favre boys would lead as he would lead, and that — beyond any other attribute — was invaluable to Irvin.

Now, however, Brett was out. Irvin asked a million questions, looked for the smallest loophole. *What if Brett . . . Maybe if he . . . Perhaps there's a way . . . How about we . . .* but accepted his son would need three to four weeks of rest and an avoidance of all contact sports.

Brett was inconsolable. The boy who rarely cried sobbed like an infant. Come late summer, the Hancock North Central varsity football team commenced practice without its presumed starting quarterback. In his place stood sophomore Melton Lewis, a converted running back with a quick first step, an average football IQ, and a soggy noodle for a throwing arm. Expectations for the team were low. Wrote Heathcock in the *Echo:* "[Irvin] Favre's Hawks lost most of their skill players through graduation last year, and inexperienced players are now filling those positions."

For Brett, 15 and itching for contact, it was pure hell. On the bright side, he spent much of his recovery time lifting weights and eating, gaining 25 pounds of muscle by season's end. He posed for the team photograph, hiding in the back row between Drew Malley and Byron Ladner, eyes to the side, chin tucked. During most games he would stand along the sidelines in blue jeans and his No. 10 jersey, watching, advising, pretending to be more engaged than he actually was. It's a tricky spot for any athlete, and a particularly difficult one for a teenager. Did he want Lewis to do well? Did he want Lewis to struggle? What if the Hawks dominated without him? Would he regain the quarterback job? Would he switch positions? Play only safety?

How would this whole scenario play out?

The young Hawks struggled, winning 4 of 10 games. Though Burton was a revelation at halfback, Lewis — the first black player to start at quarterback for the Hawks — was nothing more than a mediocre stand-in, there to hand off without screwing up. His season could be summed up in the Hawks' ugly 7–2 win over lowly Vancleave High, during which the Hancock offense failed to capitalize on three fumbles and an interception. Or maybe a better example was the 21–0 home loss to Stone County, when Lewis's longest completion went for 4 yards.

"Melton was a very nice guy," said Burton. "But Brett had nothing to worry about."

Although Brett Favre was going through the most dispiriting year of his life, there was some good news for the temporarily sidelined sophomore.

Namely, he had himself a girlfriend.

Her name was Deanna Tynes, and although she lived in Kiln and attended Hancock North Central, growing up, the two had rarely crossed paths. "I've been told that I first met Brett in catechism class when I was seven years old," she recalled. Then, somewhat skeptically, "The story could be true."

Deanna was a year older than Brett. She was the daughter of a single mother, Ann, and adopted by a stepfather, Kerry Tynes. Deanna had a raven's dark hair, with brown eyes and thin lips. Some said she bore a resemblance to the actress Winona Ryder. She was No. 12 on the Hawks' girls' basketball team, and one day — when she was a sophomore and Brett a freshman — she spotted him in the stands at a boys' basketball game inside the high school gymnasium. Deanna thought it odd that Brett's high-top sneakers were untied and flopped open. Her friends laughed and challenged her to question his fashion choice. "Realizing that I wasn't going to get any relief until I did what they said," she recalled, "I sighed and climbed up to the bench where Brett was sitting."

"Hey," Deanna shouted, "why don't you tie your shoes?"

"I don't know," mumbled Brett.

"Oh," she said. "OK, then."

A week later, Deanna and some other members of the basketball team were changing into their uniforms. Deanna had just pulled her shirt over her shoulders when the door flew open. She expected it to be a coach. Instead, it was Brett. He and Scott had been goofing around, and his older brother shoved him into the room. Brett spotted Deanna and was mortified.

Although he was reluctant to admit such, Brett had known about Deanna for some time; he'd kept his jealous eye on her from afar as she dated Drew Malley, his friend and the football team's fullback. Burton egged him on to ask her out. "But Brett didn't wanna mess with Drew," Burton said. "Then Drew started up with another girl. I was like, 'There you go, Brett! Here's your opportunity! Take it!'"

Scott was to turn 17 on December 22, 1983, and four days earlier Bonita held a surprise birthday party at the house, inviting the Hancock boys' and girls' basketball teams to attend. Deanna and her cousin, Vanessa, bought a shirt for Scott, then drove to the Favre household. Brett and his father had taken Scott to the Los Angeles Rams vs. New Orleans Saints game at the Superdome, and when the three returned they were greeted by a couple of dozen people and a vivacious "Surprise!" Brett didn't know Deanna had been invited. He looked across the room at her. She stared back. As gifts were exchanged and candles extinguished, Deanna excused herself to shoot baskets in the driveway. Brett spotted her from the window and worked up the courage to approach. He had yet to kiss a girl, hold a girl's hand, go on any sort of date. As he finished off a hot dog, he and Deanna shot baskets and played one-on-one. Vanessa asked if they wanted to take a ride, so she drove them around town — Brett and

Deanna in the backseat, alone. "At one point Brett's hand brushed against mine," Deanna recalled, "and he jerked his hand back like my skin was made of poison ivy."

Later that night, Vanessa dropped Brett off at his house. Deanna walked him to the front door as her cousin waited in the car. When he finally got up the nerve to ask her out, she accepted. He leaned in for his first kiss. It was predictably awkward. His head went right, her head went left. Then his head went left and hers went right. Finally, after a goofy laugh, their lips met. A few days later Brett called and asked, officially, "Will you go with me?"

"Yes," she said.

Their first official date was a dance in nearby Dedeaux. There was a DJ, some liters of soda, a tray of supermarket cookies. They danced for the first time to "Time Will Reveal" by DeBarge. Brett hated dancing but didn't mind with Deanna.

Brett was a chronic notebook scribbler, and before long BRETT FAVRE #10 LOVES DEANNA TYNES #12 was etched onto hundreds of slivers of paper. "If you sat next to Brett in class," recalled Jesse Dupree, a friend, "he'd steel your notebook and write it." As a sullen sophomore with mono, he depended on Deanna's positivity and companionship. Because the Tynes family lived 18 miles away, much of the communication took place via phone. "Deanna and I talked nonstop every night," Brett recalled. "It was always about the future, and how great it was going to be." Their dates weren't typical dates — movies, burgers, video arcade. "One day," she recalled, "he gave me a catcher's mask and mitt because he wanted me to catch for him while he practiced pitching." When Irv looked out the window to see Deanna squatting behind an imaginary plate, he ripped into his son. "Boy," he screamed, "you can't throw that hard to a girl!"

"Why not?" Brett replied. "She's catchin' it."

By the time spring of his sophomore year rolled around, Brett was healthy enough to join the Hawks' varsity baseball team. He started at third base, pitched some, and relished the opportunity to finally play under his father, the head coach. This came with its own set of complications.

Irv Favre was notoriously tough. He didn't explain so much as scream. "He'd be 100 yards away, and you'd hear him call you out," said Jesse Dupree. "He was anything but soft." Burton recalled an incident from his junior year, when he lied to his mother about having walked down to the Jourdan River for a swim. "She found out that I hadn't told the truth, and I had to go home instead of going to football practice," Burton said. "Then Irv found out, and that was all she wrote for me." The coach called his star halfback into his office, removed a strap from a desk drawer, and repeatedly beat Burton across the rear.

"Coach would rarely compliment you," said Cuevas. "You could run for 200 yards, and on Monday it'd be everything you did wrong."

That sort of treatment was the norm for Hancock North Central athletes, and it was a thousand times worse for the Favre children. Irv viewed his kids as reinforcements of his philosophy, and refused to accept mistakes or injuries with anything but utter contempt. Brett spent many of his summers participating in American Legion baseball for Irv. One year, the team traveled to Ponchatoula, Louisiana, for a game. It was 95 degrees outside, and Brett was playing third base. The batter stepped to the plate and hit a liner that nailed Favre directly in his protective cup. "Brett fell to his knees, Irvin came running out of the dugout, yelling for him to get up and throw him out," said Mark Ross, a coach with the team. "Brett got up, threw him out, then fell back on all fours." He proceeded to vomit, but remained in the game.

"That's just how it was done," said Ross. "That was Irv."

With a postrecovery return to sports, Brett felt rejuvenated. Yet it was also a disorienting time — new girlfriend, stubborn illness, and the absence of his hero and protector. Throughout his life, Brett had always turned to Scott Favre when he struggled. If Brett was awkward and occasionally bewildered by social arrangements, Scott was cool and confident. He was more handsome than his younger brother. More affable, too. He walked with a breeze to his back. "Scott was the best all-around athlete in our family," said Brandi. "He did everything he was supposed to do, followed all the rules. He was a model of how a kid should be."

Now, though, Brett's difficulties were being shared by Scott. Following an impressive baseball and football career at Hancock North Central, Scott accepted a scholarship to Mississippi State, and moved 250 miles north to Starkville. Although he packed only 165 pounds on his six-foot-two-inch frame, the oldest Favre boy hoped to take Bulldog football by storm. Instead, Emory Bellard, the team's head coach, paid Scott little mind, burying him deep on the quarterback depth chart and leaving him scratching for plays in freshman scrimmages. It hardly helped that football newcomers were mercilessly hazed. "It was so bad, it changed Scott," said Brandi. "You could see it. It made him a different person. Not in a good way."

"In hindsight, I should have gone to a junior college for two years to grow and work on my game," Scott said. "But Lydell Curry had gone to Mississippi State, some other friends went there, and I followed. Dumb mistake."

One afternoon, after wrapping up at practice, Scott returned from the field to find local police officers waiting for him. He was arrested for writing fraudulent checks to purchase an expensive car stereo at the nearby Walmart, and was placed in Oktibbeha County Jail. "Very few people from the college took up for me," he said. "Everyone seemed to be trying to figure out why I did it. Was I on drugs? Was I selling drugs? The thing nobody asked was, 'Why would a guy without a car steal a car stereo?'"

It was later confirmed that someone had stolen Scott's checkbook and gone on a Walmart spending spree. The fiasco capped a miserable half year, and Scott Favre packed his belongings, bid Bellard a cold farewell, and transferred to Pearl River Community College.

The mother tends to be overlooked. Isn't this often the case with sports figures? We look back fondly at the lessons imparted by the paternal figure, praising him for all the lectures, all the drills, all the doggedness and toughness. And we minimize the woman who created and nurtured the little man.

Bonita Favre never taught her offspring how to throw spirals or fastballs. She was a sound girls' basketball coach with good coordination. She attended nearly every game of every Favre child, sitting in the stands, cigarette between her lips, cheering with the rest of the attendees. ("Sometimes it was just impossible to do," she allows. "You'd have three games going at once, and only one me.")

"Mom was always there for us," said Brandi. "Always."

Bonita's greatest gift to her children was not availability, however, but empathy. In her 16 years as a special education teacher at Hancock North Central, Bonita went out of her way to expose her students to a world they rarely saw. She was compassionate, detailed, softhearted. "I did all kinds of things I wasn't supposed to," Bonita said. "I'd take the kids into grocery stores so they'd get some exposure to everyday things that maybe they wouldn't have any other way. One time, I took a class of special education kids on a ferry-boat ride. I didn't have permission to do it, and Lord knows what would have happened if one of them had fallen overboard or something. I just thought: *These kids probably won't ever have a chance to do this if I don't take them myself.* And I knew if I asked ahead of time, somebody would tell me I couldn't do it."

Bonita refused to shield her own children from her job. She knew the sway sports stardom carried in determining high school status, and she insisted Brett serve as a defender for her students and make certain nobody picked on them. He would visit her classes, talk sports and movies and whatever crossed their minds. "He looked after them, just as all my kids did," Bonita said. "When I went to the Special Olympics, the kids came too. You can't teach empathy and understanding without exposing people to those who need empathy and understanding."

In the fall of 1985, Brett was finally able to take his place as quarterback for the Hancock North Central Hawks. By virtue of being asked to throw five or six passes per game, he wasn't a star. But he was the head coach's son and a student body leader, and his parents asked for him to behave as one. During summers, when Brett played American Legion ball under Irv, he shared road lodging with Ronnie Herbert, the team's developmentally delayed manager. "Nobody wanted to have a room with him," said Brandi. "But Brett did, and he never complained or minded. He knew it was the right thing." In football, the team's water boy was a kid named Kenneth Garcia. Better known as Turtle, he was also developmentally impaired. Some of the students taunted him. Many ignored him. Brett befriended him. "It came naturally," said Bonita. "He could be very understanding."

With his son now starting at quarterback, safety, and punter, and a large number of new, high-caliber players joining the roster, Irv Favre's Hawks were, after a half-decade drought, competitive. The team featured two running backs — Burton and Stanley Jordan — who exceeded 1,000 yards on the ground, and a quarterback who could launch a ball 70 yards in the air without so much as a trickle of sweat. Not that it mattered. There was never any chance of Irvin Favre letting the boy drop back and wing it. Years later, it remains fodder for what would make a fantastic gridiron-themed mystery series — *The Coach-Dad Who Never Threw.* Irv had witnessed enough backyard football to know Brett possessed a fabulous arm. Yet when it came to game planning, Brett's role was no different from that of the Wing-T quarterbacks at Delaware. Handoff left, handoff right, keep the ball and run left, keep the ball and run right. Pass once every solar eclipse and don't get in Charles Burton's way. *Yawn.*

The father insisted he knew what he was doing. And, as a motivator, there were few better than Irvin Favre. His pregame pep talks were inspiring and feisty — *They say they're gonna kick your rears! They say you guys can't bring it! Is that how you wanna go down?* He also grasped the psychology of the teenage boy. "He'd write letters to his own players, pretending they were from the other team," Brett recalled. "They'd say stuff like, 'You no-good so-and-so, we're going to whip you.' And the players believed it. We'd get so mad we'd want to kick some ass."

Strategy-wise, though, Irv Favre was done in by a stubborn adherence to running at all costs. "It's weird, no question," said Vincent Cuevas, the Hawks' top receiver. "It's not like Brett developed his arm strength in college. He had it in high school, and we all hoped Coach would air it out. But it wasn't an option for him. I never understood."

Against the majority of the Hawks' schedule, it mattered not. Hancock North Central operated a wishbone/Wing-T hybrid, and Burton's merging of speed and toughness resulted in high-scoring games that suggested offensive genius. Through its first three contests, the team scored 11 touchdowns — all but one via the run. The Hawks gained 342 yards of total offense in a 32–7 crushing of St. Stanislaus, then scored six touchdowns on 350 total yards while humiliating St. Martin, 39–6 (Burton ran for 301 yards on 13 carries against the Yellow Jackets). It was easy work, made easy by one of the smoothest halfbacks anyone had ever seen.

"I remember after one game, we were sitting in the office and Irv said to me, 'Why are we throwing the ball so much?'" Shaw recalled. "I said, 'We only threw it four times tonight.'"

The team's three defeats, though, told the story of a head coach unwilling to recognize the potential greatness of a boy living beneath his roof. During practices, Brett unleashed passes that sailed far into the Mississippi sky — high, awe-inspiring rainbows that caused people to stop and watch. He threw finger-crunching outs and slants; "the kind of tosses NFL quarterbacks probably made," said Cuevas. In one game, he rifled a touchdown pass to Tommy Lull that knocked the receiver back two feet. "I had," Brett recalled, "a little to learn about touch." Another time, his pass hit Delano Lewis in the chest with such force that his helmet popped off his head. "The only way to catch his balls was with your body," said Jacob Dupree, a teammate. "You couldn't catch with your hands." The quarterback made certain his father was watching. The throws were un-spoken pleas to open things up. Irv, however, would not budge. "Irv's basic philosophy of football was that the team that runs the best and plays the best defense wins," said Rocky Gaudin, his assistant coach. "We knew we had a kid who could be a real good quarterback. But Charles Burton was a Walter Payton–type runner."

In a 14–6 Hawks loss at Stone County High in Perkinston, the Tomcats played eight men at the line, dared Burton to run, then knocked Brett out of the game when he plunged into the teeth of the defense and was slammed to the ground. He threw a total of seven balls, three of which were completed. Even when it was clear Chris Calcote, the Stone County coach, knew what was coming, Irv refused to throw. Against Long Beach, the Hawks led 14–0 in the second quarter, then went 17 straight plays without a pass as the Bearcats — also playing the majority of defenders at the line of scrimmage — charged back for a 15–14 triumph. "I guess we didn't want it bad enough," Irvin Favre said afterward, chalking up the loss to lack of effort, not lack of vision.

The most egregious setback came on November 16, in the 11th annual Wendell Ladner Bowl against Forrest County Agricultural High. The Aggies took a 15–8 halftime advantage and led 22–15 at the end of the third quarter. The Hawks received the ball early in the fourth quarter, and promptly ran three straight plays for minimal yardage before punting. Standing alongside his father on the sidelines, Brett begged for the offense to open up. Like most other schools, Forrest County had devoted itself to stopping Burton. "Dad," Brett pleaded, "I can throw on these guys. Lemme go deep, please . . ."

"Boy," Irvin responded, "shut your mouth."

The outcome was sealed with 58 seconds left in the fourth, when Brett's desperation heave to Cuevas was intercepted near the end zone. As he walked off the field, the quarterback's shoulders were slumped, his eyes glued to the ground. Hancock finished 7-3. Brett Favre loved the game of football more than anything else in life, but he wasn't allowed to do what he did best.

Throw.

4

VARSITY BLUES

THE CLOAK of invisibility fit young Brett Favre like a snug Champion sweatshirt, and no matter what people say about his frenzied recruitment by colleges back in the fall and winter of 1985 and spring of 1986, well, there was no such frenzy.

On page 110 of his very own autobiography, for example, Brett wrote of receiving an offer to play football at the University of Alabama.* Nobody at the school seemed to remember this.

He also wrote that Pearl River Junior College offered him a scholarship to play quarterback. Ditto.

In multiple interviews with multiple people, Irvin Favre said his son was pursued by Delta State and Mississippi College. "They both wanted him bad," Irvin told a reporter. Louisiana State, he insisted, "was interested for a while." As was Florida. False, false, false.

Brett Favre was neither wanted nor unwanted by America's Division I, II, and III college football programs. To be wanted or unwanted one must exist. And if you walked into the offices at the University of Alabama, or Auburn, or LSU, or Georgia, or Bucknell, Duke, Brown, Clemson, San Diego State, Arkansas—Brett Favre was a phantom. A nonfigment of nonimaginations. All college football programs have boards ranking the top desired high school prospects at every position. Brett Favre wasn't merely on the bottom of the boards, or just to the south of the boards. No, he wasn't even considered for the boards. Within the athletic departments of the state's three major Division I universities (University of Mis-

---

* In his defense, Favre wrote nary a word of *Favre: For the Record*. The book was entirely the product of Chris Havel, a Green Bay media personality.

sissippi, Mississippi State, Southern Miss), Brett Lorenzo Favre failed to register. Pearl River College's starting quarterback was a kid named Scott Favre — *and the Wildcats could not have cared less.*

"Brett was a fun kid to cover," said Brenda Heathcock of the *Sea Coast Echo.* "But the scouts were never there to see him."

Entering his senior year of high school, Brett Favre was fully aware of this fact. He had the arm, and he had the work ethic, and he even had the dream. In their nightly phone conversations, Brett assured Deanna he would wind up playing "big-time" college football. "You watch," he'd say. And she told him she believed it to be true, too. Which, perhaps, she did. But not rationally.

Scouts *did* descend upon Hancock North Central's campus, notepads in hand, to decide whether the school's best player warranted a scholarship and roster spot. Ultimately, all deemed Charles Burton — owner of nearly 2,200 rushing yards in two varsity seasons — too small (at the time, five-foot-six running backs barely existed) and not quite fast enough (he had 4.6-ish speed in the 40-yard dash). "It didn't help that my test scores were low," said Burton. "I blew any chance by not studying hard enough."

Brett Favre studied hard enough. His grades were solid, and he went his first three years of high school with perfect attendance. But, at six feet two and 200 pounds, he was too slow to draw any real interest as a safety, and too unaccomplished to intrigue recruiters as a quarterback. His one hope was that the 1986 Hawks would need him to throw enough that some college *might* notice. Granted, in the *Sea Coast Echo* football preview of the Hawks, Brett Favre is mentioned but once, in the third-to-last paragraph midway through a listing of all the team's players. And granted, Doug Barber of the Biloxi-based *Sun-Herald* limited his take on the Hawks to praise for Burton. And granted, Irvin Favre had no plans on deviating from the cozy confines of his limited offensive knowledge. Still, if scouts could observe his arm strength, Brett Favre *knew* he had a shot. "He wanted to be seen," said Scott Favre. "He needed exposure to have an opportunity."

Any morsels of optimism surely died on the night of September 5, 1986, when the Hawks opened with a 20–7 home win against the St. John Eagles. Before every game, Irvin Favre had his players walk the field in search of divots, holes, slick spots. Burton always refused. Instead, he would stand in the two end zones. "This is where I expect to wind up," he explained. Facing St. John, Burton compiled touchdown runs of 43,

58, and 55 yards, en route to 191 total rushing yards. When asked why his team lost, St. John coach Mike Gavin sighed and said, simply, "Too much Charles Burton." Favre, meanwhile, threw five passes — six if you include the 28-yard touchdown strike to Vincent Cuevas that was overturned by an illegal-procedure penalty. He completed two, for zero yards. The front page of the next day's *Sea Coast Echo* featured an enormous photograph of Burton, slicing through the Eagles' defense. Inside the sports section, Heathcock — surely inadvertently — excluded Brett Favre's name, writing in the game recap that the "quarterback tossed the ball to Casey Hoda for a two-point conversion." The *Picayune Item,* another local newspaper, referred to Brett as "Scott Favre."

Through three games, Brett threw 17 passes, completing 8. He also tallied 40 rushing yards on 18 carries. But what could he say? The team was soaring.

In the lead-up to a Week 4 clash with Pass Christian, Brett decided to have some fun. With his father's attention elsewhere, he gathered the offense around and declared that, instead of clapping and saying "Break!" upon leaving the huddle before every play, they would clap and say "Banana!" or "Horse!" or "Fish!" Whatever word came to mind. Most of the Hawks chuckled, but Jesse Dupree, an offensive tackle nicknamed Mongo, did not. "We're losing focus!" he screamed at Brett. "You wanna goof off and lose this game? Fine! Not me!" Irv overheard the confrontation and ordered his players to run five punishment laps after practice.

"Well, we take a break for water and Brett comes right up to me and said, 'After practice — you and me, it's on.' And I said, 'OK, no problem,' even though he was bigger. I mean, we're in pads. How bad can it be?" When practice concluded, Irv called the team together. "Jesse's right — y'all need to focus more," he said. "But it ain't worth running laps over. But you better not lose this fucking game."

The fight never happened.

The Hawks won, 53–14.

On the sidelines, Brett pleaded with his father to let him throw. *Dad, we're winning by three touchdowns! Dad, send Charles on a post!* Even Scott, who regularly came home from Pearl River Junior College, took up his brother's cause. During the fourth quarter of the Pearl River Central clash, Brett begged his brother, who was standing on the sideline, to convince Irv to open up the offense. When the game was in hand, Scott turned to his father and said, "Dad, let Brett throw a bit."

Irv, decked out in his requisite coaching attire (dark collared shirt with COACH FAVRE embroidered above the right pocket; beige polyester pants with a pullover snap), chestnut-dark eyes focused on the field, was not a fan of unsolicited advice. "Hey," he snapped, "why don't you get up in the stands with your mom!"

That was that. The Hawks were ranked 11th in the state's latest 4A football poll. Why mess with a good thing?

"It's just how Dad was," Scott said. "He wasn't the type who would showboat. He'd never put his son out there and try to make him star."

In case one is under the impression that Brett Favre — big-armed, non-throwing signal caller — was living in a state of misery, worry not. He wasn't. Even with meager statistics, few positions in American culture hold more status than starting high school quarterback. Especially during autumn in the Deep South.

On the Friday afternoons before games, Brett cruised down the long gray hallways of Hancock North Central, his red-and-white No. 10 game jersey screaming, I AM IMPORTANT! He was both a cliché and an enigma. Favre seemed to spend all his free time either lifting weights in the garage and listening to Phil Collins's "Against All Odds" or hanging with Deanna. There wasn't much to do in Hancock County, so students flocked to two local bars, Henry's and Diego's — both popular with underage patrons. Sometimes the football players would sneak into the local VFW hall for a beer. Brett did not. On occasion he'd visit Skater's Paradise in Waveland. Sometimes he'd catch a flick at the Choctaw Theater 4. There was a local arcade with Pac-Man and Space Invaders. Our Lady Academy in Bay Saint Louis held dances every month. He didn't have a car, and rode to school with his parents. His last scheduled class of the day was physical education, and Brett begged the teachers to arrange a game of football — "just because he loved it more than anything in the world," said Jason Dupree, a classmate.

"He wasn't *that* guy," said Cuevas, the wide receiver. "The party guy, the bigger-than-everyone-else guy. He was just Brett."

Kristin Hjelm, Deanna's friend, remembers Brett as "obnoxious and really gross. He farted loud and thought it was funny. He had a weird sense of humor that could be mean." The football team sometimes held practices during sixth period, when Hjelm was in phys ed. "This one time we were doing hook shots, and Brett was watching," she said. "He'd clap every time my sister or I caught the ball. But not in a nice way. I also thought he could be a jerk to Deanna. Kind of a dick. Just rude to her, not always so kind. He was basically the cracking-jokes, farting, not-paying-attention-to-anyone guy."

Favre systematically alternated warm moments with cruel ones. He complimented Burton one minute, ridiculed a teammate's sneaker choice the next. He could pull a friend aside and reassure him everything would work out, then come home and burn his sister's socks. One never knew. There were white students at Hancock who viewed blacks warily, who felt comfortable dropping "nigger" in casual conversation. Favre was not one of them. During his senior year, a classmate named Jackie Bush was nominated for homecoming queen, and a handful of white teammates insisted they would never vote for a black girl. Favre considered Bush a friend, and implored his fellow Hawks to support her. "I'm not what you would call a civil rights leader," he recalled years later. "But I do know that I did the right thing."

At the same time Irvin Favre and his Hancock North Central coaches had been readying for their 1986 season, Jim Carmody and his University of Southern Mississippi coaches had been preparing for *their* 1986 season.

Expectations were high at the Hattiesburg-based school, what with a loaded roster returning to a program that finished 7-4. With all the talk of great things to come, few noticed a shift on the coaching staff, where a former East Carolina assistant named Mark McHale was taking over offensive-line duties for Bill D'Andrea, who'd left for Clemson.

McHale had been hired by Keith Daniels, the Southern Miss offensive coordinator, in June. The interview and negotiations were conducted entirely via phone, and McHale's subsequent move to Mississippi was also his first trip to the state. Which was somewhat peculiar, considering McHale was immediately assigned the recruiting area that encompassed New Orleans's 75 high schools, as well as the entirety of Mississippi from Hattiesburg to the Gulf Coast.

To help McHale make the adjustment, Thamas Coleman, an assistant with the program, handed him a list of top regional prospects, as determined by a national scouting service, plus a large pile of completed questionnaires from local football stars. Inside the corner of his small office sat a cardboard box stuffed with VHS tapes of prospects. The recruiting period for soon-to-be high school seniors had only just concluded in

May, so McHale was woefully behind. "I had a whole bunch of names to consider," he said. "But Brett Favre wasn't one of them. I didn't know who he was. And if you showed me his name on paper, I wouldn't even know how to pronounce it."

On his first Friday on the job, McHale drove from the Southern Miss campus down along the Gulf Coast. He was armed with a list, a pen, a Coca-Cola, and minimal knowledge of the area's players. He stopped at a handful of schools and explained his precarious status. "One coach asked if I had seen the quarterback from Hancock North Central," McHale recalled. "I asked his name."

"Brett Favre," he was told.

He checked his list — nothing.

McHale assumed this was simply the case of a coach overhyping an opponent. Then a second coach mentioned Brett Favre. And a third. Their assessments were limited, and often accompanied by some variation of the sentence, "I really only saw him warm up, but . . ."

Here is a moment that changes everything. You're Mark McHale, sitting in your car in Nowhere, Mississippi, hearing about a wishbone/Wing-T quarterback opposing high school coaches both love and know nothing about. You're way behind in your work. There are 40 other kids to see. You're hungry. You're tired. You haven't even moved into your new apartment.

Do you call? Or do you ignore?

"I called," said McHale.

He introduced himself and told Irv Favre that he'd like to stop by Hancock North Central. The Hawks coach was euphoric. Nobody had expressed a morsel of interest in his son, and now a Division I coach wanted to talk! Upon arriving at the athletic facilities, McHale was underwhelmed. The stadium was small, the stands dumpy. He entered the football office and came across one of the most unique-looking people he'd seen in some time — square head, buzz cut, everything meaty. He sat down on a vinyl couch with foam bursting from the seams. Irv's oak desk was sloppy, covered with papers and notepads. Suddenly, McHale — whose brain had been overwhelmed by 12,471 tasks — realized the coach was both the father and a Southern Miss alum. "This wasn't good," he recalled. "I figured next I'd get the ol' speech — 'He can play for you even though he's my son.'"

Irvin Favre's next words: "Brett's my son, but he can play for you."

McHale asked to see tapes, and Irvin found some VHS footage of games from Brett's junior season. The first one was popped into the VCR. Irvin pressed Play, then excitedly noted, "That's him wearing No. 10 in the white jersey!" It was preposterous. There was Brett handing off to Charles Burton. And Brett handing off to Charles Burton. Oh, wait! There was Brett — handing off to Charles Burton. McHale was speechless. What the hell was he supposed to do with *this*? He saw Favre make four throws. As McHale rose to leave for his next appointment, Irv begged him to attend Friday's game against Pass Christian. "I'll try," he said. "But I can't make any promises."

As McHale walked to his car, he was approached by a tall, sturdy boy with light brown hair. This, Irvin said, was Brett, his son. "Coach McHale," the kid said, "I know I can play for you and I want to go to Southern Mississippi."

McHale promised he would be back on Friday.

"That's great," Brett said. "You won't be sorry."

When he returned to campus, McHale added the name "Brett Favre" to the master recruiting list and told the staff that, sure, he was unknown, but he was also big and strong and eager. "And you never have enough good quarterbacks," McHale said. "It's not like recruiting kickers."

The following Friday evening, he was back at Hancock North Central. He arrived a half hour early for the 7:30 game and made certain to check in with Irvin while his players stretched. "I wanted to emphasize how important it was that Brett throw," he recalled. In his book, *10 to 4*, McHale wrote of watching Brett Favre during warmups — his first exposure to the kid in action:

> He started out throwing from a three-step drop. The receivers went downfield six yards and broke out. Brett's throws were crisp, on target and had a perfect spiral. The receivers dropped most of them. He threw the out cut like it was his deepest ball — hard. He progressed to throwing to his backs and I noticed the same thing. They were having trouble catching the ball. It was obvious Brett didn't have what coaches call a grading mechanism. A grading mechanism is controlling the velocity of the ball, having a soft touch on short passes and throwing harder on deeper routes. Brett started throwing some deep balls. It was unbelievable! He could throw it deep and it had smoke on it. His throws were pretty, with the right arc and nose path. I was impressed. Very impressed.

McHale couldn't wait for kickoff. He found a seat, grabbed his notebook, and readied for an aerial bonanza.

Pfft.

The 53–14 Hawks victory featured five Brett Favre passes. When the game ended, Irv asked McHale whether he had been won over. *Won over?* "Um, no," he replied. "I didn't see what I needed."

Irv Favre was crestfallen. "Coach McHale," he said, "if you come back next week I promise to throw the ball more. I'll do whatever it takes to get him a scholarship. I promise!"

Irvin was not one to put his son's interests over the team's. The Favre boys were to be pieces of the puzzle, not superstars. McHale was on the fence: the Favre kid was intriguing, but equally mysterious. The recruiter retreated to campus with the intention of trying to see him again, "and hopefully he'll throw some more," McHale said. "Because I need to see what he can do in a game."

The best thing that ever happened to Brett Favre during his high school career was one of the worst things that ever happened to Charles Burton during *his* high school career.

On the evening of October 18, 1986, the Hawks traveled 23 miles to Long Beach High to play a team it had never defeated, in a hostile environment, on homecoming, in 90-degree heat, before a standing-room-only crowd. Hancock County *desperately* wanted to beat up Coach Paul Magee's Bearcats. "When you always lose," said Burton, "you hunger to win."

On the first play of the second quarter, with his team leading 22–7, Burton, playing cornerback, went in for a head-first takeout of Todd Sims, Long Beach's scrambling quarterback. He popped to his feet, heard a whistle, and looked toward the official — who was ejecting him from the game for spearing. Irvin Favre couldn't believe it, and launched into an expletive-filled tirade. Before Burton left the field, his quarterback grabbed him around the waist. "Don't worry, big brother," Brett whispered. "We *will* win this."

Irv finally allowed Brett to use his arm, and the results were glorious. He tossed 11 of his 13 passes in the second half, completing 7 for 105 yards. There was a 39-yard beauty to Cuevas, another 37-yarder to Frank Miller. Late in the fourth quarter, with the score tied at 22, Favre and Co. took over at the Hawks 41-yard line. The quarterback's legs were cramping. He felt nauseated. On first down he fired a 17-yard completion to Tim Cox, then hit Miller for 12. Donald Vince, normally Burton's blocking fullback, carried three straight times, taking the offense down to the Bearcats 4. With 38 seconds remaining, Favre rammed a sneak 3 yards into the defense, down to the lip of the goal line. There were now 29 seconds left in the game. Favre glanced at the sideline for the call. It was a handoff to Vince. He didn't want to hand off to Vince. The Hawks approached the line. Favre looked to the left, looked to the right, barked out the signals. Vince expected the football, his moment of heroism in the Year of Charles Burton. Instead, Favre took the snap from center and drove straight toward the end zone.

Touchdown!

On the sideline, Irvin Favre pumped his fist, hugged an assistant, then remembered his son had ignored him. A lecture followed—but not a particularly stern one. "I am glad he was sharp enough to select the right play," Irv said afterward. "Although I had called a different one."

The 29–22 victory improved the Hawks to 7-0 and a No. 5 state ranking. Brett proved he could not only make big passes in tight spots, but lead the team down the field with his arm. Though McHale hadn't attended the Long Beach clash, he read the recap and was pleased. He called Irvin to tell him he'd once again be in attendance when the Hawks hosted George County that Friday. "He assured me," McHale recalled, "he would have Brett throw the ball more."

Throughout the week's practices, Irvin incorporated an increased number of passing plays into the game plan. About 48 hours before kickoff, however, the coach reconsidered. Rain was in the forecast, and a wet football, Irvin believed, was not meant to travel via air. Once again McHale settled into a seat along the 50-yard line, removed a notepad from his pocket, and proceeded to watch in disbelief: "It was run, run, run, run." Favre booted a 45-yard punt. He made a touchdown-saving tackle on Rebels halfback Johnny Sargent. He ran several keepers for medium gains. "I was frustrated," said McHale. "What was I doing there?"

Then it happened. With the score tied at 8 late in the second quarter, Brett faked a handoff, dropped back, and under pressure scrambled to his right. Cuevas was covered. So was Miller. But Burton slipped through a seam and into the end zone, 21 yards away. Brett set his feet on the right hash and unleashed a rocket. "The ball had flames and smoke coming off it," McHale recalled. "[Burton] caught it and I could hear the crack." The Hawks won, 29–21.

"I was convinced," McHale said, "that Brett Favre was for real."

The season didn't end well for Hancock North Central, which lost its final two games, then declined an invitation to participate in something called the Shrimp Bowl. McHale, however, was 100 percent in on Brett Favre, and devoted himself to convincing his colleagues to offer a scholarship. He brought Favre's name up in every meeting, in every one-on-one conversation. The greatest skeptic among the Golden Eagles decision makers was Keith Daniels, the offensive coordinator. In his six years at Southern Miss, Daniels had committed the program to an option-styled attack that relied upon run-first quarterbacks. When McHale collected all the world's Brett Favre footage, he presented Daniels with a compilation.

"Did you get a chance to look at the tapes?" he asked.

"I sure did," Daniels replied.

And?

"He can't play for us, Mark," he replied. "He looks too slow on film. I'm not sure about his throwing ability because there weren't too many passes on the tapes I looked at, and the only passes I got to see were short."

McHale was torn up, but there was still hope. Daniels was being considered for a job at the University of Mississippi, and when he accepted, McHale squealed with delight. Daniels's replacement was Jack White, the Southern Miss receivers coach and a man exasperated with the team's predictable offensive schemes. White loved the idea of opening things up, but knew the Golden Eagles lacked anything resembling a drop-back quarterback. Their top-rated recruit was a quarterback out of Tangipahoa, Louisiana, named Michael Jackson, who ran for more than 1,400 yards as a senior, while passing for only 900. "I wanted to throw the ball down the field, and I wanted to throw it often," said White. "Michael Jackson was supposed to be the future, but he was an option guy. Mark kept talking about this kid named Favor, or Favray, or whatever it was. Nobody could pronounce the damn name. But the tapes were inconclusive. I told Mark I needed to meet him."

When high school athletes are being recruited, they're allowed to make official visits to five colleges. For big-time prospects, it's an arduous process of narrowing down hundreds of schools. Brett Favre faced no such dilemma. There was a single university sniffing around, and he was wait- ing (praying, really) for a legitimate invitation. As the weeks passed, from late November to early December to late December, more and more of the quarterbacks on Southern Miss's board committed elsewhere. Mickey Joseph from Marrero, Louisiana, was Nebraska-bound. Deems May of Lexington, North Carolina, would be a UNC Tar Heel. Matt Vogler from Tallahassee, Florida, picked Auburn, and Ricky Vestal of Houston was set to attend Baylor. The official signing day was February 12, 1987, and Southern Miss was running out of options. When McHale *again* men- tioned Favre to Carmody, the Southern Miss head coach asked whether he could play other positions.

Um . . . *sure.* Favre could be a safety. Maybe even a linebacker. Hell, he once made a 26-yard field goal. Punted the ball 43 yards. "My goal was to get him in the program," said McHale, "by any means necessary."

On the weekend of January 31, Brett Favre was finally brought to cam- pus for his official visit. He and his parents loaded into the family van, made the hour-and-15-minute drive from Hancock County, and enjoyed dinner with McHale at the Wagon Wheel restaurant. That Friday night, Brett hit a couple of local bars with some of the Southern Miss players while Irvin and Bonita met with McHale. The next morning, Brett con- vened with White for the first time. "I spent a lot of time with Brett that day, chatting, talking football," said White. "There was something about him. A sparkle. I can't place a finger on it, but it was there. A special feeling." White tried making small talk with Brett. The kid promised the coach he would be great, and wanted to know if a scholarship awaited. "He didn't lack confidence," said White. "It's usually a turnoff. But not in a quarterback. You want that." The next time he saw McHale, White pulled him to the side. "You're right," he said. "We should get this kid."

Carmody's hope was to sign three quarterbacks. Two had already agreed to scholarships — Jackson and Jay Stokes, an all-city standout from the Bolles School in Jacksonville, Florida. On Sunday, the last day of his visit, Brett had a scheduled 10:00 a.m. meeting with Carmody. He and his parents arrived at 9:30 — no Carmody. At 10:00 — no Carmody. At 10:30 — still no Carmody. At 11:00 . . . 11:30 . . . 12:00 . . . 12:30 . . . Finally, at 1:00 p.m., Carmody opened his door and greeted the Favres, who were miffed and embarrassed. It was the clearest signal to date that Southern Miss viewed Brett Favre as a last-minute option, not a prized possibility.

"Look, we knew he was a good athlete with good size," said Carmody. "But he never threw. So how am I supposed to be overly excited over a high school quarterback who never had to make big throws?"

His meeting with Brett lasted 15 minutes, and the young quarterback exited the coach's office with no promises. Known for his bluntness, Carmody told the family it would be a last-minute decision, and indeed it was. On signing day, Southern Miss coaches were scrambling throughout the office, trying to fill the final five vacant slots. A couple of defensive backs had committed elsewhere, as had a linebacker from Georgia. Around four o'clock that afternoon, a somewhat resigned Carmody motioned for McHale. "Mark," he said, "I want you to call Brett Favre and tell him we have a scholarship for him. I'm going to fill out that defensive slot with him. We'll take him as a free safety."

After a few misplaced calls, McHale had Brett on the phone. Favre was inside his Aunt Lane's house, babysitting her two children. His voice had the nervous crackling of a teenager sitting on the verge of a dream. "Here's a question," said McHale. "Are you still interested in coming to Southern Miss to play football?"

"Hell yeah, I'm still interested," Favre replied.

McHale asked if he'd be willing to work his rear off; to give 100 percent to the program.

"You won't be sorry, Coach McHale," Favre said.

"OK," he replied. "Welcome to the University of Southern Mississippi."

McHale couldn't tell whether he heard laughter or tears on the other end of the line.

It might have been both.

5

COLLEGE-BOUND

H IS NAME WAS Ailrick Young, and he was the University of Southern Mississippi's starting quarterback.

That's what Brett Favre was told before arriving on the Hattiesburg campus for his freshman year, and that's what he was expected to believe. And really, why not? Young possessed everything the Golden Eagles needed and Favre lacked—he was a returning junior with experience running the wishbone attack. He was fast and quick and—at six feet one, 200 pounds—built like some sort of chiseled ode to the Roman gods. He clocked the fastest mile time on the team and, as an ROTC enlistee, seemed to be in perpetually top shape. Teammates nicknamed him Rambo. "The lowest body fat of anyone, anywhere," said Tim Hallman, an offensive lineman. "Nobody was more physically fit than Ailrick Young."

Meanwhile, the obscure, unwanted, unaccomplished incoming 17-year-old freshman was just that—obscure, unwanted, and unaccomplished. Coach Jim Carmody's newest class featured 27 players, all from Southern states, all with résumés highlighting All-This and All-That selections. Alphabetically, Brett Favre placed 7th, right behind a linebacker out of Hattiesburg named David Dawkins and immediately before a wide receiver from Tuscaloosa named Anthony Harris. On expected importance to the future of the program, however, Brett Favre was 27th. "I would be lying," said Nick Floyd, the school's assistant athletic director, "if I told you I knew at the start of the season that he existed."

On April 18, Favre and the other incoming recruits attended the annual spring game between two squads of returning players. With Andrew

Anderson, the Golden Eagles' outgoing quarterback, having wrapped up his eligibility, the starters were Young and a freshman speedster named Simmie Carter. Standing along the sidelines, Favre was unimpressed. Both of the quarterbacks had Flash-like speed. But they were clearly mediocre passers. When the game ended, Favre located Mark McHale, the assistant coach who had recruited him, and said, "I can play quarterback this coming season."

It was one of the dumbest things McHale had ever heard. Sure, he was the coach who wanted Brett Favre. But the kid had no idea what he was stepping into. Although Southern Miss was the state's fourth-most-successful collegiate program (trailing Ole Miss, Mississippi State, and Jackson State) and far from a national power, its 74 years of football had produced 55 professional players, six bowl appearances, and a handful of upsets over Division I powers. Just five years earlier the Golden Eagles had been quarterbacked by Reggie Collier, a third-team All-American who guided the school to stunners over Mississippi State, Florida State, and Alabama. Collier went on to spend three years in the United States Football League before jumping to the NFL, and was regarded as one of the greatest college players of the decade. Now here was Favre, the thrower of a whopping 32 passes as a high school senior, thinking himself ready for Alabama and Auburn? It was farcical.

Four months later, on the afternoon of August 12, the freshman members of the Southern Miss football team reported to school. For many, like Brett Favre, coming to Hattiesburg from scattered small towns across the South was akin to a trip to London or Paris. Located 106 miles north of New Orleans, Hattiesburg had a population of 45,000 people. The once-thriving lumber town was best known as the home of Camp Shelby, the largest National Guard training base east of the Mississippi River. Hattiesburg was nicknamed Hub City in 1912 due to its proximity to a number of important rail lines. It had multiple hotels and restaurants, nearly all revolving, one way or another, around the 300-acre Southern Miss campus.

Except for a handful of drives to New Orleans, and a senior class trip to Boston and New York, Brett had spent precious little time away from home. During the recruiting process he had bonded with Chris Ryals, an offensive tackle from Purvis, Mississippi, and requested they become roommates. Carmody, however, placed Brett with a linebacker from Slidell, Louisiana, named Alan Anderson. "I think Coach Carmody thought Brett would be a linebacker before the end of summer camp," McHale recalled. "I couldn't work things out for Chris and Brett."

The football players all lived in Vann Hall, a three-story athletic dormitory on the northeastern portion of campus. Favre and Anderson were on the second floor, four rooms down on the left. The players lived in two-bedroom, one-bathroom suites. Each resident had his own California-sized king bed. "The beds were sort of side by side," said Anderson. "The older guys figured out how to make them into bunk beds so there was more space. We didn't do that." Favre kept things simple — his side of the room was filled with shorts, cutoff T-shirts, a couple of worn baseball caps, and, Ryals recalled, "maybe a book . . . maybe." (Favre majored in special education, and generally attended classes.)

Throughout his high school career, Brett wore uniform No. 10. There was no terrific backstory to his marriage to the digits — growing up, his two favorite quarterbacks were Dallas's Roger Staubach (No. 12) and the Saints' Archie Manning (No. 8). Brett arrived on campus assuming he would keep the number. David Bounds, an assistant to the athletic director and the man in charge of uniform distribution, told Favre that Collier had been No. 10, and it was permanently unavailable. "I told Carmody what Brett wanted and he dismissed it immediately," said Bounds. "First, we were about to retire Reggie's number. But Coach said to me, 'He's a quarterback now, but he'll probably wind up playing somewhere else. So the number isn't important.'" For whatever reason, Bounds assigned Brett uniform No. 7, which had been worn a year earlier by a defensive back named Darrell Williams. He dressed in the number in his first official team photograph, but wasn't happy. "He hated it," said Bounds. "Just hated it."

The freshmen players had four days of workouts before the entire roster arrived. Southern Miss ritual dictates that all newbies practice on both sides of the ball. "The defensive staff observed the players in the morning," recalled McHale, "and the offense got a look in the afternoon. This helped ensure that the players were in the right positions to help our football team." Steve Davis, the Golden Eagles' secondary coach, inserted Favre at safety and was moderately pleased with what he saw. "Good hands, solid feet," Davis said. "He did everything good." On offense, Favre raised few first-day eyebrows, especially when compared to Michael Jackson, another freshman quarterback. Unlike Favre, Jackson was a run-first, throw-second operator, and his speed was blurring. Whereas Favre was clocked at 5.0 seconds in the 40-yard dash, Jackson burst through the tape at 4.47 — on a muddy surface. He was electric, and even Jack White, the new offensive coordinator and a lover of the vertical passing game, was enthralled. Jackson received the vast majority of the looks at quarterback, as Brett stood to the side. "Michael fit what they were trying to do," Favre recalled. "I had a lot to learn. They could tell me what to do, but I needed the reps to get it and I wasn't getting many reps." Carmody pitted Favre's and Jackson's measurables against each other and suggested the kid from Hancock County be relocated to linebacker. "No," White replied. "Let's not do that just yet. Let me see some more of him at quarterback and see how he does when the varsity comes in." A couple of days later, Carmody was standing with his back to the field, observing the defense, when he picked up on a soft whirling noise. "Man, what is that?" he said — then turned. It was Brett Favre's football, slicing through the moist Hattiesburg air. "I coached in the NFL, and I never heard the football before or since," Carmody said. "But Brett was doing something unheard of. I was definitely intrigued."

Carmody's observation was coupled with a lingering concern that Jackson — the program's No. 1 recruit and future quarterback — appeared to be terrified. "I mean, it was striking," said White. "He couldn't get the snap from center, and we were just in shorts. He could barely get the 'Hut! Hut!' out of his mouth."

Favre, on the other hand, was cool, confident. He was also, apparently, bionic. "I knew Brett was different the very first day of freshman practice," said Alan Anderson. "Michael Jackson was ridiculously fast, and he and Brett were goofing around. We were all out there in shorts and helmets, throwing the ball around. Brett told Michael to take off running and he'd throw him the ball." Jackson jogged 20 yards, and Favre waved him farther. He went another 15 yards, and Favre again waved. "He went 40 yards, then 50," said Anderson. "I thought Brett was juking the guy. Just making him run far as a gag. Well, he cocked his shoulder and threw an absolute laser. I mean, it never got more than 15 yards off the ground, and he overthrew Michael by a good 20 yards." Silence overtook the field. "His arm," said Anderson, "was a freak of nature."

Later that evening, Nick Floyd, an assistant athletic director, was talking with Doc Harrington, beginning his 30th year as the team trainer. He asked whether any of the freshmen caught the old man's eye. "The Jackson kid can fly," Harrington said. "But there's that boy from the coast . . . boy, can he really throw it. I think his named is Favor. Or Favray. Whatever it is, Jesus Christ, he has an arm on him."

On August 15, 1987, the returning members of the Southern Miss football team reported to campus. For years, legend has held that Brett Favre was the seventh quarterback on the depth chart, closer to lint than Ailrick Young in readiness.

This is not true.

He was fifth.

Having dutifully backed up Andrew Anderson in 1986, Young was Carmody's opening-game starter. The second-stringer was Carter, the redshirt freshman who nearly accepted a scholarship to attend Nebraska before deciding to stay closer to his Louisiana home. The third quarterback was David Forbes, a 5-foot-11 sophomore, followed by the anxious Jackson. Then came Jay Stokes, an incoming freshman from Jacksonville, Florida, who completed 59 percent of his passes as a senior at the Bolles School. Lastly, there was Brett Favre.

"When I first came here, I was depressed," Favre recalled. "You sit there and you think about the fact that you were a starter in high school and all of a sudden you're a nobody. It really gets you down."

The good news trickled in. First, Stokes flamed out, so much so that, years later, most members of the Golden Eagles had to be reminded of his existence. Second, Forbes suffered a knee injury that ended both his season and career at Southern Miss. Third, coaches and players took notice of the quarterback who quietly swapped uniform numbers, from 7 to 4.

"During this one practice we were just throwing three-step hitches and the varsity wide receivers were out there with Gerald Goodman, our receivers coach," said White. "Brett takes his pretend snap — one, two, three — and fires it out there. Robbie Weeks was one of our better receivers, and before he got his hands up, the ball hit him in the chest plate of the shoulder pads and it sounded like a 12-gauge shotgun going off. Just, *Boom!* All the receivers were screaming. Well, I looked over at Gerald, and we looked at each other like we had just seen the nuclear test treaty being signed. It was, 'Did you see that shit?'" When practice ended, Goodman and White retreated behind the old field house and spontaneously jumped up and down like little children. "We've got one!" White yelped. "We've really got one!"

"You *heard* his ball go by," said Ben Washington, a Southern Miss defensive back. "I mean, guys were talking about how hard this Brett Something guy threw it, but I was skeptical. Then I stood there one day and he's throwing balls to the wide receivers, and they're whistling by. *Whistling.* Like, the noise of someone whistling . . ."

Favre didn't begin as a phenomenon, but word spread. There was a mythmaking quality to the banter — a *You're not going to believe this, but . . .* sense of wonder. Carter, the backup quarterback, initially thought nothing of the freshman — "a tall, sort of skinny kid who looked like a hundred other quarterbacks. When you're doing two-a-day practices, you mainly worry about yourself." Then one day, Carter asked Favre to help warm him up before practice. He didn't even know his name — "Hey, you." Carter grabbed a ball, walked about 15 yards away, and tossed it toward the freshman. Favre fired back a heater. "It was a spiral right to my face," said Carter. "The velocity of that pass rammed my hands into my throat. It *hurt.* I told him we were never playing catch again."

Carter's recollection is hardly an isolated moment:

Stephen Helms, redshirt freshman wide receiver: "He was trying to make an impression. So how do you do that? You throw it really hard. We'd run these drills where you'd run a 5-yard out and he'd break your fingers. He broke my finger. *Crack!* Then he broke [receiver] Darryl Tillman's finger — and Darryl's fingers were taped, with gloves on. *Crack!* Broken."

Chris McGee, senior wide receiver: "He split my hands open a couple of times during practice. Not 10 yards from me, he threw the ball as hard as he could. He did not have any touch. I caught the ball and threw it back to him. I said, 'What the heck are you trying to do?' I think I earned his respect that day because I caught the ball."

Carl Jones, senior fullback: "I can tell you this, and this is not lore. I saw Brett throw the ball 80 yards in the air. He was standing in one end zone and the ball landed on the 20-yard line."

Joel Singleton, junior linebacker: "A coach told the wide receivers to stop whining about Brett's velocity and put their fingers in icy water to numb the pain. That was a first for me . . ."

Jimmy Rosato, scout team coach: "I was coming out of the office and going to the practice field, and I see this person pick the ball up on the sideline, and there was a guy 20 yards up the field on the other side. Brett throws it on a rope and knocked him down. Then he picked up another ball, threw it to the kid, knocked him down again."

Over the course of camp, the Golden Eagles had three major scrimmages. The first two games came and went, and Favre did little. If a fifth-string freshman quarterback drops back to pass, and nobody's watching, do his throws make sounds?

The third scrimmage was scheduled for a Saturday afternoon. Generally, the games pitted the first team against the second team, with third-string players earning small nuggets of fourth-quarter action. This time Carmody announced that the first team would be facing the third string. A loud, visceral taunting immediately overtook the meeting room — veteran players graciously explaining to the rookies that they were about to turn into roadkill. "It was going to be ugly," said McHale. "You had a group of players who knew the system inside out, going against a bunch of new kids with no clue."

On the morning of the game, White told Favre he would not only start for the third team, but play at least three quarters. What followed, McHale recalled, "was one of the most amazing feats I'd ever witnessed." The third-teamers began the game with the ball on their own 35-yard line, and on first down a tailback named Kerry Valrie slammed into the line for no gain. The varsity starters rained insults upon the pile, and the third-stringers already looked defeated — heads bowed, bodies sagging. Favre wanted none of it. He approached White on the sideline, pleading, "Please let me throw the ball, Coach." McHale later wrote of what transpired:

> Brett stepped under center and took the snap. In a flash, one of the defensive linemen broke through the line and came up the middle to try for a sack, but Brett shook him off and scrambled to his right. Brett was running as hard as he could and pointing to where he wanted the receiver to run the pattern. Several defenders gained on Brett but he drew back his arm and launched a rocket. We all could hear the ball hit the receiver's shoulder pads. It was a 15-yard completion. You could see the eyes of the offensive players light up as they felt pride in gaining a first down against the first-team defense.

Throughout the game, a defensive back named John Baylor chanted, "Elway! Elway! Elway!" as Favre scrambled around the field, looking much like the Denver Broncos quarterback. It wasn't mocking, but homage. The third-stringers lost badly. But Brett Favre won. He threw a couple of touchdown passes, ran the offense to perfection, and earned the respect of the defensive starters, who slapped him on the helmet and punched him on the pads. "I don't think I've ever seen anything like this," Gene Smith, the team's defensive ends coach, told McHale.

Standing along the sideline, Young and Carter marveled at the arm strength and the moxie. A few days earlier neither had known the third-stringer's name. He was "Freshman" or "Kid." Now Brett Favre wasn't a stranger and wasn't No. 4 and wasn't the guy who would hold the clipboard and signal in plays.

He was the competition.

From the time Brett Favre signed his scholarship, the plan was to stick him on a shelf and redshirt him for the season. Even as his arm turned heads and his confidence won over disciples, Carmody thought it best to wait. Ailrick Young was the starting quarterback. So what if his passes fluttered? And so what if his deep-passing game did not exist? And so what if he was one-dimensional? And uninspired? And a below-average Division I football player?

Now in his sixth year as the Golden Eagles' head coach, the 54-year-old Carmody was a model of stability and consistency. The attributes most enthusiastically noted in a Southern Miss media-guide profile were "detailed organization and the ability to sustain long hours of hard work." He was smart and loyal, but rarely took chances or made drastic changes. The defense he ran as a coordinator at Ole Miss in the mid-1970s was the same one Southern Miss employed in 1987. He liked offensive coordinators who operated the option, primarily because it was safe.

That's why, in the lead-up to the season opener at the University of Alabama on September 5, White and McHale were stupefied when, during a staff meeting, Carmody abandoned the "Redshirt Brett Favre" plan, implying he'd like to get the true freshman a few snaps against the Crimson Tide. "Coach, I don't know how he can be ready," White replied. "He doesn't even know our plays."

Carmody, a man who made cardboard seem enrapturing, uttered words that no one in the room would soon forget. "Jack," he said, "anybody that gets my defense as excited as he does, I don't care if he knows the plays or not. Just see what you can do to get him some experience."

The days before the opener were filled with local newspaper stories concerning the Golden Eagles' prospects. In particular, much scrutiny was heaped upon Young, who, according to Doug Barber in the *Sun-Herald*, "displayed a strong arm in the USM spring game and has good quickness to the corner in an attack that depends on the speed and ball-handling ability of the quarterback." The assessment could have come straight from Carmody's mouth — and almost certainly did. Behind the scenes, Southern Miss players had little to no confidence in Young. "He was a very nice guy," said Pat Ferrell, a senior offensive tackle. "But as a quarterback, he was merely fair. I didn't think he was that good. And when he played, we did the same old stuff we always did. Predictable run-first nothing. We could win some games, but we weren't going to ever dominate."

Of the 11 games on the schedule, the Alabama matchup reigned supreme. The majority of Southern Miss's players had aspired to attend larger football schools. If you were a kid growing up in Mississippi, you dreamed of Ole Miss or Mississippi State. If you were a kid growing up in Louisiana, LSU was the holy grail. And if you were a kid from Alabama — as was the case with 42 members of the Golden Eagles' roster — you worshipped at the altar of Bear Bryant and the Crimson Tide.

Because Southern Miss didn't belong to a conference, it had few real rivalries. In Alabama, Carmody and his staff saw the program they aspired to be. In Southern Miss, the Crimson Tide saw an easy win to start the season. The Golden Eagles captured just 3 of 25 all-time meetings, and lacked the resources and cachet to keep up. The Alabamians who wound up committing to Southern Miss were a bit small or a bit slow or a bit dumb to ever play for the Tide. "We used to call ourselves the Alabama rejects," said Hallman, a native of Centreville, Alabama. "We knew that school didn't want us, and we'd be able to get some revenge by playing against them for Southern Miss."

When Favre found out he would dress for the game in Birmingham, he phoned home, blabbering excitedly about the journey and the new uniform and the chance — slight, yes, but still a chance — that he might play. Beginning with Scott's freshman year at Mississippi State, Irvin and Bonita committed themselves to attending all of their sons' college games, and routinely loaded up the family van with children, cousins, grandparents, aunts, uncles, nephews, and friends. In Hattiesburg, the news was barely news at all — toward the end of a *Sun-Herald* game preview, Barber wrote, "Freshman Brett Favre of Hancock North Central will travel to Birmingham as the No. 3 quarterback behind Young and redshirt freshman Simmie Carter of New Orleans." It was the first time he was ever mentioned in any sort of Southern Miss–related article.

Because Alabama lost most of the starters from a team that finished 10-3 and was, at one point, ranked No. 2 in the country, Southern Miss players convinced themselves an upset was possible. Bill Curry was in his first season as coach of the Tide, and his defense scared no one. "We always felt we could play with those guys," said Hallman. "We never thought of this huge talent gap."

The game began at 1:30 p.m. at Legion Field. And it was ugly. Before a sellout crowd of 75,808 crimson-and-white-clad fans, Alabama jumped out to a 24–0 halftime lead en route to a 38–6 blowout. For the media members in attendance, the obvious story line was Bobby Humphrey, the Tide halfback who scored three touchdowns and ran for 84 yards on 17 carries. For those pulling for Southern Miss, on the other hand, the story line was simple: Ailrick Young's debut proved disastrous. He completed 5 of 11 passes for 60 yards, and the offense didn't record a first down or cross midfield until 12:22 remained in the second quarter. Carmody considered pulling him on multiple occasions, but thought better of it. Carter, the backup, was a run-first Young clone who would fare little better. Favre, meanwhile, was 17 and raw. What better way to crush a boy's confidence than by feeding him to the monsters? When asked about his starter's performance, Carmody put on a brave face and said, "I thought Ailrick did a good job . . . at times."

Behind closed doors, the coach was at a loss. The Golden Eagles hadn't played in a bowl game in six years, and boosters and alumni were increasingly frustrated by Carmody's unwillingness (or lack of ability) to sell the program. Carmody viewed himself as solely a football coach. Which, in an earlier age, might have been fine. But in the 1980s, Division I teams required their coaches to shake hands and attend rubber chicken banquets and excite the loyalists with promises (legitimate or not) of bright futures. That simply wasn't Carmody's style, and if he wasn't winning, he wasn't viable.

Minus a legitimate quarterback, Southern Miss would not be winning. Once Alabama took the lead, it dared Southern Miss to throw the ball.

Only, Young couldn't. The Tide stacked the line, played single coverage on the Golden Eagles receivers, and taunted at will. "Ailrick was more of a track guy playing quarterback for us," said Kerry Williams, a defensive back. "He wasn't a thrower."

It has been suggested that watching the Alabama game was the height of frustration for young Favre. This is not true. The team was losing and Young was a catastrophe, but Brett — born of a town of 2,134 residents — was in pigskin heaven. The sights, the sounds, the crowds, the smells. Yes, he knew he was superior to Ailrick Young. But this was an amazing high. "It was exciting to be on the sideline," he said afterward. "I couldn't really explain it." After the game, Brett briefly met up with his family members, all of whom agreed the Golden Eagles would have been better served by a quarterback with a throwing arm.

"At some point," Brett said, "I'll probably get my chance."

The Southern Miss football team had two weeks off before hosting Tulane at M. M. Roberts Stadium, and Brett Favre used the interim to immerse himself in the time-honored rituals of collegiate existence.

A nondrinker throughout high school, he suddenly found himself gleefully intrigued by the cold canned beverage known as beer. He sought out every wild and crazy corner of Vann Hall, the athletic dormitory. From a structural viewpoint, the facility was an ugly cobbling of concrete and cement, of grays and browns. It was closer to a correctional institution than luxury living, but the players — away from home, surrounded by peers — loved it. "It was a crappy place," said Toby Watts, a defensive tackle. "It was smelly, cold, uninviting. But it was ours." The seniors were placed on the first floor, with the remaining players relegated to the second and third (many members of the men's basketball team also lived on the third). Jim Ferrell, a senior center, led a covert movement to splice the cable TV feed from the Vann lounge, and before long everyone had access in their rooms. The Hall was attached to an athletes-only cafeteria (Thursday was always steak night!), and one of the players stole a key, had copies made, and doled them out. "We'd swipe food from there and cook it in our rooms," said Ferrell. "I don't think we ever got caught." Because Vann Hall had three separate exits, it was fairly simple to sneak out. "Sometimes the coaches would ask me to try and calm [Brett] down a little," Ryals said. "One night we're about two minutes from curfew and I check his bed and he doesn't move, so I pull down the covers and there are six pillows zigzagged down his bed. The coaches peek in and say, 'Young Favre went to bed kind of early tonight,' and I say, 'Yes, sir, he did.' He got in about four. That's when I knew I couldn't even try to stay with him."

Brett shared the suite with Alan Anderson, Ryals, and another player. After a couple of weeks, though, Favre tired of Anderson, who always seemed to be on the phone with his girlfriend, Vanessa. "He'd have a big dip in his mouth that made him sound like he had a speech impediment," Favre recalled. "He'd sit on the phone for hours saying, 'I love you, Vanetha.' Good Lord, it made me about puke." Favre and Ryals removed the mattresses from their beds, placed them side by side on the floor in one of the rooms, and banished Anderson to the other. When McHale walked in on the arrangement, he frowned. "One of you is going to have to live with [Anderson]," he said. "Whether you like it or not." One night, while Anderson was out, Favre gathered a handful of tacks and stuck them through the cover sheet of his bed. "I had about five friends hiding when he came into the room," Favre recalled. "He got undressed, hopped into bed and started to scream. Everyone was laughing their asses off. Everyone except for Alan." Problem solved: Anderson moved out.

With rare exception, freshmen are to be seen, not heard. Such was certainly the case for many of the new players at Southern Miss, who tiptoed past the juniors and seniors while hoping not to be called out. Favre, however, never allowed himself to be defined. He bounded from room to room like an excitable puppy, throwing out nicknames, putting guys in headlocks, farting loudly, burping even louder, telling off-color jokes, talking trash. He kept a jar of pickled pigs' feet below his bed, and shared the unique delicacy with any interested parties. He particularly gravitated toward the offensive linemen — purveyors of large muscles and large quantities of alcohol. "One time all the linemen — offensive and defensive — were in someone's room, taking shots at each other, fighting," said Watts. "We had a tight end named Billy Schrider, a pretty big guy [six feet four, 216 pounds], and we got to wrestling. It was a tough fight, but I finally got him down. Well, Brett walks up and he said, 'I want a crack at you.'" Watts was six five and 242 pounds, a lean, muscular kid who placed second in the Texas state shot-put championship as a senior at Aledo High in Fort Worth. "You don't want this," he sneered.

"Yeah," Favre said, laughing. "I do."

The two took to the floor, surrounded by a ring of teammates. Favre flipped Watts over. Watts flipped Favre over. Back and forth, bodies pressed against the cold concrete floor. "I couldn't believe it," Watts said. "He was tall and lanky. It probably took 10 minutes, but he got the better of me. He was tough — exactly what you want from a quarterback."

The victory helped endear Favre to the team's linemen. When the elephants gathered in a dorm room to drink and watch TV, Brett was with them. When they hit up a fraternity party, Brett tagged along. Hattiesburg is one of Mississippi's finest cities, but there aren't 1,001 nightlife destinations. When the players went out it was usually to the End Zone, a sports pub located across the street from campus. For members of the football team, drinks were on the cheap. "Brett never drank in high school," said Scott Favre, his brother. "College was when he got out, saw what the real world was about. So he kind of went crazy with it."

The fact was Brett grew up around alcohol. His grandfather owned a bar, and when he died, the wife took over. Brett spent many boyhood days at the saloon as the gamblers and drunkards went about their lives. At family gatherings, nearly everyone held a beer in their hand. The two constants were crawfish and alcohol. It wasn't so much choice as cultural predetermination.

At Southern Miss, Favre's family was the football team, and Ryals was his brother. The two knew — unless something absolutely crazy occurred — neither would play in that week's home opener against Tulane. Ryals was being redshirted, and Favre spent the two weeks post-Alabama taking precious few reps during practice. Everyone inside the program presumed Carmody's plan was the same as it had been for Week 1 — Ailrick Young as the starter, Simmie Carter as the backup, Brett Favre in uniform in the case of emergency. Even when the coach mentioned in his weekly press conference that he'd like to see Favre play, few bought in. "But truthfully, I thought I might put him in if things weren't going well," Carmody said. "I didn't make a big deal of it to the other coaches or any of the players. It was mainly something in my head."

The night before the game, the entire Southern Miss football team headed to a nearby cinema for a showing of *RoboCop*. When the film ended, Ryals and Favre stopped at a package store to purchase a case and a half of Schaefer Light. "Six bucks a case," Favre recalled. "It was the beer of choice because we didn't have any money." Over the next five hours, the teammates watched Johnny Carson and David Letterman while playing quarters, the drinking game that involves trying to bounce a quarter off a table and into a cup. If the quarter finds its mark, the other person drinks. If it doesn't, you drink. "We didn't have any change," Brett recalled, "so we used a washer."

Favre had never consumed *this* much alcohol. Neither had Ryals. "We sat there and just got drunk, drunk, drunk," Ryals said. "We figured if we drank eight beers, then seven, then six . . . we figured 36 would make the perfect pyramid." Each player downed 18 beers, went to bed at 3:00 a.m. and awoke four and a half hours later for team breakfast and meetings. At six eight and 310 pounds, Ryals seemed relatively unfazed. Favre, on the other hand, wore a shade of toad-gray. He wasn't hung over when he stepped out of bed. He was still drunk.

Though far from a national power, Tulane made the two-hour drive from New Orleans to Hattiesburg accompanied by expectations of a win. In quarterback Terrence Jones and wide receiver Marc Zeno, the Green Wave featured two explosive stars, both of whom had recently been featured inside the pages of *Sports Illustrated*. Through two games, Zeno had 16 receptions for 244 yards and four touchdowns. "We," coach Mack Brown said at the time, "have firepower."

Which, he believed, the Golden Eagles lacked. "We knew their personnel, they knew ours," said Jones, the junior quarterback. "We were close enough, geographically, that a lot of the guys from both teams played in high school. It wasn't a blood rivalry, but you didn't want to lose that game, then have to hear about it."

It was a typical early September day on the Southern Miss campus. The temperature was 94 degrees, but 110 with the heat index. M. M. Roberts Stadium held 33,000 spectators, and a mere 16,023 showed up. Though they'd only played one game, the Golden Eagles were already cold product. Terrence Jones and Marc Zeno brought fans to New Orleans's Superdome. Ailrick Young did not have the same cachet — *or any cachet* — in Hattiesburg.

Tulane jumped out to a 3–0 lead, and with Young and Carter both receiving time at quarterback, Southern Miss kept the score tight. Neither played particularly well, but Tulane committed a series of costly turnovers, and the Golden Eagles entered the locker room at halftime deadlocked with the Green Wave at 10. "[Tulane] had scouted us well against

Alabama and they were shutting us down," said Chris McGee. "Ailrick and Simmie were terrible." During the intermission, McHale said White (the offensive coordinator) asked him for any suggestions concerning blocking schemes or altering the game plan. "All I could think of was how much trouble our quarterbacks were having and that Tulane wasn't having the same problem," McHale recalled. "I blurted that I didn't think any adjustments would make a difference and that we needed to put Brett in."

Is this the way it *truly* happened? Hard to say. McHale said Favre asked to be placed in the game — which is a strange recollection, considering he still had beer coursing through his system. Neither White nor Carmody recall McHale speaking up for Favre's debut. In fact, the head coach said McHale "sort of exaggerates some of the things about Brett." Whatever the case, as the players exited the locker room for the field, Carmody grabbed Carter by the pads and pulled him aside. "I think I'm gonna give the freshman a chance," Carmody said. "It's not a reflection of how I feel about you." Carter nodded. What could he say? "I wanted to play," Carter said. "But coaches coach."

The Golden Eagles returned to the field with Young at quarterback, hoping for the best, expecting adequacy. Carmody wanted to give his starter one final chance. He felt he owed it to him. So Young jogged out to the huddle, called the designated play, stood behind center — and nothing.

Three plays, no first down.

"And that was basically it for Ailrick Young as our quarterback," said White. "Nice kid. But we had to look for something better."

With about seven minutes remaining in the third quarter, and his team trailing 16–10, Carmody yanked his headset over his ears and called up to White, who was sitting in a box above the field. "Let's put Favor in," he said.

White: "Do you mean Favre?"

Carmody: "Yes, Favre. We're putting him in."

White: "Um, are you sure?"

Carmody: "Put him in."

White: "Coach, he doesn't know left from right."

Carmody: "Put him in."

White: "Coach, he doesn't really know the playbook."

Carmody: "Don't worry, it'll be OK."

White: "I figured we were gonna redshirt him."

Carmody: "Plan's changed."

White: "Coach, I don't think this is fair to him."

Carmody: "We're putting him in. Those guys love him. They'll take care of him."

A moment later, Carmody scanned the sideline for the freshman. Brett Favre was standing alone, still burping up the aftershocks of 18 Schaefer Lights. "Take some snaps from center and warm up!" the coach yelled. "You're going in!"

Favre misheard. "You want me to punt?" he said.

"No," Carmody said, "you're going in."

"Oh, shit," Favre said.

"Oh, shit."

"Oh, shit."

"Oh, shit."

One hour earlier, as he jogged onto the field from the locker room, Favre had vomited. "He went over to the wall and bent over and ralphed," Ryals said. "Just vomits his guts up right there. He looks like he's about to drop warming up. He's sweating bullets, white as a sheet."

"He wasn't prepared to play," said Scott Favre, who was watching from the stands. "He didn't know it would happen."

With 5:48 remaining in the third quarter, Brett Favre stood alongside Carmody and listened as the coach told him, simply, "Take it easy, have fun, don't make any mistakes." He pushed Favre onto the field, placing his right hand square in the black No. 4 on the middle of his gold jersey. Tim Hallman, the starting right guard, looked up, perplexed by the sight of the freshman jogging into the huddle, head bobbing, arms pumping. He turned toward Jim Ferrell, the center, and said, "That's the cocky kid from the coast, right?"

Ferrell nodded.

"What the hell is he doing here?" Hallman said.

"My first thought was, *Has Coach lost his mind?*" Hallman recalled. "I can't believe he's gonna try and throw a fourth-stringer in the game. I didn't even know his name. Was it Favree or Fahvor?"

In the stands, Bonita Favre was talking when she felt an elbow jabbing into her ribs. It was Irvin. There were about 20 Favre family members in the stands. "Brett's going in!" he yelled. "Brett's going in the game!"

"What?" she screamed. "He's what?"

Around them, a chant accompanied their son's steps toward the center of the field. "Great! White! Hope! Great! White! Hope!" Young and Carter were African Americans, as had been most of the option quarterbacks employed by Carmody through the years. "I'm not proud of the chanting," Bonita said. "It wasn't people at their finest."

Favre reached the huddle, breath smelling of beer and puke, hands quivering. He clapped, said, "OK, let's go! We're gonna score!" and called some sort of a play that included numbers and letters he didn't fully understand. "He was wide-eyed," said Jay Sherron, the starting left guard, "but he was instant energy. He took charge like he'd been there for years."

Because we live in a world of sports mythology, much has been written of Brett Favre immediately marching Southern Miss down the field in a powerful display of leadership; of throwing a 50-yard touchdown pass and screaming, "I'm Brett Favre, and this is my team!" Al Jones, a respected Mississippi journalist covering the game for the *Biloxi Sun-Herald*, vividly recalled Favre's first pass — "He got the ball and overthrew the receiver by a good 15, 20 yards, and everyone went crazy because it went so far."

Never happened.

On first and 10 from the Southern Miss 21, Favre took his first official snap as a college football player, turning to his right and perfectly handing off to halfback Shelton Gandy for a 1-yard gain. On second down he dropped back, tucked the ball, and plowed into the line, advancing three inches. "I just didn't know where to throw," he said afterward. "My mind just felt like it was blown." Finally, with Southern Miss facing a third and 9, White called for a pass to Eugene Rowell, a sophomore wide receiver with no Division I receptions. If anyone on the field could feel Favre's nervousness, it was Rowell, who had been lightly recruited out of Auburn (Alabama) High and whose blazing speed was marred by iffy hands and poor route running. This time, Favre dropped back, rolled slightly to his right, and spotted Rowell 7 yards away. His pass hit the receiver in the chest, a refreshing change from Young's rickety ducks. Even though the Golden Eagles fell a yard short of a first down and had to punt, the small crowd let loose a standing ovation.

Here was their quarterback.

The Southern Miss defense returned to the field, and when Kerry Valrie picked off an errant Jones pass, Favre found himself back in the huddle. He guided the offense 32 yards on four plays, then avoided a full-out Tulane blitz, slid right, and rifled a 9-yard scoring pass to Chris McGee, the senior receiver, who broke free when a Green Wave cornerback collided with a teammate and fell to the ground. Favre leapt into the air, pumped his fist, sprinted into the end zone, and slammed into McGee. White was incredulous — Favre had executed the wrong play. The touchdown gave Southern Miss a 17–16 lead. "He injected us with energy and confidence," said Chris Seroka, the kicker. "It was like, 'Whoa. We've got this thing going now.'"

Tulane countered when Jones scrambled through the Southern Miss defense for a 52-yard touchdown, then hit Zeno for the two-point conversion and a 24–17 advantage. The Golden Eagles rebounded, and a 2-yard sweep by Gandy again tied the score with 11:49 remaining. After Carmody's defensive unit held the Green Wave to three plays and a punt, Favre sauntered into the huddle, stared down his five senior offensive linemen, and said, "OK, shut up and listen. Here's what we're about to do . . ."

He guided the team on a symphonic 55-yard drive — barking at teammates, taking his time, walking with the confident strut of a seasoned veteran. Sometimes he took seven-step drops when they were supposed to be nine. Sometimes he took five-step drops when they were supposed to be seven. He punctuated play calls with statements like, "You know, just go left!" or "Run over there to the big guy!" On third and 10 at the Tulane 23, Favre dropped back. And back. And back. The pocket collapsed around him from both sides. With defensive end Darius DeClouette charging from the blind side, Favre rolled to his right past the outstretched arms of defensive end Lonnie Marts. Favre ran, ran, ran, ran, closer to the sideline, football gripped tightly in his right hand. With Marts inches away and two other defenders approaching and the head linesman in his path, he squeezed the ball in both hands, cocked his arm, and flipped it high into the air and toward the end zone. "My problem," Favre recalled, "was when I saw he was pretty wide open I had to compose myself to get the ball to him." The pass seemed to hang forever — more helium balloon than bullet — before it fell into the arms of Alfred Williams, the sophomore receiver from Meridian. The building went berserk — fans jumping, hugging, screaming, stomping their feet and clapping their hands. It was the loudest anyone had heard M. M. Roberts Stadium in years.

"This," McGee said afterward, "is one of the most exciting games I've ever played in."

The Golden Eagles held on for the 31–24 win. Their new quarterback completed 6 of 10 passes for 85 yards and two touchdowns, while running for 22 more yards. When Mack Brown, Tulane's coach, was asked afterward whether he had had a plan to stop Brett Favre, he admitted, with a grin, that he'd never actually heard of Brett Favre.

6

THE MAN

I N   T H E   I M M E D I A T E   aftermath of the victory over Tulane, Jim Carmody and Jack White stood in the locker room shower, basking in the glow of serendipity. As the water streamed over their heads, the head coach turned to his offensive coordinator, smiled, and in his thick Southern drawl said, "We're gonna start him next week."

"Favre?" White asked.

"Is there someone else I don't know about?" Carmody cracked.

Though only 36, with the cherubic cheeks and boyish grin of a teenager, White had been around enough to know young, charismatic, strong-armed quarterbacks weren't a commodity to be taken for granted. Since graduating from the University of California–Santa Barbara in 1972, White had coached at East Carolina, Kansas, Jacksonville State, and Oregon State, and his quarterbacks formed an uncoordinated conga line of awfulness. There was Mike Weaver at East Carolina, who passed for two touchdowns, 9 interceptions, and 443 yards in 1974. There was Scott McMichael at Kansas, whose one touchdown was coupled by 7 interceptions in 1976. There was, perhaps most memorably (or forgettable), Ladd McKittrick at Oregon State, whose four touchdowns and 18 interceptions helped lead the 1983 Beavers to a 2-8-1 record.

Now, suddenly, he had Brett Favre.

"The freshman is starting next week," Carmody told White. "Why don't you let the boys know . . ."

The first quarterback White spoke with was Young, who took the news professionally but was quietly crushed. "You're important and we need you," White told him. "You're one of our leaders." Young nodded, exiting with his head down. He later spoke with Larry Davis, the Southern Miss noseguard. "He was upset, which was understandable," said Davis. "I told him you don't have to be a quarterback to get the ladies."

When he was done with Young, White summoned Favre, who bounded into the coach's office, peppy and high off his football emergence. "We're starting you next week," White said.

"OK, that's great," Favre said. "Who are we playing?"

"Texas A&M," White said.

"Ah, Texas A&M," Favre replied. Pause. "Are they any good?"

The Aggies were ranked No. 16 in the nation. Four players would be selected in the upcoming NFL draft. "Yeah," White said. "They're not bad."

The next week included some of the most fun days of practice in recent team history. White and the assistants worked on adjusting the playbook to Favre's skill set. "We didn't have an advanced passing game by any means," White said. "So we kept it simple: downfield, flat, inside. We did those routes over and over." Balls soared through the air, receivers bolted downfield, running backs went out for patterns. It was like spending months preparing for a Spanish guest and then learning, at the last minute, that he speaks French. "Brett wasn't Ailrick," said Rick Slater, an offensive tackle. "So we couldn't prepare as if he was the same type of player." The plays White introduced were relatively simple, but not to a kid used to handing off 30 times per game. These included 75 XYZ Cross, with 75 being the protection and X and Y the crossing wide receivers. There was also 75 Right Z Hook, fancy lingo for the Z receiver running a hook. "It was pretty basic," Favre recalled.

During the week of Favre's rise to starter, the *Student Printz,* the university's student newspaper, ran a lengthy piece about Southern Miss potentially losing its Division I-A designation due to poor attendance figures. A school needed to average at least 17,000 spectators per game, and of late the Golden Eagles were struggling to hit the number. Wrote Cliff Kirkland, a *Sun-Herald* columnist: "Southern *must* address the serious problem of dwindling fan support." Suggestions were offered, including better opponents, cheaper tickets, family-friendly promotions, and joining a conference.

Then, on the morning of September 23, 1987, the *Sun-Herald* ran this headline on the front of its sports section: FAVRE EARNS STARTING JOB FOR USM AGAINST TEXAS A&M.

Problem solved.

A whopping 22,150 fans traveled 90 miles north to Jackson's Memorial Stadium, where the Texas A&M game would be held. Some surely came to see the Aggies and their famed coach, Jackie Sherrill. Most, however, were there because of the 17-year-old quarterback with the thunderous arm.

During warmups, a Texas A&M coach named Curley Hallman paid special attention to the freshman. He watched him throw, watched him walk, watched him jog. "He looked cocky as hell," said Hallman, the Aggies' secondary coach. "He had this pigeon-toed walk, sort of a strut. And I thought, *This kid's 17? Hell, our wrecking crew is about to give him a rude awakening.*"

On paper, the game was not a particularly good one. Texas A&M won 27–14, using long second-half runs from tailback Darren Lewis and quarterback Bucky Richardson to seal what was, briefly, a close contest. Favre completed only 6 of 22 passes for 143 yards, two touchdowns, and two interceptions. "That makes it sound like he wasn't good," said Carmody. "That's very misleading."

Favre was the most jaw-dropping sight on a sloppy field. His offensive linemen played abysmally, and he spent 80 percent of his time evading defensive ends. His wideouts dropped so many passes that, at one point, a reporter in the press box cracked, "Did Southern leave its receivers in Hattiesburg?" One writer glowingly compared Favre to Archie Manning from the Ole Miss days. "In essence," Doug Barber of the *Sun-Herald* wrote, "Favre ran 40 yards under duress to gain six yards." In the second quarter, Favre dropped back and launched an exhilarating 52-yard spiral to Darryl Tillman, who burst past the defensive back, caught the ball in stride, and cruised into the end zone. "I just reared back and threw it," Favre said with a shrug. "And he caught it."

About 20 minutes after time expired, Hallman found himself in the Aggies' dressing room, changing alongside Sherrill and R. C. Slocum, the defensive coordinator. "I'm gonna tell you something," he said. "That kid they've got is gonna be something special."

Neither man agreed. "Ah, shit," said Sherrill, "he's just a boy who had a pretty good game. He ain't gonna be much of anything."

Favre was a different player from practice to practice and game to game. Hot, cold, high, low, precise, erratic. He had both the strongest arm and the worst touch anyone had ever seen. Whether he was throwing a 5-yard screen to tailback Shelton Gandy or a go route to Tillman, the velocity was always the same. "There were wide receivers coming in with the laces from the football imprinted on their chests," recalled Jarrod Bohannon, an offensive tackle. "Brett threw one speed: superhuman hard." In the pocket, he was sloppy and unpredictable. Having rarely passed in high school, Favre didn't fully grasp the intricacies of stepping forward to escape the rush. He led the world in 360-degree twists. He zeroed in on one receiver, failing to gaze elsewhere if the primary target was covered. At times, Carmody and White thought they were witnessing the second coming of Billy Kilmer. Then, in other situations, they'd pull him for Young.

Off the field, Favre devoted time to studying game plans. But not an overwhelming amount of time. He possessed both a 17-year-old quarterback's confidence and a 17-year-old quarterback's knowledge of the sport. He believed in arm strength over game plans. "You have to remember, he was very young," said Simmie Carter, the backup quarterback. "He was really just a kid."

Scott Favre, Brett's older brother, was now a student at Southern Miss. He'd given up intercollegiate sports after quarterbacking for Pearl River Junior College to focus on pursuing his degree and his beer. He and Brett were often inseparable inside Vann Hall, at fraternity parties, at bars. Along with cold beverages, Brett tried to commit himself to Deanna Tynes, his high school girlfriend. A sophomore basketball player at Pearl River, Deanna called Brett every day, and saw him as often as possible. It was a 39-mile drive from Hattiesburg to the Poplarville junior college campus. Kerry Williams, a sophomore defensive back at Southern Miss, was dating a coed on the Pearl River women's basketball team. "So we'd sneak out after curfew together and drive down to see them," said Williams. "No one had to know." Brett and Deanna were on again, off again. There was love, but Brett's availability (emotionally, physically) was limited. He was a college football player. All else came second.

Carmody didn't concern himself with the details of his quarterback's social life, but he believed the boy needed to mature. His reckless play was a cover for limited knowledge, and every time Brett twisted right, slipped left, rose, and threw off his back foot, the coach covered his eyes and sighed. The only saving grace was the results. One week after the Texas A&M loss, Southern Miss traveled north to Louisville to spar with a high-flying Cardinals squad haunted by five straight losses to the

Golden Eagles. "We considered them our big rivalry game, because we could never beat them," said Craig Swabek, a Louisville running back. "Every year we played them we were convinced we'd win. And every year the same thing happened . . ."

The final score was 65–6. Barber, the *Sun-Herald*'s excellent beat writer, called it "a nuking." When the Golden Eagles took a 24–0 first-quarter lead, half the fans began to exit. Favre threw for three touchdown passes, including two long ones (22 yards and 38 yards) to Chris McGee, his new favorite receiver. His finest moment came midway through the first quarter, when he marched his team 80 yards down the field before capping the drive by (*gasp!*) looking off two covered targets and hitting tight end Preston Hansford with a slug to the chest.

"I didn't know who he was before that game," said Howard Schnellenberger, Louisville's legendary head coach. "Two things stood out. First, he wore his uniform like one would a pair of Wranglers. And second, he was the right man for the right job in the right system. After getting beaten up like that, we could see what they had was pretty special."

There were highs, there were lows. The next week Southern Miss hosted No. 6 Florida State, and lost 61–10. Favre celebrated his 18th birthday by completing a mere 5 of 30 passes for 40 yards. Among his four interceptions was one to a Seminoles cornerback named Deion Sanders. Toward the end of the play, a defensive lineman clubbed Favre in the chin with his forearm, knocking him unconscious. Afterward, Carmody and White were terrified that the freshman would lose confidence. Yet as soon as the game ended, and the media dispersed, Brett was farting, laughing, making jokes at his own expense, cracking open a beer, and throwing his feet up on a sofa. "He used to do an impression of Tom Cruise from *Risky Business,*" said White. "He'd slide into team meetings wearing only underwear and socks. He'd look at you and say, 'Made it by three seconds!' He was just really relaxed for someone with his inexperience."

"He was a lot like Charles Barkley in personality," said Joe Courtney, a Southern Miss basketball player. "He'd make comments, and you'd laugh 20 minutes later because they were sharp. He could say a few words and make a paragraph. I played with Michael Jordan later in the NBA, and he and Brett both had a quality where they seem to know what's going on at all times."

At the conclusion of most games, Brett received an inevitable lecture from Irvin, who arrived with a mental list of mistakes. The Favre family traveled everywhere Southern Miss played, and Dad considered it his duty to break his son's performance down. He was relentless and rarely complimentary, but Brett took it all in. He knew what his father was, and that the words were as much for the old man's benefit as for his. He also surely realized that, deep down, there had to be some mitigating feelings of incompetence. Irvin coached Brett for two full high school football seasons and rarely had his son throw. Now, less than a year later, Brett Favre was the nation's hottest freshman quarterback, discovered by his college coaches in less than a month of exposure. How could that have made Irvin Favre look? Like a genius, for raising such a boy? Or a fool, for not knowing what he had?

If the Florida State game was a rough endeavor for Favre, the next week's matchup — against Mississippi State in an emotional clash at Mississippi Veterans Memorial Stadium in Jackson — was embarrassing. After being told how the Golden Eagles' season could be made with a win over the Bulldogs, Favre charged onto the field and flopped. With less than three minutes remaining in the third quarter, and his team trailing 14–3, Carmody pulled Favre, inserted Young, and then watched as the onetime starter led Southern Miss on two fourth-quarter scoring drives in a magical 18–14 victory before 40,000 spectators. "We got to a point where I could see we had stagnated," Carmody said. "You feel you need to do something to get it going."

That evening, Carmody returned home and debated whether it was time to reinstate Ailrick Young as the starter. After two straight subpar showings, Favre seemed to be regressing. "You always worry about killing a guy's confidence," said Carmody. "Brett was resilient, no question. But I'm sure he had some doubts creeping in."

A decision was made: one more chance. Were the freshman to struggle at Memphis State, he would spend the remainder of the season on the bench, learning and preparing for 1988.

Was he nervous and uptight? Hardly. The morning of the game, the entire team — dressed in mandatory shirt-and-tie attire — took a trip to Graceland. While walking past Steve Davis, the Golden Eagles' secondary coach, Favre smiled and said, "Thanks for the autograph, Mr. Gatlin."

What?

Moments later, Davis was approached by two young women. "Mr. Gatlin, do you think we can have your autograph?" Favre had told them that Davis was Larry Gatlin, the famed country singer. "What makes it really funny," said David, "is I don't even look like Larry Gatlin."

Southern Miss won, 17–14, behind Favre's two touchdown passes and 123 yards. His starting job was secure.

With the freshman leading the way, the Golden Eagles wound up with a 6-5 record, and Favre's statistics (a school-record 15 touchdown passes, 13 interceptions, 1,264 yards) made him one of the nation's most accomplished freshman passers.

"We weren't a great team," said White. "We had OK talent. But when you worked with Brett every day, it became clear we had a quarterback who could take us to pretty big places. When the season ended I was just excited to see what he would do next."

There are things 18-year-old college quarterbacks want to hear, and things 18-year-old college quarterbacks don't want to hear.

Want to hear: You have an amazing arm and a bright future!

Don't want to hear: We're dismantling the program.

Want to hear: We have some exciting freshman receivers joining the team!

Don't want to hear: They're all five feet three.

Want to hear: We're planning on throwing the ball more than ever!

Don't want to hear: I'm pregnant.

Silence.

I'm pregnant.

That last one—those words hit Brett Favre like an anvil to the jaw. They were delivered via Deanna Tynes in the early summer days of 1988. At the time, she was planning on transferring from Pearl River Junior College to Southern Miss to pursue her four-year degree. She had been experiencing slight vaginal bleeding, however, and made an appointment with her gynecologist. "After the results came back positive," she recalled, "a social worker took me into her small office, sat me in a chair, and looked at me with a concerned expression." The woman had a simple question: *What do you want to do?*

Deanna's first thoughts were of her mother and grandmother, and their inevitable disappointment. Her second thought was that, even at age 19, there was no way she would have an abortion. When she told Brett the news, he was surprisingly calm and reasoned. He, too, didn't believe in abortion (both were raised Catholic), and assured Deanna all would be OK. They discussed marriage, but dismissed the idea as foolish, and agreed to hold off informing Brett's parents.

Brett reported to Hattiesburg with the rest of his teammates, greeted by a new head coach (Curley Hallman, the former Texas A&M assistant who had admired the young quarterback just that past September), a new staff, and hopes for a winning season. But he wasn't the normal happy-go-lucky quarterback, and it was obvious to all who knew his game and personality. In particular, Irvin Favre — who made the occasional drive to Southern Miss to watch workouts — wondered aloud what was wrong with his son. The passes were crisp, but the demeanor was sullen. This wasn't the football-obsessed son he raised. Finally, after several weeks of nervousness, Brett told his father. They were home in Kiln, sitting in the living room. "I just blurted it out," Brett recalled. "It was the hardest thing I had ever done in my life." Irv didn't yell, berate, or console. He simply rose from the couch, walked into the kitchen, and cleaned the dishes. After 10 of the most emotionally tortured minutes of Brett's life, Irvin returned and sat down next to his son. "I'm not going to preach to you," he said. "I'm not going to scold you. All I'm going to say is that I expect you to step up and be a man about this. Your mom and I will do everything we can to help you, but this is your responsibility, OK? Now how are you going to handle this?"

According to Brett and Deanna, the news was greeted by relatives with peaceful contemplation. Bonita, however, remembered things quite differently. "The girls [Irvin's sister, Kay Kay, and Brandi, her daughter] told me Deanna was pregnant," she said. "I blew a gasket. I was raising Cain. My first thought was he ruined his life and his career. He was so young, just a boy." Bonita liked Deanna ("Very quiet, very polite"). But the idea of her son as a father? "He didn't know anything about being a mature adult yet," she said. "It was not the type of news we wanted to hear."

Instead of transferring to Southern Miss, Deanna dropped out of college and moved home with her parents. Brett visited when he could, spoke with Deanna regularly, and pretended, when strangers inquired, to be an excited soon-to-be father. Truth be told, however, after the shock of a pregnant girlfriend wore off, he showed minimal interest in the plight of the woman who was carrying his child.

Baby? What baby? There was football to worry about.

· · ·

In the lead-up to the 1988 season, the Southern Miss sports information department asked its athletes to fill out a questionnaire. Some of the data was helpful (Brett's goal was to "play pro football"; he resided in Vann Hall room No. 209, and his phone number was 266-2532) and some was trivial (his hometown radio station of choice was WZKX; his preferred TV network was WLOX).

All, however, was eagerly consumed by Hudson "Curley" Hallman.

At age 40, the new head coach had been something of a surprising hire. A former cornerback at Texas A&M, he'd spent the previous 15 years bouncing around the college ranks, from a defensive backs coach for four years at Alabama to a running backs coach at Memphis State for two years to a linebackers and defensive backs coach for three years at Clemson to six more seasons as the defensive backs coach at Texas A&M.

Having grown up in Northport, Alabama, just five miles from the University of Alabama campus, young Curley's dream was to play defensive back for Bear Bryant and the Crimson Tide. When he went unrecruited by the school, however, he turned toward Texas A&M and Coach Gene Stallings. It was there, while playing football and basketball, that Hallman looked around and saw guys just like him — undersized, ignored, desperate to achieve. "I learned that motivation is far more important than natural talent," he said. "And when I later worked for Coach Bryant, I loved his approach. He concerned himself with making the good player great, the average player play good. So my focus became lifting talent from a lower level to a higher level, through hard work and preparation. I came to Southern Miss with that attitude. We wouldn't get Alabama-, Florida State-, Auburn-level players often at Southern Miss. But that was OK, because we had men who'd kill to win."

Hallman watched as much tape of the 1987 Golden Eagles as possible and spotted an opening for greatness. He saw the quarterbacks listed as Favre's backups, and considered them poor fits for what was to become a high-powered pro-style passing offense. Jeff Bower, the new offensive coordinator, agreed. Simmie Carter was fast, quick, and powerful, but lacking in arm strength. Michael Jackson ran like a rocket and threw like one, too (rockets have no arms). "We needed help in the secondary, and Simmie struck me as someone with all the skills of a defensive back," Hallman said. "And Jackson — nobody could run with him. So why not try at wide receiver?" Both players agreed to make the switch and were later drafted by NFL teams. "We moved a lot of guys around," said Hallman. "We took three or four players who were third team on the defensive line and moved them to offensive line. We also played lots and lots of people. If you worked hard, I felt like you deserved to play. I don't think any teams used more people than we did."

Like many of his teammates, Favre didn't mind having a new coach. Inside Vann Hall, the dismissal of Carmody, who knew his football but was overly strict and unemotional, had been greeted with New Year's Eve–like vigor. "We had a three-day party in the dorm," said Marty Williams, the team's center. "There were kegs sitting in the middle of the dorm and when Carmody was fired we went crazy. He was just a prick to play for. And nobody wants to play for a prick."

Hallman was the exact opposite. He talked trash. He schmoozed. He had an open-door policy for everyone on the team. He refused to embarrass his men for underwhelming performances. "You'll be better tomorrow" was a common refrain, and the Golden Eagles bought in. None more eagerly than the sophomore quarterback.

Hallman knew the basics about Favre (strong arm, good vision) when he arrived, but little more. His first prolonged exposure came in spring drills, when he watched the quarterback drop back and throw. "I'll tell you what stood out," said Hallman. "If receivers were dropping his passes in practice, he wouldn't make it easier. No, he'd crank it up. That was his way of saying, 'If you can't catch that one, try catching this!'" In particular, Hallman recalled Favre throwing to Alfred Williams, a five-foot-seven, 168-pound junior receiver from Meridian. Teammates nicknamed Williams "Mud Bug" because he always seemed to rise from the ground to catch passes. "So one day Brett throws one of them bullets at him," Hallman said. "Ol' Mud Bug jumps up, and he gets hit right in the sternum. *Pop!* I mean, he busted his pads open and bruised his sternum. I thought, *OK, I can work with this quarterback.*"

In another episode, Favre and the first-team offense was practicing against the scout team defense when Keith Loescher, a linebacker lined up at defensive end, burst past the tight end and had a clear shot at the quarterback. He wasn't allowed to hit Favre, of course, but Loescher ran past and slapped him hard on the back of the helmet. "Just to let him know I could have knocked the shit out of him," said Loescher. "I kept running, I hadn't even stopped, and he threw the ball and hit me in the back of the head. It was his message." Hallman loved it.

Carmody had not been one to banter with his players. They were kids, he was the boss, and the divide was made of steel. Hallman operated differently. He had stories to tell and examples to offer. He possessed an encyclopedic memory for games and players, and he wasn't afraid to take risks in order to motivate. Southern Miss players still remember a team meeting the day after a loss. Simmie Carter had committed a series of boneheaded personal fouls, and Hallman called him to the front of the room. "Simmie," he said loudly, "if I do this . . ." — he shoved the six-foot-one, 175-pound cornerback in the chest — "how do you feel?"

"Mad," Carter said.

"Right, mad," replied Hallman, who then pushed Carter again. And again. "You want to respond, right? You want to hit me, right?"

"Yeah," said Carter, pacing back and forth, steam rising from his ears.

Hallman leaned in for another shove. "Coach," Carter said, "do not do that."

Hallman ignored Carter and rammed the player in the chest.

"Oh, man, was it tense in there," said Lehman Braley, an offensive lineman. "We all thought Simmie was about to knock him out."

He didn't. He exited the room, returned, took a deep breath, stared angrily at Hallman. "Look," the coach said, "there's always someone you wanna hit, you wanna punch, you wanna hurt. But you have to be able to control the impulse. You understand?"

Carter nodded. He understood.

Favre needed no such lessons. But from the start of their partnership, Hallman regularly evoked the mystique of Kenny Stabler, the former Alabama signal caller who went on to a fabulous 15-year NFL career. The two were old friends,* and Hallman raved of the left-handed quarterback's poker-faced approach to the position. "He never let his opponents see frustration, he never showed signs of stress or nervousness," said Hallman. "I talked to Brett about that all the time, because he had that, too. Just like Kenny."

The Golden Eagles kicked off the year by winning two of their first three games (the loss was an expected 49–13 road thrashing at the hands

---

* Hallman liked to tell people that he was the answer to the trivia question, "Who caught Kenny Stabler's last college pass?" And while it was a trivia question no one ever thought to ask, the answer was, indeed, Curley Hallman, who intercepted Stabler twice for Texas A&M in the 1968 Cotton Bowl.

of No. 10 Florida State), and on September 24 the team traveled to Green-
ville, North Carolina, to face East Carolina. On paper, it wasn't much
of a matchup. The Pirates were in the midst of their fifth straight losing season. Yet somehow, Southern Miss trailed 42–38 with less than two
minutes remaining. When he jogged back onto the field, Favre was ordered by Hallman to "get us this win." Favre moved the Golden Eagles
into Pirates territory, and with 30 seconds left took the snap at the 47-
yard line, dropped back, and surveyed the field. His third read was Williams, the five-foot-seven gnat who found an opening sprinting down
the right sideline. Favre glanced away from a covered Michael Jackson,
felt pressure from the right side, pumped slightly, and let loose a 44-yard
pass that blasted straight through the air — no arc, no wobble. The ball
slammed into Williams's chest, and he tumbled down at the 5-yard line
with 22 seconds left. "It was a laser," said Nick Floyd, the assistant athletic
director. "And the receiver wasn't even looking up." Moments later, Ailrick Young — inserted to throw off the defense — hit Preston Hansford
with a 5-yard touchdown pass, and Southern Miss won, 45–42.

Afterward, Rick Cleveland of the *Clarion-Ledger* asked Williams about
the catch. "I heard the ball humming about five yards from me," he said.
"I mean, I heard it coming at me."

Cleveland had covered hundreds of football games throughout his one
and a half decades in media. Williams *heard* the ball? C'mon. No way . . .

"I swear, I'm not joking," he said. "I heard it. I guess it was the laces
whirling in the wind, but I heard it."

With that throw and those words, Favre rose from good young quarterback to Paul Bunyan. Wrote Chuck Abadie in the *Hattiesburg American:* "USM is a football team that's fun to watch. It's a football team that
has won coming from behind. It's a football team that's getting better
each week. Maybe it is time USM began doing more to promote this football team. Get the word out to voting members of the polls that there's
something brewing here."

Five weeks later, after Southern Miss came from behind to beat Memphis State on a 45-yard Favre to Eugene Rowell touchdown pass with 39
seconds remaining, the Golden Eagles were a hot topic in the college
football universe. They clinched a berth in the Independence Bowl, the
school's first postseason appearance in seven years. Hallman's team was
8-1, and its seven-game winning streak was the longest since the school
won the 1958 small-college national championship. In the following

morning's *USA Today,* Southern Miss was ranked No. 25 in the newspaper's weekly poll. The *New York Times,* which used a computer to determine its list, had the Golden Eagles 8th, behind seven national powers (USC, Notre Dame, UCLA, West Virginia, Clemson, Florida State, and Michigan) and 10 slots ahead of Auburn, its upcoming opponent.

Which was probably a mistake.

Because so many of Hallman's players hailed from the state of Alabama, and so many of those players hailing from the state of Alabama had been ignored by Auburn, the journey to Jordan-Hare Stadium carried great significance. This was, like the clashes against the University of Alabama, about retribution. "We wanted to destroy them," said Marty Williams, the center from Eufaula, Alabama. "Not just win, not just come away with a three-point victory. We wanted to kill them and leave a bruise."

With their stellar record and their national ranking, the Golden Eagles players and coaches had never been more confident. This would be their national coming of age. "The game," said Hallman, "to show we belonged with the best." Auburn, however, was ridiculously good. The Tigers boasted college football's top-ranked defense (they finished No. 1 nationally in total defense and scoring defense), and would place seven players on the All–Southeastern Conference team. In particular, Southern Miss was worried about Tracy Rocker, a two-time All-American defensive tackle who, at six foot three and 288 pounds, was faster, stronger, and meaner than any of Hallman's offensive linemen.

Before 73,787 die-hards, Auburn jumped out to a 21–0 first-quarter lead, then added 10 more points to enter halftime up 31–0. It was football beauty vs. football ugliness, and as Auburn scored its second touchdown on a perfect 38-yard pass from Reggie Slack to Freddy Weygand, a shell-shocked Hallman knew the Tigers were too much. Somehow Favre remained unruffled. Despite being harassed on every other play, he completed 25 of 43 passes for 212 yards and a meaningless fourth-quarter touchdown. Throughout the afternoon Rocker stomped through the Golden Eagles' huddle, swinging his arms, challenging opponents to fights. "I'm the baddest motherfucker out here!" he screamed. "Can't nobody block me!" Finally, late in the game, Favre looked up at Ryals, whose muddied uniform and turf-stuffed helmet bars told the sad story of a one-sided destruction. "Chris," the quarterback bellowed, "can't you please shut that sonofabitch up?"

"Man, he ain't lying," Ryals replied. "He *is* the baddest motherfucker out here."

Favre broke up laughing.

"He would always find a way to keep us loose — win or lose," said Williams. "Whether it was something stupid he said, or a joke, we always had fun. Even while getting our asses kicked."

Southern Miss rebounded from the embarrassing loss to beat Louisiana Tech, 26–19, then play in the December 23 Independence Bowl against the University of Texas–El Paso in Shreveport, Louisiana. Of the nation's 17 bowl games, the Independence may well have been the least hyped or, for that matter, interesting. The 10-2 Miners competed in the lightly regarded Western Athletic Conference, and built their record by feasting on creampuffs like Mankato State and Weber State. While watching tape of UTEP, Hallman and his assistants knew this was a ridiculous mismatch. So, too, did Favre, who brought his characteristic sense of levity to the affair. A couple of days before the game, while the team was staying in the Clarion Hotel, Favre called Marty Williams and pretended to be a reporter for the *Shreveport Times*. For 10 minutes he peppered his center with questions about the team, the game, the "amazing, fabulous, talented, future Pro Bowl quarterback named Brett Favre!" Having rarely been requested by the media, Williams was thrilled, and blathered on about life as a Southern Mississippi Golden Eagle. "Well, he has me on speaker phone and I hear the guys start laughing," Williams said. "I was so excited to be interviewed, because nobody ever cares about linemen. We went into the hall and I was pissed. I whupped his ass. He deserved it, too."

The game was as close as the fight. The Miners opened the scoring with a 30-yard first-quarter touchdown pass from Pat Hegarty to Reggie Barrett, then vanished. James Henry, a Southern Miss cornerback, returned two punts for touchdowns, Shelton Gandy ran for two scores, and Favre completed 15 of 26 passes for 157 yards and one touchdown. The final score was 38–18, and as Curley Hallman walked off the field, he could have made a serious run for the mayorship of Hattiesburg.

The program was back.

Less than two months after the Independence Bowl, on February 6, 1989, Brittany Nicole Favre was born. She weighed seven pounds, two ounces, and when Deanna Tynes held her, "I knew I'd made the right decision."

How did Brett feel, standing there at his girlfriend's bedside, looking down at the pinkish infant who was now his responsibility? It's a question he has never fully addressed. Scared? Certainly. Happy? Probably. Confused how this would all play out? Without a doubt. "We agreed to love our daughter and take care of her without getting married," Favre said. "When I was at Southern Miss I went out partying with the guys, then drove all night to see Deanna and Brittany. Here I was, [19]-years old, changing diapers in the middle of the night and playing football the next day."

The memory — conveyed to *Playboy*'s Kevin Cook in 1997 — was warm and likely well intended, but not entirely true. The Brett Favre who became a father eight months shy of his 20th birthday may well have been a burgeoning football legend, but he was ill equipped to parent. Save for a brief try at cohabitating with his girlfriend (it lasted only a few months), Brett was a bit player in Brittany's early life. The primary caretaker was Deanna, who resided in a small apartment in Poplarville and, shortly after his daughter's arrival, took a job in the collections department of a bank. As Brett was living life as the big man on the Southern Miss campus — drinking and partying and having peers ask for autographs and coeds seek his attention — Deanna dwelled in a small gray cubicle, phoning customers whose mortgages or loans were near foreclosure. "The people I called would inevitably launch into a story about their sick children or invalid mothers," she recalled. "My heart would break, of course, because I could relate to their problems."

Irv and Bonita helped pay some of the bills, but Deanna still struggled to afford rent, groceries, diapers. She left the bank to become a waitress at a local golf club. The money was better, but the life no easier. Dreams of a four-year college education died. Social experiences withered. Most of her friends were off at universities, getting drunk, meeting young men, filling in the blanks of their dreams. Deanna, meanwhile, had a screaming baby and Brett's wild stories from Southern Miss. It was the loneliest time of her life.

Favre tried to empathize. Truly, he did. On the following season's player questionnaire, he filled in the blank space alongside IF MARRIED LIST WIFE'S MAIDEN NAME AND HOMETOWN with "Deanna Lynn Tynes, Poplarville." But the couple was neither married nor engaged. A year later, the same space was left blank. In the August 27, 1989, *Clarion-Ledger*, Favre said — not entirely convincingly — that Brittany was the most important thing in his life. He added of Deanna, "We've sort of broke up right now, but I hope we can get things worked out and get married some day. I care a lot, I really do. I want to be with my daughter. I want to be a daddy." For Favre, however, the allure of single life proved irresistible. He had spent the first 17 years of existence as a sports-obsessed choirboy, and now he wanted to eat from the buffet. Keith Loescher, his pal and team-mate, remembered the night he received a call from Deanna, who des-perately wanted him to collect Brett from her apartment and take him back to campus. "He's been in the bathroom for two or three hours," she told him. "You have to get him out." Loescher arrived to find Favre drunk and passed out. He lugged him to his car and tossed him in the backseat. "If you puke," Loescher said, "I'm gonna beat your ass."

Once the season ended, Favre went wild. He was out most nights, ei-ther at bars or fraternity parties, usually drinking either in someone's dorm room or at the end of a dirt road. "We also spent a lot of time in New Orleans down in the French Quarter," Loescher said. "It was only a two-hour drive from school, and Steve Helms [a little-used wide receiver] had an uncle who owned Johnny O's, the bar across from Pat O'Brien's." Brett and Scott Favre, Ryals, Loescher, and Co. began the evenings with a couple of cherry bomb shots, then progressed to beer and more beer and more beer. "Sometimes we'd shut a place down," said Loescher. "Those were some of the best nights of my life."

Although he came to love Favre as much as any player he coached, Hallman lived in fear of the calls he inevitably received. The stories of the quarterback's wild ways could have filled a 200-page book, and of-ten involved his No. 1 running buddy, his older brother. In particular, there was a hellacious brawl at the Phi Delta Tau fraternity house. At the time, football players and fraternity members mingled like lions and ti-gers. They were parts of the same campus social circles, but warily eyeing one another, waiting for an opportunity to pounce. "Those Phi Taus were always being pricks, or at least that's what we told ourselves before going down to their house and wreaking havoc," said Pete Antoniou, a defen-sive tackle. "So one night they were having a bash and we forced our way in. All hell broke loose . . ."

The fraternity members saw the football players — the Favre broth-ers, Antoniou, Ryals, defensive tackle Buddy King — and demanded they leave. The football players saw the fraternity brothers and laughed. *Who's gonna make us?* For a solid 15 minutes, the front lawn of the fraternity house served as the state's largest boxing ring. Punches were thrown, choke holds administered. Scott, drunk and out of control, went after any fraternity brother he could find. "It was the classic story of someone talking shit, and the shit talk escalating," said Clark Henegan, Brett's friend and a participant in the melee. "Brett wasn't one to shy away from action, but he didn't start it. He was just involved, fighting, like we all were."

When members of the Hattiesburg Police Department arrived, sirens blaring, a handful of football players and fraternity members darted up the street and into nearby bushes. Many simply froze in their tracks. The fraternity members were ordered back into the house, the party officially ended. The football players were placed in the rear of the cars and brought back to Vann Hall. No charges filed.

"We were so stupid," said Antoniou, "that as soon as the cops drove off we went right back to the frat house for more."

They were greeted by a jarring sight. During the fight, Scott somehow lost his favorite pair of white Bucks shoes, and returned to Vann Hall in socks. Now, as they glanced toward the front yard, the players spotted a bright flame and some smoke. It was the shoes, on fire and charred to the insoles.

The morning after the brawl, Hallman held a team meeting and demanded that those involved in the incident identify themselves. One player had a black eye. A couple of others featured cuts and small bruises. He didn't blame Brett Favre, but he held him accountable. What sort of leader winds up in a fraternity brawl with a shoeless sibling? "After that fight I talked to Bonita and Irvin, and I said, 'I'm going to alert you ahead of time now,'" Hallman said. "Because I heard word that Scott and Brett were raising a lot of cane. I said, 'We can do one of two things. You can talk to Scott, but I'm not sure that'll help. But what's gonna happen real soon is I'm gonna suspend Brett Favre. Can you help me for that not to happen?' They got Scott to move back home or something. I said, 'I know you love both sons. But he either has to stop running around with Scott, or I'm gonna have to take action.'"

Brett Favre — part-time father, full-time quarterback — was far from done running around.

Hell, he was just beginning.

7

LEGEND

WE NEED to get a Heisman Trophy campaign going."

The nine words emerged from the mouth of Chuck Bennett, marketing and promotions coordinator for the Southern Miss athletic department. They were not greeted warmly.

There were plenty of other statements that would have made far more sense. We need to send a student to Mercury. We need to purchase Scott Baio's slippers. We need to reunite the original members of Pseudo Echo. We need to change our university's name to Bob's Souvlaki Palace.

But . . . *a Heisman campaign?* "Southern Miss ain't gonna win no Heisman," snapped Bill McLellan, the fourth-year athletic director. "No fucking chance in hell. Why even bring it up?"

This was during a staff meeting in the spring of 1989, shortly after Favre wrapped a season that saw him set school records for touchdown passes (16), passing yards (2,271), and total yards (2,256). Bennett had watched as other mid-level schools mounted fruitless campaigns on behalf of their players. Just one year earlier Tulane spent thousands of dollars promoting the candidacy of quarterback Terrence Jones, who lacked Favre's skill and charisma. The result: tons of media attention, including a (highly coveted) *Sports Illustrated* photo shoot. So, who cared if no Southern Miss player had ever placed near the top of Heisman voting? Who cared if Houston had Andre Ware and West Virginia had Major Harris and Notre Dame had Tony Rice and Florida had Emmitt Smith and Michigan State had Percy Snow and Penn State had Blair Thomas? Who cared if a solid 70 percent of college football fans couldn't properly pronounce Brett Favre's last name?

"We're Southern Miss!" Bennett replied. "To be mentioned, or even to just be considered, would be huge to us. Just in terms of getting attention for our program . . ."

"How much?" said McLellan.

"How much what?" asked Bennett.

"How much money do you need?"

Though he'd never actually kick-started a Heisman campaign, Bennett suggested $10,000 to begin. Begrudgingly (and shockingly), McLellan acquiesced. Within days, Bennett ordered 100,000 1989 football-schedule cards featuring Favre's photograph, 500 slick Favre photographs for the media, 5,000 posters featuring a full-length Favre image, and 5,000 FAVRE4HEISMAN bumper stickers. John Cox, the school's director of sports broadcasting, was enlisted to write a letter on the quarterback's behalf . . .

To Whom It May Concern:

Let me take a few moments to introduce you to Brett Favre (Farv) the junior quarterback at the University of Southern Mississippi.

Over his first two seasons with the Golden Eagles, Favre has established himself as one of the top young quarterbacks in the nation and a legitimate All-American and Heisman Trophy candidate.

Enclosed you will find a ¾ inch video that will give you some idea of what type of player Favre is. Please take a few minutes (the tape lasts only four and a half minutes) to watch this tape. I think you will enjoy it. I also believe the tape will be useful in order to provide you with some file footage on this young man to use for whatever purpose necessary.

Thanks for your time and should you need any further information or video footage on Favre or Southern Miss, please don't hesitate to let me know.

Warmest regards,
John Cox
Director of Sports Broadcasting

The efforts paid dividends. A CNN anchor held one of the bumper stickers on air and said, "Here's the best player you have never heard of." *The Sporting News*'s nationally syndicated radio show highlighted five players to follow, and selected Favre for a Tuesday profile. The idea of Brett Favre actually winning the Heisman Trophy was laughable, but when asked by Van Arnold of the *Hattiesburg American* whether his quarterback had a shot, Hallman did not hesitate. "When you talk about the top players in the country and what the Heisman Trophy stands for," he said, "you've got to add his name to the list." Why, as soon as his team wrapped the Independence Bowl, Hallman was plotting an even greater 1989 season. With 14 starters returning from the 10-win Golden Eagles, there was hope of a Top 10 finish and maybe — just maybe — a chance at a top-shelf bowl game.

To make the dreams reality, Hallman and his staff spent the winter months beating the Southern Miss players into pulp. When he first arrived at the school, many mistook the coach's casual demeanor for softness. They were terribly mistaken. Hallman's money line was, "I'm here to make you do the things you don't wanna do so you can be who you wanna be." If one missed a class, he paid Hallman back in "Curley Bucks" — aka: run the stadium steps at 4:30 a.m. The "winter workouts," as they were called, began every morning at six o'clock in the campus gym. If you were late, you were punished. If you were on time, you were also punished. Every Southern Miss player was gifted a cotton yellow sweatshirt and cotton yellow sweatpants, as thick and warm as a polar bear's fur. Hallman would turn the thermostat to 90 degrees, drag a garbage can to the middle of the room, then drop it — *Thud!* "If y'all need to use a bathroom," he'd yell, "here you go!" With that, the players spent the hour running, jumping, sprinting, pushing. "The hardest workouts imaginable, at the hardest time of day," said Leon Anderson, an offensive guard from Grapeland, Texas. "You'd have guys leaning over the can, puking up everything inside."

By the time the players reported back for fall workouts, football expectations were as high as they had ever been at the school. In Favre, there was a Heisman-worthy quarterback. In Michael Jackson and Darryl Tillman, there were a pair of top-flight wide receivers. The offensive line was experienced and skilled, the defense (a question mark at the end of 1988) looked phenomenal. Southern Miss's annual spring football game — normally a showcase for the offense — ended with a 14–6 score. The *Hattiesburg American* headline: DEFENSES DOMINATE USM GAME. "There was no reason to think we couldn't be a terrific team," said Reggie Russell, an offensive lineman. "If you look at all we had going for us."

The Golden Eagles merely had to survive their opener.

· · ·

Back in the spring of 1987, when he was a junior at A. Crawford Mosley High in Lynn Haven, Florida, Keith Loescher signed a letter of intent to play college football at Florida State University.

Although he had actually grown up rooting for the University of Florida Gators, playing Division I for a national power was a dream come true. Plus, with the commitment, Loescher — a highly recruited six-foot, 220-pound linebacker/fullback — could relax and enjoy his senior season. "I was really excited to be a Seminole," he said. "So was my family."

In the final game of his high school career, however, Loescher was carrying the ball when a defensive tackle for Pensacola's Washington High charged forward and pushed Craig Harris, A. Crawford Mosley's halfback, into Loescher's left leg. "It just snapped," Loescher said. "I knew immediately. I rolled over, and everybody was reaching down to help me up. But I wasn't getting up."

Fortunately, he had the security of the scholarship.

"On National Signing Day [Florida State defensive coordinator] Mickey Andrews came and got me out of English class to tell me they wouldn't be keeping their word," Loescher recalled. "I was devastated. I remember he said, 'Are you going to be OK? You should be home with your family tonight.' Yeah, like I wanted *his* advice."

Loescher was, in fact, home that night when the phone rang.

"Can I speak to Keith?" the strange voice said.

"This is him," Loescher replied.

"Keith, this is Curley Hallman at Southern Miss. I've never heard of you, I've never seen you play, and don't know anything about you. But you've got a full ride to my school if you want it."

Loescher and his parents visited Hattiesburg the following weekend, and committed on the spot. With that, the Golden Eagles added a player who would become one of their best linebackers, and Florida State added a lifetime enemy. "All I wanted to do," he said, "was beat them."

When Loescher initially learned Southern Miss faced Florida State most every year, he was thrilled. Especially when he looked at the future schedules and saw that, in 1989, the damned Seminoles were slated to come to M. M. Roberts Stadium. That elation, however, was lessened when McLellan took a call from C. W. "Hootie" Ingram, Florida State's athletic director. He wanted to know if the Golden Eagles would consider changing the location of the game from Hattiesburg to the Gator Bowl in

Jacksonville, Florida. McLellan said he would have to take the request to Hallman.

"Curley," McLellan said, "Florida State wants the game to be in Jacksonville, but they say we'll still be the home team."

"That's crazy," Hallman replied. "Are they offering anything?"

"Yes," said McLellan, "$525,000."

"OK," said Hallman. "Book it."

Click.

"Did I prefer the game be at our place? Of course," said Hallman. "But our entire athletic department budget was only $2.7 million."

Coming off of an 11-1 season that concluded with a Sugar Bowl victory over Auburn, Florida State was a 22-point favorite. The Seminoles had outscored the Golden Eagles 110–23 in wins the previous two years. Three of the team's quarterbacks (Peter Tom Willis, Brad Johnson, Casey Weldon) would play in the NFL, and a fourth (Charlie Ward) would win the Heisman Trophy. Three of its running backs (Edgar Bennett, Dexter Carter, Amp Lee) also played professionally. "They were more talented than we were," said Hallman. "And it wasn't close."

On the morning of the biggest game of their lives, the Southern Miss players were terrified. Lehman Braley, a backup offensive lineman and long snapper, was stretching alongside Renegade, the horse that served as one of Florida State's mascots. He'd never seen a stadium this enormous, and his blank facial expression oozed terror. Hallman looked at the sophomore, slapped him on the rear, and said, "Welcome to Division I football, son!"

The clash would be broadcast nationally on TBS — a first for many of the Golden Eagles. The night before, Favre dreamed of Southern Miss winning in the final seconds. Now he strutted onto the field with a broad smile plastered to his face. The stadium seated 80,126, and when the Golden Eagles came out for initial stretching and warmups, the seats were only about a tenth filled. Favre was standing alongside Ben Washington, a junior cornerback, when he looked up to gauge the atmosphere. "Man, there ain't a lot of people here," Favre said, grinning. "But that's all right. Fuck them." When he returned to the field a half hour later, 48,746 spectators — nearly all Florida State supporters — were watching. Many held signs reading ONE DOWN AND 11 TO GO. "Still," Favre cracked, "fuck 'em."

"Players were sweating as they put on their shoulder pads," Mark McHale, the offensive line coach, recalled. "One of our managers asked a trainer to find out the temperature. He came back and told us it was 110 degrees. I'd never coached in a game where it was that hot. The locker room was getting stuffy. There was no air flow. We heard the crowd noise muffled through the walls and the national anthem began to play."

When Southern Miss's Chuck Davis launched the opening kickoff, the temperature inside the stadium was 107 degrees. The Seminoles were wearing white uniforms. The Golden Eagles were dressed in black jerseys and gold pants. "The first thing I thought was that we'd wear them down in the all-black," said LeRoy Butler, one of Florida State's starting cornerbacks. "Black uniforms, black helmets? In the heat? Forget about it. They were dead."

On its first series of the day, Southern Miss drove to the Florida State 26 before halfback Ricky Bradley fumbled away the ball. The Seminoles scored a touchdown two minutes later on Dexter Carter's 11-yard run, then added a 24-yard field goal to lead 10–0 late in the first quarter.

It was the beginning of an inevitable rout. "To us, Southern Miss was like playing a junior college," said Butler. "A fly on our shoe — that was Southern Miss."

"We knew they had this quarterback who was very good," said Willis, the Seminoles' starter. "But I don't think any of us knew how to pronounce his name."

Then — *Boom!* On the Golden Eagles' third series of the afternoon, Favre dropped back and found Darryl Tillman for a 64-yard completion. Four plays later Davis hit a 22-yard field goal, and the score was 10–3 at the end of the opening quarter. "After the long pass we were on the 3-yard line, and Brett's under center, and the fans are screaming so loud that we can barely hear anything," said Leon Anderson, an offensive guard. "We have all these checks, and for us linemen, once he started barking, 'Blue 58! Blue 58!' — the check is coming. Well, his call to check off was 'Easy! Easy!' And in this heated moment in time, with all the pressure in the world and the linemen just ready to fire off the ball, he's barking, 'Easy! Easy!' with all the command in the world. We didn't score, we just kicked the field goal. But it was his team."

Southern Miss's Gerald Blake recovered a fumble on the kickoff that followed, and within two minutes the underdogs scored again, this time on a nifty 3-yard touchdown scamper from Eddie Ray Jackson. With 13:43 remaining in the second quarter, Florida State and Southern Miss were tied at 10.

Wait. Florida State and Southern Miss were . . . *tied?*

"It's all about sticking around," said Simmie Carter, the defensive back. "When you play teams like Florida State, you need to destroy their confidence. You do that by taking their best punches and not fading."

When Jackson entered the end zone, the Gator Bowl went quiet. Moments later, it went dead. The football was coated in a grotesque brew of collective perspiration, and Dexter Carter — the sublime Seminoles halfback — took a handoff from Willis, swept to his left, and dropped it when Simmie Carter charged from the opposite side of the field and slammed into his arm. Free safety Kerry Valrie recovered on the Southern Miss 39, and Favre hit Eugene Rowell for 43 yards, Reggie Warnsley for 11, and, lastly, a lob to Alfred Williams in the end zone, who burst past Butler for the 4-yard touchdown completion. A scan of the Florida State sideline showed 60 young men in collective shock. A team predicted by many to challenge for the national championship had reached halftime trailing Southern Miss, 17–10.

"They didn't have a ton of talent," said Willis. "Really, they didn't."

The Golden Eagles' locker room was quiet, but no longer in a nervous way. Confidence is infectious, and the Seminoles seemed neither big nor bad. Toward the end of the half, Florida State's linemen were often bent at the waist, gasping for breath. Eric Hayes, a 300-pound star defensive tackle, could barely make it back to the huddle. Many of the Florida State players spent halftime attached to IV tubes. "Their guys were leaving the field with cramps," said Hallman. "I wouldn't even let our players take a knee during time-outs. It's all about body language. So while Florida State's guys were on the ground, my players were standing, looking at them."

"We endured our days running and running and running in the Mississippi heat," said Toby Watts, a Southern Miss defensive end. "We wore Florida State out."

Not completely. The Seminoles refused to give up, and with 6:57 left in the game found themselves winning, 26–24. It was time for Brett Favre — Heisman Trophy candidate — to announce himself. Before jogging back onto the field, the quarterback spoke via headset with Jeff Bower, the offensive coordinator, who urged him to stay calm, stay in control, make nothing approximating a dumb toss toward anyone wearing white. Across the line of scrimmage, Butler glanced at No. 4 and inhaled deeply. Earlier in the game, on the scoring pass to Williams, the cornerback came off the edge on a blitz and barely missed slamming into Favre. "I remember Brett giving me that look," Butler said. "It was like, 'Dude, these black jerseys and this heat — they ain't making me tired. I'm here *all* day.'"

By now, everyone was exhausted. Long-ago dry uniforms were hot water pillows. Cleats spouted liquid through the lace holes. Some players vomited, others merely dry-heaved. It was the 15th round of Apollo Creed vs. Rocky Balboa I, and the upstart lug from nowhere had an opportunity to land the knockout punch.

The Golden Eagles took over on their own 42-yard line. "Their fans were stunned," said Tony Johnson, a Southern Miss wide receiver. "I just remember stunned silence." Favre glanced toward Butler and Corian Freeman, the Seminoles cornerbacks. Both appeared drained. The safeties, Dedrick Dodge and Bill Ragans, were normally fast and tough and hard-hitting. But now, with the pressure on, they looked meek. It had not been the absolute best of times for Favre. He rushed some throws, had two passes intercepted. But with the game on the line, he was smiling, laughing, ribbing teammates, humming "Candy Girl" by New Edition. With a methodical brilliance, Favre marched the Golden Eagles down the field, using 12 plays to reach the Florida State 2-yard line. There were 27 seconds remaining, and only a field goal was needed to capture the lead. It was third down. Hallman called for a running play that would conclude (he presumed) with the ball centrally placed for a short Davis kick. Which made perfect sense, save for the fact that Davis was an erratic walk-on freshman who had taken off two years of football after high school (he would conclude the season by making only 9 of 21 field goal attempts). From the booth, Bower pleaded with Hallman to change the play. "I just figured that FSU would be jamming down the middle and some kind of rollout pass would be wide open for the touchdown," he said. "I wouldn't have called a pass with another quarterback, but I felt Brett could pull it off."

Hallman refused to budge. Bower insisted. Hallman still refused to budge. Bower insisted. Bobby Bowden, the Florida State coach, signaled for a time-out. Favre wanted the game to rest with him, not a first-year kicker. He pleaded his case to Hallman, who finally nodded and pushed his quarterback back onto the field. The Golden Eagles lined up in a power formation, with three running backs positioned behind Favre. He took the snap, faked a handoff to Bradley, and rolled five steps to his left. Butler, the Seminoles All-American cornerback, wasn't tricked, and came charging full speed at the backpedaling quarterback. With an inch separating him from Butler, Favre — standing on the 8-yard line — spotted tight end Anthony Harris crossing the end zone. A six-foot-two, 230-pound junior from Tuscaloosa, Harris was the absolute wrong man. One season earlier, he went 11 games without a single reception. "Harris was just a terrible tight end," said Ben Washington, the Southern Miss defensive back. "He couldn't catch."

The pass was perfectly thrown. Harris glided into its path, extended his arms, and used two meaty hands to cradle the football as he stepped across the white *G* (for Gator Bowl) painted on the turf. He lofted both arms in the air. Soon, he and Favre were besieged by an ocean of black uniforms. The TBS cameraman immediately shifted to the Florida State sideline, where wide receiver Matt Frier stood, hands on his hips, dumbfounded. *What in the world had just happened?*

The aftermath was mayhem.

Upon entering the Gator Bowl with two dozen other relatives that morning, Karen Favre, Brett's aunt, was asked by a Florida State fan, "What are you people even doing here?" Now exiting, she spotted the man again. "We kicked your ass," she snapped, "and now we're leaving!"

Inside the Southern Miss locker room the players were sprawled out on the floor, in the bathroom, anywhere there was space. It was exhaustion mixed with euphoria, and Brett Favre wore both. Chris Ryals, his closest friend on the team, leaned to the side on a neighboring chair, steam rising from his scalp. Every couple of minutes another player would walk by, place his hand in the quarterback's wet brown hair, and ruffle it. He completed 21 of 39 passes for 282 yards. It wasn't the best game of his career, but it was the most rewarding. A cornucopia of thoughts darted through his brain. Elation. Disbelief. A few days earlier, a *Sports Illustrated* writer had arrived in Hattiesburg to write a lengthy Favre profile. He told him the piece was sure to run should the Golden Eagles trump the Seminoles. Now Favre was giddy with anticipation — a real lengthy story in his favorite magazine! "I remember standing there, looking at him," said Billy Watkins, who covered the game for the *Clarion-Ledger*.

"And he was wearing a big gold chain around his neck. His grandma had given it to him. And I thought, *When do you ever see a football player wearing a gold chain during a game?*"

The Golden Eagles took a seven-hour bus ride to travel to Jacksonville for the game. The 54-minute return flight to Hattiesburg is an event most Golden Eagles never forgot. It was filled with laughter, shouting, relief. Throughout the game, Florida State fans repeatedly broke out their famed "Tomahawk Chop" chant to intimidate the visitors. Now the Southern Miss players and coaches did their own derisive Tomahawk Chop. More than 20,000 fans greeted the plane at Hattiesburg–Laurel Regional Airport, and Favre and many of his teammates headed straight to the End Zone bar. The following afternoon, the team met to review film of the game. Usually, such gatherings are businesslike. This was a party.

Before the replaying commenced, Pete Antoniou, a defensive tackle, tapped Hallman on the shoulder. During the win, Antoniou's father, Constantinos, sat in the stands, wearing a sweat-soaked white tank top and shorts. He had arrived from Greece in the mid-1950s, opened up Dino's Spaghetti House and Lounge, and knew nothing about American football. Yet that Saturday in the Gator Bowl, he shed tears of happiness. *This,* he told those who would listen, was his son realizing the American dream.

"Coach, I came here to play football and to contribute to winning," Pete Antoniou said. "But that was one of the best times I've had in my life, and one of the best times my dad has had in his life, and I want you to know how proud I am to play here at Southern Miss."

Hallman's eyes grew moist. He was proud, too.

The week that followed was bliss.

The journalists came, and Southern Miss was ranked 18th in the latest Top 25 poll. Favre was asked oddball questions by oddball reporters about his favorite music (New Edition, Kool and the Gang), favorite food (shrimp po'boys), favorite TV program (*The Tonight Show*), and greatest dislike (working). He was hailed as a sudden Heisman contender and a potential NFL draft pick.

Then, as quickly as it began, it ended. For only the second time since 1979, Mississippi State and Southern Miss met outside Jackson. The game was held in Hattiesburg, and a record 34,189 filled a normally half-empty stadium to see one of the nation's hottest teams. The Bulldogs had been a trainwreck for years — 1-10 in 1988, 4-7 the year before. But, to the shock of everyone, they ran the ball freely through the Golden Eagles' defense while beating up Favre, who completed 18 of 39 passes for 182 yards, no touchdowns, and one interception. When Joel Logan's 34-yard field goal passed through the uprights with eight seconds remaining, Mississippi State left with a 26–23 win and Southern Miss lost everything. You don't remain in the top 25 with a loss to one of the worst teams in the nation, and you don't make a case for the Heisman by delivering a stinker. "Honestly, I think we blew our entire wad against Florida State," said Antoniou. "We didn't have anything left."

After the game, Hallman called a 2:00 a.m. team meeting. It was the worst beatdown most of the players had ever heard. They were soft. They were quitters. They had an opportunity, and they lost an opportunity. "It's up to you!" he said, veins bulging from his neck. "It's up to you! You can make this season something special, or you can make this season a waste! You decide!"

The next week Southern Miss traveled to No. 5 Auburn and suffered a humiliating 24–3 thrashing. The week after that, Texas Christian, in the midst of a 4-7 season, pulled out a 19–17 squeaker. Then it was a trip to Texas A&M, Hallman's alma mater, and a 31–14 pulverizing.

Even as Southern Miss dragged its way to a 5-6 season, scouts from across the NFL landscape were beginning to descend upon Hattiesburg to watch the Golden Eagles quarterback flex his golden arm. To the nation's football-talent evaluators, wins and loses are irrelevant, especially when compared to strength, durability, and moxie. Not that there weren't concerns. The first time Favre worked out for an NFL scout, he arrived late, ran the 40-yard dash with a turtle's speed, reached the end, fell to his knees, and vomited. "Jeez," the personnel official asked, "what did you drink last night?"

Favre grinned. Beer. He drank beer.

The scouts were particularly abuzz after a heavily attended October 14 game at Louisville. Although neither team was a traditional power, both featured junior quarterbacks who were thought to be potential franchise-makers — Favre and Cardinals starter Browning Nagle. Because the teams played each other every season, there was an ongoing debate over which man had the more powerful arm and the brighter future. Both were right-handed flamethrowers with a love of action and a love of the nightlife. Both were athletic marvels somehow overlooked by bigger schools.

"Browning was a much better college quarterback than Brett," said Howard Schnellenberger, the Louisville coach. "Nagle made some of the best defenses in the country look like children. It wasn't close."

"If you asked back then who was better, it was probably a flip of the coin," said Rick Lantz, the Louisville defensive coordinator. "Browning was a great quarterback. He could do 100 different things physically. But Brett . . . I mean, c'mon."

This time, Favre and Nagle spent 59 minutes and 51 seconds as near equals. Each quarterback threw for a bunch of yards (232 for Nagle, 224 for Favre) and suffered a fair share of drops. Then, with nine seconds remaining and the game tied at 10, a miracle occurred. Southern Miss had the ball on its own 21-yard line. Terry Lantz, a backup defensive back for the Cardinals, told Derek Hawthorne, one of the starting safeties, "Whatever you do, don't go for the ball, don't jump. Just stay behind the pile." Hawthorne rejected the advice. "Man," he said, "I'm gonna intercept *that* ball."

Favre dropped back 11 steps, drifted right toward the sideline, and was partially swamped by Ted Washington, the six-foot-five, 320-pound defensive lineman. Somehow, Favre broke free with a stiff arm, stepped forward, cocked twice, and let loose a high, deep Hail Mary that soared through the air before landing in a sea of white and red jerseys. The ball glided over Hawthorne (Lantz: "Christ, I warned him!") and came down atop Michael Jackson's hands. He tipped it behind him to Tillman, who was crossing the center of the field. After breaking one tackle, the senior sprinted into the end zone with no time remaining. "It was an absolute fluke," John Gainey, Louisville's cornerback, said afterward. "Things like that aren't supposed to happen."

With that throw, in that moment, Brett Favre officially placed himself on the NFL map of top junior prospects to watch. Did the university's Heisman campaign pay off? Hardly. For a mere $10,000, Favre received zero votes. His 2,588 passing yards were a school record, but 14 touchdowns and 10 inceptions hardly jumped from the page. "The numbers didn't matter," said Jim Hay, who worked as a vice president with the Atlanta Falcons. "It was more like, 'There's this kid at an OK football program, and every game he doesn't look good for two or three quarters, but all of a sudden he does something completely amazing. And we need to know more about him.

"'We needed to know everything about Brett Favre.'"

8

NEAR DEATH

ON THE AFTERNOON of July 14, 1990, Brett Favre, his older brother Scott, and two Golden Eagles teammates, Toby Watts and Keith Loescher, met on Dauphin Island, Alabama, for a day of fishing in the Gulf of Mexico.

There was nothing particularly unique or special about the plans — "A boat, lunch meat, beer," said Watts, a defensive end who had transferred to Southern Miss after a year at Southern Methodist. "Just a college day of it, hanging out" — and after several hours of eating and fishing and drinking and drinking and drinking and drinking, the young men split up. Watts returned to his hotel room, and the three others made the 95-mile trek back to Kiln, where they were to have dinner with Bonita and Irv. Keith and Scott were in one car; Brett drove his white 1989 Maxima.

The straight shot along I-10 West was scenic, but hardly noteworthy. Before long, the cars were rolling through the Diamondhead resort development, a stone's throw from the Favre home. What happened next — at approximately 7:45 p.m. on Kapalama Drive — is somewhat confusing. In 1997 Brett told Steve Cameron, author of the book *Brett Favre: Huck Finn Grows Up,* that he was distracted by the high beams of an oncoming vehicle and was not speeding. In 2007 he told Mark McHale — his former coach and the author of *10 to 4* — that he merely "slid off the road" (high beams never noted). In his 1997 autobiography, he also failed to mention an oncoming car, simply that he was traveling above the speed limit (about 70 mph in a 35 mph zone) and that his right front tire "hit some loose gravel on the shoulder." Favre wrote that he straightened the wheel, but, "because I was going so fast, the car shot across the road." When asked about the accident by Russ Brown of the *Louisville Courier-Journal,* he said he might have been blinded by "the setting sun." In 1991 he told the *Atlanta Journal-Constitution* that "they'd been repairing the road and I forgot it."

Loescher, trailing Favre by no more than 20 feet, witnessed the entire incident. "Brett was probably going 60, and he just kind of went off the edge of the road," Loescher said. "He overcorrected and his car just shot across the road and started flipping sideways and it rolled up to a stop at a telephone pole. There was actually a point when it was flipping, where if we hadn't hit the brakes we could have driven right underneath his car. It went off the side of the road and into a telephone pole and up on its side."

Loescher slammed the breaks and backed up. He sprinted toward the Nissan, glanced through a window, and saw no Brett. "He was gone," Loescher said. "He wasn't anywhere in the front." Loescher shifted his view to the rear of the vehicle and spotted his friend, crumpled behind the backseat along the shelf. Blood covered his left knee. Shards of splintered glass were everywhere. "I punched the window—the driver's side window—three or four times," Loescher said. "I couldn't break it. So I ran to Scott's car and opened the back." An avid golfer, Scott kept his clubs in the trunk. Loescher grabbed a 3-iron and hammered it into Brett's window, causing a slight crack in the glass before the clubhead broke off and flew through the air. "I'm standing there with the shaft of the club, and I started stabbing the window," Loescher said. "Before I got all the glass out Scott jumped into the car."

"I drug him out the back as quick as possible," Scott said, "because I had no idea whether the car would catch on fire." The two men grabbed Brett beneath his shoulders and laid him on the side of the road. They screamed his name, but he did not respond. "I thought he could have been dead," said Loescher. After a couple of seconds, Brett mumbled a handful of nonsensical words. Then—"Scott, stay right here, don't leave me. Am I gonna be alright, Scott?"

"Hell, yeah, you're gonna be alright," his brother replied. "You'll be fine."

Scott and Keith tried to flag down a bypasser. A woman finally stopped, and immediately lectured Scott on safe driving. "She was bitching about how we ended up there," Loescher said. "We were driving too fast or too recklessly or whatever. I remember Scott started yelling back at her." Brett, still on the ground, tugged at Scott's leg. "Be nice," he said in a whisper. He then complained about severe stomach pain, so Loescher pulled his shirt off. A purplish-red steering wheel imprint was embedded in Brett's torso. At long last, the sound of sirens could be heard.

"I remember Scott screaming at me, 'Are you alright?'" Brett recalled. "I had one of those concussions where you don't know who or where you are, but I was talking."

Bonita Favre was attending a function at St. Paul Catholic Church in Pass Christian. Karen, Irvin's sister, excused herself to take a phone call. She returned moments later, her face ashen. "We've gotta go!" she said. "Brett's been in a wreck not far from the house." They rushed to the scene. Lights were flashing; police officers and firemen lingered. "I saw the car," Bonita said, "and thought, 'Oh my, they're dead.'"

Bonita rushed toward Brett, who was on a stretcher. "Mama, I'm alright!" he said. "I'm alright!" He was taken to Gulfport Memorial Hospital. "I screamed with every bump we hit because it hurt so badly," he recalled. "I'd scream every time they moved me."

Shortly after he reached the emergency room, a groggy Favre was told by the attending physician that, with his injuries, football wasn't an option for the upcoming season.

"Just watch me," he replied.

The next morning, readers of the *Clarion-Ledger* opened up their newspapers to the frightening headline FAVRE HURT IN WRECK. Staff writer Robert Wilson, who learned of the accident two hours after it happened, filed a detailed piece, explaining that Southern Miss's star quarterback suffered a hematoma (a swelling caused by a collection of blood) on his liver. "He has a lot of soreness in his abdominal wall," Dr. Jare Barkley, the treating physician, said. "We hope his body can absorb it. He is in a lot of pain and under medication, but he is alert and in full possession of his faculties. He had a concussion briefly. He was like a prize fighter being knocked out. He doesn't remember the accident."

The article quoted multiple sources, filled in myriad gaps (he had six stitches in his left kneecap, a severely bruised left arm, a bruised vertebra, and a right side that was black and blue from ribs to hip), and left Southern Miss fans to wonder whether Brett Favre would recover in time for the upcoming season. Two days later, a piece from Billy Watkins in the *Clarion-Ledger* added a bit more information, including that the cause of the wreck "is under investigation."

One detail remained secret for the next two and a half decades. After the accident, Slim Smith, sports editor of the *Sun-Herald,* called the hospital to find out whether Favre's blood alcohol content had been above the legal limit of .08 percent. Smith found a hospital employee who was willing to share the information but then, according to Smith, backed out with cold feet. It was made clear he was not allowed to speak with the press. The reason: Brett measured above the legal limit, but benefited from a system that had long protected local athletic heroes. "Brett almost certainly got preferential treatment from law enforcement," said Smith. "It's not a big surprise."

"We were all shitfaced," said Loescher, never asked about the specifics of that night until years later. "I can just hold up a little better."

Brett Favre should have been arrested on DUI charges. In a region that loved and protected its football stars, however, he never was.

Division I college football players are slabs of meat, and if you don't believe it, see how popular a big-time halfback or superstar linebacker is three months after suffering a career-ending injury. It's one of the central themes of Willie Morris's landmark book, *The Courting of Marcus Dupree,* and it's long held true. You're only as valued as your last play.

Having been largely ignored throughout his high school career, then suddenly thrust into Heisman dialogue, Brett Favre fully understood the fickle nature of sports fame. That's why, despite an accident that left him hospitalized, bloodied, bruised, and in severe pain, he never entertained the idea of redshirting the season in order to recover. "His resolve was amazing," said Mark McHale. "I first presumed he'd have to sit out. To Brett, there was no way."

The Golden Eagles began two-a-day practices while Favre was hospitalized. McHale visited a couple of days after the wreck, and turned visibly agitated when Bonita suggested Brett might not return. He had yet to walk, after all, and she, her husband, and Deanna (who, despite their on-again, off-again difficulties, was at Brett's disposal throughout the recovery) were taking turns feeding him food, taking him to the bathroom, wiping his rear. "Oh, Coach McHale," she told him, "this doesn't look good. All we ever worked for is over." McHale entered Brett's room. There was a small grease board, intended for the day's menu, at the base of the bed, and McHale started drawing up plays. "[Brett's] eyes were wide open," McHale recalled, "and getting bigger."

On July 17, 1990, Southern Miss football fans exhaled a collective sigh of relief. FAVRE SHOULD RECOVER FOR '90 SEASON read the headline atop the *Clarion-Ledger* sports section. Brett Favre was not only fine and dandy; he'd almost certainly suit up for Southern Miss in the coming weeks. "His liver is still bleeding, and we're watching that," said Barkley, his physician. "But it doesn't seem to be a problem. I'd say that barring any unexpected problems, Brett would be able to participate [in football] this season." One day later, Favre guaranteed his return for the September 1 season opener against Delta State. "I'll be there," he said.

On July 22, following eight days in the hospital, Favre was released. He returned to the Southern Miss campus, to the off-campus apartment he called home. The Golden Eagles training staff kept it simple — some walking, some light swimming, and low weights. After a week, Favre transitioned to throwing the football. He looked great, and it seemed he would, amazingly, start the opener.

Until the gas came.

Not just gas. Cramps. Jolts. Pangs. On the morning of August 6, Favre thought his stomach was being attacked by an army of pitchforks *from the inside*. He ate, felt awful, vomited. Ate again, felt awful, vomited. A school physician suggested it was a reaction to the trauma of the accident. "Screw that," Favre said. "I'm dying." He was taken to Forrest General Hospital in Hattiesburg, where the only person speaking to the media was Irvin, his father. "There seems to be an obstruction in his lower intestine," he said. "The doctors are trying to treat it. There's a 50-50 chance it could get worse. If so, they might have to operate. This is something new. This wasn't on the X-rays when he was released."

Two days later, Favre underwent one and a half hours of surgery. Dr. George McGee determined the car accident caused a blockage that constricted the blood flow in the small intestine. He removed a 30-inch section of his intestine. Afterward, McGee held what still goes down as the largest press conference in Forrest General's history. All 25 chairs were filled, and the operating physician explained that Favre could begin "full, unrestricted activity" in five weeks. He might *possibly* rejoin the Golden Eagles for the third game of the season, a September 15 matchup with Georgia. "It's good to know at this point where we and Brett are headed," Hallman said. "Things certainly look brighter than they have in recent days."

Later that day, the phone rang in Favre's hospital room. A nurse answered and said the head football coach at the University of Alabama wanted to speak with him. "Young man," he said, "we're scheduled to play

you. Hopefully you can make it, but more importantly hopefully everything works out and you get back on your feet again. Just know we're
pulling for you."

When the conversation ended, Favre, high on painkillers, said to his
parents, "I just spoke to Bear Bryant!" Bryant had died in 1983. It was
Gene Stallings, the new Crimson Tide head coach.

By now, the local media was All Favre, All the Time. Newspaper readers would rise, walk to the end of the driveway, pick up the *Clarion-Ledger* or *Hattiesburg American* and see (almost always on page 1A) what was
happening that day with the Southern Miss quarterback. He was home
recuperating under the watchful eye of his mother. He took a short walk.
He ate some soup. He ate some more soup. He napped. Some subscribers
expressed their displeasure via letters to the editor. ("This is ridiculous,"
one read. "I wonder if there would be this kind of headline if the same
thing happened to a Rhodes scholar that was attending USM.") But for
most it was *General Hospital* brought to life. There was drama! There was
intrigue! There was heartbreak! There was jubilation! "It was huge," said
Watkins, the *Clarion-Ledger* beat writer who covered the accident recovery as he would a presidential election. "Easily the biggest story around
for that span of time."

A small number of writers suggested Southern Miss should redshirt
Favre, that the university's first priority needed to be the health of its
quarterback. That opinion, however, was drowned out by the thrilling
vision of August 21, when Brett Favre—dressed in black shorts, black
helmet, and a gold No. 4 jersey—returned to practice. He weighed 192
pounds (down 34 pounds from his normal measure), with toothpicks for
legs and the shoulders of a prepubescent teenage boy on a juice diet. But
there he was, jogging, tossing, smiling. "Right now I couldn't go out there
and play," he told the media after a brief workout. "I'm just trying to sit
back and do what doctors tell me to do."

"He feels good," added Rodney Allison, the quarterbacks coach. "Just
having him out there is a positive influence for the other guys."

There was hope that come September 1, Brett Lorenzo Favre would jog
onto the field for Southern Miss's opening game and start at quarterback
against Delta State.

It sure beat Plan B.

• • •

He was home in Chipley, Florida, when the call came. John Whitcomb doesn't remember the exact words, but they concerned Brett Favre, a car accident, an opportunity. "Get ready," Curley Hallman told the redshirt freshman quarterback. "Because you're up."

You're up? What the hell was he talking about? All summer, Whitcomb was comfortable with the idea of returning to Southern Miss, standing along the sideline, watching Favre set records, possibly mopping up at the end of a blowout. "I was ready," he said. "But I wasn't *mentally* ready. There is a difference."

Although they weren't particularly close, Favre and Whitcomb had a lot in common. Like Brett, John grew up knowing only sports. Like Brett, John's football coach for as long as he could remember was his father, Skeebo Whitcomb, a local legend. Like Brett, John spent the majority of his high school career handing off. Brett Favre had Charles Burton standing behind him at Hancock North Central; John Whitcomb had Amp Lee — a future star at Florida State, then with the San Francisco 49ers — standing behind him at Chipley High.

Finally, with his son a senior, Skeebo Whitcomb opened up the offense, and the results were breathtaking. Using a run-and-shoot system, the Tigers outscored their opponents 311 to 121, and John threw 16 touchdowns with only two interceptions. He was named All-State but — because nobody knew of him as a junior — went lightly recruited. Just like Brett Favre.

Now the six-foot-one, 190-pounder would make his first collegiate start. Four days before kickoff, Favre told the *Clarion-Ledger* that he expected to play, but it was wishful thinking. Inside the football offices, the goal was to make do without Brett for a week, maybe two. Although Delta State went 6-3-1 in 1989, it was a mere Division II program, and an easy triumph was the expectation of Hallman and his players (Delta State was paid $50,000 by the university to come to Hattiesburg). *Even with Whitcomb.* * "John was a very intelligent player," said Honoroe Britton, a freshman quarterback. "That was his strength. He reminded me of a Joe Montana. Analytical. He didn't have Brett's arm, but who did?"

---

* Interestingly, Whitcomb wore uniform No. 10, which Favre had been denied upon arriving at Southern Miss. With 139 players on the roster, numbers were at a premium, and past standards were set aside. In other words, Reggie Collier's retired number was no longer retired.

Favre dressed for the game. He stood along the sideline beforehand, throwing lightly to Eric Estes, a backup, and looking thin but fit. He had started 32 straight games for the Golden Eagles, and this was torture. Favre wanted to play. He floated the suggestion to Hallman — *How about a few snaps? A series?* "No," Hallman said, repeatedly. "You're watching."

So, begrudgingly, Favre watched. And as torturous as the pregame felt, this was 1,000 times worse. The Golden Eagles won 12–0 behind two field goals and a late touchdown pass from holder Stacy Dennis to tight end Anthony Harris on a botched field-goal snap. Whitcomb completed 8 of 17 passes for 111 yards, but played poorly. Hallman, meeting with his coaches a few hours after the final whistle, put it best. "Men," he said, "we need Favre back. Now."

Although they are loath to admit it, most college and professional coaches know there are games they will win, and games they will lose. Against Delta State, for example, Curley Hallman was certain his team would not fall to a Division II squad. It was a near certainty.

As the second game of the season approached, Hallman was equally certain that Southern Miss was likely to lose. This had nothing to do with a lack of faith in his players, or shortcomings in finances or manpower. It was matters of circumstance and reality. His team would be traveling to Birmingham to face the University of Alabama in a colossal mismatch. First, the Crimson Tide was coming off a 10-2 season that included a 37–14 rout of the Golden Eagles and ended with a close loss to Miami in the Sugar Bowl. Second, this would be Alabama's opening game, as well as the debut of head coach Gene Stallings. Third, the contest would be played before a sellout crowd of 75,962 people — 99.9 percent Alabama loyalists. Fourth, the Crimson Tide roster — loaded with 16 returning starters — was a who's who of future NFL players. Fifth, there was this little issue with the quarterback, and his 30 inches of missing intestine. "Southern Miss was the sacrificial lamb," said Robert Wilson, who covered the game for the *Clarion-Ledger*. "Alabama was the lion."

In the days following the Delta State contest, Favre spent the majority of his time either throwing footballs or breaking wind. The first was mandatory preparation for what he hoped would be a triumphant return to the field. The second was a result of the intestinal surgery. Suddenly, Brett Favre was a farting machine — in the morning, at night, during meetings, midway through meals. Because he was embarrassed by seemingly nothing, Favre let loose with an eight-year-old's delight, often lifting a leg for dramatic gaseous accompaniment, or approaching a teammate with a look of seriousness, only to follow with a noxious reminder of his presence. "All that farting started with the surgery," said Bonita Favre. "The doctor actually told him, 'Now Brett, if you have gas you need to expel it. Don't hold it in.' Buddy, he expelled it. It didn't matter who was in the room or who was nearby, he just let it rip."

When Favre wasn't stinking up the Southern Miss facilities, he was trying to show Hallman he was prepared. Every throw was dedicated to getting his coach's attention. Every rollout, every drop-back, every hand-off. "I want to play," Favre told the *Hattiesburg American* — more plea than statement. "Hopefully I'll get an opportunity."

He wasn't just battling against the suggestions of doctors and a training staff. No, Favre was fighting his own coach's history. Back in the late 1970s, before he emerged as a coaching prospect in the collegiate ranks, Curley Hallman was a little-known running backs coach at Memphis State. On October 29, 1977, the Tigers were playing Southern Miss in Hattiesburg. It was late in the first half, and a member of Memphis State's special teams unit went down with an injury. "We had a kid named Bill Crumby who didn't play much," said Hallman. "We needed somebody, so I said, 'Well, let's put the tall string bean in there!'" The six-foot-two, 175-pound Crumby rushed onto the field, tried to make a tackle, and sustained a fractured dislocation of the fifth cervical vertebra. He was paralyzed from the shoulders down and never walked again. Hallman had inserted the boy into the game. The burden was *his*. "That sticks with a coach," said Hallman. "It always sticks with you. After that, I never took the health and safety of my players for granted. I'll put you in the game, but only if I know you can be safe and protect yourself."

Could Brett now be safe and protect himself? Hard to say. Three days before kickoff, the *Sun-Herald* ran the disappointing headline, WHITCOMB TO START AGAINST TIDE. Southern Miss wouldn't beat Alabama with Brett Favre. But with the robotic freshman, they'd lose by . . . what? Fifty? Sixty? "Honestly, I probably wasn't ready to do much against a team that good," said Whitcomb. "Not at that point in my football career."

What those outside the program didn't know was that, by the time the article hit newspapers, Favre was all but locked in as the starter. The unofficial anointment came that Thursday afternoon, when the Golden Eagles held a physical full-contact practice inside the stadium. The team ran a drill called pass under pressure, which entailed the first-team defense blitzing the first-team offense for 10 straight minutes. Hallman saw it as a proving ground. Survive, and he'd consider. "Now keep in mind, Brett still didn't look too healthy," said Estes. "Not that much earlier he could only walk one lap around the football field and he was puny. And here he was, leading the first-team unit." With the defensive linemen and linebackers charging at full speed, Favre went to work, completing eight of eight passes before hitting Michael Jackson for a touchdown. "It was unbelievable," said Estes. "He had barely practiced, and they were perfect throws, perfect placement. I knew he was good. I didn't know he was *that* good."

Later that evening, Favre convinced a handful of teammates to accompany him to the Silver Saddle, a Hattiesburg bar with a $5 All You Can Drink night. Until that moment, Favre had been recovering on nightly milk-and-egg protein shakes — "which tasted like crap," said Reed Wainwright, the strength coach who prepared the beverages. "I'd sit there and watch him drink, to make sure he finished it all." Now, protein shake or no protein shake, the quarterback was getting drunk. "I was like, 'Dude, we're *not* going to the Silver Saddle!'" said Pete Antoniou, the defensive tackle. "Of course, we went and we drank, and Brett didn't even have the five bucks. I had to pay for him."

The Southern Miss football team planned to make the four-hour bus ride to Birmingham on the Friday morning before the game. Hallman was committed to Favre, but nervous about it. "Brett, we're gonna start you," he told him. "And I think it'll be a big boost for our football team. But after the first series it'll be series by series for you, and we'll see how it goes." The quarterback was quietly giddy. Under National Collegiate Athletic Association rules, teams cannot keep a player's availability a secret. This was a secret. Throughout the week in Tuscaloosa, home to the Crimson Tide, Stallings prepared his team to face Whitcomb, with only a slight emphasis on Favre. Asked by the local paper for his thoughts on the rival quarterback, Stallings slipped and said, "I'm not concerned about Mississippi Southern." When roving regional college scouts stopped by campus, the Alabama coaches would ask what they heard about Southern Miss. All said Whitcomb was the guy. The words were accepted as gospel by all but Ellis Johnson, Alabama's linebackers coach and Southern Miss's defensive coordinator the two previous seasons.

"I haven't talked to anyone, but I bet Brett plays," Ellis told Brother Oliver, the Tide defensive backs coach. "He doesn't miss games like this."

"C'mon," said Oliver. "There's no way."

"OK," said Johnson. "Just watch."

On the morning of September 8, the members of the Southern Miss football team walked out onto the Legion Field Astroturf, knowing little about their pending fates. On the other side of the 50-yard line, the Alabama Crimson Tide players stretched, jogged, played catch. Although it was the season opener, as well as their head coach's debut, the team appeared calm. This wasn't a matchup against Auburn, after all, or even Florida, Georgia, or Louisiana State. It was Southern Miss, and a game they scheduled for the win.

Brett Favre was emaciated and physically untested. How would he hold up against John Sullins and Eric Curry, two of America's elite pass rushers? Nobody was quite sure. "That was my first college game, and I was pretty terrified," said Darian Smith, a Golden Eagles offensive tackle. "You grow up watching Alabama, loving or hating Alabama. And now you're playing Alabama, *at Alabama*."

When the team returned to the locker room for final preparations, Hallman gathered everyone around for last thoughts. The players sat on wood stools. It was brutally hot (95 degrees), without air-conditioning or fan. "OK," Hallman said, "I want all of the offensive linemen to stand up. First team, second team, third team — actually, all of y'all. Stand."

The 76 young men rose. Still, silence. "Boys, it's on you," Hallman said. "Brett's about 70 percent and he's going. And he better not get touched."

A pause.

"A lot of you boys are from the state of Alabama, a lot of you boys dreamed of playing for Alabama. But they didn't want you. You were too small or too slow or whatever. Well, we wanted you. We want you. Today is your chance to show them what they're missing . . . to show them what kind of stupid mistake they made . . ."

With that, the Southern Miss players charged through the tunnel and onto the field. Favre walked to the sideline, gripped a ball, and began to warm up. "To watch him throw — wow," said Gary Hollingsworth, Alabama's quarterback. "When a guy throws from college hash marks to the other side of the field, and the ball never gets lower than head high off the ground . . . as quarterback you sit and watch that and just go, 'Damn. I can't do that.' And he wasn't even healthy." By now, Stallings, who later described Favre as looking "like a damned scarecrow, his uniform hanging all loose around him and stuff," was fully aware of whom his team would be facing. Before kickoff, he spoke to his defensive starters. "Go hard," he said, "but don't hit Favre after he releases the ball." The words shocked Alabama's pass rushers, but not Hallman, who played under Stallings at Texas A&M and later coached with him. "Gene is a quality man," Hallman said. "He did things the right way."

Alabama received the opening kickoff, marched down the field, and easily reached the end zone on an 18-yard Derrick Lassic touchdown run with 12:07 remaining in the first quarter.

It was Southern Miss's turn. Favre took a deep breath and prepared for the most meaningful jog of his young football life. Several months earlier, before the wreck, Favre had volunteered to work at a summer high school football camp held on the Louisiana State campus in Baton Rouge. The counselors—hired by a Golden Eagles assistant coach named Daryl Daye—were all regional college players, including a large number of LSU standouts. Favre gravitated toward Shawn Burks, a linebacker who enjoyed a cup of coffee with the Washington Redskins. Whenever Burks completed a drill, or coached a successful play, he would scream out, "Whiskey!" Nobody knew why, but the exclamation alone—expressed with such gusto—reduced Favre to hysteria.

Now, as he jogged out onto the field, trailing 7–0, the pressure of a football program heaped upon his shoulder pads, Favre looked at Daye, grinned slyly, and screamed, "Whiskey!"

Favre entered the huddle and was choked up by the tears streaming down his teammates' cheeks. "It was a great reception," he recalled. "Right up to the snap." On the first play, Favre dropped back and was drilled into the ground. When he failed to rise, Doc Harrington, the trainer, sprinted toward his side. "Oh, God, Brett, what's wrong?" he asked.

Favre struggled for breath. "Doc," he gasped, "I got hit in the balls."

"Oh, good," Harrington said. "Stay down."

"No," he replied, "not good."

Favre played terribly throughout the first two quarters. Alabama held a 17–10 halftime lead, and outgained Southern Miss by 241 yards to 36 yards. The Southern Miss quarterback returned to the locker room exhausted and beaten up. Save for the three series where Whitcomb provided a breather, Favre took all the snaps. His numbers were awful, his impact immeasurable. "You could see the emotion he brought to those players," said Hollingsworth. "Shit, he'd roll out, duck, move, spin, run, drop back and throw it, and somehow the receiver would be there. That team believed in Brett, and believed they could always win as long as he was playing."

During his halftime speech, Hallman pleaded with his players to keep the score close. "If we can stay within a touchdown, we'll win this," he said. "The pressure is entirely on them. The closer we are, the more nervous they'll feel."

Thanks to a series of brilliant runs from halfback Tony Smith, Southern Miss entered the fourth quarter tied with Alabama at 24. This was supposed to be Stallings's coronation as the heir apparent to Bear Bryant. Instead, the Alabama offensive line looked inept, and its defense couldn't make big stops. Alabama had four turnovers and 54 yards in penalties. "At times," wrote Chuck Abadie in the *Hattiesburg American,* "[the Tide] had trouble even getting the proper 11 players on the field." With 7:23 left in the game and the score still deadlocked, Southern Miss took over at its own 20. There would be no more Whitcomb insertions, and no more questioning Favre's readiness. This was his game.

Slowly, meticulously, the Golden Eagles drove down the field behind a series of runs and short passes. Favre's moment came five plays into the series, when he danced around the pocket, avoided a charging Sullins, ducked, pumped, and threw a laser to halfback Eddie Ray Jackson over the middle for 34 yards. Shortly thereafter Jim Taylor — "a straight-on kicker with one of those clown shoes," said Daryl Daye — booted a career-long 52-yard field goal, and Southern Miss somehow escaped with a 27–24 victory. "This isn't supposed to be happening!" Allison screamed to McHale in the coaches' box. "This is Alabama, Hoss! Alabama!"

At midfield, Hallman and Stallings embraced. "Curley," Stallings said, "I just hope your quarterback is OK."

Hallman laughed.

"Coach," he replied, "my quarterback is fine."

9

SENIORITIS

THEY BEGAN ARRIVING in the middle of September, shortly after the win over Alabama reminded people that Brett Favre was alive and well. By now, the Golden Eagles' senior quarterback was enough of a national name that a good number of NFL scouts were familiar with his strengths and weaknesses. They knew, when he escaped the pocket, he tended to sway toward the right and throw against the grain. They knew he had a bad habit of forcing balls into double coverage. They knew he played above the level of his surrounding peers; that Favre belonged at Miami or UCLA, not slumming with C-level talent at Southern Miss.

What they did not know, however, was whether post–car accident Brett Favre was still NFL-worthy.

So they came to games and practices. They sat down with Curley Hallman, who insisted his quarterback was destined for big things, and with Mark McHale, who told the story of a high school nobody finding himself. Then they watched him throw from the pocket, throw on the run, check off one wideout, another wideout, dump the ball to a halfback out of the backfield.

And they thought, collectively . . . *meh*.

Just *meh*.

It was hard to blame them. The Brett Favre with Heisman ambitions no longer seemed to exist on the Southern Miss campus. Oh, the cockiness was still there. As was the bowlegged strut and the undying belief of his teammates. But if the car accident didn't sap his arm strength, it did sap much of the hype among pro football executives, who now viewed him as the nation's fourth- or fifth-most-NFL-ready college signal caller.

For many teams in need of quarterbacking help, the place to be was

Southern California, where San Diego State's Dan McGwire was compiling one of the best seasons in Western Athletic Conference history. The brother of Mark McGwire, the Oakland A's slugging first baseman, Dan's size (six feet eight, 240 pounds) had scouts imagining him towering over defenses, throwing deep bombs with gusto. "McGwire has the talent to be a great quarterback," Charlie Armey, the Atlanta Falcons' player personnel scout, told the *New York Times*. "He has the stand-up courage like a John Elway or a Dan Marino or a Johnny Unitas. He sets back in the pocket, stands there and reads the coverage. He throws the football and doesn't worry about the pressure. He knows he's going to take the hit, but he stands tall and takes it. Some guys won't do that."

By comparison, Favre was frail and damaged. Scouts loved his arm strength (even in his depleted state, he could muster velocity McGwire only dreamed of), but wondered whether he could survive on the next level.

In keeping with their recent tradition of playing an impossibly hard schedule, the Golden Eagles followed the Alabama win with a lovely bus trip to Athens, Georgia, home to the University of Georgia. The Bulldogs, 0-1 but favored by 12 points, did not seem overly concerned. "We were supposed to beat the living shit out of them," said Paul Etheridge, Georgia's tight end. "I don't think any of us knew shit about Southern Miss, except they were on the schedule to serve as an easy game. Concerned? Um, no."

Located one and a half hours to the west of Athens was the headquarters of the Atlanta Falcons, where Ken Herock was serving in his third year as the team's vice president of player personnel. A onetime tight end with the Oakland Raiders, Herock loved his job, and particularly the challenge of prospecting hard-to-find diamonds at college games. He knew of Southern Miss, of course, and had heard a few things about the quarterback with the oddly spelled name. "But I didn't have much information," Herock said. "He was a guy on a list." As opposed to many NFL franchises, the Falcons also had little need for a new quarterback. The team's starter, Chris Miller, was 25 and already one of the league's better players. His backup, Scott Campbell, was more than serviceable. Still, on the morning of September 15 Herock made the drive, arriving at Sanford Stadium in plenty of time for the 1:00 p.m. kickoff. "I got there for warmups," Herock said. "I had no idea what type of quarterback he was. I'm watching the pregame, and he's skinny. Really skinny, almost frail. He had the intestine thing and he lost all this weight. And I'm thinking, 'I don't know about this. I just don't know . . .'"

He quickly knew.

Brett Favre completed 11 of 20 passes for 136 yards and two touchdowns and was the best player on the field. There was a magnificent 31-yard should-be-touchdown sling to Michael Jackson that was erroneously ruled a fumble by officials. On one particularly dazzling third-quarter play, he was captured in the backfield by a Georgia defensive lineman named Mike Steele, who outweighed Favre by at least 80 pounds. Steele yanked the quarterback toward the ground, but Favre somehow freed himself, shimmied, and launched a 62-yard touchdown pass to Jackson. Southern Miss led, 17–6. "From that point," Favre said, "I felt like we were going to win."

Under constant pressure, Favre spun his thin body away from defenders. It was like watching the magical Doug Flutie during his Boston College days, only with Jeff George's cannon arm. "He was just a tough son of a gun," said Ray Goff, the Georgia coach. "You hit him, he came back at you. His toughness was at a new level."

The Bulldogs fought back to take an 18–17 fourth-quarter advantage, but Favre was not done. A fabulous Tony Smith kick return, along with a Georgia penalty, gave Southern Miss the ball on the Bulldogs 25 with 1 minute, 40 seconds remaining. After Smith lost a yard on first down, Favre roped a pinpoint pass to receiver Ron Baham on the left sideline. The junior caught the ball at the 15, but fell out of bounds for an incompletion. On the next play, Favre again targeted Baham on an out pattern to the right side. The throw was perfect, but Baham turned a second late and the football trickled off his fingertips. On fourth down, Hallman had Jim Taylor attempt a 42-yard field goal. The kick traveled long, high — and directly into the right upright. "That's my biggest miss of all time," said Taylor. "If I don't hit the upright, we beat Alabama and Georgia. Not bad for a bunch of packrats, huh?"

Favre was devastated. He retreated to the locker room in near tears. He was exhausted, battered, and somewhat nauseated. He'd probably dropped 10 pounds of sweat off an already reduced frame, and greeted his 20 family members in attendance after the game with an uncomfortable dispiritedness. Favre could generally laugh at himself, win or lose. This time, there was no laughing. "I felt real good today," he said afterward. "But there were a few plays that I may have made before that I couldn't today. But that was no excuse for us losing this game."

Herock had planned on sticking around only for the first half. He stayed for all four quarters. "He's beating Georgia by himself!" he recalled. "He gets them in a position toward the end of the game to kick a field goal and win, and they miss. But he took them there, singlehandedly. I liked everything I saw."

Ron Wolf wasn't so certain. The New York Jets' personnel director visited Southern Miss shortly after the Georgia game, and watched Favre work out. Unlike Atlanta, the Jets—with an aging and immobile Ken O'Brien at quarterback—needed new blood. Wolf was relatively unimpressed. Favre's velocity was good, but not up to the usual otherworldly standards. Compared to the Herculean McGwire, he seemed small and erratic. The tapes from Alabama and Georgia only mildly interested him. "I remember being intrigued by Brett, because the coaches loved him and everybody talked about the way he carried himself, the way he was such a winner," recalled Wolf. "But then I got in with those tapes and it just wasn't anything really special." The whole visit was a disappointment. Where was the Brett Favre people had raved about? Where was the sparkle? This guy looked like just another solid college quarterback. Before he had the chance to depart for a scouting trip to Jackson State, Wolf was stopped by Thamas Coleman, a Southern Miss administrative assistant. He urged him to watch some footage from Favre's junior season, pre-accident. "I told him he wasn't really seeing Brett Favre," Coleman said. "I told him if he just saw one game from the season before, he might have a different opinion."

Wolf acquiesced, and like Herock, he was thunderstruck. He was a fan of the untraditional, Fran Tarkenton/Billy Kilmer/Ken Stabler model of weird-yet-successful quarterbacking. Favre, always in motion, always jabbering, always weaving and skipping and hopping, fit the bill. "As far as throwing the football is concerned, he was the perfect quarterback," said Wolf. "There were several movies out back then about what to look for in a quarterback, and how to do certain things, and Brett Favre had it all covered." Wolf was scheduled to stay one night in Hattiesburg. He spent two— "To see more tape, see what else there was. You can't skimp on a quarterback. You need to know everything."

With Favre, there was *a lot* of everything. First, potential employers would want to know whether the quarterback (*their future quarterback*) was mature enough to serve as the face of an NFL franchise. Teams were well aware of the car accident, obviously, and his proclivity for beer was increasingly common knowledge. What remained hush-hush, however, was the existence, back in Hancock County, of Brittany Favre, his daughter. This was not a ploy of any sort. When asked in his day-to-day life, Favre talked openly about the little girl, now a year old with the dimples and giggles to prove it. But he was rarely asked, and even a large number of teammates did not know their fast-living leader was a father.

By his own later admissions, Favre was minimally involved, available for visits and cuddles between games and practices and classes and parties. It wasn't indifference so much as immaturity. He loved the girl, just as he loved Deanna. But he also loved the spotlight, and the buzz, and being with his teammates their final year together. Brett was now the biggest celebrity in Hattiesburg, and everyone wanted a piece of him. *Come to this party! Visit this bar! Free food! Free drinks!* He was a regular at the Sigma Chi house, home to shindigs that featured flowing taps and the prettiest coeds on campus. During the season, the hottest spot was the End Zone, the popular sports bar on West 4th Street where Southern Miss football jerseys adorned the walls and pitchers of beer were dirt-cheap and *Monday Night Football* telecasts were weekly holidays. "Man, I would eat about 20 chili dogs, they were so good," Favre recalled of his visits. "Best of all, they were free, which was key when you're a college student."

The Golden Eagles lost a 13–10 heartbreaker at Mississippi State the week after Georgia,* then hosted Louisville in a game hyped as the final showdown between Favre and Browning Nagle. By now, despite Southern Miss having won the last eight meetings between the schools, the Golden Eagles and Cardinals considered themselves to be heated rivals. This was, in large part, because both teams believed they featured the best quarterback in college football. Like Favre, Nagle had traveled an untraditional route toward collegiate stardom — a highly recruited standout out of St.

---

* The game was most memorable for the aftermath, when Mississippi State players — during a victory-lap walk around Scott Field — stopped in front of the Southern Miss fan section and taunted, according to Tim Doherty of the *Hattiesburg American*, "with graphic gestures emanating from body parts below the waist."

Petersburg, Florida, he attended three different high schools, committed to West Virginia, and transferred when the coaching staff switched from a pass-first attack to the option. "I guess," he said, "I'm a survivor." Nagle sat out a redshirt season at Louisville, then backed up quarterback Jay Gruden for another, before finally getting his chance as a junior. His 2,503 passing yards and 16 touchdowns told the story of a quarterback on the rise. "The comparisons were pretty right on," said Gary Hollingsworth, the Alabama quarterback who played against both men. "Browning had a cannon for an arm, a lot like Brett did."

If, in anticipation of the matchup, fans sought some sort of personal animus to fuel their sense of the rivalry, they would be terribly disappointed. A couple of days after his car accident, Favre had received an unexpected call from Nagle. "I wanted to make sure I gave him my condolences," Nagle said, "and tell him that I was pulling for him." There were a handful of follow-up conversations, and both were elated to be nominated side by side for the annual Johnny Unitas Golden Arm Award, presented to the country's top senior quarterback (Miami's Craig Erickson wound up winning). "That was special," Nagle said. "To be on that list together."

On the night of September 29 inside M. M. Roberts Stadium, they were together again, along with two dozen NFL scouts. For the first time in recent history, Louisville (3-0-1) was a clear favorite to beat the 2-2 Golden Eagles, whose offensive ineptitude against Mississippi State prompted the *Biloxi Sun-Herald*'s John Bialas to write, "A yard looks like a mile to this attack."

A crowd of 20,545 came to the stadium, more to see Favre–Nagle than Southern Miss–Louisville. And, in one sense, they were not disappointed. The physical incarnations of Brett Favre and Browning Nagle did, indeed, appear on the field, and they even tossed footballs through the air. But the game was awful. The Golden Eagles won, 25–13, because a backup walk-on fullback named Roland Johnson ran for 102 yards on 14 carries, including a 47-yard first-quarter touchdown burst. Neither quarterback did much of anything, though at least Favre had an excuse: he was sacked six times, hurried repeatedly, and leading one of the flattest offenses in Division I football. "Look how awful we were," said one anonymous offensive player. "How do you have Brett Favre as your quarterback and have one of the worst offenses in the country? We had a shift in philosophy, and it made no sense. The general idea was to keep it simple and win with defense. But we had Brett, Michael Jackson, Tony Smith, and we didn't take advantage of the firepower."

The Golden Eagles won their next three games, but the offense was so dull and unimaginative that, in the midst of home victories against Tulane and Memphis State, fans booed when the unit took the field. When Southern Miss scored 23 points against an awful Memphis State defense, the *Sun-Herald* referred to the offense as a "good-looking machine." A week later, against Virginia Tech (a team only slightly better than Memphis State), Southern Miss gained 81 first-half yards in a 20–16 setback. An hour after the game, every Southern Miss player was on the bus and ready to go, save Brett. "I'm asking everyone, 'Where the hell is Brett? Where is he?'" said Hallman. "Finally I see him walking across the field." Favre was dressed like a slob. His shirt untucked, shoelaces flailing, belt buckle undone. "Lemme tell you something, young man," Hallman said. "You're dressed about how you played today." Favre reached to tuck in his shirt. "I'm serious," Hallman said. "How you're dressed is how you played."

Irvin Favre overheard the exchange, and asked the coach whether all was OK. "I was getting on him pretty good," Hallman explained. "Just because—" Hallman stopped. He saw furor cross Irvin's face. "Irvin," he said, "Brett's gonna be OK. I promise you, he's OK. Relax."

Somehow, the Golden Eagles wound up with an 8-3 record, including a shocking win over No. 15 Auburn before 85,214 fans at Jordan Hare Stadium. It was Favre's best statistical showing of the season (24 of 40, 207 yards, two touchdowns), and was capped by a game-winning 10-yard touchdown pass to tight end Anthony Harris with 46 seconds remaining. The victory ruined Auburn's homecoming festivities, and gave Favre's team—filled with players from Alabama—bragging rights over the state's two football powers. "No Southern Miss team had ever done that," said Hallman. "You can always brag about beating Alabama and Auburn in the same year."

Thanks to the win, Southern Miss was invited to play North Carolina State in the All-American Bowl. However, 17 days after the victory, Hallman accepted a five-year, $85,000 contract to replace Mike Archer as the head coach at Louisiana State. In the blink of an eye, the Golden Eagles were a surging bowl-bound team without a coach. Then, five days after Hallman and most of his staff departed for Baton Rouge, the administration hired back Jeff Bower, the former offensive coordinator who had left four years earlier, to be his immediate replacement. Many of the Southern Miss players were crushed. Hallman was more than a coach. He was a father figure; a guide. Favre, though, *loved* Bower. Especially when the new coach met with Favre and told him, "I've got you for one game, and we're gonna open this offense up and see what happens."

The words were cotton candy to the quarterback's palate. Favre's arm was as strong as ever. Hallman and Allison simply were not letting him use it properly, replacing deep throws down the sidelines and 20-yard outs with dump offs and draw plays. Every time he heard of an NFL scout attending one of the team's underwhelming offensive showings, Favre surely wondered whether his future was taking a hit. "I'm not sure all of Brett's strengths were fully utilized," said Whitcomb. "I could see that being frustrating."

The final game of Favre's college career was, from a cinematic standpoint, perfectly placed. Now in its 14th season, the All-American Bowl would be played in Birmingham, at Legion Field, home to *Southern Miss 27, Alabama 24* a mere three months earlier. The Golden Eagles players and coaches checked in to the Wynfrey Hotel four days before the game, and Bower — back on the scene, trying to get his footing — made it clear that his guys should have fun.

Though Birmingham is hardly New Orleans or Atlanta, its bars and restaurants were tantalizing destinations for Favre and the other Southern Miss seniors, all liberated by the imminent end of their collegiate careers. So, when practices were over and the obligatory appearances concluded, the players hit the town, drinking as if their spirals and tackles were powered by hops. Meanwhile, during the day, Bower and Favre worked side by side on turning the offense on its head, planning three- and four-receiver sets and hoping to fully utilize Jackson, whose blazing speed could exploit a plodding Wolfpack secondary.

The result was *the* bowl game of the year, one Favre would look back upon as one of the most joyful — and heartbreaking — moments of his collegiate career. Wolfpack quarterback Terry Jordan was just as captivating as Southern Miss's star, and the two went back and forth exchanging brilliant throws. The Golden Eagles opened the scoring on a 10-yard touchdown pass from Favre to Mark Montgomery. Jordan returned fire with a 10-yard option keeper into the end zone. Back and forth, back and forth. Favre threw for 341 yards and two scores. Jordan threw for

166 yards and one touchdown. On the final play of the game, with North Carolina State leading 31–27, Favre — who frantically marched his team 48 yards down the field — dropped back at the Wolfpack 20, convinced he was about to go out a winner. Instead, with eight seconds left, he was chased toward the sidelines by defensive end Corey Edmond. With nowhere to turn, Favre fumbled the ball forward and out of bounds, trying to stop the clock. Time, though, expired. On Southern Miss. On Brett Favre.

As the white-and-red-clad Wolfpack players swarmed the turf in ecstasy, the greatest quarterback in Southern Miss history lay sprawled out on the field, crushed in disbelief. He would be named the game's MVP, but took no pride in the honor.

"You always think you can pull it out at the end," he said afterward. "But tonight, we didn't."

On January 19, 1991, Brett Favre headed to Mobile, Alabama, for the 42nd Senior Bowl. He felt the pressure. After an up-and-down season with up-and-down results against (with some obvious exceptions) mediocre competition, here was a chance to face the best players in the country. So what if he was listed as McGwire's backup on the AFC squad? He would play, and — dammit — he would play well. To hell with USC and Miami and Alabama and Texas. This was Brett Favre's time to shine. In the days before kickoff, Favre met with executives from a half-dozen franchises, including Denver, Washington, Cleveland, Buffalo, and the Jets and Giants. That Thursday, he even went to dinner with Mike Holovak, the Houston Oilers' general manager, who was seeking a young backup for Warren Moon. This was turning into a good week. A great week.

And then . . . it wasn't. As McGwire lit up the NFC squad for 165 yards and two touchdowns, Favre played terribly. He attempted 15 throws. He completed 7. They covered 62 yards. There were several other quarterbacks in the game (Alabama's Hollingsworth, Louisville's Nagle, Rice's Donald Hollas), and Favre was easily the most inept. It was even worse afterward, when instead of spouting off a bunch of clichés to the press, he fumed. "Hell, I got killed," he said of shoddy protection from the offensive line. "What I need is a cold beer. That's what I need. It wasn't fun. I didn't enjoy it. I'm glad I came, but I'm coming away with a lot of bruises. All [an all-star game] is really is a game of pitch and catch. I didn't get the protection that some of the other guys got, though. For me it was more a game of getting killed than pitch and catch."

Afterward, Joe Mendes, the New England Patriots' personnel director, spoke about what he had just witnessed. "There's no complete player in this draft like a Troy Aikman or a Terry Bradshaw," said Mendes, whose team had the No. 1 selection. "Jeff George [the Illinois quarterback who went to Indianapolis as the 1990 No. 1 pick] lacked the real good movement, but had a strong arm and quick release. There isn't a Jeff George in this draft."

Favre wondered whether he'd blown his golden ticket. Never before had he played in front of so many scouts, and never before had he played so badly in front of such a large crowd. "It wasn't good," said Ricky Watters, the Notre Dame tailback and Favre's Senior Bowl teammate. "I didn't know who Brett was, but I wasn't impressed. He threw everything 100 miles per hour. There was no touch. His balls were impossible to catch. Maybe it was nerves."

One week later, Favre found himself in Palo Alto, California, for the East-West Shrine Game, yet another college all-star fest for those entering the draft. Although he was scarred from the misery of Mobile, Favre didn't show it. This was his first-ever trip to California, and the week was dreamy. The bowl organizers supplied cars for every player. They stayed in hotel suites, with a generous daily food per diem. Trips were arranged to Alcatraz and San Francisco. Practices didn't begin until 2:00 p.m., so there was no pressure for early bedtimes or set alarm clocks. "We all went out and drank lots of beer," said Blake Miller, Louisiana State's center and East teammate. "You'd be out all night, hanging with these guys you never met before, having a lot of fun. It was pretty sweet."

To many, Brett Favre remained a mystery. Teammates from the South knew the legend of his 70-yard throws, but others had never heard of him. The majority of the West roster couldn't pronounce his name. "He was a small-school guy," said Joe Valerio, a center from the University of Pennsylvania. "I felt out of place being from Penn. But he was just like me, so we probably bonded a little. Nobody knew who I was, nobody knew who Brett Favre was."

For as awful as he played in Mobile, the Brett Favre who stepped onto the field at Stanford Stadium was nothing short of brilliant. He completed 15 of 26 passes for 218 yards, and launched a 54-yard bomb to Alabama receiver Lamonde Russell for a touchdown. He also ran for a 7-yard score after pump faking, juking, and bolting toward the end zone. Favre was named the game's co-offensive MVP with Stanford wide receiver Ed McCaffrey. The confidence returned.

Sitting in the stands, notebook in hand, the Jets' Wolf could hardly contain his excitement. There had been great debate inside the team's headquarters about the upcoming draft, and what they should do with limited resources. The Jets lost what would have been their first-round pick when they drafted Syracuse wide receiver Rob Moore with a supplemental selection in 1990, so they didn't have to worry until the seventh spot in the second round. Wolf returned to New York, entered the office of Dick Steinberg, the New York general manager, and said, "Brett Favre is the best player in this draft. We need to get him."

"You mean the best *quarterback?*" Steinberg replied.

"No," said Wolf, "the best player."

"What?" Steinberg said. Some had Favre ranked *fifth* among senior quarterbacks, behind McGwire, Arizona State's Paul Justin, Rice's Hollas, and Duke's Billy Ray.

"Dick, trust me," Wolf said. "This kid will be our quarterback for the next decade."

Steinberg remained unconvinced.

Buoyed by the Stanford experience, Favre created some serious buzz at the February NFL Scouting Combine in Indianapolis. People knew of his strength, but witnessing it was a different experience. Sammy Walker was a defensive back from Texas Tech who opened eyes by clocking less than 10 seconds in the 100. One of the drills involved standing 10 yards from the quarterback, turning on the blow of a whistle, and catching the football. "Three guys are in front of me, and Brett's the quarterback," Walker said. "The first guy, the ball hits him in the hands and his finger goes sideways. The second guy just dodges it. The third guy gets hit in the eye and needs ice. I'd been told I couldn't catch AIDS if I had sex with the virus, and I sure as hell can't catch this fire. So I'm terrified, and as soon as he throws the ball I just duck and it sails over my head."

Favre also held his own predraft workout on the Southern Miss campus. A cast of 20 coaches and scouts showed up for the morning activities, including Wolf, Green Bay head coach Lindy Infante, June Jones, the Atlanta Falcons' offensive coordinator, and Mike Holmgren, offensive coordinator of the 49ers. Favre threw to a couple of receivers, showed off his arm strength. Nothing new. With a roster featuring Joe Montana and Steve Young, San Francisco needed a quarterback less than any team in the league. Still, Holmgren was a passing junkie, and he wanted to see what all the fuss was about. "Somebody will probably take you fairly early," he said before leaving. "I wish you luck."

They gathered at the house at the end of Irvin Farve Lane, as they always gathered at the house at the end of Irvin Farve Lane.

In Kiln, Mississippi, where there seems to be a Favre for every grain of dirt, the afternoon of April 21, 1991, was Christmas and Easter and a birthday rolled into one.

Although ESPN's televising of the NFL draft would not commence until 10:00 a.m., relatives and friends began arriving hours earlier, replete with crawfish, chips, dip, beer, whiskey. Deanna was there, of course, with little Brittany. Many wore matching T-shirts that read DRAFT DAY 4-21-91. This was to be the ultimate celebration: Brett Favre's introduction to the world as a first-round NFL draft selection. Just 10 days earlier, Allan Malamud of the *Los Angeles Times* wrote that Favre "probably will be the first quarterback taken," and shortly thereafter United Press International's Dave Raffo hailed him as "the best" thrower in the country and the *Miami Herald* rated him "the No. 1 QB available." Steinberg, finally swayed by Wolf, told *Newsday* that Favre has "the passing skills, athletic ability, and toughness to be a winning NFL quarterback." Alas, he anticipated the quarterback would be long gone by the time they had a chance to pick. The UPI's annual mock draft had him going 21st to Kansas City.

By now, Brett Favre had an agent. A Hattiesburg-based attorney with a general law practice, James "Bus" Cook met Brett two years earlier, when a friend asked if he would take a couple of college kids out for an afternoon of golf. While walking the greens, Favre — not yet 20 years old — said to Cook, "I've heard a lot of good things about you, and I wanted to know if you might be interested in helping me."

Cook was confused. "What kind of trouble are you in?" he replied.

Favre laughed. He explained that he had a potential future in the NFL, and he wanted an agent who was trustworthy and down-home. "Son," Cook said, "I don't know anything about that business."

"Sir," Favre replied, "I don't know anything about playing pro football. But I'd love for you to talk to my parents and help me."

Now they were side by side in the Favre household, pots boiling, beer being poured, 100 or so relatives filling the rooms, no real clue as to what was about to transpire. In recent days, the Seahawks and Falcons had sent representatives to Mississippi to meet with Favre one final time. Both teams possessed high first-round slots (Atlanta held the 3rd and 13th picks, Seattle the 16th), which boded well, Cook presumed. But maybe it didn't. Maybe they were bluffing, or thinking second-round. He had no real clue.

The draft was held in New York City at the Marriott Marquis Hotel, and the sense of mystery was greater than usual. In the weeks leading up to the event, the consensus No. 1 pick was Notre Dame wide receiver Raghib Ismail — who ruined all plans days before by signing a four-year, $26.2 million deal to play for the Toronto Argonauts of the Canadian Football League. The Dallas Cowboys, holders of the golden ticket, were left to select Russell Maryland, an underwhelming defensive lineman from the University of Miami. With that, all bets were off. The Browns, second up, grabbed a UCLA safety named Eric Turner,* and for the first time all day silence befell the Favre household. The Atlanta Falcons, picking third, loved Brett Favre. They loved his arm, his moxie, his Southern charm. Ken Herock, the vice president of player personnel, was close friends with the Jets' Wolf, and the executives agreed he was probably the prize bull of the entire herd. But . . . the team already featured a quality quarterback in Chris Miller, as well as a number of defensive holes. Finally Pete Rozelle, the NFL commissioner, stepped to the podium and announced the Falcons were drafting Bruce Pickens, a cornerback from the University of Nebraska.

A collective groan could be heard through the Favre household.

A low-pitched groan could be heard from Herock.

"I wasn't a fan of Pickens," he said. "But the coaching staff thought he'd be a good cover guy, and we needed that. But he wasn't a good kid." Pickens lasted three unexceptional years in Atlanta. He goes down as one of the biggest busts in franchise history. "He was lazy and not very smart," said Taylor Smith, the team president. "That's a bad combination."

As most of the Favre attendees hovered around a large television, Brett sat in his old bedroom, the one with the wood-paneled walls and the ceiling covered with posters of Michael Jordan and Jose Canseco and Dwight Gooden and Jerry Rice and Al Toon. He wore jean shorts, a white

---

* Turner died of intestinal cancer in 2000, at age 31.

T-shirt, and a white Southern Miss baseball cap. Wrote Robert Wilson in the *Clarion-Ledger:* "He didn't watch the draft or eat. Instead, he opted for Nintendo on an empty stomach."

From time to time, Favre glanced at a small television, or a relative knocked on his door to offer an update. As the hours passed, the news was never particularly good. The Falcons used a second first-round pick to select a wide receiver from Colorado named Mike Pritchard. "Every receiver we had on the roster ran slower than I did," said Jerry Glanville, Atlanta's second-year head coach. "We needed speed." Three slots later, the Seahawks — an organization thought to be hot for Southern Miss's quarterback — grabbed McGwire.

"Dan McGwire?" Favre yelled.

He'd worked with McGwire in two all-star games, and liked San Diego State's tall quarterback. But Favre *knew* he was better — just as he knew he was better than the 24th overall selection, a sophomore quarterback from Southern Cal named Todd Marinovich.

Wait. *Todd Marinovich?**

The new Raiders quarterback was, according to the *Los Angeles Times,* "perceived [by NFL teams] as immature, erratic and a possible substance abuser who would have been better served by remaining in school." During his senior year of high school, Marinovich kicked off his days by doing bong hits with classmates. By college, he had moved on to heavier drugs. On January 20, 1991, he was arrested on Balboa Peninsula, California, with a bag of cocaine. He was charged with two misdemeanors and allowed into a program for first-time offenders. He was also suspended by the Trojans for missing classes. It was all public information, there for every team executive to digest.

And now, baggage be damned, *Marinovich* was a high NFL draft pick.

The first round lasted nearly five hours, and it was pure torture. Beer and food kept the mood relatively light inside the Favre household, but Irvin, Brett's father, was particularly incensed. Dan McGwire? Todd Ma-

---

* In a 2010 *Esquire* profile, Marinovich spoke with a group of children and introduced himself like this: "I was the first freshman in Orange County to ever start a varsity game at quarterback. I broke a lot of records. Then I chose to go to USC. We beat UCLA. We won a Rose Bowl. It's quite an experience playing in front of a hundred thousand people. It's a real rush. Everyone is holding their breath, wondering, What's he gonna do next? After my third year of college, I turned pro. Here's a name you'll recognize: I was drafted ahead of Brett Favre in the 1991 draft."

rinovich? How hadn't teams seen what he knew? That his son was the best quarterback in the draft? How could they be so blind?

The second round began, and one team after another selected players nobody in the state of Mississippi had ever heard of. The Oilers grabbed a safety from Indiana named Mike Dumas. *Tick*. The Browns took an Auburn guard named Ed King. *Tick*. The Broncos snagged a tight end — a flippin' tight end! — named Reggie Johnson, from Florida State. *Tick*. Roman Phifer, UCLA's best linebacker, became a Los Angeles Ram. *Tick*. The Phoenix Cardinals went for Mike Jones, the defensive end out of North Carolina State. *Tick*.

And now, a moment. The next two teams on the board were the At-lanta Falcons, picking 33rd, and the New York Jets, picking 34th. They had always been the most likely Brett Favre landing spots. Inside the New York war room, Wolf spent the afternoon urging Steinberg to move up by any means necessary. At one point, the team reached a deal with the Cardinals to slide two slots ahead of Atlanta. But when Jones remained on the board, Phoenix backed out. Herock, meanwhile, was overruled by ownership on the 3rd and 13th selections. At one point Taylor Smith, the team president, demanded Herock calm down. "I understand you like this guy," he said, "but we have a good quarterback."

"I know," Herock replied, "but I think this guy might be a franchise quarterback. A *franchise* quarterback."

Here, finally, was his chance. Inside the Falcons' room, Herock posted a board ranking the team's top prospects, 1 through 100. He was con-stantly working the list — scratching names off, jotting down arrows, phrases, question marks. A team had 10 minutes to decide upon a player, so as soon as the Cardinals (to Herock's great relief) selected Jones, he re-turned to the board and said, for all 13 people in the room to hear, "Listen, our top-rated player on the board is Brett Favre, the quarterback. I really like him, I think he'll be a quality player in the league."

Herock then turned to Glanville. An ornery man who thrived upon social unpredictability, Glanville repeatedly assured Herock that he, too, liked Favre's style. As long as other positional needs were filled, Glanville would gladly add the young quarterback. Hence, Herock looked at the coach and said, "Jerry, you onboard with this?"

"You know, Ken," Glanville replied, "I wouldn't take him."

"What?" Herock said.

"Yeah, I wouldn't take him," Glanville said. "We should get Browning Nagle."

Herock waited for the punch line. Browning Nagle? "I couldn't believe it," Herock said. "I mean, there was no comparison between the quarterbacks." He let Glanville's words sink in, then looked toward June Jones, the offensive coordinator. "June, you saw both these guys," he said. "What do you think?" Herock figured this to be the world's easiest question. "OK, so I like Brett for some reasons," Jones replied, "and I like Nagle for some reasons. It's your decision, but I'm a bit torn."

Four minutes passed.

Five minutes passed.

Six minutes passed.

In New York, Wolf—hoping the Falcons were about to commit a colossal blunder—called the Favre household to speak to Brett. When the phone rang, an ocean of relatives poured into the small bedroom. Wolf insisted he was their guy, and Brett would love the Big Apple, and he could learn behind Ken O'Brien and everything would be fantastic. "If Atlanta's not taking me, the Jets are taking me," Favre announced to the room.

"Nagle was OK," Wolf said. "But Favre was special. Clearly."

For the Falcons, six and a half minutes passed.

Seven minutes passed.

Eight minutes passed.

"The room is silent," said Herock. "And that's usually not a good thing. Silence, silence, silence, silence. I'm thinking to myself, *What do you do now?* Here your coach doesn't want the player, your coordinator said he doesn't know if he wants the player now. But in the meetings they did want him."

With one minute remaining, Herock gathered his courage and said aloud, "Gentlemen, we're going to take Brett Favre. I think he can be a great player."

Glanville flashed a piercing look that Herock would never forget. "He was clearly pissed," he said. "And I think he harbored that resentment for Brett far beyond the draft."

Favre was talking with Wolf when he heard the call waiting click.

"I've gotta take this," he said.

"Don't answer," Wolf replied with a laugh.

It was Jerry Glanville on the line. Even though he hated the pick, he insisted, as head coach, that he be the one to welcome new players. "Hey Brett! It's Jerry Glanville from the Atlanta Falcons! How do you feel about playing for us?"

"That'd be great, Coach," Favre said.

"We wanted to take you in the first round," Glanville said, "but we needed to take a receiver and Pritchard's a good one. When you were there in the second, we were thrilled."

It was ludicrous.

"He didn't want Brett," said Herock. "No matter what nonsense he said later on. He didn't want him."

When Brett told everyone the news, the house shook. Despair and anxiety were replaced by hugging and laughter. Don Weiss, an NFL official, leaned into the microphone at the draft and said, "Atlanta has selected Brett *Favor*, quarterback, Southern Mississippi." It was one of the proudest moments of Bonita Favre's life. "I was just thrilled he'd be near home," she said. "Atlanta was pretty close." On the outside, Favre smiled and accepted congratulations. On the inside, however, he was hurt. "I still believe I'm the best quarterback in the draft," he told Robert Wilson of the *Clarion-Ledger*. "I'm disappointed I wasn't the first one taken, especially with Marinovich. He hasn't played but two years. But it's not the end of the world. Joe Montana and Boomer Esiason were [not first-round] picks and look what they did."

In New York, Wolf was crushed. The best player in the entire draft had lasted for five and a half hours, and somehow the Jets were unable to get him. Moments later, New York announced the selection of Browning Nagle. He lasted three seasons in New York, threw seven touchdowns and 17 interceptions, and now sells medical supplies.

"I think Brett wound up the better quarterback," said Herock. "But just by a little."

10

HOTLANTA

THE LOST YEAR of Brett Favre's football career is, in many ways, the most fascinating year of Brett Favre's football career. Which is quite peculiar, because nobody ever seems to discuss it.

Just look through the magazines, the newspapers, the books, the documentaries. When it comes to the 1991 season, it's as if everything can be summed up in 10 words or less. Even in his own autobiography, Favre devotes nine paragraphs to life as an Atlanta Falcon — and two of those are single sentences.

Traditionally speaking, the days that follow the draft serve as a period of mental adjustment. Young players come to grips with relocating to foreign cities and organizations start the process of figuring out who fits where, and how. There are press conferences to attend and papers to sign and jerseys to hoist and pose behind. Although Jerry Glanville was far from enamored by the addition of a quarterback he didn't want, he had no choice in the matter. Brett Favre was coming to Atlanta.

Before bread could be broken, though, Bus Cook — Favre's naive agent — committed a classic rookie mistake. Having watched his client's heartbreak over being a second-round pick, and also seeing Raghib Ismail, the presumptive first overall selection in the draft, take big money from the Canadian Football League, Cook reached out to the Toronto Argonauts and Winnipeg Blue Bombers. Then he informed the media. "That Canada stuff, it's just us talking right now," Cook told the *Atlanta Journal-Constitution* on April 23. "Brett wants badly to play in Atlanta, but we have to explore all the options in case things don't work out."

The resulting lengthy freeze between player and franchise involved Glanville uttering the phrase "Fuck that kid" inside the Atlanta offices an estimated 2,762,211 times. During his time *not* under contract, Favre remained home in Kiln, kicking back in his childhood bedroom, casually throwing the football around with friends, and watching *New Jack City*, his all-time favorite movie, on a near-endless loop. In mid-May he received a visit from Len Pasquarelli, the Falcons beat writer for the *Atlanta Journal-Constitution*. It remains one of the greatest (and weirdest) experiences of his journalistic career.

Recalled Pasquarelli: "This place was hard to describe — like a scene out of the *Dukes of Hazzard*. And Brett was like Li'l Abner and one of the Hazzard boys. It was just another world. I don't know what people did for a living, but I suspect they mostly held factory jobs where they worked until three, then came home to work on their cars the rest of the day. I drove to Brett's family's house, way in the middle of nowhere. And when I walked in Brett was sitting there with a bunch of buddies watching *New Jack City*. It was their second or third viewing that day. Finally me and the photographer asked if they wanted to go to lunch. Well, Brett, all his buddies, me, and a photographer packed into the rental car. We drove over to Bay Saint Louis to a little fish place. He introduced me to a shrimp po'boy. We played catch in the yard right near Rotten Bayou, and they told us all these stories about alligators eating dogs, so they never had dogs for long. Then we toured the town, which took 15 minutes. The best part of it came when Brett said, 'Let's go down to the VFW.' Everybody there knew Brett — probably five or six guys at the bar, all drinking draft beers. We go into the backroom and the wall is filled with slot machines, and all these women are illegally playing the slots. They have blue hair, and some teeth, and rolls of quarters, drinking beers. And they all had salt shakers next to them, and they'd throw salt over their shoulders for good luck."

The story ran on May 21, beneath the headline FALCONS' SEARCH FOR A BACKUP QB LEADS TO A BACKWOODS TOWN FOR ONE. It was funny, well written, and received in Kiln like a Taser to the spine. Favre later lamented that the piece "made me look like a goofy redneck."

At long last, on July 17, Favre and the Falcons agreed to a three-year, $1.4 million deal that included a signing bonus somewhere between $350,000 and $400,000. He placed 70 percent of the money in stocks and bonds, and used the rest to purchase a $30,000 maroon Acura. Favre reported to Suwanee, Georgia, the next day for the opening of training camp, commencing his one-year apprenticeship at the strangest and most dysfunctional shop in the National Football League.

Beginning with the Falcons' debut season in 1966, the team forged a well-deserved reputation for spirited ineptitude. The franchise was owned by Rankin Smith, a former U.S. Army combat pilot who made his money in the family life-insurance business, and ultimately run by Taylor Smith, the fourth of his five children. "In public they were called the Clampetts," said Terence Moore, a longtime sports columnist for the *Atlanta Journal-Constitution.* "They were nice people who couldn't figure it out." Upon Favre's arrival Atlanta had but one double-digit-win season.

The team was notoriously cheap with contracts and notoriously indifferent when it came to the quality of the facilities. Their final home game of the 1989 season drew 7,792 fans to Atlanta–Fulton County Stadium. Falcons employees were named in seven different paternity suits over four seasons. "We may not be good," a player's wife once noted, "but at least we're fertile."

By the time Favre arrived, however, some around the league felt Atlanta was turning a corner. The roster featured a slew of young, exciting players, including quarterback Chris Miller, wide receiver Andre Rison, and a dynamic defensive back from Florida State named Deion Sanders. And while Atlanta finished 5-11 in 1990, fans seemed to genuinely believe in the vision of the head coach. Glanville was, in the words of *Sports Illustrated*'s Rick Reilly, "a scalawag and a raconteur and a pretty fair coach and a man who has too much fun and laughs too loud for some people." He was loved by a few in the NFL and abhorred by the vast majority. Sometimes he told the truth. Oftentimes he stretched it out. "You can listen to 100 percent of what Jerry said," said Taylor Smith, "and believe 30 percent of it."

In 1985 Glanville was working as the defensive coordinator with the Houston Oilers when, with two games remaining, he took over for the fired head coach, Hugh Campbell. The team was, in his opinion, "a joke — smack 'em in the mouth, pee on their pants, and they still wouldn't hit anybody. Their mamas loved 'em. Their daddies loved 'em. But they wouldn't hit if you handed them sticks."

Glanville called himself "the dark prince" and issued a challenge to his players — break 100 facemasks per season. He spoke of developing "trained killers." The Oilers were a dirty team that specialized in late hits and illegal shots. "If the sucker's moving, our goal is to get 11 guys on him," Robert Lyles, a linebacker, said. "Put the flag up. Surrender. He's dead. It's over. He's a landmark. It's hit, crunch, and burn." Were Glanville unhappy with a player, he'd let him know. When a defensive lineman held out for more money, Glanville ripped the nameplate from above his locker and stuck it over the entranceway to the bathroom.

Glanville dressed in all black, drove Harley-Davidsons, listened to rock and roll, and left tickets at the front gate for Elvis and James Dean. It was all dramatic and thrilling as the Oilers went 9-6 in 1987 and 10-6 in 1988, but carnivals run their course, and by the time Houston lost to the Steelers in the first round of the 1989 playoffs, the front office had tired of his antics.

As soon as Glanville was fired, the Falcons swooped him up. In his introductory press conference, he was asked about the terms of his contract. He had no idea. The uniform and helmet colors went from primarily red to primarily black. He encouraged Rison and Sanders to dance. "He was the ultimate player's coach in many ways," said Ken Herock. "He bullshits with the players, he has fun with the players. But if he didn't like you, or he didn't want you around, it was a different thing entirely."

From the day he checked into camp, Favre was an object of Glanville's derision. Their opening exchange said it all . . .

Glanville: "Hey, Mississippi!"

Favre: "Hey, Coach, how are you doing?"

Glanville: "Call me Jerry."

Favre: "OK. Hey Jerry."

Glanville: "What school are you from, Mississippi?"

Favre: "Southern Miss."

Glanville: "Aw, damn, we drafted the wrong guy. We wanted the guy from Mississippi State."

"I was standing next to Brett," said George Koonce, a rookie free agent linebacker. "And I remember the look on his face was devastation."

To Glanville, Favre projected an unjustified cockiness. The coach relished bravado, only *not* from rookies. There were four other quarterbacks in camp — Miller, the established starter; Scott Campbell, a veteran backup; Gilbert Renfroe, a Canadian Football League refugee; Mike Rhodes, a former Arena League star — and Favre made it clear he was the best of the bunch. "I'd played in six Pro Bowls by that point, and this kid comes up to me in camp and tells me he has the strongest arm in the NFL," said Chris Hinton, the offensive lineman. "I'm like, 'Yeah, whatever.'"

"Every week, if I was there on Friday, Brett would find me and start bitching," said Herock. "He would always say, 'Mr. Herock, I'm better than the guys you have here. I'm better.'"

When Herock responded that Miller was the established starter, Favre snapped, "I'm better than *him!*"

For the first two weeks of camp, Favre could not throw a spiral. He would drop back, release, and — *wobble, wobble.* A man known for his fastball was suddenly Phil Niekro. He chalked it up to nervousness. Then a lack of reps. When seven-on-seven drills commenced after a few days, June Jones, the offensive coordinator, increased Favre's reps. It wasn't a status thing. He hoped more passes would equal more comfort. "Throwing a football's something I never had to think about," Favre said at the time. "But, man, there's some ugly ones, aren't there?"

Glanville ran the least-disciplined training camp in the NFL, as well as the most colorful. No team featured more beer drinkers, more renegades, more trash talkers, more larger-than-life personalities. Sanders, brash and outspoken, bought Favre his first dress-up outfits — two garish suits straight out of Pimp 101. Rison purchased luxury cars as if he was buying cups of coffee.

There was also a dark side. His name was Bill Fralic.

A 1985 first-round draft pick out of the University of Pittsburgh, Fralic was both a four-time Pro Bowler and one of the locker room's more sadistic ringleaders. If his No. 1 goal was to win football games, it often felt as if a close second was teaming with his fellow offensive linemen to make life miserable for young Falcons. Sympathetic veterans warned rookies to steer clear, and with good reason. The offensive linemen lived to humiliate.

In 1990, for example, members of the unit grabbed a young player as he was showering, taped his arms to a metal bench, and carried both (the man and the bench) onto the field. "He's out there naked, in front of people, and he can't move," said one Falcon. "The fans watched it all."

Favre's draft class included a 10th-round pick from Wisconsin–Stevens Point named Pete Lucas. A six-foot-three, 320-pound offensive tackle, Lucas graduated from high school and spent several years working at Swaggart Furniture, a Wisconsin-based family business. When his grandfather sold the company, Lucas enrolled in college and emerged as a *Football Gazette* First Team All-American. By the time he was picked by the Falcons, he was 25 and unusually mature for an NFL rookie.

Fralic and several of his line cohorts made Lucas the target of their aggressions. He arrived in the mornings aspiring to work in peace, then faced a daily nightmare. "I was threatened to have my knees taken out in practice if I didn't do as I was told to," Lucas said. "And that was basically to take my clothes off, sing, dance, perform — naked, any time, any place. I don't know if it was because I intimidated them with my size and strength, but it happened to me all the time. On airplanes, on buses. You expect some hazing from time to time. But when the coaches stop meetings so guys can force you to strip and do something, it's a different level. Literally, in offensive-line meetings the coach would call for a break and I'd take my clothes off."

One awful night, Lucas and another rookie lineman, Mark Tucker out of Southern Cal, were commanded to strip naked in front of the entire offensive line, hold each other tight, and sing "Ebony and Ivory," the Stevie Wonder–Paul McCartney ode to racial unity. Lucas is white, Tucker African American. "It was always the same thing — 'Do this or your knees are taken out,'" said Lucas. "There were times I'd be on an airplane sleeping, and I'd get knocked in the head and told, 'Guess what? It's time to get naked.' I felt sexually violated and humiliated. There was one night where they made all the rookies get up and do a song and dance. I drank as much as I could beforehand, because I was told, 'I better see nuts hanging out, or your knees are gone.'"

Lucas's accounts are confirmed by other Falcons players. Bob Christian, a rookie fullback who roomed with Lucas and went on to a 10-year NFL career, calls the offensive line "perverted," and said members of the unit threatened to shave off his pubic hair if he didn't sit for a veteran-administered haircut. "Pete is not lying," said Christian. "Something was really wrong with the offensive linemen." Tucker, too, said Lucas is telling the truth. "It was what we had to go through," he said. "I hate that he was so scarred."

The Falcons eventually released Pete Lucas, ending his NFL career before it ever began. "It was," he said, "the greatest relief of my life."

Not yet 22 and naive to the world, Favre was in no position to step in and help a battered teammate. Not that he would have. Much like when he arrived at Southern Miss out of high school, the offensive linemen (and Fralic in particular) took a liking to Favre. He was one of them — a drinker, an airplane poker player. His shower routine involved bending over, naked, and pretending to chat with his butt crack. "It sounds gross," said Scott Fulhage, the punter, "but it was hilarious." As other rookies had their haircuts butchered into mortifying clumps and unimaginable angles, Favre bribed his way out of the fate. "He came and asked us whether he could avoid a Mohawk in exchange for a night out at dinner for all the linemen," said Hinton. "We went for it." Favre took the entire unit to Bone's, a fancy steakhouse on Piedmont Road in Atlanta. It cost him a couple of thousand dollars, but his shaggy brown hair went untouched. "He ordered fish and drowned it in ketchup," said Hinton. "I remember that."

Even though he didn't want Favre, Glanville knew he had to keep him. After a couple of bad weeks of camp, the quarterback started to find his groove. Miller's arm strength was terrific, but Favre's throws were events. As was the case in college, his power, combined with a lack of touch, left many a training camp wide receiver wounded. "He didn't make many right reads," said Naz Worthen, a free agent receiver. "But, boy, he could sting your fingers."

Even with the ups and downs of the preseason, Favre presumed he would wind up the No. 2 quarterback. Sure, he struggled to grasp June Jones's complex red-gun offense, but things were starting to make sense. The Falcons' 1991 regular season was scheduled to open at Kansas City on September 1, and Favre told family and friends that, barring an alien invasion, he would be playing behind Miller, one of the league's most fragile quarterbacks.

On August 28, the aliens landed.

The headline attached to the Associated Press story read CHARGERS' TOLLIVER TRADED TO FALCONS, but it could have been FALCONS' FAVRE NOW FREE TO GET FAT AND DRUNK. Atlanta sent a fourth-round pick to San Diego for Billy Joe Tolliver. A third-year quarterback out of Texas Tech, Tolliver started 14 games for the Chargers in 1990, throwing 16 touchdowns and 16 interceptions for a 6-10 club. Tolliver had been nicknamed "Billy Joe Terrible" by the *Los Angeles Times*'s Brian Hewitt, and it was justified. He was just good enough to play and just bad enough to lose. Herock made the exchange with the understanding that Favre would remain the backup. That's how it went for the season opener at Kansas City—Miller started in the 14–3 loss, and Favre stood on the sideline, holding a clipboard and appearing mildly interested. Then Herock read the depth chart for the second-week battle against Minnesota and saw Glanville now listed Tolliver as the top reserve. He barged into Glanville's office. "I thought we agreed Brett was No. 2 and Billy Joe would be third," Herock said. "That's the reason I made the trade."

Glanville didn't like Herock and he didn't like Favre. He also had final say on lineups. "Well, Billy Joe just knows so much more than Brett," he crowed. "He's more ready to play."

At that moment, the Herock-Glanville relationship — never terrific to begin with — was permanently damaged. "I never really trusted him," Herock said. "He lied a lot."*

When Favre learned of Tolliver's acquisition, he was indifferent. Quarterbacks come, quarterbacks go. It was only *after* the Minnesota game — when Miller, Tolliver, and Favre all wore uniforms — that he realized his plight. Under a new NFL rule, a team could dress a third quarterback and still designate him as inactive and only available in case of injury to the starter and backup. Nobody bothered to fill Favre in. He learned he had been deactivated only when Pasquarelli, the *Journal-Constitution* beat writer, approached in the locker room to ask whether he was upset. "I was third?" Favre said. An awkward pause. "Oh, well. I'll just keep plugging away, I guess."

"It was the beginning of the end," said Herock. "Brett lost interest."

There are good teams for young players and bad teams for young players, and the '91 Falcons were the all-time worst. Although Glanville's squad wound up compiling a 10-6 record en route to a rare playoff berth, everything seemed to be about brashness and arrogance and individual liberties. Glanville regularly invited celebrities to stand along the sideline during games, and granted rapper MC Hammer carte blanche to the team facilities. One of Glanville's favorite quotes — "If you ain't cheatin', you ain't tryin'" — was interpreted literally by a roster filled with cheapshot artists. Glanville continued to humiliate his rookie quarterback in ways big and small. When the team traveled, Glanville kept warmups loose by betting any takers that Favre could launch a football into a stadium's highest decks. Favre always succeeded, but did not enjoy being part of the dog and pony show.

Scott Favre, Brett's sibling and college running buddy, moved to Atlanta to keep his kid brother company. He took a job teaching learning-disabled middle-schoolers in the Clayton County School District, and

---

* "Ken Herock said that about me?" said Glanville in 2015. "The only time that man tells the truth is when his lips don't move."

Brett and Scott rented an apartment. Two of their friends attended a nearby chiropractic college, and the four hit the city *hard*. Brett knew he wouldn't play on Sundays, so he went on a nonstop drinking and eating binge. Lots of pineapple and vodka, lots of pizza and steak and dough-nuts. "He didn't think he'd ever get a chance that season, so he probably didn't take it very seriously," said Scott. "Plus, you're young and dumb and in a big, exciting city. We took advantage of it."

"I just said, 'The hell with it,'" said Brett. "I went out every night, gained weight and was out of shape. I didn't study, I didn't care. I'd show up just in time for the meetings and I'd be out of there the second the meetings were over."

Glanville reached out to the Falcons' favorite night spots and requested they deny his third-string quarterback service. "I went to downtown At-lanta, to a place called Frankie's, to a bunch of other spots," Glanville said. "I went to all of them and asked them not to give him free drinks, not to let him party, that he needed to be at home. Well, in Atlanta they don't care who you are, what you want. No bar would agree to help me.

"People think I didn't like Brett Favre. Not true. It wasn't about like or hate. Shit, I saw him do things with a football nobody did. I've seen him, in the wind, throw strikes when nobody could get heat on the ball. He could play. But he didn't want to play. He wanted to party."

His regular-season NFL debut came on October 27, against the Rams at Fulton County Stadium. Miller had left the game with a bruised right thigh, and Tolliver went 5-for-5 for 45 yards before a hip pointer forced him out, too. With 1:54 remaining in the fourth quarter, and his team leading 31–14, Brett Favre walked onto the field under the Glanville direc-tive, "Don't do anything stupid, Mississippi." Favre successfully handed off three times. "Hey, I came in and ran out the clock pretty good, didn't I?" he joked afterward, a sad resignation attached to his words. "I think I found me a new role. I'll be our kill-the-clock guy."

At one o'clock on the afternoon of November 10, 1991, two weeks after Favre executed those three marvelous handoffs, the Falcons and Redskins faced off in Washington, DC—two teams with playoff expectations. At 9-0, the Redskins were an NFL powerhouse. At 5-4, the Falcons were on the rise and confident. Before the game, Glanville framed the contest as a test. "Are you men enough," he asked his players, "to beat the best?"

The answer: No. With Chris Miller out because of a rib injury, Tolliver started and completed a mere 14 of 31 passes. The Falcons opened the game with a Norm Johnson field goal to take a 3–0 lead, then sat back and watched Washington score the next 28 points. By the late fourth quarter, the Redskins were up 49–17 and the 56,454 fans at RFK Stadium were filing out to go about their days.

A few weeks earlier Glanville had said that in order for Favre to play, "we gotta have two plane wrecks and four quarterbacks go down." This was neither an airline crash nor four battered quarterbacks, but Tolliver had been sacked on five occasions. So, with nowhere else to turn, Glanville let Favre take over for the final 55 seconds. Wearing his black No. 4 jersey above a white long-sleeve shirt (it was 35 degrees), Favre trotted onto the muddy green field, approached the line, ducked behind center, and — for reasons only he probably knows — grinned boyishly. Perhaps it had to do with the realization of a lifelong dream. More likely, it was the preposterousness of an oddball rookie season. The PA announcer, Charlie Brotman, blared, "In at quarterback, Brett Favre!" Steam rose from the rookie's breath as he barked the signals. Two wide receivers stood to the right, two to the far left. Rison jogged in motion behind him, the lackluster trot of a man itching for a hot shower. Favre took the snap and dropped nine steps back. With the pocket collapsing, the quarterback lifted his arm and shot a pass — high and hard but not completely uncatchable — to Pritchard. The football slipped through the wide receiver's hands and into the waiting arms of linebacker Andre Collins, who was playing 4 yards back. He bobbled the ball, controlled it, burst through Pritchard's weak grasp, and sprinted 15 yards for the score. As Collins gleefully spiked the ball onto the white end zone paint, Favre walked off the field. "Well, Brett Favre, you ever have the Redskins on your schedule at Southern Mississippi?" crowed Randy Cross, a former NFL star now working color commentary for CBS. "Welcome to RFK and the NFL!"

Favre wandered through his teammates along the sideline, all silent and glancing awkwardly in other directions. He finally reached his head coach, who couldn't stomach his team being crushed so badly.

"Can you believe that, Coach?" the quarterback said. "My first pass in an NFL game went for a touchdown!"

Glanville was in no mood. "Yeah," he said. "But it was for them, not us."

"Eh, that doesn't matter," Favre replied. "It's still a touchdown pass. That's what they'll remember."

Glanville cackled. Moments later, Favre returned to the field for the final 47 seconds. On first down, his pass landed three feet short of Rison's toes. On second down, his pass jetted high above the outstretched arms of Rison for an ugly (and nearly intercepted) incompletion. On third down, he rolled right, repeatedly bounced on his toes, escaped two defensive linemen, swiveled left, and was smothered by a 297-pound defensive tackle named Bobby Wilson for the sack. On fourth down, with eight seconds remaining in the game, Favre escaped pressure, drifted to his left, and lofted a 55-yard Hail Mary that was picked off by cornerback Sidney Johnson.

Brett Favre's life as an Atlanta Falcons quarterback began.

Brett Favre's life as an Atlanta Falcons quarterback ended.

He never again played for the franchise. Miller returned to health, threw for 3,103 yards and 26 touchdowns while carrying Atlanta to a wild card berth and earning the only Pro Bowl nod of his career. Favre's statistical line was complete (0-for-4, two interceptions), but his antics were not. There were still six regular-season games left in the season, and with Miller back Favre knew he was useless. He arrived at team meetings with alcohol on his breath, and on one occasion was sent home by the coaching staff. "I went into a meeting and he was sound asleep," Glanville said. "And I went to go over and raise all kinds of difficulties and the closer I got to him, I could tell why he was asleep." Sometimes he reached the facility on time. Usually he was late. It was only in the final weeks of the season that anyone with the Falcons knew he had a daughter and girlfriend back home. Meanwhile, Favre's understanding of the playbook was at a kindergarten level; his waistline continued to expand. "He absolutely could not run a 40-yard dash," said Glanville. "It was a joke."

If there's one moment that perfectly encapsulates Brett Favre's Falcon existence, it is the annual official team photograph at the Suwanee training facility. On this day, as Jimmy Cribb, the photographer, assembled the players and coaches in five neatly organized rows, Favre was nowhere to be found. He skidded into the parking lot nearly an hour after the photo shoot ended, spotted Glanville's van pulling out, caught his attention, and explained he was stuck behind an awful traffic accident and then he got lost and . . . and . . . and — it was all garbage. Favre had been out partying late into the night, and failed to set the alarm. "I was hung over," he said. "I tell people I played for Atlanta and if they get the team picture they say, 'What a liar. You didn't play for them.'" Favre was fined $1,500.

For Glanville, it was the last of the last straws.

"I got trapped behind a car wreck," Favre told the coach.

"You *are* a car wreck," Glanville replied.

A couple of weeks after the season ended with a 24–7 playoff loss at Washington, Ken Herock steeled himself for the conversation he did not wish to have.

Throughout the year, Glanville's weekly Favre reports broke his heart. They were usually entertaining, but always negative. "I'd be on the road three or four days a week during the season, scouting," said Herock. "I'd come back Friday and it'd be, 'You should see what your boy did this week. Oh, he was drunk at a meeting. Oh, that son of a bitch is 20 pounds overweight. He doesn't even know the damn scout plays.' They showed me one tape and they go, 'Watch this! You've gotta watch what he did in practice! Watch this ball! We've never seen a ball curve before. This guy can't play.'"

Glanville insisted he was OK with Favre as a person, but couldn't stomach his attitude and approach. The main Atlanta Falcons' rules involved punctuality and effort, and he adhered to neither. "You can't tolerate this stuff," said Glanville. "Not from a veteran, definitely not from a rookie."

So now, sitting across from one another, Herock listened again to the coach's complaints, swallowed hard, and said, "I'll see what we can get for him."

When Glanville exited the room, Herock dialed a familiar number. Ron Wolf, his longtime friend, had recently left the Jets to take over as the general manager in Green Bay.

The Packers needed a quarterback.

11

ARRIVAL

THERE IS a little-known journalistic law regarding the Green Bay Packers, and it involves history, reverence, and at least 253 evocations of Vince Lombardi per hour.

It is, after all, the NFL's most storied franchise, dating back to 1919 and filled with legendary names, legendary games, legendary settings, legendary accomplishments. So when one writes about Lombardi and Bart Starr and Paul Hornung and 13 championships and 24 Hall of Famers, we are required to kneel, make the sign of the crucifix, and speak in hushed tones.

Shhhh.

Thank you.

Now that that's done, let's turn to Billy Ard.

Yes, Billy Ard — a man who arrived in Green Bay as a free agent in the fall of 1989 after spending eight years as the New York Giants' starting left guard. Having won a Super Bowl under Bill Parcells, Ard thought he understood what it meant to play in the NFL. You worked hard, you endured injuries, you overcame obstacles, you were richly rewarded with lucrative contracts and sweet perks. It was a plum gig, and he was thrilled to have it.

"Then I came to Green Bay," he said, "and they gave you one pair of shoes."

Ard doesn't mean a member of the Packers would receive one pair of shoes per game, or per month. No, if you were on the Green Bay roster in the 1980s, Bob Noel, the equipment manager, asked your size, then dropped off one pair of athletic shoes for the entire season. "In New York, footwear was unlimited," said Ard. "In Green Bay, you were on your own."

That wasn't the worst of it. As the majority of NFL franchises played in palatial stadiums that seated 70,000 fans, the Packers held their home games in charming-yet-antiquated Lambeau Field — an enormous Erector-set construction plopped down in the heart of a barren village. "I played my college football at USC," said Ken Ruettgers, an offensive tackle and Green Bay's first-round pick in 1985. "Reaching the NFL was a huge downgrade. The weight room was a downgrade, the locker room was a downgrade. Guys were packing up their boxes to be sent home with two or three games still left in the season. My Packer teammates threw in the towel all the time. They didn't care."

In the 24 years that followed Lombardi's glorious final season in 1967 (the Packers beat the Raiders to win Super Bowl II), Green Bay endured five head coaches, each one accompanied by his own special blend of awfulness. The team won 10 or more games just twice, and made two playoff appearances. The tales of misadventure are endless. John Brockington, a star running back from 1971–77, recalled that before games, Dan Devine, the head coach for four dreadful years, would open his pep talk with, *If I could build a franchise around one player, I'd pick* . . . "And it was never one of us," Brockington said. "Never." Starr, the legendary quarterback, took over as coach in 1975, and optimism didn't equal success. Midway through a 1980 preseason contest, a defensive end named Ezra Johnson was spotted eating a hot dog on the bench. Things turned so ugly that, after home games, Jerry Parins, a security worker for the team, would pull Starr's Lincoln beneath the stadium so the coach could avoid the catcalls and threats from intoxicated fans. There were rumors that Starr's son, Bret, was dealing cocaine to the players, and the coach once pleaded to Parins, "Jerry, please let me know if you hear about him doing anything."

Forrest Gregg, another magnificent ex-Packer, became head coach in 1984, and promptly ended Family Photo Day, an annual fan-favorite event. In 1985, defensive back Mossy Cade was charged with assaulting a woman — who happened to be his aunt — then wide receiver James Lofton was charged with sexually assaulting a woman in a stairwell. Gregg seemed to greet both incidents with dismissive shrugs.

After four uninspired seasons, Gregg was replaced by Lindy Infante, former head of the USFL's Jacksonville Bulls and a man whose modest coaching abilities were yanked downward by the organization's repeated personnel gaffes.

Unlike the other 27 franchises, all of which featured an owner (or

owners) who paid the bills and a general manager in charge of personnel decisions, the Packers — the league's lone publicly owned team — was
run by a 45-member board of directors and a 7-man executive committee charged with providing input on all organizational moves. There was
a president and a general manager, but neither position came with auton-
omy. As a result, the Packers could not make decisions. Or, at least, good
decisions. In 1979, Red Cochran, one of the team's scouts, repeatedly
begged the Packers to draft a quarterback he had watched and loved. Finally, with the 82nd pick, the San Francisco 49ers grabbed Notre Dame's
Joe Montana.

Between 1980 and 1991, just 3 of 13 first-round picks ever appeared in
a Pro Bowl. The absolute lowest moment came on April 23, 1989, when
the Packers used the No. 2 overall pick in the NFL draft to take a Michigan State offensive tackle named Tony Mandarich. At six feet six and 330
pounds, with the quickness of a halfback and the strength of a weight-
lifter, Mandarich was hailed by *Sports Illustrated*'s Rick Telander as "the
best offensive line prospect ever." Yet while four of the first five selections
from the draft wound up in the Pro Football Hall of Fame, Mandarich
— plagued by addiction issues and a body fueled by illegal performance-
enhancing drugs — lasted but three dreadful seasons as a Packer.

There was also the matter of race. Really, lack of race. Green Bay is a
city of 100,000 residents, a solid 3½ percent of whom are nonwhite. In
the dark ages that followed Lombardi's departure, a trade to Green Bay
was used as a threat against black players. "My first experience in Green
Bay came right after I was drafted in 1971," said Brockington, who is African American. "I went to the Midway Motor Lodge on Lombardi Ave.
and asked for a room. They told me they didn't have one." Brockington asked Rollie Dotsch, an assistant coach, for another option. Dotsch
marched Brockington back into the Midway lobby. "This is John Brockington," he told the clerk. "He is our No. 1 draft choice. Give him a room."

Black Packers players traveled to Milwaukee (120 miles away) or Chicago (180 miles away) for haircuts, food, and women. There was (and still
is) a running joke among the African American players over the number
of times in a season local white residents confuse them for other members of the squad. "Everyone who comes into contact with you knows
you're affiliated with the team because you're black," said Patrick Dendy, a
defensive back in the mid-2000s. "That's not a bad thing. It's just a shock
at first to see so few people who look like you."

One more issue was the weather. Arctic cold, piles upon piles of snow, ice-coated roads. Young players from warm-weather climates arrived in town with only a few sweatshirts and, maybe, a thermal. They learned quickly. "The snow, the ice, the lack of other black people — it all gets to you," said Johnny Holland, a Packers linebacker from 1987–93. "Try being a guy from Florida or Alabama or California, coming to Green Bay, Wisconsin, for a winter. It's not a selling point."

By October 1991, Bob Harlan had had enough. The Packers' president and CEO had been with the organization since 1971. Through the years, Harlan hopped from one position to another to another, always accompanied by a blinding smile and irrepressible enthusiasm, always convinced this season would be the one. "I genuinely believed in the things we did," he said. "But more often than not, they didn't seem to work out."

Now, with the 1990 Packers headed toward a 6-10 finish, Harlan decided something big had to be done. For nearly five years, Green Bay's key decision maker was Tom Braatz, the executive vice president of football operations. He was a by-the-book thinker — steady, hardened, and as creative as a turnip. Every move the Packers made was predictable. No surprises. "We needed a spark of life," said Harlan. "Really, we needed Ron Wolf."

The men first met in 1987, when Harlan was interviewing candidates for the vacant general manager position. At the time, Wolf was working for the Raiders, and Judge Robert Parins, the Green Bay president, only wanted a GM who would split personnel authority with the head coach. Harlan flew Wolf into town, and they spent three hours chatting over hamburgers and Coca-Colas at Denny's, one of the few restaurants open past nine o'clock. Wolf talked about his boyhood in New Freedom, Pennsylvania; about three years in the Army. He talked about the craziness of working under Al Davis in Oakland and Los Angeles; about serving as general manager for the Tampa Bay Buccaneers. Harlan was mesmerized by Wolf's knowledge, but reached the sad conclusion he would never take a position where he didn't have full authority. That's why Braatz was hired.

This time, though, Harlan came armed to the GM search with the new title of president and CEO of the Green Bay Packers. He told the executive committee that he wanted to let Braatz go and pursue Wolf, and scored the green light. He then received permission from Dick Steinberg, the Jets general manager, to speak with Wolf. "I said I wanted to give him full authority over the football operation," Harlan recalled. "It would be his team to run. There would be absolutely no interference, and we would make sure he had everything he needed to succeed. I also told him that I didn't even have a second choice for the job. I intended to do everything I had to do to get him to say yes."

That conversation was held on a Friday. One day later, Harlan and Wolf agreed to a deal. At 52, he was among the oldest first-time general managers in league history.

The timing was unusual. New general managers are generally hired once a season is completed. Harlan, though, wanted Wolf to evaluate the Packers as they operated. "They were mired in bad," said Wolf. "That was the biggest problem. They were mired in bad and they couldn't escape." He arrived in Green Bay for a Tuesday press conference but had to complete a handful of scouting assignments for the Jets before fully diving into the gig. On December 1, the Packers were scheduled to fly to Atlanta to face the Falcons. Wolf agreed to connect with Harlan at the game. They met up in the Fulton County Stadium press box three hours before the 1:00 p.m. kickoff. Wolf set his briefcase down next to Harlan and said, "I'm gonna go watch Atlanta's backup quarterback. If his arm is as strong now as it was coming out of college, we're gonna go after him." Wolf walked off and as soon as he exited, Harlan grabbed the nearest Falcons roster. "I thought his name was Fav-*ray*," said Harlan. "Who was Brett Fav-*ray*?"

En route to the playing field, Wolf ran into Ken Herock, the Falcons' general manager. "If you wanna see Favre throw, you've gotta watch now," Herock said. "Because once the whole team comes out for practice, Jerry [Glanville] probably won't let him throw. He's being a dick to the kid."

The Packers lost 35–31 on a late touchdown, and the next afternoon Wolf attended his first Green Bay practice. He wandered from spot to spot, taking mental notes without saying much. Later, he met with Harlan. "You have a problem on your practice field," he said. "This team is 3-10 walking around like it's 10-3." Wolf grabbed a yellow pad and drew columns — one marked "All Pro," one "Star," one "Starter," one "Backup" and one "Can't Do It." He placed every Packers player into a category, and was shocked by how many simply couldn't do it. "They had too many athletes whom I hadn't considered seriously as draft possibilities for either the Raiders or the Jets," he recalled. "Wherever I looked, the mediocrity had become as routine as eating macaroni and cheese once a week for dinner. Everyone was polite and nice. The staff did their jobs — and then they went home every night promptly at 5:30."

The season ended on December 21, 1991, and Infante was fired the following day. One month later, after being rebuffed by Bill Parcells, Wolf hired Mike Holmgren to be the organization's 11th head coach. The San Francisco 49ers' offensive coordinator was 43 and the hottest assistant in the league. Unlike the Packers coaches of the past decade, who worked with such nonlegendary signal callers as Anthony Dilweg and Randy Wright, Holmgren's time with the 49ers was spent learning and teaching a master class on inventive offensive football with two future Hall of Famers, Joe Montana and Steve Young. He came to Green Bay not only eager to lead the moribund franchise back to glory, but armed with an unrivaled knowledge of the West Coast offensive system that helped the 49ers to three Super Bowl titles in six years. "Mike wasn't just your average assistant," said Roger Craig, the former 49ers halfback. "He was the innovative guy. He always had a big idea."

Actually, the big idea belonged to Jerry Glanville, the Falcons coach who badgered Herock into action. In mid-January, with the Redskins and Bills preparing for Super Bowl XXVI, Herock called Wolf, the only man he knew who loved Brett Favre's potential as much as he did. "So, Ron, we have this quarterback here and he's available," Herock said. "You know we already have a Pro Bowl quarterback in Chris [Miller], and there are none in this draft. I'd be willing to do something, but I'm looking for two firsts." The Packers, not coincidentally, owned a pair of first-round picks.

Wolf laughed. "Two firsts?" he said. "You're kidding me. Look what he did this year."

"Well," Herock replied, "what would you be willing to offer for Favre?"

"A second," he said. "Best offer."

Herock returned to the conversation after a few days. He demanded a first-round selection, or no deal.

"One first," said Wolf. "The 19th pick, not the 5th."

Herock told Wolf he'd have to check back with the Falcons. A day later, he met with Glanville and June Jones, the offensive coordinator, and told them of the offer. "Oh my gosh," Glanville said. "You'd be a genius. A first for *that* guy?"

Herock was raised in Pittsburgh. He lived and died with the Steelers, and could never grasp the organization releasing Johnny Unitas in 1955. "I used to think Pittsburgh was so freakin' dumb," he said. "How do you dump Johnny Unitas?" Following the session with Glanville and Jones, Herock debated whether he was now the one about to commit a similar blunder. "But then I calmed down," he said. "I mean, there was no way he'd be another Johnny Unitas."

On February 11, 1992, Green Bay and Atlanta reached an agreement. Brett Favre became a member of the Packers, and the Falcons owned the 19th slot in the first round. The quarterback was sitting inside the kitchen of his parents' house in Kiln when the phone rang. It was Jones, the Falcons' offensive coordinator. "Brett, you've been traded and I wanted to call and tell you before anyone else did," Jones said. "I know it wasn't a great year for you with us, and I know you and Jerry had your problems. But I think this will be great for you."

Brett was stunned. "I've . . . I've been traded?" he said.

"Yeah," said Jones. "To Green Bay."

Click.

Scott Favre was also in the kitchen. "I'm going to the Packers," Brett told him, nary a trace of emotion in his words.

Bonita overhead the conversation and rushed in. "The Packers?" she said. "The Packers? Where do they play?"

"Green Bay," Brett replied.

"Green Bay?" A pause. "Where's Green Bay?"

The phone rang again. This time it was Wolf. "We just traded for you," he said, "and I want you to know that we're very excited about having you and having you lead our team."

Favre proceeded to pour himself another pitcher of beer. Yes, the Falcons were dumping him. But the Packers sought him out, and Wolf even said they saw him as a future starter. "I was real excited," he said. "It was like turning over a new leaf for my career."

As was the case when he first arrived in Atlanta, Favre figured he'd report to Green Bay and — "future starter" talk be damned — challenge for the No. 1 job.

If only there wasn't someone formidable standing in his way.

Back in the late 1980s and early 1990s, the hottest hangout for members of the Green Bay Packers was Knights on Main, a sports-themed pub at 401 Main Avenue in the nearby city of De Pere. If the team didn't happen to be playing on *Monday Night Football* (and Lord knows, the nation wasn't clamoring to watch the Packers), one could find a solid 15 to 20 players that night at Knights on Main, drinking beers, hitting on women, taking to the dance floor. The owner, Kevin Burkel, was a Packers fan, and he even allowed members of the team to slide behind the bar and serve drinks to patrons.

A warm man with thick brown hair and a wide smile, Burkel meets few people he dislikes — and almost no Packers. From Sterling Sharpe and Ron Hallstrom to Ken Ruettgers and LeRoy Butler, anyone who wore the green and gold was not only welcome into Knights on Main, but assured protection and special treatment.

"There was just one guy who didn't always do it for me," Burkel said. "Majik."

Before Brett Favre established himself as *the* quarterback in Green Bay, there was already *the* quarterback in Green Bay. He was handsome. He was nimble. He was (relatively) strong-armed. He was popular. His name was Don Majkowski, and the onetime 10th-round draft pick from Virginia somehow led the predicted-to-be-woeful 1989 Packers to a 10-6 record by throwing for 27 touchdowns and a league-best 4,318 yards. "He just had a great feel for it all," said Sharpe. "He was smart, athletic, savvy." Majkowski rallied Green Bay to five come-from-behind fourth-quarter triumphs. *Sports Illustrated* responded by writing, in a glowing profile, "The transformation from Don Majkowski to Majik Man occurs on game day . . . Majik can afford to be cocky; he is the most athletic quarterback in the NFL."

Majik, though, was also a pretty boy, prone to blow-drying his blond hair in the mirror before games and staring longingly at his reflection. He referred to himself as Majik, and seemed to believe the hype of a city longing for a hero. "He was a very arrogant guy," said Burkel. "Very arrogant. He was just a real . . . if he walked into the bar, he'd be sitting over to one side, and there'd be a couple of good-looking women on the other side. He'd say to me, 'Hey, Kevin, go tell them I'm here.' Like I was his employee and they would automatically fall over themselves to meet Don Majkowski."

One would think, with struggles and trials, ego subsides. But it didn't seem to with Majkowski, who held out for a $1.5 million contract until four days before the 1990 kickoff, played poorly as Green Bay opened the year 4-5, then suffered a torn rotator cuff against the Cardinals. Majkowski missed the remainder of the year, and returned for the 1991 season with all the predictable athlete-back-from-an-injury redemptive story lines. His performance, though, was pitiful. Majkowski started eight games for Green Bay, throwing three touchdowns and eight interceptions. It took Ron Wolf but a couple of days on the job to see the Packers had a genuine quarterback dilemma. "With guys like that, you have these flashes of greatness and you always hope it'll happen again," said John Jurkovic, a Packers defensive tackle. "You get reminiscent for the old days, but you also realize — sadly — the old days are over. And you're left with something half of what it used to be."

As he readied for the 1992 season, Majkowski once again walked with the confidence of a seven-time Super Bowl winner. When the Packers sent the first-round pick to Atlanta for Favre, the reaction around town was muted and somewhat perplexed. Why, loyalists wondered, would a team in need of young blood surrender a high draft selection for a backup quarterback? This was Majkowski's take as well, and with good reason: he'd never heard of Brett Favre. "Almost no one knew about Brett," said LeRoy Butler, the third-year safety. "Weird name, unknown guy."

He came to Green Bay on March 7, stepped off the airplane, and was greeted by 14 inches of snow and a temperature of minus 13. "The coldest I've ever played in was 32 degrees," Favre cracked, "and I thought that was bitter." The Packers sent Jon Gruden, the young quality-control coach, to pick him up. "I couldn't believe how loose he was for a young guy who had just been traded for a first-round pick," Gruden recalled. "He felt no pressure, no responsibility. None. Zero." In fact, after Gruden introduced himself, he was bowled over by Favre's first question: "Do they have any fried okra around here?" Then, the second: "So where does a guy get a beer?"

Favre's early arrival was an effort to start rightly in Green Bay. Which didn't quite happen. To begin with, Favre failed the team-administered physical when Clarence Novotny, the Packers' physician, discovered that his left hip was degenerative; the diagnosis was avascular necrosis, the death of bone tissue due to a lack of blood supply to the socket. The condition had contributed to the end of Bo Jackson's football career two seasons earlier, and was an automatic red flag. Yet Wolf demanded a second opinion, looked over the charts, and said, "No, we're not failing him." Patrick McKenzie, an orthopedic surgeon, figured Favre could last four or five years before being destroyed via injury. Wolf considered it a risk worth taking.

Minicamp was scheduled to commence on April 5 at the team's practice facility, and the angel on Favre's right shoulder told him to get plenty of sleep and show up wide-eyed and eager. The devil on the left (non-throwing) shoulder, however, whispered sinister thoughts. He was staying at the Best Western, and that day a young woman at the front desk told him she had an extra ticket for the evening's concert at the Brown County Arena. The lineup was Brooks and Dunn, Reba McEntire, and Travis Tritt—and while Favre wasn't a huge country music fan, he'd met Tritt in Atlanta and considered him a casual pal. "Well, we went to the concert and had a big time," Favre recalled. "We walked around the arena, drank some beers, and got to go backstage with Travis." When the concert ended, Tritt invited Favre onto his tour bus, where the men, in Favre's words, "partied until Lord knows how late."

The next morning, he arrived at the facility with the scent of alcohol adhered to his body. Steve Mariucci, the Packers' quarterbacks coach, picked up the smell, but presumed he was misunderstanding. There's no way the quarterback would show up drunk for his first day, right? Mariucci let Favre participate in the practice, and watched aghast as his balls wobbled and fluttered through the air. Afterward, he grabbed Favre for a stern lecture. "You can't do that," Mariucci said. "You've got to tighten up. This whole organization has a lot invested in you."

Favre nodded, said all the right things, promised it wouldn't happen again. A mere three days later, it sort of happened again. Favre and some teammates went out for dinner at a Mexican restaurant, then headed to McSwiggin's, a pub on the east side of the city. Rich Moran, a Green Bay offensive lineman, was minding his own business when a bar patron started to pester him. "Next thing you know," Moran said, "Brett flew over my shoulder, grabbed the guy and pinned him against the wall. It was unbelievable, because I really didn't even know Brett yet."

"He was willing to mix it up for his teammates," said Ruettgers. "That showed us something."

Favre was able to ease doubts about his maturity by showing off an arm that, according to a *Sporting News* report, "is far better than anyone on the team." His first Wisconsin-based broken-finger victim was Orlando McKay, the fifth-round pick out of the University of Washington. "I was 6 yards away," said McKay of the minicamp route, "and he just lit me up with the ball. *Pop!*"

Unlike Majkowski, Favre (who was making $310,000) was easily embraceable. Although he knew nobody in the locker room, he quickly established himself as the team prankster — shaving cream in shoes, talcum powder in jocks. "You'd just look at his face and laugh," said Paul McJulien, the Green Bay punter. "It was like a little kid hiding something." Favre formed a particularly tight bond with Esera Tuaolo, a second-year defensive tackle who was born and raised in Hawaii, then played collegiately at Oregon State. When Favre and Tuaolo weren't on the minicamp field or in the locker room, they were exploring Wisconsin bars and their myriad beer offerings. "We connected well because we're both from small towns," Tuaolo said. "It was one of those things where we met and just clicked."

A couple of weeks before the start of training camp, Favre invited Tuaolo down to Mississippi for some relaxation on Irvin Farve Road. It was, for the six-foot-two, 281-pound Polynesian, among the greatest (and strangest) experiences of his life. "I was introduced to a crawfish boil," he said. "When I was little in Hawaii, we'd catch crawfish in streams, but I never thought I'd eat them. Well, I go down and Brett's family is boiling giant pots of crawfish, throwing them onto the middle of the table, everyone's eating this weird food." Tuaolo was astonished by the love and warmth of Favre's family members and friends. Life was a never-ending party, and free time existed to get drunk.

On the night of June 23, 1992, Favre and Deanna, his younger brother Jeff, Tuaolo, and two pickup trucks filled with friends traveled the 1 hour, 15 minutes to Hattiesburg for an evening of wildness at Ropers nightclub, a popular hangout for Southern Miss students. As soon as they entered, Tuaolo knew there might be trouble. "We walk in, and there's a bunch of . . . um, country folk," said Tuaolo. "We're drinking, having a good time, minding our own business." According to police reports, Brett and Deanna started screaming at each other, and a patron attempted to intervene.

This is what, according to a Favre representative, happened next:

When Favre told the man to get lost, the man charged him and the two began wrestling. While Favre tried to throw the man off him, another man snuck up on him and punched him three times in the nose, eye, and ear. The fight was broken up without Favre throwing a single punch. The police arrived a short time later and Favre tried to have them arrest the man who punched him. The police told him they did not have any evidence to arrest anybody and ordered him to leave immediately or face arrest. Favre argued but then left with Tuaolo and drove around for 20 minutes before returning to pick up Favre's girlfriend. When they pulled into the parking lot, Favre saw his girlfriend and began yelling for her. The police saw him, ran to the car, pulled him out, and put him in handcuffs. Favre said he argued briefly with the police, especially when they told him they were arresting him for public drunkenness.

That take, said Tuaolo, is only partially true. After someone sucker punched Favre, Tuaolo said he jumped in and slammed the man to the ground. "Brett gets up, we both start hitting him," Tuaolo said. "We finally got up to run but by the time we reached the door the cops were there." Favre's face was covered in blood and both eyes were black-and-blue. After initially being released with a warning, Favre and Co. returned to the Ropers parking lot looking for more action. That's when they were arrested and sent to the local jail. Favre was charged with public drunkenness, disorderly conduct, and profanity. Tuaolo was charged with disorderly conduct. Jeff was cited for interfering with a police officer, and Deanna was charged with profanity and interfering with an officer. En route to the holding facility, Favre — intoxicated, bloodied, furious — barked at the officer driving the car, "Why don't you just pull over and drop your gun? We'll take these cuffs off, step out of the car, and I'll whup your ass."

The policeman paid him no mind as he made the drop-off. Tuaolo was mortified, and wondered whether he'd still have an NFL job come morning. "They put us in a cell with a bunch of African American guys," Tuaolo recalled. "I remember walking in there, he's drunk, I'm drunk, and he's yelling at the top of his lungs, 'This is my boy from Hawaii!' I was like, 'Shut up, Brett. Just shut up.'" After a few hours Tuaolo was released from his cell and was greeted by a surprisingly warm law enforcement official. "Don't worry about this, kid," the man said. "When he was in college this was Brett's second home."

Tuaolo thinks he was kidding. Maybe. Four hours later they were bailed out by Bus Cook, Brett's agent. The mayhem was all over the next day's national news circuit, and generated front-page placement in Wisconsin.

For Favre, the worst moment came when he spoke via phone with Holmgren, who was vacationing with his family in California. "We just can't have this," the coach said. "You can't play for me and do all the things you did all your life." Holmgren was well versed in Favre's résumé as a hell raiser, and he didn't like it. What was he supposed to do with a 22-year-old kid who seemed determined to drink himself out of football?

He had no idea.

Much like major-league baseball's annual spring awakening, the opening of NFL training camp serves as a renewal of optimism and hope. Whether a team went 0-16 the previous season, or lost its best running back to free agency, or suffered the death of a head coach, there's always reason to believe, once the grass is watered and the whistles blow.

This seemed especially true in Green Bay, where on July 14 the Packers kicked off camp at the team training facilities. After a solid 25 years of mostly subpar football, there was a new sense of optimism in the air, only it had nothing to do with the drunkard second-year quarterback. No, this was all about Holmgren, who arrived with a bold walk, bold talk, and stated expectations of excellence. The Green Bay Packers weren't here to win eight or nine games. They were here to win Super Bowls.

"It was different," said Sharpe. "I knew Mike would be great beginning with our first meeting in camp. He told me, 'We don't have a lot of pieces, so we can only be as great as you take us. But I think you're gonna like this offense, because we'll stay out of long yardage, keep our offense on the field, and allow us to move the ball.' He just had a confidence that made you believe."

Holmgren was 44 and shared little in common with those he coached. Professional sports tend to draw athletes who have a singular focus. One doesn't merely play football, one *lives* football. Holmgren, however, was a Renaissance man among Neanderthals. He grew up in San Francisco's West Portal neighborhood, one of the six kids of Linc Holmgren (a real estate executive who helped found Century 21) and his wife, Barbara (a nurse). At Lincoln High School, Mike Holmgren played center in basketball, quarterback in football, and served as the student body president. At six feet five and 220 pounds, he was a sturdy kid who agreed to attend the University of Southern California on a football scholarship, then spent four years as a backup to Steve Sogge and Jimmy Jones. He completed eight collegiate passes.

In 1971 Holmgren served as a substitute history teacher and part-time football coach at Lincoln High. The following year he became a full-time football coach at San Francisco's Sacred Heart Cathedral Prep. A decade after beginning his career, he was named the offensive coordinator at San Francisco State, and a year later joined LaVell Edwards as the quarterbacks coach at Brigham Young University. It was here, in Provo, Utah, where Holmgren morphed from offensive thinker to budding offensive mastermind. The Cougars were known for throwing and throwing and throwing some more, and Holmgren specialized in developing routes and formations that had opposing defenses pleading for mercy. Bill Walsh, the 49ers' head coach, referred to BYU's attack as, "the most sophisticated passing offense in college football," and when he needed a quarterbacks coach heading into the 1986 season, he knew where to turn. "He had a better feel for football than anyone I knew," Walsh raved of Holmgren. "He was obviously the man."

If BYU was a master class in offensive football, Walsh and the 49ers comprised an Einsteinian think tank. In six years by the Bay, Holmgren absorbed an eternity of knowledge about football and leadership. Perhaps the number one thing that prepared him for the Green Bay job was Walsh's oft-stated organizational philosophy. Writes David Harris in his excellent Walsh biography, *The Genius*: "The premise was that all the components of the Forty Niners' structure had to be a single unitary construction, all pointed toward the same direction, all generating the same energy, independent in the goal of creating a great football team, from the janitors on up. Everything it did would be funneled toward advancing the Niners to the Super Bowl, the team a seamless extension of the organization that supported it."

Holmgren carried this idea to Green Bay, and Wolf seconded it. But it required commitment and adherence, two things they worried Favre might lack. That's why, of the five passers who attended training camp, Favre was one of the least likely to emerge as the starter for the September 6 opener against Minnesota. Officially, Majkowski was listed as No. 1, followed by Favre, backup Mike Tomczak (who was holding out in a contract dispute, but expected to report), Ty Detmer, the Heisman Trophy winner from Brigham Young, and Jeff Bridewell, a free agent from Cal–Davis.

"There are always a lot of quarterbacks in training camp, and it's easy for guys to get lost in the shuffle," said Greg Bell, a veteran halfback who was trying to make the Packers as a free agent. "I watched Brett from a distance at first, and there was something special about him. I played with Jim Kelly in Buffalo. I'd worked out with Dan Marino. But when Brett threw the ball — *whew*. Different."

When he entered the league with Atlanta, Favre struggled to grasp the complexities of NFL offenses, both because he was intoxicated 50 percent of the time and because June Jones's red-gun system was dizzying for the young mind. In Green Bay, Holmgren installed the West Coast offense, which involved quick drops and quick reads, and it fit Favre well. "It was quicker for Brett than you might think," said Kitrick Taylor, a fifth-year wide receiver. "He was a coach's son. Smart. I remember, very early in training camp, Sterling Sharpe warning me to be ready when Brett was throwing, to snap my head around quick. So I ran my first route with him, and I didn't get my hands up quickly enough and he jammed my left pinky. Ever since that moment, I've had a crooked pinky top. He threw the ball so hard, with such power . . ."

Majkowski treated Favre as a veteran might treat a new threat. *Hello. Goodbye. Nice throw. See you later.* Nothing intimate, nothing overly jerky. "You could see he had a tremendous arm," Majkowski said years later. "But . . . he was immature and very green." Unlike Atlanta, where the inmates ran the asylum, Holmgren insisted there would be no hazing and no deliberate hostilities. He also made clear that Majkowski was the No. 1 quarterback and would receive the majority of the reps in practice. Which allowed teammates to see his limitations. "I was shocked at Don's lack of arm strength," said George Koonce, a Green Bay linebacker. "There was no comparison between him and Brett. None."

"Don had taken a lot of shots, had been beaten up pretty good," said Darrell Thompson, a Packers halfback. "Now along comes Brett and he's throwing the ball hard. Like balls shooting from a JUGS machine. He wasn't satisfied being there; he wanted to play." During one practice, Thompson was standing near Favre when he completed a pass that wound up breaking the receiver's finger. He was shocked — yet oddly pleased — when Favre snickered and said, "Add it to the collection."

Majkowski felt stale. Favre felt like a birthday party. Mariucci, the quarterbacks coach, and Andy Reid, the tight end coach, encouraged the receivers to use the young quarterback as a hand-strength test. "They'd start off standing far away, and they'd walk closer and closer as Brett threw rockets at them," said Andrew Oberg, an offensive tackle and 10th-round draft choice from North Carolina. "The goal was to not get hit, and it was insane to watch." The other thing Favre did was throw underhand behind-the-back spirals with perfect placement. "I've never seen anyone do that," Oberg said. "Before or since."

The Packers kicked off their exhibition schedule by hosting the Chiefs at Lambeau Field. In the local newspapers, the game was billed as the genius head coach's debut and the veteran quarterback's return to possible stardom, and both narratives took early beatings. On Green Bay's very first offensive play, Majkowski was intercepted by Albert Lewis. His next two series were also failures. Favre was inserted to begin the second half, and the anticipation inside Lambeau was nonexistent. He was an unknown quantity with an unknown skill set. But after methodically guiding the Packers down the field in the fourth quarter, he hit Dexter McNabb, the rookie fullback, for a 9-yard completion, followed with an 8-yard scramble up the middle, then found free agent tight end Jerry Evans for a 5-yard score and his first touchdown pass as a Packer. "He was loose, carefree, relaxed," said McNabb. "Even then, as a kid starting out, he had a way of guiding a team."

Green Bay's 1992 season would officially open at home against the Minnesota Vikings, and while everyone agreed Brett Favre was the most talented quarterback in camp, Holmgren did not consider him ready. His passer rating for the exhibition run was 45.96. His one touchdown pass was coupled with six interceptions. So when Majkowski jogged onto the field for the noon start, he received a standing ovation from the sellout crowd of 58,617.

The Vikings were the far-superior team, but Majkowski played fairly well, completing 13 straight passes in Minnesota's 23–20 win. One week later Green Bay went to Florida to face the lowly Tampa Bay Buccaneers, and the second game of Holmgren's Packers career was also the worst. Losing 31–3 was bad. But losing 31–3 to Tampa Bay (with a flu-stricken Vinny Testaverde at quarterback) was unforgivable. "After the Bucs dominated them," Chris Havel wrote in the *Green Bay Press-Gazette,* "the Packers somehow resisted any temptation to wrestle the gun away from the referee and put it to their heads."

From a mere statistical viewpoint, Majkowski was OK. He completed 10 of 15 passes for 75 yards. But he couldn't orchestrate any drives, and after Tampa Bay jumped out to a 17–0 halftime lead, Holmgren and Mariucci conferred in the locker room about giving Favre some action in the second half. What was the risk?

That's why, with the opening of the second half, Favre jogged onto the field to make his Green Bay Packers debut. The name meant nothing to the majority of Tampa's players. Keith McCants, the star defensive end, however, shuddered slightly. He had played against Southern Miss as an All-American at Alabama. "I immediately told the guys, 'Hey, Brett Favre is a hell of a lot better than Don Majkowski,'" he said. "The game plan was normally to get the starter out. But I did not want to see Brett Favre again. Not after what he did to my college team."

On the first official play of his Packers career, Favre stepped to the line on Green Bay's 17. Matt Millen, calling the game for CBS, sounded baffled. "Maybe Majkowski got dinged or something," he said, "or maybe they just want another look." Favre took the snap, faked a handoff to halfback Edgar Bennett, and rolled to his right. He was approached by Ray Seals, the six-foot-three, 296-pound defensive end, and drew back his arm to throw to fullback Harry Sydney. As Favre released the ball, Seals leapt and batted it high into the air. Favre looked up, plucked it, and ran 2 yards up the field before Seals and linebacker Broderick Thomas brought him down. "This is what's gonna make Brett Favre a good player," Millen said. "See, he never stopped. Very competitive. He doesn't wanna go down. He's gonna make something happen. The book on Brett Favre — he has a rocket for an arm. He's gotta learn some touch."

Lost in Millen's praise was the fact that Brett Favre's first NFL completion went minus-7 yards, and to himself.

He didn't play poorly the rest of the day, completing 8 of 14 passes for 73 yards and an interception. Afterward, Majkowski was livid, and went off in front of the assembled media. "[Holmgren] said he wanted to experiment," he said. "I'm obviously not happy about it. I didn't think he was the kind of coach that would have an early hook. I've come back from more than 17 points down in the second half. The decision that he made, it didn't make a difference. I'm angry."

12

A PACKER EMERGES

WHEN THE CINCINNATI BENGALS used the 276th pick in the 1983 NFL draft on a slow, undersized University of Wisconsin defensive lineman, they presumed — best-case scenario — he would stick around a year or two before fading in favor of stronger, faster players.

It's the way the league generally works. Less talented guys might plug a hole for a spell, but ultimately talent and prestige win out.

That's not how Tim Krumrie saw things.

"The computer said I was too short, too slow, and too light," he said. "The only thing I could do was play football."

What franchises failed to see was that inside, Krumrie was a violence-charged motor incapable of being stopped. Growing up on a farm in Mondovi, Wisconsin, he spent nearly all his nonworking hours either blasting people on the football field or slamming them into a wrestling mat. He competed in both sports in college, and was reliably terrifying. "I have seen some very, very tough and aggressive men," said Kim Wood, the longtime Bengals strength trainer, "and Tim Krumrie is at the top of that list."

After playing sparingly as a rookie, Krumrie emerged as the staple of the Cincinnati defensive line, starting every game at nose tackle from 1984 through 1989 while twice being voted to the Pro Bowl. How fierce was he? In the first quarter of Cincinnati's 20–16 loss to San Francisco in Super Bowl XXIII, Krumrie suffered a severely broken leg when pressure caused the bone above his ankle to snap. He was diagnosed with both a broken tibia and fibula, but refused to leave for the hospital until the game ended.

By the third week of the 1992 season, Krumrie was 32 and a step slower than most of the linemen he faced. The Bengals were now coached by a newcomer, David Shula, and the rebuilding effort was underway. Krumrie was playing for survival.

The Bengals arrived in Green Bay on September 18, two days before the Sunday kickoff. At 2-0, they were a surprise of the league. These were the revamped Bengals. The ferocious Bengals. "We felt like we were on to something," said Eric Thomas, a Cincinnati cornerback. "New coach, new attitude." Green Bay, on the other hand, was a mess — 0-2, coming off the Tampa Bay disaster, and playing behind a suddenly unhappy quarterback. Holmgren was not pleased with Majkowski's publicly aired complaints of his benching against the Bucs, and especially didn't like it when, in a meeting with NBC broadcaster Ahmad Rashad leading up to the Cincinnati clash, he complained that he would like to throw deep, but lacked "the horses" to do so.

Early in the first quarter, Majkowski looked predictably erratic. On a second and 7 he missed a wide-open receiver by throwing a pass that hit right guard Ron Hallstrom in the back of the head. "I think he's tentative," Rashad rightly observed. "I think he's really not yet comfortable in this offense." One play later, on a third and 7 from the Green Bay 38, Majkowski took a seven-step drop and the pocket quickly collapsed. He was slammed in the upper torso by defensive end Alonzo Mitz and ripped to the ground by Krumrie, who shoved Hallstrom aside, dove for Majkowski's left leg, and rolled atop the ankle. Majkowski's body collapsed as if someone had pushed over a bag of leaves, and he writhed in pain on the grass, facedown, hands clawing at the sides of his gold helmet. "I wish that play had ended differently," said Krumrie. "I never took pride in hurting someone. That's not the goal of football." Nevertheless, a gaggle of Packers linemen charged Krumrie, blaming him for the eradication of their leader. "Majkowski is in great pain, Ahmad," said Jim Lampley, handling the play-by-play. "As the scuffle goes on behind him."

Majkowski spent several minutes on the field before he was carried off by a couple of trainers. Holmgren approached Favre. "You're in," he said. The NBC camera panned from No. 7 exiting to a young, cleanly shaved kid on the sideline, wearing a green baseball cap and tossing a football.

Rashad: "Majkowski now being carried off the field. I think that might be it for him today. And in comes . . ." (Two seconds of awkward silence)

Lampley: "Brett Favre."

Rashad: "Brett Favre will be the next quarterback."

Because Majkowski was injured on third down, Favre did not have to immediately take over. Green Bay punted and — with the defense on the field — he conferred with Steve Mariucci, went over the Bengals' tendencies, familiarized himself with the secondary personnel. Cincinnati quarterback Boomer Esiason, however, threw a quick interception, and Favre entered the game with the ball at the Cincinnati 45-yard line. Lampley introduced him to a regional viewing audience thusly: "And here is second-year quarterback Brett Favre, out of Southern Mississippi by way of the Atlanta Falcons. He cost the Packers a first-round draft choice, they are hopeful he can succeed in the NFL."

On the Packers' sideline, safety LeRoy Butler was standing next to a teammate. "He said to me, 'Is Favre ready for this?'" recalled Butler, who was a star on the Florida State team that fell to Southern Miss. "I said, 'I'll tell you what — he showed me in college he's ready.'"

"We had won our first two games and they were putting in their backup quarterback," said Alfred Williams, a Bengals linebacker. "We thought we had the game won."

Favre walked nervously into the huddle to call a play. He was neither hung over nor drunk. Simply overwhelmed by the magnitude of the moment. He witnessed Majkowski's gruesome injury. The Majik Man would not be coming back. "[Brett] barely knew the plays," recalled Jon Gruden, the offensive quality-control assistant. "He could hardly say the ones he did know. I wasn't sure if he knew what he was doing."

Favre's first pass was a short completion to wide receiver Sterling Sharpe, and the crowd cheered wildly. Maybe, just maybe, the Packers would be OK. But for the majority of the remaining three quarters, the new quarterback performed terribly. He fumbled four times, blew myriad blitz reads, called some of the strangest formations Holmgren had ever seen. Once, while standing along the sideline, he turned to James Campen, a teammate, and said, "It's good I'm getting hit like I am, because it brings you to your senses."

"I was all over the place," he later recalled, "like a chicken with his head cut off." After three quarters, the Bengals led 17–3 and Lambeau Field was silent. "Dead," said Butler. "Rightly so. We stunk." Slowly, the Packers mounted a charge — rookie Terrell Buckley returned a punt 58 yards for a touchdown, and Favre capped off the first sustained drive of his NFL career with a 5-yard strike to Sharpe for another score. The Bengals, however, answered with Jim Breech's 41-yard field goal, and with 1:07 remaining in the game, Green Bay trailed 23–17. "It didn't look so good," said Sharpe. "Rookie quarterback, losing, bad field position."

After the kickoff Favre and Co. took over on their own 8-yard line. No time-outs remained. "Here, Brett Favre, you want a challenge?" said Lampley. "Try this one." On first down, he dropped back into the end zone and hit fullback Harry Sydney, who gained 3 yards and used just six seconds before running out of bounds to stop the clock. Favre strolled up to the line for second and 7, took a deep drop, stepped, stepped, and launched a fireball to Sharpe, who grabbed it at the Packers 45, tumbled forward, landed on the 50, and rolled 4 more yards to the Bengals 46. Sharpe fell atop the ball, and as Favre sprinted up the field, the star wide receiver — a two-time Pro Bowler — walked hunched over in agony, pawing his stomach with his left hand. His ribs were broken. "You can feel the fluid in your stomach moving — it hurts that much," Sharpe recalled. "I can't breathe, can barely talk . . ."

On the next play Favre connected with Vince Workman out of the backfield for 11 yards, and with 19 seconds left, Favre spiked the ball to halt the clock. Sharpe, now barely able to walk, shouted, "Mike! Mike! I have to come out!" He waved wildly for a backup to enter, but Holmgren hesitated. Sharpe mustered a genuine scream. "Mike! I can't breathe! I can't move! I can't do anything!"

The coach reluctantly inserted Kitrick Taylor, a fifth-year journeyman from Washington State who made the team out of camp based upon speed and special teams skills. Green Bay was Taylor's fourth pro stop, but he had never caught an NFL touchdown. As he entered the game, Taylor was quickly stopped by Sharpe. "You gotta get it done," he said.

"OK," replied the soft-spoken Taylor.

The 11 Green Bay players gathered in the huddle. The play call was "All go," where the wide receivers sprint toward the end zone. The Packers had a trio of wideouts on the field, along with tight end Jackie Harris and Workman at fullback. With the snap, Favre dropped back five steps, pumped once, looked to his right, and let loose a frozen rope to Taylor, who bolted past Rod Jones, the Bengals' top defensive back, Somehow, the pass slipped between Jones and safety Fernandus Vinson, who arrived a half second late, and Taylor caught the ball in perfect stride at the 1-yard line and burst into the end zone. "It's 'Holy mother of hell! What just happened here?'" said John Jurkovic, a Green Bay defensive lineman. The crowd exploded as Taylor raised both arms to the sky, the ball tightly secured in the neon-yellow glove that wrapped his right hand. Favre ripped off his helmet, held it aloft in his right fist, both arms — like Taylor — thrust upward. He then fell to a catcher's crouch, overcome by euphoria and disbelief. The standing ovation lasted for a solid minute, as Lampley screamed above the noise, "Number 85 is Kitrick Taylor, out of Washington State!"*

Green Bay won, 24–23, and afterward Favre — until this point relatively unknown to the local media — offered his special brand of country charm. "I couldn't bear to look," he said of the throw. "I just closed my eyes and waited for the crowd to let me know. I was shaking, put it that way. I felt like I took a laxative. Thank God I held it until afterward."

The Cincinnati locker room was a morgue. It would be the first of five straight losses for the Bengals, and Krumrie, in particular, was crestfallen. He knew what it was to win and lose in the NFL, and how one crushing defeat could spawn a season of horrors.

"What I obviously didn't know then is that my tackle of Don Majkowski kick-started the legend of Brett Favre," he said with a chuckle. "I suppose I should take full responsibility for what Brett became. It's only fair, right?"

Every week during the season, the Packers' public relations department put out a news release recapping the previous Sunday's events, as well as updating player injuries and offering small news tidbits.

After his magnificent breakout showing, Brett Favre very much looked forward to reading about his accomplishments. Then he took a gander, and noticed the spelling of his name: "Bart Favre."

This was not the staff's way of paying homage to Bart Starr, Green Bay's Hall of Fame quarterback. It was an embarrassing screwup, one *USA Today* took delight in highlighting in Gary Mihoces's Thursday notes column. Even with the big win and the miraculous throw to Taylor, Brett Favre was still Bart Favre, and "Brett Farve," and "Bret Favor." His name

---

* It was the only touchdown reception of Taylor's career. Years later, Sam Farmer of the *Los Angeles Times* visited the wide receiver, who lives in Southern California. Taylor showed Farmer the ball, which was scuffed and bloated from years of bouncing it off the asphalt in front of his house. "I figured I was gonna catch a bunch of those in my life," Taylor said, "and nobody would know who Brett Favre is."

was mangled and bungled, butchered and bastardized. It was also, briefly, the talk of the league, what with Majkowski's injury diagnosis (strained ligaments in his left ankle) assuring Favre a first NFL start against undefeated Pittsburgh. When asked by members of the media, Holmgren and Wolf said they were unsure what would happen when Majkowski regained health. But they knew the truth. Bart, eh, Brett Favre was, in this case, probably Lou Gehrig, and Don Majkowski was Wally Pipp. Green Bay was a franchise in rebuilding mode. Why not start now? "I remember after the [Bengals] game, I was saying, 'This is our quarterback right here,'" said Johnny Holland, a veteran linebacker. "Brett was different than anything we'd seen. You pretty much could see that was it for Majik. It was over."

Pittsburgh came to Lambeau Field for the afternoon game, and beforehand Holmgren invited Paul Hornung, the legendary Green Bay halfback, to address the team. As he listened to the 56-year-old Hall of Famer speak of long runs and glorious days, Favre found himself choked up. Twelve years earlier, as a sixth grader in Hancock County, Mississippi, he wrote a book report about Hornung. "Never in my life did I think I'd hear him give a speech to a team I'd be playing on," he said. "Especially a Green Bay Packer team. Man, I had to pinch myself."

The Steelers were 3-0 and favored by 3½ points. Favre, pleasantly naive, didn't care. For the first time since college, he spent the days leading up to the contest practicing with the first team, and his confidence was, in Sharpe's words, "really, really high." The general NFL game plan against Pittsburgh's high-level defense was simple: control the ball, and don't throw in the direction of Rod Woodson, the NFL's best cornerback. But in a surprisingly easy 17–3 win, Favre twice used his beloved pump-then-throw maneuver to burn Woodson for touchdown passes. One was a 76-yard beauty to Sharpe, the other an 8-yarder to Robert Brooks — the receiver's first professional score. "One of the things that makes [Woodson] great is his aggressiveness," Holmgren later said. "We thought maybe you can get him to bite."

After the throw to Sharpe, Favre sprinted down the field and jumped atop his star wide receiver, slamming him to the ground. Holmgren threatened to fine his quarterback $5,000 should he ever deck a teammate again. "That was the end of tackling my own guys," Favre recalled.

When the game concluded, a humiliated Woodson stood before his teammates and apologized. He had now joined Cincinnati's Jones and Vinson as early victims of Green Bay's rookie quarterback.

They wouldn't be the last.

Favre Fever was the feel-good disease of Green Bay, Wisconsin, just as three years earlier the Majik Man had taken over the city. That's the way these things go in sports. You're high, you're higher, you're soaring above the clouds. Then (*plop!*) you're back on the ground, covered in dirt and wondering what the heck just happened.

Enter: the Atlanta Falcons.

Favre's second career start would come back in Georgia, against the team that let him go and the coach who took pleasure in mocking him. The quarterback pretended the game was nothing special, because this is what athletes are taught to do. Yet few men took greater delight in the Falcons' 1-3 start, which included three straight losses and growing doubt that Jerry Glanville knew whereof he spoke. The Atlanta sports media had never much cared for Glanville, and now, in Favre's emergence, they had new ammunition. The draft pick acquired in the trade was used to select (coincidentally) Tony Smith, the Southern Miss running back and a man who had already shown he wasn't NFL-worthy. "He was soft," said Glanville, "and he couldn't play."

Four days before kickoff, Len Pasquarelli of the *Atlanta Journal-Constitution* published a piece that praised Favre's newfound maturity, writing that "the human laugh track/sound bite has discovered the serious side of football." Favre went along with the narrative. He was reborn and appreciative; he committed himself to the game and to studying film. "Honest, I've changed my lifestyle completely since I came up here," he said. "It's OK here. It's a football town. You could go places in Atlanta and nobody'd even know who the Falcons are. Up here, it's 'Packers this' and 'Packers that.'" The talk was ludicrous. Favre was still drinking and partying — only in a city where, unlike Atlanta, there wasn't very much to do. If a teammate was popping open a beer, Brett Favre was nearby. If there was a club to hit, he was hitting it. Deanna and Brittany visited on occasion, but only for quick stays. Mostly, he was sort of bored. And cold. His car had already been towed from a snowbank. He'd replaced flip-flops with boots. He tried getting into bratwurst, but preferred the taste of crawfish. Had Brett Favre changed, or was it merely a new environment?

By the time Sunday arrived, Favre was just happy to stop talking and play. A loud 63,769 fans filled the new Georgia Dome for the game. That figure included 12 members of the Favre family (his parents, grand-mother, aunt, and a handful of friends), who would be watching Brett for the first time as a Packers starter. What unfolded was, by most regards, the best showing of his young career — 276 passing yards and a touch-down on 33 of 43 completions. But the porous Green Bay defense allowed Chris Miller to fire at will in the Falcons' 24–10 romp. Afterward, the op-posing starting quarterbacks embraced at midfield, Falcon cornerback Tim McKyer spoke of Favre's passes "ripping the skin off your hands," and a relieved Glanville told a group of reporters that he was "real proud" of his ex-player.

When conveyed the message, Brett Favre smirked. Having grown up in a rural community, he knew well the scent of bullshit.

The Atlanta setback was followed by a bye week, then losses to Cleveland and Chicago. The Packers managed a triumph over lowly Detroit on No-vember 1 to improve to 3-5 (during which Favre suffered what appeared to be a catastrophic ankle injury, but continued to play), but fell hard at the Giants a week later (Favre tossed three interceptions in the 27–7 loss to New York), leaving folks to wonder whether a now-healthy Majkow-ski should return to his perch as the starter. It was a fair question, and one even Holmgren toyed with. The coach liked everything about Favre's physicality, and he compared his toughness to that of a linebacker. But, man, could he drive a guy to drink. Favre seemed to listen. He really did. But then he'd take the field and do . . . stuff. A play would go left; he'd run right. Sterling Sharpe would be the primary receiver; Favre looked for the tight end. He sent halfbacks in motion without being told to send half-backs in motion, and inadvertently called the wrong signals at least five times per Sunday. Sometimes his passes were more beautiful than a dove gliding through a soft breeze. Other times his balls resembled empty soda cans tossed into a stiff wind. Holmgren's two favorite quarterbacks were Joe Montana and Steve Young, and while both had their own styles, they generally followed his instructions. Sometimes, Holmgren wondered whether Favre was listening to him talk or merely watching his lips move while thinking, *Mmm . . . beer.* Once, while the coach was trying to ex-plain something to Favre during a particularly frigid game, the quarter-back stared blankly. "Will you listen to me?" Holmgren screamed. To which Favre replied, "Mike, you ought to see your [ice-coated] mustache

right now." Sydney, the veteran fullback brought in from San Francisco
as a free agent, was a Holmgren favorite, limited as a player at age 33 but
trusted to teach the 49er way. "How you win, how you watch film, how
you treat people," said Sydney. "Everyone has to pick up the approach so
there are no weak links. Really, I was there to help change the philosophy." He found the early Holmgren-Favre dynamic particularly riveting,
in the way it would be fun to listen to a Guatemalan and a Russian try
to converse in Arabic. "Brett would drive Mike crazy, but then he'd turn
around and do something amazing," Sydney said. "It was a lot of, 'Brett,
what the hell! Oh, wait! Good throw!'"

The Packers were 3-6 with the Eagles coming to Milwaukee.* Featuring an electric quarterback named Randall Cunningham, Philadelphia was considered a legitimate Super Bowl contender. By now, opponents were game-planning for Favre, which meant studying the tapes and
tracking tendencies of the man leading the NFL's 16th-ranked offense.
The early reviews were strong. Lynn, the Bengals' defensive coordinator,
compared Favre to John Elway. John Robinson, the former Los Angeles Rams coach, said he was the new Bobby Layne. And Joe Woolley, the
Eagles' personnel director, believed the league was seeing a young Terry
Bradshaw.

Thirteen minutes into the first quarter, with the thermostat reading
17 degrees and the agony of frost-powered numbness settling in, Reggie
White and Andy Harmon—two of the Eagles' star pass rushers—sand-
wiched Favre. A fire-like pain shot through his left arm as his shoulder
popped out of the socket, the arm drooping to his side. Holmgren immediately motioned for Majkowski to warm up, but Favre refused to leave
the field. He somehow manipulated his shoulder back into place and
three plays later found Sharpe for a 5-yard touchdown. It was the toughest thing anyone had ever seen. "I wondered, 'Who is this guy?'" White
recalled. "His left arm had seized up so bad he couldn't even lift it, much
less hand off to that side." At halftime Clarence Novotny, the team physician, injected the painkiller Xylocaine into the shoulder, and the pain
subsided. It wasn't the first time Favre had taken pain medication, and it
would be far from the last. Whatever was needed to stay on the field, he
willingly did.

---

* Until 1994, the Packers played three games every season at Milwaukee County Stadium.

The statistics were strong (23 of 33, 275 yards, two touchdowns, two interceptions), the lasting impression stronger. The Packers held on for a 27–24 win, and White — the man who would not have been able to distinguish Brett Favre from a grocery store clerk three hours earlier — sought the Green Bay quarterback out afterward. "You," he told him, "have as much guts as anyone in this league, and it was an honor to play against you. I won't forget it."

The victory improved the Packers to 4-6, but the infusion of confidence counted more than the record. What began as one victory over a high-quality team turned into a six-game winning streak, the longest for the organization in 26 years. The local media came up with different reasons for the roll (Holmgren's genius, Wolf's savvy, a ramped-up defense), but the greatest contributor was the odd yet perfect coupling of Favre and Sharpe — a bad movie cliché brought to life.

The quarterback and the star wide receiver were both big Southern kids (Sharpe was raised in Glennville, Georgia) who loved football, but the similarities ended there. Favre was a beer-swilling country boy. Sharpe didn't drink. Favre talked to everyone, about everything. Sharpe largely kept to himself. Favre was not one to brag. Sharpe would stand naked before a locker room mirror, inviting teammates to admire the full physical splendor that was Sterling Sharpe. When he was nabbed by Green Bay with the seventh overall pick in the 1988 NFL draft, friends presumed Sharpe would be devastated to have to play football in a cold, mostly white wasteland. Not so. "My family was all like, 'Ugh,' and I was like, 'Yes!'" Sharpe said. "I never wanted to be famous or market myself. I just wanted to play football." His first professional season was good (55 catches, 791 yards), his second, stellar. Sharpe caught 90 passes for 1,423 yards and 12 touchdowns, introducing himself as Jerry Rice's new rival for NFL's best pass catcher. Sharpe had enormous meaty hands, and wrists as strong as iron. He wasn't particularly fast, but ran precise routes. He was also one of the few Packers wide receivers to never have a finger snapped by Favre, and actually relished the challenge of catching his passes at close range. "We used to have this thing on Saturday mornings where we'd stand 10 yards from the quarterbacks and see if they could throw it through our hands," said Sharpe. "They could throw it as hard as they want, but they couldn't throw it through my hands. Never. Not even Brett, bringing it with everything he had. Why? Because I can catch."

But for all his accomplishments, Sharpe was far from beloved by Packers fans. Part of the reason was likely race — Green Bay simply did not seem to embrace black stars the way it did white ones. But the biggest factor was perceived attitude. Beginning during week 9 of his rookie season, Sharpe stopped talking to the local media. "They would write something about me without ever asking me anything," he said. "So I was like, 'OK, if you guys wanna do that, I'll do that, too.'" The boycott lasted throughout his career, and it did not go over well. Sharpe was perceived to be selfish, arrogant, indifferent, removed. He lived across the street from the stadium, and walked to practices accompanied by his pet, a rottweiler named Luger. Technically, animals were not allowed in the Green Bay facilities. Technically, Sterling Sharpe didn't give a damn. "One time we had a players-only meeting, and everyone's going around, talking about why they play football," said Sydney. "Well, Sterling stands up and says, 'I'm playing for me. I need to get the numbers. I need to get paid.'"

But Sharpe played hurt, played sick, played in the minus-10-degree winds without a moment of debate. He was a ferocious downfield blocker, and used his strength to physically beat down cornerbacks off the line. He and Majkowski emerged as one of the NFL's most dynamic connections, and often hung out to watch *Monday Night Football*. Once Favre became the starter, Sharpe deemed it his duty to give the new quarterback a security blanket. In the week following the Cincinnati game, Sharpe enrolled in Brett Favre 101, studying his drops, his mannerisms, his reactions after good throws, after bad throws. "Here's an example," Sharpe said. "In practice everyone is more relaxed and we call 22ZN — it's a 14-yard route with Brett taking a five-step drop. No hitch in his throw. But in a game everything moves faster, and that 14-yard route we practice is now 12 yards. So I'd run it 12, and Mike [Holmgren] would ask, 'What was that?' I explained my thinking. It was all good." Favre and Sharpe were emotional players, and fans presumed there was tension. They also presumed Sharpe was bullying Favre into throwing him the ball. Not true. "I never told him to get it to me," Sharpe said. "Never. Beforehand I'd always say, 'Let me help you.' People thought that was me looking out for me. No. It was me looking out for him. We understood each other, we liked each other. Best friends ever? No. But close teammates who worked well together? Without a doubt."

With Favre generating most of the national hype, and with the Packers' No. 1 receiver ducking out of the locker room after games, it was easy to overlook Sharpe putting together one of the greatest seasons in NFL history. He burned the Eagles (and star defensive back Eric Allen) for seven catches, 116 yards, and a touchdown, and a week later, in a 17–3 thrashing of the Bears, caught five more passes, including a backbreaking 49-yard touchdown bomb. The following Sunday, in a 19–14 revenge victory vs. Tampa Bay, he destroyed the Buccaneer secondary for nine receptions. His hands, decimated by arthritis, were swollen and plagued by shooting pains, and he told no one.

The capper of a surprisingly terrific season came on December 20, when the Packers won their sixth straight game with a sound 28–13 beating of the Los Angeles Rams before 57,000-plus attendees at Lambeau. The kickoff was scheduled for noon, and the temperature was 10 degrees, with a windchill of minus 15. Three hours before start time, thousands of fans could be found in the expansive parking lot, grilling bratwurst, sizzling steaks, bundled in — to cite the *Washington Post*'s Leonard Shapiro — "enough blaze-orange hunting coveralls to scare the local deer population all the way back to Minnesota." Less than a year earlier, the idea of Brett Favre excelling in such conditions was preposterous. Now he seemed to thrive in the weather. Did Favre love blistering cold? No. But he found himself enjoying the feel of brisk air surrounding his skin, and particularly liked seeing opposing defenders wrapped in thermal along the sideline, shivering like newborn penguins. Favre inherited a raw toughness from his father. To hell with the elements — this was football. Sharpe had a similarly profound approach to the cold: fuck it. He didn't care, wasn't bothered, gave it little more than a second's thought. Whether it was 90 degrees or minus 20, he always wore short sleeves. Against the Rams he caught eight passes for 110 yards and two touchdowns. The most impressive play of the game came with time ticking off the clock toward the end of the first half. "We've got 20 seconds to go, we've got no timeouts, we throw [Sterling] the ball and he's hit two yards short," recalled Gil Haskell, an assistant coach. "And he still gets in the end zone. That's pretty much his whole season for us." Haskell failed to mention the *five* Rams Sharpe dragged along for the ride

The Packers were now 9-6 heading into the season's final game at Minneapolis. A win (plus a loss by either Washington or Philadelphia) would have them in the playoffs for the first time since 1982. The good news for the Packers was that the last matchup against the Vikings — a 23–20 overtime loss in the season opener — came with Majkowski at quarterback. "If there was one game we could have back, it'd be the Minnesota game," said Brian Noble, Green Bay's standout linebacker. "It was one we probably let slip away that we should have had."

The bad news was that, at 10-5, the Vikings were the class of the NFC Central — deeper and more experienced than the Packers and hard to handle in the Metrodome. By the time the game rolled around, the Vikings' defense was ready. Tony Dungy, the defensive coordinator, knew Sharpe would inevitably get his (he caught six passes for 45 yards and set a league record with 108 receptions), but refused to allow Favre to sit back and comfortably pick the secondary apart. Minnesota's coverage packages were advanced and disguised, and Favre wound up being intercepted three times by Vencie Glenn in a lopsided (and dull) 27–7 defeat. Afterward, the Packers' looker room — usually jovial and upbeat — was silent. Chuck Cecil, the safety, sat slumped in a chair, blood dripping from his nose. Jurkovic, towel draped over his shoulders, admitted the Vikings were the superior team, but "it feels like I swallowed a rotten egg." Favre reclined by his small cubby, dejected, heartbroken. The season had surpassed all expectations, and cemented his status as one of the best young quarterbacks in the NFL. His statistics (3,227 yards, 18 touchdowns, 13 interceptions) jumped off the page. He was even a Pro Bowler. But the numbers and accolades mattered not. He didn't merely aspire to win the Vikings game. He *expected* it. "We keep telling ourselves that we had a good year, but I can't accept a loss like this," he said quietly. "We've got to work harder to become a playoff team."

With that, he turned and walked off to the shower.

The snow. The wind. The green and gold. The No. 4 — darting down the field, making something happen. Classic Brett Favre. © *Jim Biever*

Don't be fooled by the cute smile. Little Brett Favre was, in the words of his sister, "mean."
© *Hancock Schools*

Because his father/coach believed in run-first football, young Brett spent most of his time with the Hancock North Central Hawks turning to hand the ball off.
© *Hancock Schools*

Brett signing his letter of intent to attend Southern Miss — the only Division I school that knew of his existence. © *Hancock Schools*

A young Brett Favre in a Southern Miss publicity shot. The quarterback morphed from an obscure nobody into a Heisman Trophy candidate.
Courtesy of Southern Miss Athletics

A relatively unremarkable Division I football program before Brett Favre's arrival, Southern Miss began shocking traditional powerhouses and appearing on Top 25 lists. Fans responded. *Courtesy of Southern Miss Athletics*

The famous nuclear-charged right arm of Brett Favre was first deployed at Southern Miss. *Courtesy of Southern Miss Athletics*

A rare shot of Brett Favre, Atlanta Falcon. As a rookie in 1991, Favre threw four passes, two for interceptions. He devoted significantly more time to drinking than football, and was run out of town by Jerry Glanville, the head coach.
© Perry McIntyre

Much of Brett Favre's refusal to leave the field can be traced back to 1992, when he filled in for the injured Don Majkowski (right) against Cincinnati —and never surrendered the position.   *© Jim Biever*

Although he could be off-putting and cantankerous, no one made Brett Favre's early NFL days easier than Sterling Sharpe, the Packers' transcendent wide receiver. © *Jim Biever*

Some of the greatest seasons in Green Bay history can be chalked up to the pairing of Mike Holmgren (left) and Brett Favre. With Holmgren's departure after the 1998 season, everything changed. © *Jim Biever*

Green Bay's triumph over New England in Super Bowl XXXI signified the highest moment of Brett Favre's career. © *Jim Biever*

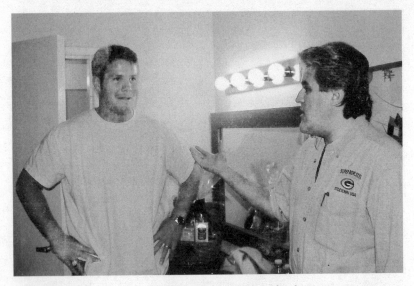

Brett with Jay Leno in 1997, before one of his many late-night television appearances.
© David Thomason

Brett Favre with Bus Cook,
his longtime agent (left), and
Joe Sweeney, an adviser, after
landing in Palm Springs,
California, in 1998. Although
his agent could be annoying
and standoffish to media members, hiring Cook was one of
the best moves Favre made.
© David Thomason

13

GOD AND THE DEVIL

I F THERE IS something particularly surprising about Brett Favre's early days with the Packers, it's this: nobody knew him.

Oh, they knew him, in the way you know a teammate who farts and burps and cracks jokes and snaps towels and cites Tupac lyrics and chows down on barbecue ribs and drinks alcohol by the crate.

But if one had asked the 80 or so men who wore Packers uniforms in 1992 whether their quarterback was a father, or had a hot-and-cold, on-again-off-again girlfriend, the vast majority would have shrugged.

It's not that Brett Favre deliberately kept Deanna Tynes a secret. Heck, she even flew in from Mississippi for a handful of games, stayed at his apartment, met some of the guys. It was just that, well, there was *soooo* much out there. So much alcohol. So many women. So many nights on the town, where the shots flowed and the midriffs were exposed and the 20-something groupies hovered around their new football god. The state of Wisconsin was long derided among NFL players for its thin (well, not so thin) selection of sexy women, yet Favre made do. The talk of settling down to focus solely upon football? *Eh . . . um . . . ah.* No. On their off days, many of the Packers traveled to Milwaukee, just 118 miles down the road, and hit the Water Street bar scene. This was also the era before iPhones and Twitter, when a celebrity's every move wasn't chronicled, then distributed to the masses in a flash.

However . . .

The video exists. It existed in 1992, but not for widespread consumption. The man at the center of the 2-minute, 38-second clip is dressed in a dark-blue collared shirt. He has brown hair and a boyish face. He holds a beer bottle in his right hand, and takes repeated swigs and chugs. He is Brett Favre, and the bar patrons surrounding him chant his name as a man with a microphone bellows, "Let me hear you all shout for Brett Favre — welcome to Milwaukee!" A thin blond woman with early '90s hair, big gold hoop earrings, jean shorts, and high stockings struts back and forth before stopping to shake and twist her slight rear end. Brett Favre takes hold of the microphone, clears his throat, and harkens back to a particular melody he enjoyed in college: a 1986 Sinatra-esque classic from 2 Live Crew titled "We Want Some Pussy."

"We used to sing this little song!" Favre says to the adoring crowd. "And I was singing it earlier! *Heeeeeeeey, we want some puuuuuusy . . .*" The men all join in as Favre repeats himself four times. Eventually, the scantily clad women arrive, and begin stripping down to their underwear.

Ah, good times.

When Brett Favre was home in Mississippi, he lived with his parents and devoted a reasonable amount of attention to Deanna and Brittany. He even encouraged his sorta girlfriend to quit working and return to college, which he paid for. But when he was back in Wisconsin, it was a different story. Drinks were free. Breasts were large. Life was a party. Did he love Deanna? Sure. But *Heeeeeeeey, we want some puuuuuusy . . .*

In 1993 Favre made some decisions befitting the status of an NFL starting quarterback. One, he and his agent, Bus Cook, wisely decided it was time (and a good investment) to purchase a house. Having spent nearly his entire life living at home with Irv and Bonita, Brett knew not the first thing about real estate. Cook hooked him up with a local agent, Lynn Blache, who happened to be the wife of Greg Blache, the Packers' defensive line coach. "The first time I went to meet Brett, I entered his apartment and someone yelled, 'Duck!'" said Lynn Blache. "A pillow flies through the air, his brother Scott comes running through the door, and Brett tackles him into a table, and the table breaks beneath them. It's my introduction to Brett."

Bus, Brett, and Lynn drove off to look at houses. The first one, located at 2114 Shady Lane in a quiet Green Bay neighborhood, was brand-new and enormous (4,450 square feet; four bedrooms, four bathrooms). It was brick, and a classic country French style. There was a two-story great room off the kitchen with a fireplace. The first-floor bathroom had a whirlpool tub. "I like this one," Brett said. "I wanna take it."

"No," said Lynn, "you have to look at more than one."

"I don't care," Brett replied. "I want this one."

Cook insisted they conduct a more extensive search, but at the second house Brett sidled up to Lynn and said, "Please, can we go back to the other house? That's the one I want."

"No," said Bus. "That's not how you do this."

The third house was a last straw. "I can't take this any longer," Brett whined. "Can we just go back to the first house now?"

The home was empty and under construction. Lots of work needed to be done. It was more expensive than homes two and three. "I'd really like this to be a finished rec room," he said, nodding to one area. "So the guys can come down, watch games, play pool. They can be in one area and not mess everything else up."

Favre bought the home for $285,000 and took the unusual step of asking Lynn and Gayle Mariucci, Steve's wife, to help decorate. "Gayle literally went through and bought every stick of furniture in the house — from the towels to the furniture to the bedroom set," Lynn said. "He was so happy, like a kid in a candy shop."

The plan was to live by himself, with guests constantly coming and going. But then Clark Henegan, a pal from Southern Miss, moved in to both party and serve as a quasi cook. He was followed by Frank Winters, the Packers offensive lineman who arrived in Green Bay in 1992 after having played for three teams in five seasons. "When Brett was talking about the house," said Lynn, "he said it was important there was a bar built in that Frank Winters could lay over if he drank too much. He was very specific on that point — the bar needed to be strong enough to hold Frank."

"With Brett, you got to experience what it was to be a rock star," said Henegan. "Deanna was in the picture, and I knew and liked her. But it wasn't my job to tell her about all the women Brett was with. He had girls come to town. Lots of girls. But he was like a brother to me — I wasn't going to tell his girlfriend what was really going on. We were having some great times."

It was a strange year for Brett Favre, who simultaneously lived the life of Green Bay's new playboy *and* served as the No. 1 promotional tool for drawing football's most important (and devoutly Christian) free agent to Green Bay. During the winter and spring months that followed the '92 season, the NFL was abuzz with talk of two related subjects: (1) unrestricted free agency for the first time in league history, and (2) Reggie

White's availability. The seven-time Pro Bowl defensive end had spent his entire NFL career in Philadelphia, and now — thanks to a recent labor settlement that included free agency — he was the hottest name on a list of 298 players able to sign wherever they chose. Without much warning, the NFL offseason became a *Price Is Right* knockoff (*Sports Illustrated* called it "The Reggie Game!") with teams itching to lure White to their cities. For example, four days after the free agency period began, the Cleveland Browns flew White and his wife, Sara, to town via private jet, ferried them by limousine to their $800-a-night suite in the Ritz-Carlton penthouse (a bouquet of red, white, pink, and yellow roses — Sara's favorites — awaited), had Jim Brown call to talk up Cleveland, gifted Sara with a $900 leather coat, and then gave the couple a tour of their magnificent $12.3 million practice facility.

In Atlanta, Georgia governor Zell Miller presented White with a black No. 92 Falcons jersey, then asked him to address the state legislature. In Philadelphia, a crowd of 2,000 held a downtown rally, imploring White to stay. In Detroit, Lions coach Wayne Fontes escorted White to a Pistons game. The Jets treated White to a fancy French restaurant and a Broadway show.

The Green Bay Packers took Reggie White to Red Lobster.

It's true. Holmgren and Wolf were the escorts. White — who had to be convinced by his agent to even make the trip — was picked up at nearby Austin Straubel International Airport in a normal car, by normal human beings. No flowers. No jacket. No call from Bart Starr. At his core, White was a simple man from Chattanooga, Tennessee; one who grew up attending a Baptist church with his parents and gave his first sermon at 17; one who believed in Jesus Christ with his entire heart and spoke up for the poor and suffering. White's first impression of the Packers came as a six-year-old Cowboys fan, watching Dallas and Green Bay play in the classic 1967 NFL Championship Game at Lambeau. It was 16-below, and White felt his hands numb from sitting too close to the screen. "I used to tell my mom I'm going to be a pro football player," White said, "but not in Green Bay." Times changed. White's needs were relatively straightforward. Did he want a big contract that would take care of his family for generations to come? Yes. Did he desire the coat and the flowers and the penthouse? No. During their meal together, Wolf and Holmgren talked football to a football player. They explained the potential greatness of a franchise on the brink. Afterward, they gave White a tour of Lambeau.

"You can go any place you want and be a great player," Wolf said. "You're already a great player. But look at the names of the legends who played here. You can come here and be a legend."

The words resonated. People didn't move to Green Bay for the amazing skiing, or the beachfront views. They moved to be a part of the Packers. The citizens owned the team. They *were* the team. "I wasn't with him, but he called me from Green Bay and said, 'This is it,'" said Sara White. "I'm from Cleveland and was sort of hoping for the Browns. I'd never even heard of the Packers. They weren't in our division, I'd never been to Wisconsin, I did not like the cold. But Green Bay was his gut feeling. I trusted that."

There was one other factor: White couldn't shake Brett Favre from his mind. The cockiness. The spunk. The toughness. ("Tougher than nine miles of detour," Jets scout Joe Collins once said.) Most quarterbacks took punishment and wilted. Not Favre. He bounced back up, patted opponents on the rear ends, whispered, "Nice hit" and "Bring it harder, big boy." White had separated Favre's shoulder, and the quarterback returned to the field as if nothing had happened. Later on, White praised Favre as the fiercest quarterback he had ever seen. Randall Cunningham, the Eagles' starter, was butter. Favre was steel.

On April 7, 1993, the *New York Times* sports section featured the banner headline PACKERS LAND WHITE WITH $17 MILLION DEAL. The four-year contract was shocking. For years, Green Bay was the last place an African American would choose to play. Much was made of Holmgren leaving a voice message for White ("Reggie, this is God. Go to Green Bay"), but the deciding factors were money, happiness, a chance to win, and a quarterback to build around. "This," White said, "is what I was looking for."

The NFL's newest odd couple were officially a pair. Favre couldn't believe the news. He welcomed White to Green Bay with an excited call, but was well aware there would be no pub crawls. Reggie was an ordained minister and a married father of two, and the Whites hosted Bible study in Philadelphia, as they would do in Green Bay. Brett Favre was more than welcome to attend.

The Packers opened training camp on July 18, and the hype was palpable. Unlike most other teams, where camp is camp, in Wisconsin the start of another Packers season is akin to a religious revival. Tradition doesn't begin with the opening weekend. No, it starts in training camp and, specifically, with a swarm of children lining up their bicycles at Lambeau Field and hoping players will choose theirs to pedal across the street to the practice facility. For jaded veterans, the ritual can become stale and burdensome. But for youngsters (and the young at heart), it's magical. "It's just so neat," said Brian McDonald, a free agent wide receiver in camp in 1993. "They didn't care who you were, as long as you had a uniform on. It was their way of getting close and personal." Had White signed with, say, Detroit, a couple of hundred die-hard fans might attend workouts. Green Bay was a sea of spectators, day after day. "The crowd would be up against the fence," said McDonald. "They would cheer you for good plays, even when the plays were meaningless."

With Majkowski now fighting to latch on with the Indianapolis Colts, Favre was king of the Packers. One year earlier, he shuffled anonymously from place to place. Now there were autograph appearances, corporate billboards, screaming fans. It's been said that Green Bay loves its football players but worships its quarterbacks. Brett Favre was worshipped.

He also stunk.

It was the nonstory story of training camp; a not-so-secret secret that concealed itself with the ubiquitous Favre catchphrase "unorthodox." Favre was unorthodox, so when his throws sailed high, or he missed targets, or he ran when he should have passed, hey, he was unorthodox. Yet Favre was a mess — drinking too much, staying out too late, behaving like a frat brother. His two backups, Ty Detmer, the second-year kid from BYU, and a left-handed rookie from the University of Washington named Mark Brunell, were woefully inexperienced. It was Favre's offense, sink or swim.

The 1993 season was supposed to be the year Favre established himself as a legitimate NFL star. The various season previews were clear in that regard. There was Dallas's Troy Aikman, there was San Francisco's Steve Young, there was Denver's John Elway, and there would be, inevitably, Brett Favre and the rising Packers. "After years of icy disappointments," raved the *Dallas Morning News,* "Green Bay is rekindling the old Title-Town fire." The Packers opened the season in Milwaukee with a 36–6 thrashing of the Rams, and Favre was artful, completing 19 of 29 passes for 264 yards, with two touchdowns and an interception.

The three weeks that followed, however, were the lowest of his young career. The Packers welcomed the Eagles to Green Bay and lost 20–17 — a crushing blow to White, who desperately wanted to beat his old team.

They then visited the Vikings and fell, 15–13, and lost to the Cowboys, 36–14. The defense was terrific, the running game solid. But Favre threw for less than 200 yards in each game and paired two touchdowns with four interceptions. At one point, during the Dallas matchup, Sharpe jogged back to the huddle and berated his quarterback for repeated awful plays. The two jawed back and forth, but the wide receiver's message was righteous: get your game going. "They got along in the same way you get along with your mother-in-law," said LeRoy Butler, the Packers safety. "You're polite, but she annoys the hell out of you."

When times were good, Sharpe and Favre were fine. Times, though, weren't good. Sharpe didn't like the way Favre seemed to approach the game—casually, like a day in the sand. He didn't moan over losses with the same emotive intensity he partied with wins. Everything seemed to be a gag to Favre; fun and shots of Jägermeister. He, Winters, and tight end Mark Chmura referred to themselves as the Three Amigos, which meant lots of beers, silly jokes, and childish pranks. Favre, who Winters and Chmura called Kid, liked to pull down pants and yank penises and pinch butts—none of which Sharpe would ever consider funny. As African American teammates were lifting weights, Favre snuck into the workout room, removed whatever hip-hop CD was playing, and slipped in some Garth Brooks or Travis Tritt. Once, on a bus ride, players were cracking on each other's hometowns. "You're from Kiln, huh?" said Gilbert Brown, a rookie defensive lineman. "Like the K is for Killing and the N is for niggers?"

Favre looked over the African American Brown's six-foot-two, 340-pound frame. "It's OK, Gilbert," he said. "They don't have a strong enough tree branch to hang you from, anyhow. Plus, you don't have a neck."

Green Bay seemed lost entering its next game against 3-1 Denver. "A win over the Broncos would change things quickly," wrote Jeff Schultz of the *Atlanta Journal-Constitution*, "but that would require some signs of life from quarterback Brett Favre." The Denver matchup seemed to be a contrast of what made NFL teams good versus what made them struggle. The Broncos were led by John Elway, the cool, studious veteran. Favre, on the other hand, seemed to be winging it. "He was a bit shaky," said Gil Haskell, the team's running backs coach. "It's hard for players to change overnight, and he had a lot of learning to do."

On a warm Green Bay afternoon, he appeared to learn. Before the game, White held a players-only meeting, imploring his teammates to dig deep and make plays. Sharpe, never one to hold his thoughts, was livid. "*You've* got to make plays!" he screamed. "*I've* got to make plays! We're the highest-paid guys on this football team. How many sacks do you have in the first four games?" White, owner of one and a half sacks, did not enjoy being challenged. The stars had to be separated — and the coaches loved it. Finally, some fire and spunk.

In a 30–27 Green Bay triumph, Favre's brilliance owned much of the day. His 66-yard touchdown pass to Jackie Harris was a throw only three or four other quarterbacks could make. He scrambled for 17 yards like a stallion galloping through a field of firecrackers, then for another 39 yards — head up, arms chugging (regrettably, the scamper was called back after a penalty). Yes, he tossed three second-half interceptions — two of which were boneheaded enough for Holmgren to pull him aside for a round of expletives. But the spectacular overshadowed the maddening. "Every once in a while he plays young," Holmgren said afterward. "It was one of those games you just hold on to."

The upcoming weeks were Favre at his best, Favre at his worst. Green Bay won five of its next six games, and on occasion the quarterback play was extraordinary. Favre's four touchdown passes to Sharpe resulted in a 37–14 win over the Buccaneers. But a week later he needed White and the defense to make up for his utter awfulness (15 of 24, 136 yards) as the Packers beat the hapless Bears, 17–3. He alternated between mastering the West Coast offense and butchering it. "Think about it," Favre later said. "I got thrown into the toughest offense in the game as a starter at 22. Every other guy who's played it sat for a year or two and learned. Joe Montana sat behind Steve DeBerg. Steve Young sat behind Joe. Steve Bono sat behind both of them. Ty Detmer and Mark Brunell sat behind me. That's why it's frustrating when people would get on me." Holmgren referred to him as a "knucklehead," and nobody stepped in to debate the point. "I want to hug him more than strangle him," the coach said. "But it's close." Sometimes Holmgren would gaze toward Favre and embrace the future. Other times, wrote Lori Nickel of the *Milwaukee Journal Sentinel,* "he looked as if he was going to burst. The crimson would begin in his cheeks, then spread to his neck, his ears, his forehead. The headset didn't always pinch his temples tightly enough to remain there."

White emerged as the locker room leader, but only in a way. There was something of a divide. Pious, serious men hung on the defensive star's every word, action, and prayer. "Reggie was all about respect," said Paul Hutchins, an offensive tackle. "When he spoke, you had to listen." Younger guys hovered toward Favre's goofiness, casualness, eagerness to seize the day. They laughed at his jokes, either because they found them funny or because he was the quarterback and they were required to find them funny. Favre could pick up baseballs with his toes and burp out long strings of words. He uttered oddball Mississippi sayings ("I was so excited I wanted to swap some spit with the guys!") and spoke at 563 words per minute. "Being with Favre was like hanging out with an over-developed seventh-grader," Ken Fuson once wrote in the *Des Moines Register.* "He loved pranks and practical jokes, liked dumping a bucket of cold water on a teammate when he was in a bathroom stall. His eyes glowed as he described parties that had gotten out of hand. He couldn't have been prouder of his locker-room reputation for being able to expel gas on command." Indeed, ever since having 30 inches of his small intestine removed as a college senior, Favre farted with the power of a bundle of dynamite and the frequency of a termite.* His fermented anal gas became the stuff of legend/tragedy in the Green Bay locker room — Favre smiling widely or announcing, "Hey, take a listen," or pulling down his pants to expose his bare buttocks before discharging the merging of hydrogen, carbon dioxide, and methane (combined with hydrogen sulfide and ammonia) into a 12-by-15-foot meeting area. In the NFL, farting has long been considered a source of levity in a pressure-packed profession, but with a single caveat: third-string running backs and reserve linemen and rookie kickers hold it in. Stars let loose.

Favre had yet to establish himself as a star, but inside the facility he was marquee and important. This was proven in a November 28 matchup with Tampa Bay at Lambeau. The Bucs were 3-7 and predictably bad; the Packers 6-4, fighting for a playoff spot, favored by 12½ points and destined for a letdown. Holmgren could feel it beforehand; an expectation among his players that the Buccaneers would die in the frigid cold. His instinct was correct. With seven minutes remaining, Tampa Bay scored on a 9-yard touchdown pass from Craig Erickson to Courtney Hawkins, and led 10–6. Despite the 23-degree temperature and a stiff-

---

* Fact: No animal or insect releases more methane.

ening wind, the stadium was filled, and all fell into silence as the Bucs celebrated. Once again, Favre had spent the afternoon looking ordinary and erratic when, with 7:25 remaining, he took over on the Green Bay 25-yard line and orchestrated the drive of the year. He used 6 minutes, 19 seconds, completed 8 of 12 passes for 69 yards, and calmly marched the Packers through the Buccaneer defense. On second down and goal, he tried scrambling for the touchdown when defensive end Shawn Price and safety Barney Bussey teamed to nail him so hard that his feet rose above his head, sending him spiraling to the ground. "I thought I could run it in," Favre said, "but I never saw the guy who hit me. Next thing I knew, I was doing a 360 in midair." He limped off the field with a bruised thigh, but after spotting Detmer warming up on the sideline, he rubbed his leg with his right hand and said to Holmgren, "Let me finish."

Seconds later, after stumbling back onto the field, Favre hit Sharpe with a game-winning 2-yard touchdown pass, and Green Bay escaped, 13–10. "It's like Jerry West, Larry Bird, Michael Jordan — the last two seconds of the game, who are you going to give the ball to," Favre said afterward. "That's what puts those guys on the top of the mountain."

The win improved the Packers to 7-4 and gave them a share of the NFC Central lead with Detroit. The rest of the regular season was typical Favre — hot and cold, hot and cold — but on December 26 the Packers destroyed the Raiders 28-0 to clinch their first playoff berth in 11 years. The win was another step forward for Green Bay's quarterback, who survived a temperature of minus 3 and windchill of minus 22 to play well enough (14 of 28, 190 yards, one touchdown). "The field was like concrete," Favre said. "It was so cold that I put Vaseline in places I never thought of before." Favre took specific pleasure in destroying the Raiders, one of two teams that selected a first-round quarterback in the 1991 draft. Todd Marinovich, the USC lefthander picked 24th, had been released in training camp after failing his third drug test.

Brett Favre and the Packers, meanwhile, were 9-6 and playoff-bound.

On January 8, 1994, Green Bay traveled to Detroit for a wild card battle with the Lions, who beat the Packers in the season's concluding week to clinch the division. (Typical of his up-and-down ways, Favre played abysmally in the finale, hoisting four interceptions in a 30–20 loss.) The Lions were, at 10-6, the slightly better team. They featured halfback Barry Sanders and a fleet cast of wide receivers. But three weeks earlier the San

Francisco 49ers hung 55 points on coach Wayne Fontes's defense, and Holmgren ran a nearly identical attack. The plan going in was quite simple — mercilessly attack Detroit's flawed secondary until it caved, and force Erik Kramer, the Lions' solid quarterback, to beat them.

It didn't work.

Before 68,479 fans in the Pontiac Silverdome, Detroit held a 24–21 fourth-quarter lead when the Packers got the ball on their own 29 with but 2:26 remaining. With a patience and calm he often lacked, Favre purposefully led the Packers — a screen to fullback Edgar Bennett for a 12-yard gain; the two-minute warning; a bullet to Ed West for 9; a Bennett 3-yard run up the middle; a time-out called by Holmgren. As Favre walked to the sideline, Guns N' Roses' "Welcome to the Jungle" blared from the speakers, and his head coach reminded him to stay in control. On the next play, first and 10 from the Lions 46, Favre spotted Sharpe crossing the middle, leaned back, and hit him for a 6-yard gain. Dick Vermeil, calling the game for ABC, couldn't contain his praise. "Great poise under pressure," he said. "Doesn't allow the negative play to affect him. He might come back and make a bad one. He might come back and make three good ones." The goal, Vermeil and Brent Musburger agreed, was to get in field goal position. Touchdown? Not even discussed. "It's funny," Sharpe said. "We only needed the field goal to tie, which was key. But I don't think Brett understood or realized the situation." With 1:05 left, the ball sat on the Detroit 40. It was second down and 4. Sharpe, who had taken two shots before the game to numb the pain from torn ligaments in his right big toe, was motioning for Robert Brooks to take his place in the game. "Robert's standing to Mike Holmgren's left, and I'm shouting," Sharpe said. "But he didn't hear me." Mark Clayton lined up in the left slot, Sharpe wide right. West was at tight end, Bennett and Darrell Thompson side by side in the backfield. Favre stepped behind center and screamed, "Red left 25! Red left 25!" — code for a double square out. The crowd noise was deafening. The Lions — participants in zero Super Bowls — had won one playoff game since 1957. This was their chance. Favre took the snap and dropped five steps. "If you draw it up on a chalkboard," said Sharpe, "Brett plants his foot, throws a square out left to Mark Clayton for 13 or 14 yards, he steps out of bounds and stops the clock." From the right, defensive end Robert Porcher shredded through the line and headed straight for the quarterback. Favre ran eight choppy steps to the left and readied himself to throw a screen to Thompson, who was loitering nearby. Then, in a half-second's span, he corkscrewed his body to face the opposite corner of the end zone and, without fully stopping, hopped and cocked back his arm . . .

Seconds earlier, Sharpe — toe brutalized, play designed for Clayton — had begun to jog. "I was supposed to run an out, but I ran a fade because the corner was in position," he said. "But I'm not really running, because [Lions free safety Harry Colon] is standing right there." Suddenly, however, Ed West's route took him toward an unmanned spot in the middle of the field, and strong safety William White charged toward the tight end. "I'm now all alone," said Sharpe. "Like, *all* alone."

Favre let go of the football with exactly one minute on the clock, and threw what may well be the most awe-inspiring pass to ever grace the inside of an NFL stadium. His body lurched forward violently with the follow-through of a shot-putter, then gravity somehow jerked him backward. The football departed Favre's right hand, soared through the air, and found Sharpe in stride just as he reached the heart of the blue-painted end zone, four steps in front of cornerback Tim McKyer. Sharpe looked up and snuggled the ball against the green No. 4 on his white jersey. Two years earlier, in a game against the Lions, he uncharacteristically dropped an easy score and was haunted by it. Not this time. "Brett's feel for the game was unreal," Sharpe said. "If I had been healthy I would have run out the back of the end zone by the time the ball gets there. But Brett knew I was slowed, and he threw it perfectly."

When Favre saw Sharpe catch the ball, he yanked the helmet off his head and sprinted toward the sideline, where he jumped into a teammate's arms before tackling him to the ground. He then bumped into Bob Noel, the team's equipment man, who was so busy packing gear he missed the play. Noel hugged Favre and said, "That's OK, kid, we'll get them next time."

What?

"Hell, Bob," Favre said. "We just won the damn game!"

"Redemption, revenge," said Musburger. "Call it what you will, but this can be a defining day for Brett Favre."

Indeed. The Packers won, 28–24, and afterward Favre looked at the assembled reporters and said, with a straight face, "It was all planned."

"Really?"

A grin. "No."

A week later the Packers fell to the Dallas Cowboys, who would go on to win Super Bowl XXVIII. They were a good team playing a great team, and the setback was expected. "We weren't ready," said Sharpe. "Not yet."

It mattered not.

The Green Bay Packers were back.

14

THE WHEELS FALL OFF

I N T H E S U M M E R of 1994, on the same week the Indianapolis Colts
waived Don Majkowski in favor of signing Browning Nagle, Brett Favre
and the Green Bay Packers agreed to a five-year, $19 million deal that in-
cluded a $2.5 million signing bonus, a $500,000 reporting bonus, and a
$1.6 million base salary for the upcoming season.

"I'm thrilled," Favre said. "This is where I want to be."

The quarterback was happy.

The franchise was happy.

The fans were happy.

Then everything went to crap.

- First, a report from, of all places, the *San Jose Mercury News*'s wire
  service suggested that, as Favre was throwing 24 interceptions in
  1993, he was "on cocaine or had become an alcoholic." No sources
  were cited, and the Packers' director of corporate security, Jerry Parins, said he never had reason to believe Favre was a drug user. But
  the drinking had, indeed, become an issue that worried many in the
  front office. Green Bay is a small city with a handful of bars and a
  rumor-generating machine that never quits. Favre imbibed — a lot.
- Second, one day before the Packers were set to open the season
  against the Vikings at Lambeau Field, Sterling Sharpe walked into
  Mike Holmgren's office and said, simply, "I'm going home." The
  player and the team had been engaged in a summer-long contract
  dispute, and Sharpe was both fed up and — in hindsight — wick-
  edly intelligent. "We were playing the Vikings, a team everyone really wanted to beat," said Sharpe. "Mike and [Vikings coach] Denny

Green were on the same staff in San Francisco, and Mike had never beaten Denny. The game plan featured a lot of me. So I walked in, told Mike I was leaving, and left."

Favre learned of the news and was abnormally apoplectic. Generally, the ins and outs of team politics interested him little. But Sharpe was also, in Favre's view, a selfish, me-first baby. "My opinion," Favre said, "was if you sign a contract, you honor it."

Sharpe and the Packers secretly worked out a new deal before kickoff, and he caught seven passes for 53 yards and a touchdown in the win. But the quarterback–wide receiver relationship was strained, and would be throughout the season. Which is how it concluded, because against Atlanta in Week 16, Sharpe suffered a neck injury that would end his career. "Holding out brought me the money I needed to survive after retirement," Sharpe said. "So anyone who hated me for doing it — they should understand it was nothing personal. Just business."

- Third, Mark Brunell.

Yes, Mark Brunell — the second-year quarterback from the University of Washington; the 23-year-old third-stringer who, having been born and raised in Southern California, approached the 1993 draft with a singular wish: *anywhere but Green Bay*. Brunell was close friends with Orlando McKay, a wide receiver selected by the Packers one year earlier, and his pal repeatedly issued warnings about the city's awfulness. "It's cold, it's miserable," McKay told Brunell. "Don't come here. Trust me."

Brunell had no choice, however, and he impressed Holmgren with his speed, smarts, and instinctiveness. Favre, on the other hand, was his frustratingly erratic self, kicking off the '94 run by alternating good games with awful games, good throws with awful throws. The thing that most irked Holmgren was his quarterback's stubborn refusal to listen. Favre seemed to think he knew everything about the sport and needed no assistance from anyone on the sideline. He ignored instruction, laughed off advice. "Brett told some reporter that he wasn't going to change his style, that the offense was good but he was the kind of playmaker, some riverboat gambler who had to take crazy chances sometimes and that's just how it was," Holmgren said. "The gist of his remarks was that we were a better team because he went winging it on his own a lot of the time instead of sticking with what the coaching staff wanted to do. Oh, I was hot." In the first quarter of a Week 8 matchup at Minnesota, Favre exited with a hip injury and Holmgren wasn't entirely disappointed. He looked toward Brunell and told him to start warming up. "Ty [Detmer] and I alternated as the backups, and it was my turn," Brunell said. "I thought, *You've gotta be kidding me. I have to go into a game in the Metrodome and play against Warren Moon? I'm not ready for this.*" With their new (albeit terrified) quarterback at the helm, the Packers led until the final seconds of regulation before suffering a 13–10 overtime loss. Holmgren was demoralized by the defeat, but delighted by the experience. There was no backtalk from Brunell; no tough-guy machismo nonsense. He got rid of the ball when under duress, communicated openly, played smart and selflessly. "Mark was shitting in his pants out there," said John Jurkovic, the defensive lineman. "But he didn't make too many mistakes."

On the sidelines, Favre internally applauded the defeat. He hated sitting, and rightly viewed Brunell as a threat. "Good," he thought. "We lose the rest of the games this year, that's fine with me."

The days that followed were awful. Favre threw a fit in Steve Mariucci's office over trying to master an impossible offense. Irv Favre called Mariucci and begged him to ask Holmgren to ease up. "I know my son," he told the team's quarterbacks coach, "and if Mike hadn't stopped butchering him after he made a mistake, Brett would have dwindled to nothing."

A few days after the Packers returned to Green Bay, Holmgren gathered his coaching staff for a meeting. "OK," he said, "So I'm thinking of making a change and I wanna have a vote. How many of you guys think Brett should stay the starter, how many of you guys think I should bench him?"

A moment for thought, then the hands were raised. There were 13 men in the room.

Three — including Steve Mariucci — voted for Favre to remain the starting quarterback.

Ten voted for the Mark Brunell era to begin.

Holmgren wasn't shocked. The defensive coaches, in particular, were fed up with having their exhausted players return to the field on short rest after yet another moronic interception. He was, however, at a loss. He felt loyal to Favre, in the way a master feels loyal to his dog — even when the mutt urinates on the floor. They arrived in Green Bay together; inspired hope together; reached the playoffs together. On the other hand, Favre was not improving. Holmgren's two San Francisco quarterbacks, Joe Montana and Steve Young, seemed to take progressive steps by the week. But Favre either stood still or drifted backward. He wasn't stupid, but he was a stupid quarterback.

A few nights later Holmgren summoned Favre into his office for a talk. This, the quarterback thought, isn't a good sign . . .

Favre was nervous. Holmgren was nervous, too. But he was also steadfast in his beliefs. "Look," the coach said, "you're too stubborn, you don't listen, you play dumb. But you're my quarterback, and we're in this together. So let's figure this out. We're taking it all the way or we're flaming out. I'm putting all my chips in with you. We're joined at the hip. Either we get to the top of the mountain together, or we're gonna wind up in the dumpster."

In the official Brett Favre narrative, sanctioned by the NFL and its merry band of half-fictionalized legend-creators, this is the moment where everything changes. The belief of a coach is a powerful force, after all, and knowing that Holmgren trusted him was all Favre needed to take the next step in his life and career.

Nonsense.

The '94 season was, on the surface, a near replica of 1993 — a 9-7 record, a second-place finish, a first-round playoff win over the Lions, a second-round loss to the Dallas Cowboys, lots of Brett Favre moments of brilliance mixed with fewer Brett Favre moments of idiocy. His statistics were eye-catching — 33 touchdowns, 14 interceptions, 3,882 yards — as was his continued growth as a leader. "Someone else could probably describe my leadership style better, but I think it's all action and very few words," he told ESPN. "When I say 'action,' that means practices, meetings and, of course, games. When it comes to giving inspirational speeches, I clam up. That's just not me. I just feel like the only way to lead is to do things right." But beneath it all, in a dark place where few witnesses were welcomed, something awful was brewing. And, even with the faith Mike Holmgren placed in Brett Favre, it couldn't be stopped.

The first time Brett Favre had unlimited access to pain medication was before his senior year at Southern Mississippi, when — while lying in a bed at Gulfport Memorial, recovering from the car accident that nearly took his life — he kept his finger glued to the button that controlled the morphine drip.

Nobody thought much of it. This is how pain was treated. Tylenol and Advil were wonderful, but not strong enough. Surgery hurts. Recovery hurts even more. Post–car accident, morphine was what the local hero needed, and morphine was what he received.

"When Brett learned about that pump, he rarely let go," said Bonita Favre, his mother. "He was in very bad shape, you have to remember. But I've always thought maybe that gave him a taste for it . . ."

Two and a half years later, in the game against Philadelphia when Eagles pass rushers Reggie White and Andy Harmon had given him the greatest thumping of his young career, dislocating his shoulder with a brutal sack, Favre played through the pain, steadfastly refusing to let Majkowski replace him. "If he'd gotten back in there, I may never have gotten my spot back," he said. After an injection of Xylocaine at halftime, Favre returned to being his old self, slinging the football (and his body) all over the field.

Later on, with the victory sealed and the pain returning, Favre asked Clarence Novotny, the team doctor, for medication. "He knew I had a separated shoulder, so he didn't even question it," Favre recalled. "He prescribed Vicodin and it eased the pain, which is the whole point of painkillers. It made me feel 100 percent better." There was nothing unusual. Dating back to the 1960s, NFL teams distributed opioids to their players as if they were M&Ms on Halloween. There were no available studies on long-term impact, and no concerns over addiction and dependency. It was about one thing: having players play. "Novotny would hand them out on the plane," said Jurkovic. "He'd just come by and hand you some. No problem, no real limit." It was, many Packer players confirm, accepted and approved by the organization. *Pain, schlaim* — take some drugs and get back on the damn field.

"In the later part of my career Vicodin was aspirin," said Darius Holland, a Packers defensive tackle. "You'd use Vicodin for practice, then Percocet for the games. We all knew what we were getting paid to do. There were guys — myself included — who would smoke marijuana between two-a-day practices, just to get through. And you can't blame them. I used it all — alcohol, Vicodin, marijuana, Percocet. Through the season I'd get shots in my knees and toes. People don't understand — there's no protocol to survive football. You do what you have to do to survive."

A few months following the first taste, Favre popped some Vicodin while nursing yet another hangover, and the discomfort vanished. The next season, after opening with a loss to the Rams, Favre and some teammates made a two-hour drive from Milwaukee to Green Bay, downing Vicodins en route. "My headache was gone," Favre recalled, "and I felt like a new man."

Favre liked Vicodin with water. He enjoyed Vicodin with beer even more. Whenever one of his players was experiencing pain, Holmgren inevitably asked, "Are you hurt or are you injured? Because if you're hurt, you can play." The message was clear — find a way. With increased frequency, Favre's games would be followed by the ingestion of multiple pills. "If I saw a teammate who was injured getting six pills," Favre recalled, "I'd stop him in the locker room and tell him I was really hurting and I wondered if I could borrow a couple." On Wednesdays and Thursdays Favre might pop a couple of Vicodins to, in his words, "just pass the time." It was, truly, no big deal. He didn't think about it as a problem. Nobody else thought of it as a problem. Because nearly all of the Packers were taking Vicodin in one dosage or another, the behavior never felt abnormal or particularly unhealthy. "It's not what people want to hear," said Jurkovic, "but with the painkillers you could kill the pain and practice and be a functioning human being. Playing football isn't a natural physical thing to do."

Late in the 1994 season, without warning, bad things began to happen to Favre. Want turned to need. Desire turned to craving. "He would routinely run stop signs in Green Bay just because he was so high and he felt so entitled," said Roy Firestone, who interviewed Favre on his ESPN show multiple times. "He was Brett Favre and they wouldn't stop him. I asked if he realized he could have killed people. He said he was so high, it didn't matter to him." Though it has never been formally diagnosed, family members believe addiction, in the form of alcoholism, probably runs deep in the Favre family veins. There are many photographs that tell the story, dating back decades upon decades, to bars and bar fights and drunken nights extending into mornings. Almost all of them seem to include a can or bottle of something cold and wet. Once, when Brett's addictions were coming into focus, Tom Silverstein, the *Milwaukee Journal Sentinel* scribe, asked Irv Favre whether his son was an alcoholic. "He paused for a really long time," Silverstein recalled. "And then he said, 'I don't know. But it's possible.'"

"If you dig far enough, every family has something they don't really want out," said Bonita. "Is it drinking with us? Maybe."

"We have to be realistic," said Brandi Favre, Brett's sister. "Addiction has been an issue."

The 1994 season was the beginning. The 1995 season was the explosion. Which is confusing, because it coincides with, arguably, the best run of Brett Favre's football career. But he was a mess, and any on-field success only helped hide the demons eating away at his innards.

In the summer months of '94, when he was back in Mississippi, spending an increased amount of time with Deanna and Brittany, Brett decided it was time to take a maturation leap. He asked his girlfriend to relocate with him to Green Bay so that they could try being a family and raising their daughter together. Deanna was overwhelmed — she knew Brett was no saint, but she also always felt the love and warmth he semiregularly offered. "I was actually excited about moving up there and becoming a family," Deanna said. "We had been dating on and off for 11 years, so we saw the coming season as a make it or break it time for us."

Brett went to Green Bay first for minicamp, and Deanna and Brittany followed in August. The girl was enrolled in first grade at the nearby elementary school, and — on the surface — everything seemed wonderful. Brett spoke with the media about the steadying influence of family; how having his girls around would only serve to keep him grounded and together in pressure-packed times. "[Brittany] was in heaven," recalled Deanna. "[She was] thrilled to be living with her daddy."

The honeymoon lasted for, oh, two days.

Deanna Tynes wanted Brett Favre to be the shy boy who'd kissed her at her front door. She wanted the courteous, caring person who looked at her as if she were the most beautiful being in the world. In short, she wanted the Brett Favre she fell in love with all those years ago.

That Brett Favre, however, seemed to be dead. "I began to realize that Brett was no longer the man I knew," she recalled. "The Brett I knew was quiet; this Brett was a party boy who stayed out all night with his friends. He was loud, rough, and often hateful. I saw the first signs of a mean streak I didn't know Brett had. I wasn't sure what had changed him, but I suspected it had something to do with drugs or alcohol. Brett didn't seem to care that Brittany and I were in the house. He started to ignore us soon after we arrived, and when I pressed him on it he became very snappish with me. I kept wondering if I should go back home, because this life was not at all what I had expected."

It's a ridiculously common tale, told in books, in movies, in seemingly 60 percent of ESPN's *30 for 30* productions. The athlete starts humbly, tastes stardom, and metamorphoses into an ugly, unrecognizable creature. By the time Deanna and Brittany relocated to Green Bay, Brett's tight social circle was firmly established, as was his well-deserved reputation as a drunk womanizer. His two primary running buddies were Frank Winters, the burly offensive lineman, and Mark Chmura, the handsome tight end, and together they formed an oddball trio. A six-foot-three, 290-pound center, Winters was born and raised in Hoboken, New Jersey, and spoke with a thick, exaggerated accent that earned him the nickname Frankie Baggadonuts. One of his favorite sayings, uttered repeatedly, was, "Beer and pizza — that's how you make it in this league." Nobody was quite sure what he meant, but it sounded right.

"Frankie and Brett were from different worlds, but they were really close," said Rob Davis, who spent a decade as the team's long snapper. "Brett was Mississippi, Frank had that New Jersey brashness to him, like a goombah. He set the tone for the offensive line — we're gonna smack people around."

Winters was squat and round, and walked like a bowling ball hoisted upon tiny legs. Chmura, on the other hand, had presence. He didn't rise from chairs, he unfolded. He carried himself with an upright gait of regalness; a six-foot-five, 248-pound model brought to the football field. But he was also insufferably arrogant; a man who thought himself smarter than he probably was. Teammates laughed with Favre, laughed at Winters, and rolled their eyes behind Chmura's back. "I always joked that if Mark was at a bar and he went unrecognized, he'd call the phone number and have himself paged," said one former running buddy. "He was that arrogant and insecure."

When it was time to work, Favre went above and beyond. Through the years, it was the one part of him that improved the most — dedication to craftsmanship. Holmgren and Wolf insisted he needed to devote himself fully to the game, and he tried. Despite his irksome (to Holmgren) need to break apart the playbook and design his own X's and O's on the fly, Favre was also a craftsman. He learned his teammates' strengths and weaknesses; he knew when and where certain receivers liked their balls.

Though far from an MIT-caliber brainiac, Favre had an unrivaled capacity to remember details. From routes to blocking schemes, it all stuck. "We were at dinner one time, and he'd seen the movie *Sling Blade* several days earlier," recalled Peter King of *Sports Illustrated*. "Well, he was doing paragraphs of dialogue from the film, in character, without missing a word. It was unbelievable." Members of the Packers vividly recall Favre staying late after practice, arriving early the next morning. He knew the reputation he had earned in Atlanta as an indifferent slacker, and he didn't much care for it. "During lunch sometimes I'd go and work out and I'd see Brett on the treadmill, studying plays at the same time," said Darrell Thompson, the Packers halfback. "Or he'd be on the StairMaster for 20 minutes, working up a stretch while looking at plays and reads. He wasn't one to rest on accomplishments. He wanted to be great."

But there was . . . *the pull.* "The 8,000-pound gorilla in the room was Brett's philandering and Brett's drinking," said Bill Michaels, host of the Packers' postgame show. "We all knew it's there. But most of us chose to ignore it." Favre went out when he wanted to go out; he had sex with whomever he wanted, whenever he wanted. There was a Milwaukee bar, Taylor's, with couches and a spare room designated for Packers players. Favre, Winters, and Chmura became frequent Tuesday-night attendees — Deanna and Brittany be damned. "It was widely known that Favre, Chmura, and Winters would come to Taylor's, and they could do whatever they desired," said Tom Silverstein. "You'd hear all types of stories."

There was a Madison bar, Buck's, overflowing with drunk, bubbly coeds from the University of Wisconsin. "I saw Brett and his guys there a lot," said one Madison native who later, as a journalist, wrote extensively about the Packers. "They'd be down on State Street, drunk, surrounded. All the stories ended with Brett with this woman, Brett with that woman. I think half of Wisconsin has some Favre-drinking-woman story. An amazingly high percentage of this state saw Brett doing something, somewhere."

Favre was trapped between being what he was supposed to be (a loyal partner and devoted father) and what he was (a 20-something football player with money to spend and women to please). Perhaps in other locations (New York, Los Angeles, Miami), the media would catch wind and investigate the titillating world of a superstar gone wild. But not Green Bay; not Wisconsin. Dating back to May 29, 1848, the day it gained statehood, Wisconsin's predominant non-Indian ethnicity was German — "and Germans are not ones to look down upon drinking," said Tom Oates, the veteran sports columnist for the *Wisconsin State Journal*. "When towns in Wisconsin were founded, they'd build a church, a mill, and a brewery. It's the odd state where drinking is celebrated." Hence, while many saw Favre and his friends stumbling from bars, or chugging pints, the behavior was never deemed problematic, even with football games to win.

The local press, meanwhile, covered the Packers with the hometown friendliness of a 500-circulation rural weekly. Most of the beat writers and columnists knew of their quarterback's off-the-field wildness, but in Green Bay such information was not to be divulged. Unless there was a direct link between Favre's partying and Favre's Sunday performances, his late-night whereabouts mattered not. "I remember struggling, asking the editors, 'How far do we take this? Do we find out details?'" said Silverstein. "We talked about sending an intern to the bars, but never did. And a lot of the stuff was exaggerated. You'd hear, 'Someone saw Brett snorting coke off the bar,' and you'd sort of sigh, assume it's not true, and move on."

"He was protected," said Kyle Cousineau, a longtime Packers blogger. "You could write about Brett Favre's play. But him drunk with some girl? Never. It wasn't allowed."

Multiple journalists who covered the Packers agree that, during Favre's heyday, the team made it clear that reporting on his hard-living ways would result in restricted access and, ultimately, no access. This wasn't New York, where the *Post* and *Daily News* would sneer at such an order, then blast the team in an editorial. No, this was Green Bay — where the townspeople owned the team, and victories trumped journalistic integrity, and being a Packer meant wide-ranging protections. "Green Bay isn't a city," said Jeff Ash of the *Green Bay Press Gazette*. "It's a *Packer* city."

Every now and then, a member of the team would get in trouble with the law. But it took something especially big for that to happen. A Packer who raped someone might wind up behind bars. Armed robbery? Also not a great decision. Otherwise, all was good. "If you're a player here and you get arrested, it has to be by a cop who doesn't want to be a cop for long," said Jerry Watson, owner of the Stadium View, a bar near Lambeau. "Because they'll fire him, and switch him to doggy patrol. Will the cops admit that? No. Is it the truth? You bet. If you're a Packer and you get picked up for drunk driving, they're gonna call the team and handle it quietly. The *G* on that building doesn't really stand for 'Green Bay'. No, it's for 'God' — because that's what the team is here."

As far as the franchise was concerned, Brett Favre was not to be touched — unless "touching" meant supplying him with pills to numb the pain. Which the training staff and teammates did. As Favre's play morphed from good to great to legendary, few people noticed that anything was awry. In the Packers locker room, he was the same guy he'd always been — snapping towels, pulling down shorts, spitting out rap lyrics like a hip-hop guru. LeRoy Butler, the star safety, calls him "the best teammate in the history of sports."

"What did Brett do that was so special?" Butler said. "This was him: We had some African American guys in the corner playing a game called spades. We had some white guys playing backgammon. We had some older guys, you know in camouflage, getting ready to go hunting after practice. We had some of the younger guys playing video games. The locker room is separated into different cultures of people doing all this stuff. Brett Favre went to every culture, and after a couple of days everybody liked the guy. He introduced himself and fit in. He didn't wait for guys to come to him. He'd go over to the younger guys and say, 'I don't really know how this game is played — but I want to play.' He went over to the brothers and said, 'I don't know a lot about hip-hop music, but I'm open to listening to it.' He'd be, 'OK, now I like hunting, but I'm used to shooting more coyotes or whatever. I'm open to shooting deer. You know what, I like country music but I don't really know that artist. But I'm open to listening to it.' And you take that on the field and you say, 'That's the guy I wanna follow through a brick wall. Because he took time out to know me as a person.' So Brett didn't just hang out with white guys. He didn't just hang out with black guys. He hung out with everybody. Not a lot of guys would do that. I would almost go out on a limb and say that no guys would do that. Certainly none in his position, as the star quarterback of the Green Bay Packers."

This was of little value to Deanna, who felt lost, alone, confused, disoriented. One day she went to the local dentist to have her wisdom teeth removed. That evening, Brett asked her to call the office and complain of mouth soreness. "Why?" she asked. "My teeth are fine."

"Because," he said, "my back is killing me and there's no other way to get pain pills."

Deanna believed Brett because she never considered him to be a liar. "What I didn't know," she recalled, "was that he was using everyone he knew — me, the team doctor, his trainers, and his teammates — to get painkillers. Anyone who might have Vicodin, or access to it, became a target. He had no trouble getting the drug, because he worked in a job where people get hurt all the time." She found white pills in plastic bags. They were Vicodin — made clear by the name neatly inscribed on each tablet. But why in a Ziploc, as opposed to a prescriptive vial? Her boyfriend was hooked. "I'd do anything to get it," he recalled. "Lie. Beg. Borrow. You name it . . . They were my diamonds, my security, my escape, and my obsession." Favre's daily routine included sneaking into the bathroom at nine o'clock at night to pop 15 Vicodins, riding the high into the night, then sticking his head out the back door to vomit. He would suppress any guilt by ignoring Deanna while staying up late to play Sega Golf and watch television. He detailed the ritual in his 1997 autobiography:

> The problem isn't getting the pills down; it's keeping them down. I'd go into the upstairs bathroom at home, take a big slug of water, and try swallowing a handful of pills. Most of the time I'd just throw them right back up and they'd land on the floor. No big deal. I'd just pick the pills out of the vomit, rinse them off and try again. It was just awful, and it went on every night.

"He behaved like some kind of high-strung superman," Deanna recalled. "He'd stay up until 3 or 4 in the morning and then get up at 7 and go to work. He was drinking, too, more heavily than I'd ever seen him drink." At long last, Deanna confronted Brett. "Are you addicted to painkillers?" she asked.

"No," he insisted. "I am not."

It was a lie. Not only was Favre struggling to sleep, but his body started to malfunction. Dehydration was a regular issue, as was constipation. Both were Vicodin side effects. "It got to the point," Favre recalled, "where sometimes I couldn't take a shit for a week." On the eve of the December 31, 1994, playoff game against the Lions, Favre had wound up inside Bellin Hospital, his stomach and midsection ravaged by crippling cramps. After several tests, the doctor said, "My God, you've got this big ball of stool built up in your intestine."

An enema removed the blockage, but Favre was momentarily scared straight. He was done with Vicodin! Never again! Really—never, ever, ever again! He learned his lesson, and this time it would stick . . .

"Sure as shit," Favre recalled, "I was back to taking the Vicodin after the game." To avoid any future blockages, he began chugging magnesium citrate—a laxative used to treat occasional constipation. "I would drink it," he recalled, "and it would blow everything out."

Against conventional logic, Brett Favre, drug addict, was a significantly better football player than Brett Favre, mere beer drinker. But, to those who know the game, it is not especially puzzling. Pain reigns in the NFL, and with less worry comes greater freedom to be daring and creative and adventurous. Favre wasn't the quarterback who dropped back and knew what would transpire next. He scrambled, shifted, danced, guessed. He has been referred to as a gunslinger in print at least 5,000 times, and with good reason. "He did whatever it took to win," said Joe Sweeney, Favre's longtime business partner. "Did it come with a price? Absolutely. I remember the day after one game, both hands were swollen, his knees were swollen, one ankle was the size of a grapefruit, and his back was killing him. You want to know why he needed the drugs? It's easy—he was getting killed."

To excel as a gunslinger, one must be some combination of insane, unaware, indifferent, and numb. You can't flinch from oncoming tacklers; you can't be afraid to make a throw that could work but might not. "People called him unorthodox, but it was more than that," said Mark Williams, a former Green Bay linebacker. "It was his willingness to try anything."

The 1995 season came with expectations. Sharpe was gone, but the roster was deeper than ever. A team that long struggled to move the ball on the ground featured a pair of underrated runners (Edgar Bennett, Dorsey Levens) who dazzled in camp. Sharpe would no longer be executing the game's best routes, but he'd also no longer be whining with every perceived slight. (Asked in camp whether he missed the star receiver, Favre noted dismissively, "Not really—Sterling never practiced or played in pre-season games anyway.") Robert Brooks, now in his fourth season, was a suitable replacement. Chmura, rock-headed but sure-handed, and Keith Jackson, acquired from the Dolphins, formed the league's best tight-end duo. The defense, featuring White and veteran Sean Jones as bookend defensive linemen, was ferocious. The general take among NFL experts was that the Packers were a legitimate Super Bowl contender.

So was Brett Favre nervous and uptight from the expectations?

"I'm the last man on the totem pole," said Lenny McGill, a little-known defensive back from Arizona State. "It's training camp and I have 15 minutes to go until a meeting starts, so I rush to the bathroom. I'm sitting on the toilet reading the playbook, preparing, and I hear somebody say, 'Well, good morning, Lenny.' And it's Brett peeping over, looking at me sitting on the toilet reading my book."

McGill didn't know what to say.

"What's up, Brett?" he said.

"You doing OK?" Favre replied.

"Sure," McGill said.

"It's kind of hot in here," Favre said, "don't you think?"

Um . . .

"He pulls out this ice bucket and proceeds to pour it all over me," McGill said. "I had no time to change, so I show up to the meeting soaking wet. People asked, 'What happened to you?' What happened? Brett happened . . ."

Favre's 1995 season was an ode to improvisational quarterbacking genius. Jon Saraceno of *USA Today* memorably called him "Opie with a robust arm — a classic overachiever with loggy legs and a scrambling style that looks more like Barney Fife than Roger Staubach." Any questions about his long-term usefulness, or whether he was a worthwhile starter, died as Green Bay jumped out to a 5-2 start. On October 22, in front of a record 60,332 fans at Lambeau, he lit up the Vikings for four touchdown passes in a 38–21 victory that kept the Packers in first place. Three weeks later he had what many consider to be the greatest performance of his career, using the 150th regular-season meeting between the Packers and Bears to announce his arrival as the NFL's best quarterback, if not player. In a game at the Metrodome a week earlier, Favre suffered a gruesome sprained ankle that was fat and plump and the color of a bowl of Froot Loops. "It was a rainbow, just disgusting," said Butler. Ty Detmer, the backup, stepped in, but was also knocked from the game with injured ligaments in his right thumb. T. J. Rubley, the journeyman third-stringer, entered to promptly commit one of the great gaffes in franchise history, calling an audible late in the game that resulted in an interception, the loss, and the unofficial end of his football career. Ron Wolf signed Bob Gagliano, a free agent quarterback of little note, and rumors circulated that either Rubley or Gagliano, the pride of Utah State, would start against the Bears in a battle for divisional supremacy. On Wednesday Favre was still on crutches, and trainers were alternating ice pumps and heat packs on the ankle. For 20 hours every day, Favre had some sort of therapeutic pack affixed to his lower leg.

The game-day temperature was 22 degrees, with the howling wind making it feel 15. Snow flurries cascaded from a pewter sky. Lambeau Field was packed, and Brett Favre — Vicodins aplenty — still walked with a limp. With a 6-3 record, Chicago held a one-game divisional lead. In the stands, loyalists unfurled a banner that read, WELCOME HUNTERS! BEAR SEASON HAS OFFICIALLY COMMENCED IN GREEN BAY.

Even as fans entered the stadium, Favre's status was unknown. Then he was introduced as the starting quarterback, and ran onto the field to a deafening roar. With his hands held above his head and his right fist pumping, Favre charged toward his teammates, drugs flowing through his veins and no limp to be seen. The tape around his ankle was thick and cast-like. He could play, but not scramble.

In a shock to the man himself, Favre torched the Bears for a career-high five touchdown passes and 336 yards — including a 16-yard strike to Bennett in the fourth quarter that sealed the 35–28 triumph. Favre used nine different receivers, a drastic change from the days of Sharpe-Sharpe-Sharpe. Afterward, Bears linebacker Vinson Smith, who sacked Favre twice, insisted the quarterback and the team were lying about the injury. "There was nothing wrong with the guy from the start," he said. "A bunch of baloney they made up."

Not true. Favre was, in fact, hurt. He just happened to be hopped up on medication. When the game ended, he popped his ever-increasing dosage of Vicodin and headed home to Deanna and Brittany, both of whom he ignored. On multiple occasions, Deanna expressed her concerns to people she hoped might help, only to be met with general indifference. The goal in Green Bay was to win football games. Brett Favre won football games.

Gayle Mariucci, the wife of quarterbacks coach Steve Mariucci, asked her husband to intercede. It did not go well. "[Brett] blasted me for talking to Gayle," Deanna recalled. "'You don't know what you're talking about,' he told me. 'I'm not on drugs.'" Sara White, Reggie's wife, told Deanna that her husband tried speaking with Brett, but to no avail. Devoutly religious, Deanna asked friends to pray for Brett. It didn't work. She reached out to Bus Cook, Favre's agent, but felt brushed aside. When

Bonita and Irvin flew in to Green Bay, she picked them up from the airport and mentioned her concerns. "They thought," she recalled, "I was only feeling insecure."

If Favre was addicted to Vicodin and alcohol, those surrounding him were addicted to the buzz. He was walking electricity — high on football, high on living, high on the chemicals filling his body. The media didn't only protect him because they were beholden to Green Bay. They did so because he was neon copy. Favre's weekly press conferences were the stuff of legend — part Huck Finn, part Winston Churchill, part Magic Johnson. "I started as a reporter when I was 19 covering the Indiana Hoosiers, and Bobby Knight would walk into a press conference and make journalists lazy," said Lori Nickel, the longtime *Milwaukee Journal Sentinel* writer. "Favre was the same exact way. It'd be 45 minutes of personal stories, football stories, bar fights. He'd tell you anything. You could pull up a chair and he'd ask you about yourself, and be genuinely interested. He was a reporter's dream." In most other cities, the stars were either walled off and inaccessible or walking clichés. Jerry Rice was a San Francisco prima donna. Troy Aikman was dull and guarded in Dallas. The Patriots' Drew Bledsoe was friendly but bland. Falcons quarterback Jeff George perfected moody arrogance. Dolphin legend Dan Marino allegedly once said something interesting. But Favre's warmth and aw-shucks Southern charm won people over. He remembered every play from every game, and was more than happy to break down the specifics. He never blew a reporter off, or cursed out an overly aggressive inquirer. There were hunting and family stories galore. The Superman tattoo on his left biceps? The product of a drunken night in Phoenix. The haircut he was sporting? Sympathy for a blind barber. The inappropriate weirdness of an NFL linesman asking him for autographs before a recent game? "That's the first time I've ever seen that," he said, laughing. "He had, like, eight cards."

"Brett was always interesting to speak with," said Rachel Nichols, the veteran print and TV reporter. "He didn't necessarily say the predictable thing. He refused to just give one-word answers." When he was told that Andre Rison, the Cleveland wide receiver who played with Favre in Atlanta, dismissively referred to him as a "hillbilly," Favre laughed and nodded. "No, Andre's right," he said. "I am."

In the week leading up to a December 3 matchup with the Cincinnati Bengals, Favre was at it again. "There are some great quarterbacks in the league," he told *USA Today,* "but I don't think none of them are asked to do what I am. Troy Aikman's great, but they don't ask him to win. Steve Young? Great quarterback, but [the 49ers] won without him. Here, they ask me to win the game. They live and die with what I do." Holmgren read the words and summoned Favre for a chat. Opponents read newspapers, too. Why give them ammo? The quarterback shrugged his shoulders, then went out and annihilated the Bengals with three touchdown passes and 339 yards in a 24–10 win. "Right now, Brett Favre is probably the hottest quarterback in the league," David Shula, the Cincinnati coach, said afterward. "And they are one of the hottest offenses."

Green Bay wrapped the season at 11-5, the franchise's finest record in 29 years and its second outright division title since 1972. Favre's numbers (his 38 touchdowns and 4,413 passing yards both led the league) made him the frontrunner in an MVP race with San Francisco's Rice (122 catches, 1848 yards, 16 touchdowns) and Dallas halfback Emmitt Smith (1,773 rushing yards, 25 touchdowns) — a battle he won.

Although Jerry Glanville was no longer Atlanta's coach and most of his old teammates were long gone, Favre took genuine delight in opening the playoffs with a decisive 37–20 New Year's Eve thumping of the Falcons. Six days later Favre again played brilliantly, and the Packers cleared an obstacle that had long sat in their way, beating the 49ers 27–17 in San Francisco to finally reach the NFC championship game. That contest would involve yet another trip to Dallas, where the Cowboys (recent winners of two Super Bowls) awaited. Because the days between games can be uneventful, the media often looks for stories to fill blank pages. Here there was an easy one: Aikman vs. Favre.

Statistically, it wasn't much of a matchup. Aikman's numbers were fairly pedestrian (16 touchdowns, seven interceptions, 3,304 yards). He also happened to be quiet and somewhat demure, and as a seventh-year veteran his story had been told ad nauseam. Favre, on the other hand, was a beacon of big words and strong throws. He was new and fresh. Kevin Mannix of the *Boston Herald* detailed Favre's rise from nobody to Aikman's heir apparent. Jean-Jacques Taylor of the *Dallas Morning News* infuriated local fans by referring to Favre as "the NFL's best quarterback." Cowboys–Packers wasn't merely a rematch of the 1967 Ice Bowl classic, it was a changing of the guard. Out with the old Aikman, in with the new Favre.

The Packers lost 38–27 in an entertaining yet ultimately fruitless battle. Favre played well, but the Cowboys were better. Smith, third-place finisher in MVP voting, tore up the Green Bay defense for 150 yards on 35 carries. The Packers briefly led, but they weren't good enough. Favre's three touchdown passes were a mirage that failed to fully disguise the fact that he threw two interceptions, was sacked four times, and hurried nine other throws. Afterward, he rightly called the loss a "step ladder — each year we go up another ring. This was one more step." The Green Bay players were saddened, but not despondent. On the flight home, White, Butler, Favre, and safety Mike Prior found themselves together at the rear of the plane, discussing what went wrong. "Next year," White said, "we're winning the Super Bowl."

Favre's mood changed, from despondent to hopeful. "Hell, yes," he said. "Hell, yes."

15

HIGH AND DRY

LIFE IS DIFFICULT when people are fully aware of your struggles.
Life is impossible when you're struggling and the world sees you as the luckiest man around.

This was Brett Favre at the end of the 1995 football season. Envied, but drowning.

On the outside, existence couldn't be sweeter. He was the toast of the NFL—the league's Most Valuable Player, the NFC's starting quarterback in the Pro Bowl; boyfriend to a gorgeous young woman and father to an adorable little girl. Wrote Tom Silverstein in the *Sporting News:* "Brett Favre was one of the most sought-after people at Super Bowl XXX, yet his team didn't even make the big show. Favre has been as busy as a bee attending dinners and interview sessions ... he is currently negotiating sponsorship deals for automobile, telephone, T-shirt, and shampoo products."

Envied.

Drowning.

The Pro Bowl was held on February 4, 1996, at Aloha Stadium in Honolulu. Brett attended with Deanna (Brittany stayed home with Deanna's mother), and the couple had a much-needed week of relaxation and five-star meals and walks on the beach. Removed from the hoopla, they were still two kids from Mississippi.

Their flight home was that night, and there was enough time for a final dip in the Royal Hawaiian hotel pool. Favre had a couple of beers, and the alcohol made him feel sluggish. He excused himself and retreated to the room to examine his drug supply. "I had about 15 pills left," he recalled. "There were some Lortabs. Vicodins. Percodans. Tylenol 3." Favre grabbed all 15, poured a cup of water, and swallowed. "By the time the plane took off," he recalled, "I was already flying."

The five-hour flight to Los Angeles was a nightmare. Favre badgered the woman sitting next to him, talked incessantly, paced the aisle, talked some more, paced, talked. Eventually, he rushed to the bathroom to vomit. From Los Angeles, the Favres caught a connector to Dallas. To this day, Brett Favre still doesn't recall the three-hour flight.

Six days later, the couple traveled to New York for Brett to be honored as Best NFL Player at the ESPY Awards at Radio City Music Hall. For Deanna, just 27 and still relatively sheltered, the lights and sounds and sights of Manhattan were a huge deal. So were the stars attending the ceremony — big names ranging from Adam Sandler and Denzel Washington to Tony Danza and Ann-Margret. Deanna wore a new dress, new shoes, had her hair done that morning.

Dennis Hopper, the *Hoosiers* actor, presented Favre with his award to kick off the evening, and while his speech was gracious, the quarterback's mind was on the bottle of pills trapped in the pocket of his suit pants. He sat through some of the ceremony, but at approximately 10:00 p.m. excused himself to use the bathroom. Ten minutes passed. Thirty minutes passed. Deanna seethed as Brett sat on a toilet in a backstage stall, forcing the requisite 13 Vicodins down his throat, then trying to vomit without making noise. "All of a sudden the buzz hit in," he recalled. "I was back. I was walking around, talking everyone's ears off."

Brett returned to the table and slurred an apology.

"Why are you acting like this?" Deanna asked. "What have you been taking?"

"I took a couple of Vicodins," he said.

"A couple," she replied. "No way."

"Well," he said, "five or six."

"How many?" she said. "Tell me the truth."

"Thirteen."

The boy she once trusted was a lying pill popper, as well as an alcoholic womanizer. He loved his Vicodins, and his beers, and good times with the guys, more than his girlfriend and his daughter. That night, in Manhattan, it was finally real, and Deanna Tynes was done. At the conclusion of Brittany's school year, she and her daughter would return to Mississippi to start a new life. It was over.

Two weeks later, according to Deanna, God took a stand. On February 27, 1996, Brett was admitted to Bellin Hospital to have a bone spur removed from his left ankle. The operation went smoothly, and Deanna brought Brittany to room 208 for a visit. A nurse entered to check Favre's IV, and he rolled his eyes toward his wife — a nod to his hatred of needles. Then he rolled his eyes again. But differently. His legs began to tremble, followed by his arms. His teeth gnashed together, then his body went hard and straight. He was having a seizure. "Get his tongue!" Deanna screamed. "Don't let him swallow his tongue!" The nurse charged forward, and Deanna removed Brittany from the room, but not before the little girl asked, "Is he going to die, Mommy?"

He didn't die. One of the first faces he saw after regaining consciousness was that of John Gray, the Packers associate team physician. "You've just suffered a seizure, Brett," he said. "People can die from those." Tests were run, and the results showed that Brett Favre — reigning NFL MVP, only 26 years old — had a toxic liver.

The apparent culprit: Vicodin.

"All sorts of crazy things were racing through my mind," Favre recalled. "Was I going to have these the rest of my life? Did I screw up my body with the Vicodin? I'd be lying if I said the seizure didn't scare me. It scared the hell out of me. Right then I decided I better tell the doctors exactly what I had been doing."

He traveled to Chicago to meet with four league-appointed doctors, and over the course of an hour was asked a series of questions. "We know you're addicted to painkillers," a doctor told him, "and we think you have a drinking problem, too."

Favre understood the Vicodin part. But alcohol? He could have a beer with dinner, he could have a 12 pack with the guys. Drinking made him feel happy and loose. Plus, it wasn't illegal. So what difference did it make? The doctors suggested that Favre go away for treatment. There was this place the NFL recommended, the Menninger Clinic in Topeka, Kansas. It was excellent and . . .

"Thanks," Favre said, "but no thanks."

As far as he was concerned, the whole Vicodin ordeal was over. He made appointments with a pair of neurologists, both of whom explained the seizure could not have been caused by the drug abuse. "They said the odds of me having another seizure were almost nonexistent," he recalled. "That reassured me."

The NFL was unmoved. The league told Favre he either report for treatment and sign the league's 10-part treatment plan or be fined four weeks' pay — roughly $900,000. Ultimately, he acquiesced to the league's demands, but begrudgingly. The call home to his parents was a low point. "After he told us I sat back on the porch and cried," said Bonita Favre.

Favre met with Mike Holmgren, who was shocked to learn of his quarterback's troubles, and Wolf, somewhat less shocked. The men wanted to know which teammates had hooked Favre up with the Vicodin — information he refused to divulge. "It doesn't even work that way," said John Jurkovic, the Packers lineman and one of the many players who slipped Favre extra pills. "If the guy needed a couple, fuck it — I gave it to him. But that didn't make me unique. Vicodin was everywhere. If you needed it, you could get it. We shared. All teams shared. It wasn't some underground network. We played a game with a lot of pain." Under NFL policy, Favre did not have to speak to the media about his rehabilitation. He could have left for the month and nobody would have known. That struck Holmgren as unwise. Favre was a superstar. Somebody would find out.

The press conference was held on the afternoon of Tuesday, May 14, inside the media hall at Lambeau Field. As the reporters filed in, Favre went over the prepared statement written for him by the Green Bay media relations team. It was direct and to the point ("My main objective is to get better for myself and my family . . .") and largely nonsense. Favre said he looked forward to getting treatment, and that he thought "that the best thing to do was seek help." He also mentioned the seizure, implying that it was caused by the Vicodin. Which he didn't believe to be true.

Holmgren added to the ridiculousness, noting (erroneously) that Favre "voluntarily referred himself to the league's doctors." He called his quarterback courageous for facing drug addiction head-on, failing to note that he didn't think he needed to face drug addiction at all. Favre spoke clearly, and Deanna — identified as his fiancée — stood by his side. They were both positioned behind a podium, and no one could see their legs shaking. "It came across like Brett stepped up and turned himself in," said Lance Lopes, the team's general counsel. "That's how it was reported, and it's still incredible nobody got it right."

Members of the Packers watched Favre's press conference with a combination of disgust and anger. They felt as if the team had sold Brett Favre out in the name of cheap publicity points — "It was, 'Look, we're handling this right! Look how wonderful we are!'" said Darius Holland, a Green

Bay defensive tackle. "It made it very clear to all of us that we should never show weakness, especially in the areas of alcohol and drugs. From that point on, if I ever went to a doctor for help I told him, directly, 'If this makes the papers, I'm suing you.'"

Brett Favre arrived in Topeka the morning after the press conference. He flew via a private plane and was accompanied by Bus Cook, Deanna, Brittany, and a babysitter. He ordered some pizzas for the hour-long flight, but nobody was hungry. His attitude, understandably, was awful. This would be six weeks of hell, and Favre wanted no part of it. The Menninger Clinic's mission statement explained that it was dedicated to treating individuals with "mood, personality, anxiety, and addictive disorders" — none of which Favre thought he had. He was embarrassed. "People look at me and say, 'I'd love to be that guy,'" he told *Sports Illustrated* hours before departing for Kansas. "I'm entering a treatment center. Would they love that?"

A clinic representative picked him up at the airport and drove him to Menninger. He was shown to his tiny room, which included a small bed, a couch, a desk, and a telephone jack.

He thought the worst.

He experienced the best.

Rehab wasn't half bad. The food was healthy and tasty. There was a gym filled with workout equipment. "Every morning I would get up at 7, do 50 pushups and 100 sit-ups, go for a three-mile run, and hit the gym," he recalled. "When I first got there I could barely touch a 10-foot basketball rim. When I left, I was dunking a basketball. My vertical had increased by six inches." It helped that among his fellow attendees were six or seven other NFL players. One, a former Dallas Cowboys defensive back named Clayton Holmes, said he ran some routes for Brett during downtime. "The experience probably brought the football players together," Holmes said. "Brett was very humble, very down to earth."

Professional athletes tend to be walled off from the real world, and Favre was no exception. His life was all about Sunday football games and parties. Now he was meeting crack addicts, sex addicts, heroin addicts. Their stories moved him, and aroused emotions that had been dulled by fame and glory. Back when he was playing football in high school and college, Brett regularly visited his mother's special education classes and talked with the kids. They were reminders of how fortunate he was, and how much he had. Now, hearing things like, "I saw my mom blow her boyfriend's head off with a shotgun," he was forced to reevaluate his life.

From time to time, Favre received visitors. He was allowed to play golf with Frank Winters, who spent offseasons in nearby Kansas City. His parents came. So, on multiple occasions, did Deanna. Every time she arrived, Brett proposed. Every time Brett proposed, Deanna brushed the words aside. "We've got a lot of wrinkles to iron out," she'd say. When they spoke via phone, it was more of the same. "Let's get married this summer before the season," he pleaded. Deanna was skeptical, and rightly so. Her man was a habitual cheater. Would he truly commit and settle down?

On June 28, a private plane flew to Topeka to retrieve Brett and return him to Mississippi. Deanna removed all the alcohol from their home, and pledged to stop drinking as a measure of solidarity. Everything about Brett seemed to be changed. He was leaner and more muscular; spoke positively of the lessons he learned; seemed upbeat about their relationship. This, at long last, was the Brett Favre Deanna fell in love with. He was back.

When the plane touched down at Stennis International Airport in Kiln, Mississippi, Favre was greeted by five friends, who welcomed him with hugs and handshakes. "Then they all went out drinking," said a person there for the landing. "Deanna was close to tears."

In other words, on the day he returned home from rehab, Favre partied. A few weeks later, in his first session with the media, Favre publicly committed himself to giving up alcohol, which he was required to do for two years under the bylaws of the NFL's substance-abuse policy. "I realize that while I am in this program I must abstain from alcohol," he said. "When I was growing up I thought an alcoholic was just a bum on the street. I thought someone who was addicted to drugs was just some bum who was a loser. It's totally the opposite.

"We've had a lot of fun in the past and probably will again," Favre said, alluding to Winters and Mark Chmura. "But as they said, Coke and pizza after the game. And that'll be fine with me."

Favre was either hopelessly optimistic, delusional, or lying, because he was already back to drinking. Deanna was torn. A devout Catholic who was raised in the church, she believed the power of prayer could touch someone's heart and change his soul. But was Brett capable of change? He again asked for her hand in marriage, and she again paused. "For the first time in a long time, I began to see his willingness to make our relationship work," Deanna recalled (somewhat delusionally). "I began to see a change in him. Instead of just going out the door to do whatever he wanted to do, he'd discuss it with me or ask if I thought it was a good idea. I began to feel like a partner instead of his caretaker. I began to feel loved again."

On July 4, 1996, Jim Biever, the Packers' team photographer, received a call from one of the team's public relations officials, asking if he'd ever worked a wedding. "Oh, I've shot a lot," he said, failing to mention the last one was decades ago.

"Great," the man replied. "Brett wants you to shoot his."

Ten days later, Biever and 11 other people gathered at St. Agnes Parish Catholic Church in Green Bay for the tiny wedding of Brett Favre and Deanna Tynes. Kent Johnson, the team's strength coach, was the best man. His wife, Pam, was the matron on honor. Brett wore a gray suit, black shoes, and a floral corsage attached to his lapel. Deanna looked lovely in a short-cut white dress, white stockings, and white high heels. Brittany, giddiness personified, served as the flower girl. En route to the church, the 7-year-old looked at her mother and squealed, "This makes me so happy!"

The ceremony was followed by a small reception. The newlyweds honeymooned that night in the village of Kohler, Wisconsin, a charming town along the Sheboygan River (Favre had to report to training camp a day later, hence the one-night getaway).

For the first time in years, everything felt right for Brett and Deanna Favre.

Training camp began on a Tuesday.

Brett Favre addressed the media that morning at Lambeau Field in what he said would be his only time discussing rehab. He was newly married, newly fit, and excited about a team that, many believed, was finally Super Bowl ready. So the last thing he wanted to dwell on was substance abuse.

Four days later, though, he had no choice. It was 1:45 a.m. in Pass Christian, Mississippi, when Scott Favre, Brett's older brother and hero, was driving his Mitsubishi van with Mark Haverty, a 26-year-old family friend, positioned in the passenger seat. The two were returning from a night out at a local bar. They had known each other for years. Mark roomed for a short time with Brett at Southern Miss, and then moved to Green Bay for a brief spell when the Favre-Packers union began. Brett and Mark shared passions for hunting, sports. "He was a bartender for me, did some cooking," said Kevin Burkel, the Green Bay bar owner. "Just a great guy, and very close with Brett."

Scott steered the van north on Third Avenue, toward Toca's Food Store. He passed three RAILROAD CROSSING signs, but any oncoming train lights were obscured by the tall, thick trees. "On summer nights," wrote Barry Meisel of the *New York Daily News*, "when the windows are rolled up for the air conditioner and the stereo is cranked loud, the intersection is deadly." Scott began to roll across the tracks when a 49-car CSX freight train slammed into the passenger side of the van, iron crumpling aluminum. Scott, 29, suffered only minor bruises and cuts. The force of the impact was so great that Haverty, wearing a seat belt, was thrown from the vehicle. He died immediately from internal injuries.

Scott's blood alcohol level was 0.23, more than twice the legal limit. Said Bobby Payne, the county prosecutor: "We're alleging that due to his negligence, he caused the death of another human being."

The phone inside Irv and Bonita's house rang around 3:00 a.m. There was an accident. No details, except that it involved a train and Scott. "We get to Memorial Hospital, and of course the reporters are there," said Bonita. "There's nothing private in your life." The news was like a brick to the skull. Scott was arrested and charged with DUI felony negligence. He faced a maximum 25 years in prison, and after being discharged from the hospital was taken three hours away to the Greene County Jail in Leakesville, then later transferred to the Harrison County Jail. According to Bonita, guards would "slap Scott upside the head and say, 'When you see your brother tell him how stupid you are.'" Bonita called Bus Cook, Brett's agent, for help, but according to her, he was largely useless. "Hey, how are you?" Cook would ask when she called, to which Bonita would respond, "How the fuck do you think I am?"

When Brett learned of the tragedy, he froze. His close friend was dead? His brother might spend the next 25 years in jail? Two days later he and Deanna flew in for the funeral. "We were all distraught," said Scott. "You're numb and lost. My friend Mark and I, we thought we were bulletproof. When I went to jail, I was just sitting there and I made a deal with myself that I was done drinking. I couldn't have anyone say I didn't learn my lesson."

Scott wound up being sentenced to 15 years in prison, with 14 suspended and the other served under house arrest. Buddy Haverty, Mark's
father, was one of his biggest defenders, blaming the railroad crossing,
not Scott. "Any further punishment would be more punishment to me,"
he said. "My family's sentiments are: I would rather it just be dropped.
Through no intent of Scott's did this occur . . . Lord knows, everybody
has been punished enough for this."

When Brett returned to training camp, he turned to the one thing athletes have long used as motivational tools during tough times: devotion.
He would devote the season to Mark Haverty and the memory of his
friend. It wouldn't bring anyone back, or even soothe the awful feelings
that crept through his brain every day. But he needed a tool to survive. He
needed *something*.

The 1996 Packers were special, in the way great teams that aren't
overtly great often are. Green Bay wasn't Dallas of the 1990s, loaded with
high-priced superstars at every position. What the Packers possessed,
more than anything, was immense confidence, as well as a quarterback
determined to carry his team to the next level. Favre had a clear-eyed
steeliness few had seen before. It was noted by veterans, it was noted by
newcomers. "He was always the first one there, the last one to leave," said
safety Eugene Robinson, then entering his 12th NFL season. "When he
stepped out to the field, it was business."

The Packers emerged from training camp as the odds-on favorite to
win the NFC Central. They jumped out to an 8-1 start, including a 37–6
pounding of the rival Bears and a 23–20 win over San Francisco, a league
power. Favre — using only Advil to ease the pain — was playing master-
fully, and it paid off. An ESPN/Chilton Sports Poll showed him to be
America's most beloved football player, and businesses lined up. Favre
endorsed Choice Hotels, Sprint, Nike; he signed objects big and small for
profit. "I have been at this many, many years," said David Burns, founder
of Burns Entertainment and Sports Marketing, "and I haven't seen a
quarterback move to the top profile-wise and endorsement-wise as fast
as [Favre] has."

In Green Bay, any worries his popularity might diminish after the
Vicodin admission vanished. Favre was bigger than ever — a married,
clean-living, drug-free hero who perfectly embodied the Midwestern vir-
tues of hard work and accountability. So what if he was neither clean living nor drug free? (Though done with Vicodin, Favre still drank plenty

of beer, and his connubial faithfulness to Deanna did not last long.) He worked with his own marketing expert, Joe Sweeney, who proved a huge help to Favre in massaging his image. "Brett spoke his mind, gave you who he was," said Sweeney. "He was immediately likable, so he wasn't a hard sell."

With the team rolling and his wife and daughter by his side, Favre was relaxed and at ease. He stole linebacker Wayne Simmons's catchphrase for the '96 season ("Shit be bringin' it, Hoss") and repeated it incessantly. "Shit be bringin' it, Hoss" could apply to a great catch, an amazing throw, a large unflushed poop in the toilet. Favre's favorite nonfootball pastime was sneaking up on teammates while they were showering and slapping them — bare-assed — as hard as he could with his right palm. The average NFL quarterback's hand measures 9.6 inches. Favre's was a ridiculous 10.38 inches. "Always when your face was under water, shampoo was in your hair," said Don Beebe, a Packers receiver. "He'd leave a red mark on your can that would send you into shock."

"You might be in the shower and you feel something warm on your leg," said Ken Ruettgers, the offensive lineman. "It'd be Brett peeing on you."

Team cohesion was put to the test in late November when the Packers went out on a limb to sign wide receiver Andre Rison off waivers. Not all that long ago, Rison had dismissed his former Atlanta teammate as a hillbilly. The slur, though, was stated when Rison, a five-time Pro Bowler, was one of the NFL's elite pass catchers. Now, having flamed out with Cleveland and Jacksonville, the 29-year-old was considered a past-his-prime punch line, best known off the field as the fool whose Atlanta mansion was burned down by Lisa "Left Eye" Lopes, the TLC singer and his on-again, off-again girlfriend (who started the blaze by setting fire to his athletic shoe collection in a bathtub). Dumped by the Jaguars and sitting home alone, Rison was desperate. "I needed a job," he said. "Any job."

Green Bay's two best wide receivers, Robert Brooks and Antonio Freeman, were injured, and Ron Wolf asked the coaches if they wanted Rison. "I was the only one to raise my hand," said Gil Haskell, the wide receivers coach. "And everyone looked at me like, 'We want that asshole in here?'" As the reigning MVP, Favre's opinion carried weight. When asked, he didn't flinch. "'Dre can help," he said. "That's what matters."

Rison signed on November 19 for a paltry $81,000 and arrived the next day. The negative perceptions immediately vanished. On the field, everything Rison did was precise and professional. "He taught me shit in two practices that I didn't learn in 20 years," said Derrick Mayes, a rookie receiver out of Notre Dame. "Just the nuances of being a wideout. It was sick to see. I mean, everything he did was about slowing the game down."

One of Favre's gifts was an ability to get along with everybody, and Rison was no exception. There was a bond over shared time in Atlanta, as well as the mutual appreciation between a strong-armed quarterback and a speedy wide receiver. "We used to talk a lot in the locker room," said Rison. "I loved Brett. He knew when and how to get you the ball, he was a cool guy who tried to know you as a person."

The coaching staff knew Mayes resided by himself in a half-empty duplex, and he was told by Holmgren that (*a*) Rison would live with him, and (*b*) he was responsible for getting the notoriously tardy player to practice every day. "Mike, are you kidding me?" Mayes said. "I'm a rookie. Why would Andre listen to me?"

The gruff Holmgren wasn't empathetic. "It's your job," he said. "Do it."

Rison made his Green Bay debut in the 24–9 win at St. Louis on November 24, starting across from Beebe and catching five passes for 44 yards. The team flew back to Green Bay, whereupon Rison turned to Mayes and said, "We have the day off tomorrow. Rook, you're coming with me." The wide receivers caught the next flight to Atlanta — "two first-class tickets, paid for by 'Dre," said Mayes — and were greeted at the terminal by a stretch limo holding Lopes and two of her friends. "We go straight to the Gold something . . . some strip club," said Mayes. "There are two magnums of Cristal on either side, and I'm talking to a girl and Lisa gets in her face and said, 'Sugar Bear, we ain't paying you to talk to him all day. You better get up and dance at the same time!'"

Lopes frequented Green Bay, and she and Rison constructed a makeshift music studio in the apartment. The earsplitting beats blasted throughout the night. There would be fighting some evenings, lovemaking other evenings. One time Michael Silver, the *Sports Illustrated* writer, came to the apartment to interview Rison. "'Dre, a reporter is here," Mayes said.

Rison: "Are you sure he's a reporter?"

Mayes: "I think so. That's what he said."

Rison: "Well, frisk the motherfucker."

Mayes: "Nah, I'm fine."

Rison: "You better fucking frisk the motherfucker right now!"

"I frisked Mike," Mayes said. "It was a little bit embarrassing."

Green Bay won its last five games with Rison as a starter, and while his 13 catches for 135 yards didn't leap off the page, his intensity did. "We needed somebody with the right swagger to get our group to understand," said LeRoy Butler. "Andre was starving. He had numbers, but no ring. And he wanted it. Our receivers were good, but we didn't have a guy with that swagger."

The Packers' locker room seemed to come alive. It was a playground for all seasons — Reggie White in one corner preaching the gospel, Rison in another talking smack, Favre telling stories about Mississippi and Oreo-eating alligators, the offensive linemen discussing hunting excursions and fishing holes. "We had an interesting dynamic, in that every section was like a neighborhood, and it almost seemed as if the locker room was organized on what type neighborhood you were from," said Chris Darkins, a defensive back. "You had the Wayne Simmons–LeRoy Butler area as the hood. They were hanging out, playing games, talking shit. So if wanted to have fun you'd walk to the hood. The only stabilizing part of the hood was Reggie White. He was smack-dab in the middle and whenever a fight broke out in the hood, Reggie stepped in. Then on the far corner, to our far-left corner, you had the suburbs. That's where you had mostly offensive linemen hanging out, chilling. Not a lot of noise. Our corner was the intellectual corner — people who observed, watched. That was kind of like Brett's demeanor. He'd watch, observe, talk to anyone, maybe pull a prank."

The Packers had a rowdiness to them, especially with Rison's addition. They talked shit and smoked pot and drank bountifully. Much like Rison, Simmons was a fiery player who never worried about holding his tongue. He found pleasure in trying to trick White into cursing or losing his cool. He would blast gangsta rap from the locker room speaker, anxious to goad White into shutting it off. Over the final two months of the season, the only music that was accepted by all parties was a well-worn Bob Marley CD. Once, the men nearly came to blows. "Reggie, in the Bible it said Jesus preached to the prostitutes, the sinners," Simmons once noted. "Why don't you come to the clubs with us?"

"Reggie tagged along one time," said a teammate. "He lasted 15 minutes."

The Packers concluded the season with an NFC-best 13-3 record. They went 8-0 at home, and were the first team since the undefeated 1972 Miami Dolphins to have both the NFL's highest-scoring offense (456 points) and stingiest defense (210 points allowed). Favre, with 39 touchdowns, 13 interceptions, and 3,899 passing yards, would yet again be voted the NFL's MVP. Green Bay lacked a 1,000-yard rusher or wide receiver, making his run all the more impressive. "[Brett is] the greatest, the best, the most unselfish, the most competitive," said Gilbert Brown, the Packers nose tackle. "You know he's going to show up, you know he's never going to leave you hanging."

Green Bay opened the playoffs at home by crushing the 49ers, 35–14. The hero was Desmond Howard, who returned the first punt for a 71-yard touchdown, then later had another 46-yard return to set up a score. Steve Young, the star San Francisco quarterback, left early with a rib injury, and hope departed with him. By the time the fourth quarter began, Lambeau's fans were chanting, "We want Dallas! We want Dallas" — the team that knocked Green Bay from the playoffs the past three seasons. Beebe, who lost two Super Bowls to the Cowboys as a Buffalo Bill, agreed. "If anyone wants to play Dallas," he said, "it's moi."

Alas, it wasn't to be. One day later the Carolina Panthers — a second-year expansion franchise with no business making it this far — somehow shocked the Cowboys, 26–17, to earn an exotic weekend trip to ice-covered Wisconsin for the NFC Championship Game. Favre watched the Dallas–Carolina game from his couch with Deanna and Bus Cook, and while the nonplayers rooted for the Panthers, Favre was indifferent. "I didn't think Dallas could beat us in Green Bay," he recalled.

Favre was probably correct, but the Carolina Panthers *definitely* couldn't beat the Packers in Green Bay. Not with the temperature at 3 degrees (minus 17 with the windchill) and the field feeling like a bed of slate. The lead-up to the game was everything one would expect from a city that oozes football. Green-and-gold-coated homes, buildings, mailboxes, binders. Every church marquee seemed to feature a Bible verse or inspirational thought geared toward the Packers. The nightly news was 95 percent football, with weather mixed in. For two days, the lead story on every local network was about the NFL importing 40 trucks filled with Maryland sod to fix a field torn apart the previous week.

By now, Rison was as much a Packer as Favre and White. Which is why Butler, the respected safety, asked Holmgren to have Rison address the team before taking the field against the Panthers. "He's got the fire," Butler said. "The young guys need to hear that."

Holmgren agreed. "I wasn't here for the Dallas game last year," Rison said in his remarks. "But I hear a lot of y'all talk about the bitter taste it left in your mouths . . . this isn't the Super Bowl — it's bigger. There's no way we can let the media intimidate us, telling our offense how it has to handle the zone blitz. To hell with that. They've got to stop us. We've got too many weapons. So let's go out there, run our offense, and kick their fucking asses!"

Green Bay's players charged the field, and even though the Panthers scored first after a Favre interception, they never had a chance. Green Bay outscored Carolina 17–3 in the second quarter, twice on Favre touchdown passes, and the blowout was on. By the end of the third quarter, following a short Bennett scoring run, the score was 27–13, and Super Bowl tickets could be safely printed. Most of the 60,216 fans stood the entire fourth quarter. Neighboring spectators were unable to hear one another over the roar of the crowd. "It was the most fantastic game I've ever been to," said Tom Lynn, a *Journal Sentinel* photographer. The final score was 30–13. The Green Bay Packers were returning to the Super Bowl for the first time in 29 years. In the boisterous locker room afterward, White sought out Favre and wrapped him in a terrifying bear hug. "Where are we going tonight?" the minister asked the rehab patient, who had just started his 86th straight NFL game while throwing for 292 yards and two scores.

"Oh, we're going partying," Favre replied.

White changed and headed for home.

Favre changed and headed to Chmura's house, where he'd be joined by Winters, teammate Aaron Taylor, members of Hootie and the Blowfish, and the comedian David Spade. Wrote Dick Schaap: "Just a typical Sunday evening at home in Green Bay."

The Packers were off to New Orleans.

16

SUPER BOWL

OVER THE COURSE of the first six years of his NFL career, Brett Favre took pleasure in having people believe he was a backwoods Mississippi redneck with three teeth and a hankering for skinned possum.

He would address members of the media with excessive insertions of "y'all"; he would play down his intelligence in an effort to have people underestimate what he could accomplish. Favre's weekly press conferences were often rambling drunk-hillbilly-uncle beauties, and more than a few reporters thought there was genius in the act. "Brett liked to play the hick thing to the hilt," said Rob Reischel, the veteran Packer beat writer. "But really he was controlling the message. If you only get 15 minutes and he rambles four minutes for each question, he steers the topic how he wants it."

Favre wasn't the first professional athlete to play the "I'm an idiot" card (former Steelers quarterback Terry Bradshaw mastered the craft), and he wouldn't be the last. But by the time the Packers beat Carolina, he had some cause to regret it.

Super Bowl XXXI would pit Green Bay against New England in a matchup that was both underwhelming and a bit disappointing. Heading into the postseason, most prognosticators had expected the Denver Broncos, featuring an AFC-best 13-3 record, to wind up facing the Packers. Then the Broncos fell to the Jacksonville Jaguars in the divisional round, and the Patriots snuck through.

Only, New England was (yawn) sort of dull. Sure, coach Bill Parcells was an all-time great, and a week before the game the *Boston Globe* published a shocking piece, headlined PARCELLS TO LEAVE, about the coach's awful relationship with Robert Kraft, the team owner. Other than the grumpy coach, however, the Patriots roster was a who's who of who cares? New England beat two so-so playoff opponents (the Steelers and the Jaguars) to reach New Orleans, and was immediately installed as a 12- to 13-point underdog. "We were riding a high, but we weren't a great team," said Lawyer Milloy, the Patriots' rookie strong safety. "Even our coaches couldn't believe we were in the game."

With gripping on-field matchup pieces a hard sell, the media turned to the best-available spin: bumpkin Brett Favre returning to the Deep South. In the two-week gap leading up to the January 26, 1997, kickoff, no fewer than 200 stories ran across America concerning Favre, Mississippi, and dumb, ignorant Southerners with pickup trucks and Confederate flags. It began with Mary Foster filing an Associated Press piece headlined PACKERS' FEVER HITS QUARTERBACK'S HOME TOWN, which painted the quaint portrait of Kiln, Mississippi, rallying around its favorite son. At Rooster's Café, a stuffed rib eye was renamed the "Brett Favre Special"! At Donna's Quick Stop, people talked of stocking a Favre doll made of cheese! "I don't think anyone in town ever gave an interview before this, but all of a sudden we're all stars," said a local named Buddy Barnett — and one could all but feel the tobacco juice dribbling from the corner of his mouth. These were real live clodhoppers, and they were *amazing* print. The *New York Times* called Hancock County, Mississippi, "ground zero of the football world."

Green Bay spent the first week after the Carolina win practicing at home, then flew to New Orleans via charter on the Sunday before the game. The temperature was, with windchill factored in, minus 35 when the plane left. It landed in 65-degree warmth. More than 3,000 media representatives from 150 countries were credentialed and charged with the task of making a relatively dull lead-up interesting. So they descended upon Favre's home turf like a pen-wielding army, knocking on Bonita and Irv's front door, badgering local businesses, seeking out any nugget of funny or quirky or (ideally) humiliating information. The tragic car accident involving Scott Favre was prime material. So was a September arrest of Brandi Favre, Brett's younger sister, for being involved with a drug-related drive-by shooting at a motel in Slidell, Louisiana. (The details — including the fact that Brandi had nothing to do with the actual crime and was largely a victim of circumstance — were conveniently omitted from most copy.) Anyone who wanted to speak about Favre's addiction issues was likely to be quoted. But mostly, the articles and TV segments concerned the image, the scene, the middle-of-nowhere Bayou presentation.

The father.

Irvin Favre ate it up. While Bonita was happy to chat, Big Irv (as he was referred to throughout town) seized the spotlight and refused to let go. You wanted a story? Hell, he'd give you a whopper. Just pull up a bar stool, order a beer (and make certain to buy him one, too), and relax for the next four hours. Irv would talk about the bayou, about Brett as a baby, about the time his son threw that pass to Charles Burton, and on and on and on. Hey, did you hear the town of Kiln just put up a wood sign honoring Brett? How about the history of the old Indian tribes? At 52, Irvin knew *exactly* what the press was after. In a sit-down with the *New York Times,* he told reporter Jere Longman that they'd be eating hamburgers, shrimp jambalaya, seafood gumbo, and "whatever else we run over between now and then." Later, pointing to an area behind a local bar called the Broke Spoke, he cracked, "Watch a woman with no teeth come running out of there." In another one-on-one session, this time with Steve Buckley of the *Boston Herald,* Irv admitted he generally walks through his house only in underwear. "Hey," he said, "I'm not a flashy person."

"By now," read an MSNBC piece, "the tale of Brett Favre, Country Boy Turned Conglomerate, has been worn to a nub." It was all kicks and giggles — only the giggles were directed at the quarterback, the region, the father. In the four days before the media tour, the Favres had 52 reporters visit their house unannounced. Most were seeking out alligators and ignorance. "It could get hurtful," said Bonita. "You sometimes read the articles and knew they were mocking us."

"They thought we were dumb," said Brandi. "It was all a joke."

None of this made Brett Favre particularly happy. He wasn't a hick, and he was tired of playing a hick. He wore shoes. Had every tooth. Whizzed through crossword puzzles and lost himself in Discovery Channel features. The NFL responded to the interest by chartering *two* loaded busses to Hancock County for a one-day media visit, and many of the reporters stuck around to witness an enormous crawfish boil at the Broke Spoke, attended by more than 5,000 people. At one point, Favre was asked how he felt about it all. "There is no private life," he said with a sigh. "Sometimes I wish I could change my identity."

By now, everybody across America knew of Favre's Vicodin addiction, as well as his pledge not to drink alcohol for two years. Had the Super Bowl been in any other city, this would have been a relative nonissue. Yet when the Super Bowl comes to town, New Orleans turns Mardi Gras plus Carnival. Eleven years earlier, the Big Easy welcomed Super Bowl XX between Chicago and New England, and Bears quarterback Jim McMahon spent much of the week partying and drinking. Now McMahon was Favre's backup with the Packers, and he still partied and drank. In the week leading up to the Super Bowl, McMahon was a wealth of information. He told teammates both the best places to get drunk and to see naked women dance. "He comes to meetings hung over," Favre said with great admiration. "And then he talks during the meetings. He doesn't give a shit about anything."

Nobody cared much about McMahon. But they did care about Favre. Which is why he assured everyone he wasn't drinking — then went out and drank. Not nearly as much as he once had (the eyes of a nation were cast upon a man thought to be sober), but he seemed to be defiantly ignoring the NFL's no-alcohol ordinance. A *Green Bay Press-Gazette* reporter spotted Favre imbibing and called Bus Cook, his agent, for comment. It turned out the NFL had changed Favre's status in its substance-abuse program from "behavioral-referred" to "self-referred." Translation: he was OK to imbibe. "The league didn't want to make a big deal out of it," Favre said, "and neither did I." That's why, beginning shortly after his release from rehab (well before the NFL approved his alcohol consumption), Favre came up with a simple method to drink in public: he would have the beverage (or whatever he was consuming) placed in either a soda can or a Styrofoam cup with a lid and a straw. If he wanted a beer, he was having a beer. "It was a joke," said one friend. "People actually thought he was always drinking Diet Pepsi." As the game approached, though, Favre lay surprisingly low. Except for one night where he was reportedly caught out at a strip club, there were no accounts of mayhem. A handful of paparazzi trailed him through the French Quarter, but got nothing. On Thursday he came down with the chills and an accompanying 101-degree fever. That night, while others were living it up, he was shivering beneath his blankets. "I was worried," he said. "I'd waited my whole life for this." The fever broke, and he was fine.

Unlike New England's players, who had no curfew for the first three days, the Packers were required to return to their rooms at the Fairmont

Hotel by 1:00 a.m. Which still allowed for plenty of wildness. Packers fans overtook the city, and no player had to pay for a drink. Dozens of Favre family members spent much of the week living the life — Irvin (beer always in hand) bragged to approximately 100,000 people he was Brett Favre's father; Brandi — at the time a student at Southern Miss — spent one memorable night drinking three bottles of Dom Pérignon with Eagles halfback Ricky Watters at an NFL-sponsored party at the House of Blues.

The Three Amigos (Favre, Chmura, and Winters) hopped from Bourbon Street bar to Bourbon Street bar, soaking in the love and adulation. On one of the excursions, they grabbed a taxi. The driver wanted to talk football, and raved about the toughness of that guy playing quarterback for Green Bay. "He can throw with two guys hanging on him," he said.

"If two guys are hanging on him," Favre replied, "he must not get much blocking." Chmura and Winters howled.

"I don't drink or smoke, but that week was the closest I came to either," said LeRoy Butler. "There was just so much of . . . *everything.*"

No player dove into the moment like Andre Rison. The team curfew meant little, as did Holmgren's request that his men maintain low profiles. One evening, Rison took Derrick Mayes and Antonio Freeman, the two young wide receivers, to the Goorin Bros. Hat Shop in the French Quarter. "'Dre bought every fucking color of derby hat they had," said Mayes. "He probably spent $1,500 just on hats. I never wore a derby hat in my life, and he even bought me one. My wife took one look at it and made me get rid of the motherfucker."

Many of the Patriots' workouts, held at Tulane, involved pads and physical contact — and lasted two and a half hours in the 80-degree heat. The Packers, meanwhile, usually went no longer than an hour. Holmgren eschewed pads and had his players exchange pants for shorts. When rain threatened Friday's practice, Holmgren simply called it off. "Fuck it," he said to Jim Lind, the linebackers coach. "They're ready." The Packers felt fresh, invigorated. They also watched plenty of tape on New England. On the record, it was all praise. The Patriots would be a formidable foe and blah blah blah. Behind closed doors, there was derision. "I've been watching them on film," Wayne Simmons said, "and they look like crap."

Three hours before the 5:30 p.m. kickoff, the Packers players and coaches boarded the buses that would ferry them from the Fairmont to the Louisiana Superdome. Throughout the season, White and Favre always rode the second bus. They weren't about to break precedent. Every man was decked out in the requisite coat and tie, save Favre, who wore his shorts/T-shirt/sandals combo. Rison bounded up the steps and, cracking the silence, shouted, "Let's go get 'em, motherfuckers!"

The Patriots' locker room was quiet and stiff. The Packers' locker room was not. There was talking, laughter, debate. Butler roamed cubby to cubby with a camcorder, enticing teammates to step toward the lens and scream, "Shit be bringin' it, Hoss!" At one point, bored by the long wait, Favre reached for his cell phone and started making plans for the victory party. His brother Scott booked a room at Mike Anderson's Seafood and Oyster Bar on Bourbon Street. With that task complete, Favre asked Kurt Fielding, an assistant trainer, to tape his ankles. Though not overly superstitious, Favre believed in ritual. Fielding not only taped his ankles before every game, he would take a black marker and scribble a game prediction on the tape. This time, Fielding etched a *W* — for win — and wrote that the quarterback would throw for four touchdowns.

In the moments before it was time to walk through the stadium bowels and onto the field, Holmgren stood to address the team. The room went quiet. "Men, I don't have to show you how to win this game," he said. "I've already shown you how to win. You don't need me to hold your hands. This is what we've worked for since that first meeting in training camp. We're here for one reason and that's to win the Super Bowl. It was a long, hard road. It's why we worked so hard in training camp. It's why we went through all the ups and downs, just to be here in this position we're in right now. So don't let it slip away. Enjoy yourself and remember this moment forever. Now let's go out there and get after it!"

Favre's heart was pounding beneath his No. 4 jersey. His hands were sweaty. Twice he dry-heaved. He and his football brothers charged onto the field, united, nervous, excited, amplified. "It was," he recalled, "an awesome sight."

The national anthem was performed by Luther Vandross, who wore an ill-fitting Super Bowl XXXI leather jacket and baggy blue jeans. His rendition was soft and elevatorish — and Rison couldn't contain his emotions. As Favre and White and Holmgren stood stoically, tears streamed down the veteran wide receiver's cheeks. His eyes reddened. "Just to be there," he said. "To finally be there . . ."

"It was just so powerful," said Jim Lind, the assistant coach. "I was in the box above, looking down with binoculars at my family, thinking about all the hard work and the setbacks and the disappointment. It hits you hard in that moment."

The Patriots won the coin toss and elected to receive. Immediately before kickoff, Bill Maas, a Fox Sports sideline reporter, wanted Parcells to divulge what he'd said to his players. His response was predictably bland and clichéd. Then Ron Pitts, standing alongside Holmgren, asked about the keys to the game. The Packers coach, too, blathered for a moment before turning surprisingly serious. "Which quarterback plays the best today," Holmgren said, "that team is gonna win."

New England's opening series went five plays before Tom Tupa's 51-yard punt was returned 32 yards by Howard. With 12:19 remaining in the quarter, Brett Favre made his Super Bowl debut. He sauntered onto the field after conferring with Holmgren. The Packers wore green jerseys and gold pants. Favre had narrow white wristbands on both arms, and a white towel dangling from his waist. On first down and 10 from the Green Bay 45, he handed the ball to Edgar Bennett for a 1-yard gain. It was now second and 9.

The Packers' first 15 offensive plays had been predetermined by Holmgren and Sherman Lewis, the offensive coordinator, one day earlier. They knew Bennett's handoff would open things, and they knew, on second down, Favre would run 322 Y Stick, a 4-yard out to Chmura. Now, however, as both teams approached the line of scrimmage, New England was doing something . . . funky. Willie Clay and Lawyer Malloy, the two safeties, were creeping forward and suggesting some sort of blitz. Parcells was an aggressive defensive coach, but it was early in the game for a move like this. Were they blitzing? Were they faking? Favre wasn't sure, and accidentally blurted out, "Oh, shit!" as he stared at the pass rushers.

So he guessed.

The audible was called Black 78 Razor — a seldom-used play where Rison lines up wide left and Freeman slides to the slot on the same side of the field. When Favre barked out the signal, his teammates all responded correctly. "Black meant we're changing it," Favre explained. "Seventy-eight was the protection. It was a two-man route. Razor means Z (flanker) runs a post and X (split end) runs a shake." Rison was now standing across from Otis Smith, a journeyman cornerback of whom the *New York Times* once wrote, "For so many offensive coordinators, quarterbacks and wide receivers, Smith's No. 45 is a neon sign that flashes:

'Throw Here.'" When the ball was snapped, Rison sprinted seven steps forward, then sliced inside of Smith while continuing to dart down the center of the field. The cornerback lacked the speed to keep up, and Favre's pass hit Rison in stride as he crossed the New England 22 and strutted, all alone, into the red-painted end zone. While Rison performed a jubilant ode to the chicken dance, Favre ripped his helmet off and sprinted toward McMahon on the sideline, hollering with glee. In one of the stadium luxury boxes, Scott and Jeff Favre leapt from their seats. "We both hit our heads on the ceiling," said Jeff. "It was unforgettable." From the television booth John Madden, a Super Bowl–winning coach who called the game for Fox, noted, "When you have a strong-armed guy and he's anxious, throw a deep one."

The Packers forced Bledsoe into an interception on the next series, and Chris Jacke's 37-yard field goal handed Green Bay a 10–0 lead with 8:42 still left in the first quarter. Yet any thoughts of a blowout were suspended when Bledsoe threw back-to-back touchdown passes on New England's next two offensive series. Fritz Shurmur, the Packers' defensive coordinator, was livid. He called Butler, White, and a handful of other players into a circle and let loose. "Pull your head out of your asses and go do what you're supposed to do!" he screamed. "Go get Bledsoe! Do whatever it takes!" When the first quarter came to an end, the Patriots were actually leading, 14–10. "We had momentum," said Ty Law, the New England cornerback. "People don't talk about this, but we pretty much outplayed the Packers most of the game. But a Super Bowl is a thing of big singular plays adding up. And they had some big singular plays."

The Packers and Patriots exchanged scoreless possessions to begin the second quarter, and with 14:14 left, Green Bay received the football on its own 19. Earlier in the game Freeman, the second-year wide receiver from Virginia Tech, stood alongside Law after a play and said, "You ain't gonna get no balls today." The Patriots cornerback, who would go on to play in five Pro Bowls, didn't know whether he was being set up, or if Favre truly planned to avoid him. "You never know for sure," Law said.

As he stepped to the line, the quarterback looked toward his right and saw Don Beebe in the slot, facing Law, while Freeman — a stone's throw from the sideline — was covered by Milloy, the bulky strong safety. "I started licking my chops," Freeman said. Since being selected in the third round out of Virginia Tech, Freeman had both impressed and infuriated teammates and coaches. As a rookie he was used almost exclusively as a

punt returner, but Haskell, the receivers coach, urged Holmgren to give
him a chance. "When he caught the ball he was exceptional at making
the first guy miss," said Haskell. "And he was always running for a touchdown. It wasn't about a first down for Freeman. He wanted to score."
But Freeman was sometimes considered lazy and absentminded. He'd go
hard for three plays, then take a fourth off. "He was phenomenal," said
Allen DeGraffenreid, a free agent receiver in camp in 1996. "But if he'd
worked harder he'd be much more impressive." Despite the criticisms,
Favre took an immediate liking to the kid from inner-city Baltimore, who
picked up the playbook quickly. "I was in heaven with Brett," Freeman
said. "As a wide receiver, it's all about having a quarterback who can get
you the ball. Well, Brett didn't have a problem with that."

Now, Favre glanced toward Freeman, glanced toward Milloy, and
knew where the ball would wind up. He dropped back and looked right.
Milloy was supposed to jam Freeman at the line, but whiffed. The wide
receiver scampered past and Favre hit him in stride near midfield. "Once
I caught the ball," Freeman said, "all I thought about was quieting all the
critics who said I wasn't fast enough when I came out of college, who said
I didn't have the heart to go across the middle. I knew the whole world
was watching and it was my opportunity to quiet those critics." Freeman
burst down the sideline past Milloy and Clay (who had talked much trash
about Favre during the week) for an 81-yard touchdown, the longest in
Super Bowl history. He jogged into the end zone, dunked the ball over
the goalpost, and did a boogie with Rison. The Packers were back on top,
17–14, and added a field goal and a 2-yard Favre touchdown run to carry
a 27–14 lead into the halftime break. "Even though the Patriots still had
some fight left in 'em," Favre recalled, "I was pretty sure the game was
ours."

The halftime locker room was jovial, almost festive. One player, however, wasn't happy. Howard, the marvelous kick returner, had been the
1991 Heisman Trophy winner at Michigan, then the fourth overall pick in
the 1992 NFL draft, by Washington. Joe Gibbs, the Redskins coach, raved,
"This guy doesn't have any flaws," then uncovered the flaws. Howard's
hands were bad. His routes sloppy. He worked, but not especially hard.
He was one of the first NFL players to own his own cell phone, and — for
some odd reason — it irked the organization. The Redskins left Howard
unprotected in the 1995 expansion draft, and after a bad year in Jacksonville, Howard wound up in Green Bay. Barely. "The idea was we'd cut

him after the fourth preseason game," said Haskell. "But guys kept getting hurt, and in that fourth preseason game he took a kickoff and returned it for a touchdown. That took care of that. He didn't really see himself as a receiver. He was a returner, and proud to be one."

Now, in the locker room, Howard was incredulous. New England's players had been barking at him throughout the first half ("Nothing for you today!" one said. "We're gonna shut you down!") and enough was enough. Standing next to Favre, he said, "Brett, I'm gonna take one of these kicks back. It's only a matter of time."

New England scored late in the third quarter on Curtis Martin's 18-yard touchdown run, and with the extra point the Packer lead shrank to 27–21. The kickoff that followed was a long one — the Patriots' Adam Vinatieri had one of the league's strongest legs, and he booted a ball that sent Howard back to the 1. He caught it, sprinted down the middle of the field through an ocean of green and white jerseys, past Vinatieri and defensive back Michael McGruder and into the end zone. The 99-yard return was another NFL record, and Howard pounded his chest and barked deliriously toward the Patriot players as they retreated from the field.

"That was the moment when everything unraveled for New England," said Darius Holland, the Packers' defensive tackle. "Any momentum, any hope — it died for them right there."

"It was a dagger that put us away," said Vinatieri. "We just could not come back from that."

The 35–21 score held up, and Howard — he of 244 combined return yards — was named Super Bowl MVP. The Packers' offense had possession for the final 50 seconds of the game, and Favre took the last snap and fell to his right knee. As the last ticks rolled off the clock, Beebe approached from behind. The 32-year-old was an improbable NFL success story. He'd played at three small colleges (Western Illinois, Aurora, and Chadron State) before the Bills selected him with the 82nd pick in the 1989 draft. Beebe lost four Super Bowls in six years in Buffalo, and came to Green Bay as a free agent because he desperately craved victory. Now he asked Favre for a favor. "Brett," he said, "any chance I can have that ball?"

Favre didn't hesitate. "Beebs," he said, "no one deserves this more than you." Beebe walked off the field with his son Chad in one arm, his daughter Amanda in the other, and a ball — *the ball* — tucked beneath an elbow. Favre, meanwhile, hugged everyone in sight. His numbers were merely OK (14 for 27 passes, 246 yards, two touchdowns, no turnovers), but Bledsoe's four interceptions provided a striking contrast. Holmgren had been right: the better quarterbacking won.

In the locker room, Favre hugged the Vince Lombardi Trophy. "I've done everything I possibly can," he said. "I hope too many people didn't bet against me, because they're broke right now."

Eight months earlier, he'd flown to Topeka as the NFL's drug-addict quarterback.

Now he was a Super Bowl champion.

17

LOW

THE CURSE OF REACHING an immeasurable high is the inevitable plummet.

That night in New Orleans, following the Packers' Super Bowl win, Brett Favre and his friends and family members partied like the biggest rock stars who ever lived. They prowled Bourbon Street and drank into the wee hours of the morning. Even those who wondered whether Favre was wise to imbibe were willing to make an exception. The toughest stretch of his life concluded with a Super Bowl crown. Cut the guy some slack.

The fall began but a day later, when the Packers flew back from New Orleans to Green Bay for a victory parade. As soon as the plane landed at Austin Straubel International Airport, the players and coaches loaded onto five buses and drove through the city toward Lambeau Field.

It was awful.

Actually, scratch that. Awful is having your leg gnawed off by a shark. Or Mike Tyson punching you in the gut. Awful is the smell of old salmon, the taste of castor oil, the musical stylings of Rick Astley. This was significantly worse.

The temperature was 20. With the windchill, it felt 10 below. Snow covered the ground. The air was dry and bitter. Breathing burned. The Packers' marketing department planned the entire day, including the *three-hour* trek from the airport to the stadium, including the players and officials who would speak at Lambeau, including the bus's *open* windows.

Yes, the windows were locked in the open position, so the fans could feel closer to the players. Which would have been digestible had the Packers been warned, or had winter jackets been provided. "I would say it was freezing," said Don Beebe, "but that doesn't do it justice."

"We're all in suits," said John Michels, the offensive lineman. "Suits! Not prepared at all."

Reggie White was the first to board a bus, and he cradled the Lombardi Trophy in his arms. The driver popped in a CD, *Queen's Greatest Hits,* and blasted "We Are The Champions." Tremendous choice. "That was great," Bob Kuberski, a defensive tackle. "But when we're moving, the cold cuts through your body like a friggin' knife." Reebok had gifted the players with purple Super Bowl XXXI athletic suits, and before long everyone was slicing open the packets and draping the clothing over their outfits. "I'm leaning out the window, and this kid reaches out his hand," said Kuberski. "He has a glove on, and I take it off his hand. He's yelling at me, 'Hey! My glove! My glove!' Sorry, kid."

Approximately 60,000 fans filled Lambeau Field. The ground was brick-hard and covered by six inches of snow, and the players were in dress shoes. Favre — warmed by several beers — said a few words, as did White, Mike Holmgren, and Ron Wolf. "Whoever planned that thing should have been canned," said Wolf. "When Mike and I talked, we both sounded like we were drunk. A doctor later explained to me it was from the cold. It was just awful."

"I just wanted to fucking go home," said Derrick Mayes. "It was like, 'OK, we won. Awesome. Now I want to be warm.'"

In the aftermath of the Super Bowl and the parade and Favre's fourth Pro Bowl appearance, the predictable onslaught of Packer- and Favre-related books hit the shelves. There was *Brett Favre: Huck Finn Grows Up* by Steve Cameron.* There was *Titletown Again* by Chuck Carlson. There was *A Year of Champions* by Gilbert Brown. The one that most stood out — and appeared on multiple national best-seller lists — was *Favre: For the Record,* which he wrote with a local media personality named Chris Havel. Reading the autobiography, one comes away thinking the superstar had found his inner goodness and learned how to be a devoted spouse and worthy role model. Around the time of the release, Favre's hometown newspaper, the *Biloxi Sun-Herald,* ran a piece on the Brett-

---

* A good read that features one of the most tasteless chapter titles in the history of the written word. Cameron named the segment on Favre's near-death car accident "Say Hello to Mr. Tree."

Deanna marriage that included this gem: "But to [Deanna], Brett Favre is the perfect husband and father, not the famous quarterback."

Um . . .

Despite Deanna's outward optimism ("Brett hasn't changed as a person. He's just matured as a person and grew up"), her husband was drowning — and she surely knew it. The hope of reformation that emerged post-rehab had long since died. The image of a perfect marriage was pure mirage. Favre was drinking more than ever; partying more than ever; sleeping around more than ever. Because Green Bay protects its icons, and the Packers built a Plexiglas shield around their superstar, few spoke of Favre's indiscretions. (Said Jerry Watson, owner of the Stadium View bar: "If you ever hear of anything going on here, you missed 90 percent of what didn't get reported.") But they were numerous, and they were ugly. Through the years, he had a regular hookup in California whom he would see on West Coast swings. There was a another woman in Green Bay — young, pretty, somewhat eccentric — who fooled around with Favre, then told everyone who would listen that her son belonged to the quarterback (it turns out he did not). He did a growing number of autograph signings in Green Bay, and afterward was often picked up by a breathtaking woman who would drive him off to who knows where. "Every girl around here was throwing themselves at Brett," said Watson. "That's the truth."

A woman Favre had allegedly engaged with in an improper relationship began stalking the family. One day she showed up at the house and knocked on the door. Only Brittany and the family babysitter were home. "She was coming to Brett's [steakhouse, which opened in 1998 near Lambeau Field], telling people she had an affair with Brett, that she had Brett's illegitimate child," said Maggie Mahoney, the steakhouse manager. "It got so ugly that Deanna called me to ask she not be allowed in the restaurant."

Mahoney, who loved working with Favre and genuinely liked him as a person, recalled Brett in the steakhouse's banquet room, shouting, "Show me your tits!" to female visitors. "He was drinking, and I told him he shouldn't do that," Mahoney recalled.

"Because I'm married?" he asked her.

"No," she replied, "because you're a prominent person, and those women could leave here and say you tried to rape them."

What made Favre's transgressions particularly dramatic was that, inevitably, he would find himself overtaken by guilt. A devout Catholic, Favre routinely attended team chapel services and went to church as often as possible. He believed in God, accepted Jesus, knew much of the Bible, and grasped the concept of sin. He fully understood drunkenness and infidelity were morally unacceptable, but continued the behavior. "Afterward he would always say to me, 'That's the last time! That's the last time!'" said a friend. "I mean, he could have passed a polygraph that he was done with women. And then he'd do it again. And feel horrible again. He lacked impulse control, but I'm also not sure, back then, he *truly* wanted to stop."

When he wasn't playing football, Favre was often engaged in various corporate appearances and signings. He would, according to an associate, have bogus schedules faxed to the house, so Deanna would see what he was (supposedly) up to — 8:00 a.m. flight; 10:00 a.m. meeting; 1:00 p.m. lunch. On and on. "So he'd travel, and maybe he'd have one or two things to do," said the friend. "But the rest of the time it'd be drinking, women, partying. Whatever." According to two people close with the family, things got so out of control that, ultimately, Deanna tapped his mobile phone and learned he was being dishonest and disloyal. She called him in Milwaukee one night and, said a friend, demanded he return to Green Bay immediately. "I know what you're up to," she said. "Get home now."

Deanna was particularly cold to Favre's nonfootball pals, many of whom she considered to be enablers of a lifestyle that was ruining her marriage. She grew weary of Mark Chmura and Frank Winters, the two Packers players who accompanied Favre on many escapades. She was dismissive of Joe Sweeney, the marketing expert who often traveled with him on the road. "I do a lot of speaking," said Sweeney, "and one thing I always say is, 'We're the average of the five people we spend the most time with.' Frankie and Mark and Brett loved alcohol, they loved the camaraderie, they loved the action and the bar hopping. So did they contribute to his troubles? Probably. But it's Brett's fault. He made choices." In particular, Deanna urged Favre to break all ties with Clark Henegan, the friend from Mississippi now living in Wisconsin and handling Brett's autograph-show requests. Of all the nonfootball pals in his life, Henegan was most involved in Favre's off-the-field activities. A well-known night owl, he accompanied Brett to bars, to clubs. He knew about the sexual conquests . . . was often there *for* the sexual conquests. "I was always gonna do whatever it took to have my brother's back," he said. "I was loyal."

Like Favre, Henegan struggled with drinking and, years later, acknowledged his problems and found sobriety. His life has not been an easy one — in 2008 his brother Mark was sentenced to life in prison for murdering two men while in the midst of a crack cocaine binge. Clark was fiercely loyal to Favre; he refers to Bonita as "my second mother." But at the time, when Brett couldn't help himself, Henegan was along for the ride. "My friends who have met Clark say he looks like the banjo player in *Deliverance*," said Sweeney. "Brett got in the most trouble when Clark was around. And you know who had to pick him up from wherever he was? You know who would catch the blame? Me. But Clark was like the dog you'd kick, and he'd come back and lick you. Brett kept the company of people who weren't the most upstanding citizens."

In the public eye, Deanna maintained an image of the contented spouse and mother. She posed for photos, signed autographs, attended team functions. Quietly she was miserable. "You have a normal life," she confided to one person. "Don't underestimate how special that is."

In sports, plenty of athlete wives understand the unspoken condition of in-season infidelity. But Brett wasn't a famous jock she met at a Tampa strip club or on line at an autograph signing. He was a kid from Hancock County, just as she was a kid from Hancock County. It wasn't supposed to happen this way. "Everyone wants to blame the athlete for changing," said David Thomason, Favre's pilot and friend. "But think about it. Everywhere we went, someone wanted to buy Brett a drink. Everywhere we went, somebody wanted to do a shot with Brett. Everybody wanted to be seen with him, to say they had a moment with him, a beer with him, two or three beers with him. And Brett was very accommodating by nature."

On paper, the 1997 season — much like the Favre marriage — looked to be a thing of beauty. In July he inked the largest contract in NFL history, a seven-year, $47.25 million deal that included a $12 million bonus and far surpassed the No. 2 earner, Detroit halfback Barry Sanders (he made $34 million over six years).* "I feel very strongly that he's the best player in the National Football League," said Ron Wolf, the general manager. "What better way to acknowledge that than the way we've just done?" Unmentioned in the reports was that, on the same day the deal was signed, Favre missed the morning walk-through for an exhibi-

---

* A few weeks later quarterback Steve Young and the 49ers agreed to a six-year, $45 million deal. And Favre was the second-highest-paid player.

tion game against the Dolphins with a "stomach issue" caused by "bad chicken wings" — a thinly veiled euphemism for *hung over after a night out*. "The team protected him a lot," said Greg Bedard, a longtime football writer. "Like, a whole lot."

In 1997 Favre won his third-straight MVP (he shared the honor with Detroit's Sanders) and Lambeau sold out every game for the 38th straight season — but it felt different. In the years leading up to the Super Bowl, Favre charged $30 per autograph at shows. Now he was asking $40,000 per hour to sit and sign. He inked an endorsement deal with Mountain Dew, debuted the Brett Favre chocolate bar. He even earned a spot on the Forbes sports rich list, which ranked America's 40th wealthiest athletes. Many members of the franchise were outraged when, in late March, Andre Rison was released, then — along with Howard (who signed with the Raiders) and kicker Chris Jacke (signed with Pittsburgh) — not invited to join the team trip to the White House to meet President Bill Clinton. "It was really insulting," said Rison. "We were guys who played key roles in winning the Super Bowl, and now we're not wanted? I thought Brett could have stood up for us and said something. He didn't."

The Packers rolled to a 38-24 season-opening win over Chicago, but few moments came easily. They suffered an ugly 10-9 Week 2 loss at Philadelphia, barely beat Miami and Minnesota in the next few weeks, and were crushed by the Lions, 26-15. Suddenly, the defending champions were 3-2 and limping along, and the predictable search for scapegoats commenced. "Look, we spoiled ourselves, our coaches, and our fans with the season we had," said LeRoy Butler, the safety. "We're fighting against that. Sometimes it's good to have standards like that. Sometimes it's not so good."

Inside the Packers' locker room, the players became disenchanted with Holmgren, now in his sixth season as head coach. If you were a star, like Favre or Reggie White, he would treat you well. But with winning came an ego, and with an ego came a dismissiveness that rubbed many the wrong way. Holmgren would pass a practice squad receiver or third tight end in the hallway, be greeted by a "Hey, Coach!" and refuse to respond. Not because he didn't hear, or because he was busy. No, because he was Mike Holmgren, Super Bowl–winning coach. "He and I had a great relationship, but I can see why some struggled with him," said Steve Bono, Favre's backup. "There was an expectation of work ethic and focus, and if you didn't live up to that standard you were gone and forgotten."

Even with an egomaniacal coach and a reduced roster, the Packers were still the NFC's most talented team. And, in professional football, talent (plus health) tends to win out. Antonio Freeman, one of the Super Bowl heroes, emerged as a No. 1 receiver, catching 81 passes for 1,243 yards and 12 touchdowns. Robert Brooks, back from injury, added 60 catches for 1,010 yards. Dorsey Levens had his first 1,000-yard rushing season, White tossed in 11 sacks, and Butler, the league's elite strong safety, picked off five passes. Following the Detroit loss, the Packers went on a five-game winning streak, punctuated by a 28–10 demolishing of New England in a Super Bowl rematch.

On December 1, the Packers found themselves in Minnesota for a key NFC Central clash with the Vikings, who were 8-4 and one game behind in the playoff race. The game was important from a mere win-loss standpoint, but carried extra emphasis for Holmgren. One week earlier the Packers beat the Cowboys, 45–17, for the coach's first win over America's Team. Now was an opportunity (on *Monday Night Football*, no less) to triumph for the first time in six tries inside the dreaded Metrodome. "I've exorcised one demon," Holmgren said after the Dallas win. "Now I have to exorcise another."

Because the Packers and Vikings were archrivals fighting for postseason positioning, the hype leading up to kickoff was predictably excessive. Would Favre torch Minnesota? Could the Brad Johnson–Cris Carter connection break through the Green Bay secondary? Would Holmgren finally trump Denny Green, his former colleague with the 49ers, outside of Wisconsin? Would the . . .

Stop.

Wait.

The questions ceased. The hypotheticals halted. On the morning of the game, KQRS-FM, a Minneapolis classic-rock radio station, sent a reporter named Lee Mroszak to the downtown Marriott to knock on Favre's door while pretending to deliver room service. He did so — live on the air — and a woman answered.

"You must be the lovely Mrs. Favre . . ." Mroszak said.

She was horrified. "What?" the woman screamed. "He's married? He can't be married!"

With that, the connection went fuzzy and, ultimately, cut off.

A nuclear explosion followed.

The news went viral, throughout the city, down Interstate 94 to Green Bay, across the United States. Brett Favre, the NFL's greatest player, had been caught cheating on his wife! Live! On the radio! KQRS played the clip throughout the day. The news could not have been any more shocking, and the Packers immediately contacted Favre to find out how such an embarrassing episode wound up in such a public forum.

The call woke Favre. He'd been asleep in his room — and alone.

The whole thing was a hoax. Mroszak (real name: Lee Siegfried) was best known by his radio nickname "Cabe." His official job title was the respectable-sounding "street reporter," but his daily task was to stir it up. "They wanted me to do more wild things," said Mroszak, a 28-year-old Gulf War veteran with a lengthy radio career. "I went to the hotel but there was security everywhere and I didn't know what room he was in." Favre, for the record, always checked in under the name "Leo Yelle" — a special-needs team employee he'd befriended. "So I went to my girlfriend Rebecca's apartment and said, 'You're a woman, but not Brett Favre's wife. I knock on the door, you react . . .' OK, let's do it."

That night, throughout the Packers' 27–11 win, the announcers alluded to the alleged infidelity, which both Favre and the team were denying. When asked by the station whether the skit was legitimate, Mroszak lied. "I should have admitted it was a fake," he said. "But the media grabbed onto it, and everyone was talking about it as if it had happened. I guess I panicked."

Finally, KQRS was contacted by Favre's attorney, who made clear the quarterback's intent to file a defamation suit. Dave Hamilton, the station manager, called Mroszak into his office and peppered him with questions. *What floor had Favre been on? How did you get into the hotel? What was the woman wearing?* Finally, he caved. "Look man, it was a bit," he said. "It happened, but it didn't really happen."

Mroszak was fired on the spot.

"He got what he deserved," Favre said. "It just never ceases to amaze me what people will do."

The lawsuit failed to materialize. Had he dared file, KQRS attorneys (not to mention the media) would have inevitably dug deep into his life, his marriage, his indiscretions. There's a reason Packer executives initially gasped when they learned of the report. Not because it was so shocking, but because they presumed it to be true. "Look, there were rumors all over the place that he was a philanderer," said Mroszak. "That's what inspired the bit. It was his secret, but secrets don't usually last."

Green Bay concluded the regular season with a 13-3 mark, and Favre seemed as good as ever. His 35 touchdown passes led the league, and even though many of his 16 interceptions were predictably ill-advised, it was hard to fault a player who had now started 93 straight games. That he was no longer using Vicodin to suppress the pain was amazing — "Nobody was tougher than Brett, nobody will ever be tougher than Brett," said Bono. That he was regularly drinking heavily, and staying out deep into many nights, was astounding. According to the National Sleep Foundation, "The quality and amount of sleep athletes get is often the key to winning. If sleep is cut short, the body doesn't have time to repair memory, consolidate memory, and release hormones." Favre slept here and there, and never went out the night before games, but he was deep into (undiagnosed) alcoholism that would have rendered weaker men useless. He simply couldn't say no to a drink. And one drink turned into three, three into five. When confronted by Deanna, he denied any problem. "But," said Sweeney, "there was definitely a problem."

It was masked by success. Green Bay opened the playoffs by stomping Tampa Bay 21–7 in the divisional round, then traveled to San Francisco and thrashed the 49ers, 23–10, in the NFC Championship Game. Afterward, Favre was giddy. He later revealed he had played with a torn rotator cuff in his left shoulder, only adding to his legacy of unstoppable toughness.

The Packers were returning to the Super Bowl, and he was the reason why.

One might think appearing in the NFL's championship game would be the greatest thing to happen to a professional football player. It is, after all, the pinnacle of the profession, the reason men subject their bodies to ungodly pounding, their brains to repeated head trauma.

One might be wrong.

Super Bowl XXXII — featuring the Packers and the Denver Broncos — was to be played on January 25, 1998, in San Diego, California. It was a matchup that, outside of two cities, seemed to excite few people. At 12-4, the Broncos were soaring, but they'd been down this road before. John

Elway, the bowlegged 37-year-old quarterback, had already appeared in (and lost) three Super Bowls, and the experts presumed this would be the worst of the setbacks. "Oddsmakers envision another trouncing," wrote Jon Saraceno in *USA Today*. "Green Bay is favored to beat Denver by nearly two touchdowns."

The Packers were the more talented, more successful operation. They featured a bevy of stars and a locker room filled with champions. "We were better than the Broncos," said LeRoy Butler. "Now, were we *so* much better that we didn't have to worry? No. But we had the better players."

The problem for Green Bay, though, had nothing to do with skill, and everything to do with complacency. Super Bowl XXXI had been played in New Orleans, and Packer Nation traveled in droves to witness its first title game since the Lombardi days. It was phenomenal.

This, by comparison, felt like a pretty big game. "But for us," said Byron Chamberlain, Denver's tight end, "it was special. We knew the Broncos had been embarrassed in other Super Bowls, and we were convinced that wouldn't happen again. We were very determined not to lose."

The Packers arrived in San Diego a week before kickoff. They took a handful of buses from the airport to the Sheraton Torrey Pines, which was located 19 miles to the north of downtown. If one loved golf, as Favre did, it was a terrific location. If one loved partying, as Favre did, it was awful. The resort was a secluded paradise, wonderful for honeymooners and 70-year-old outdoorsmen. "It was like being in training camp in eastern Washington," said Gil Haskell, the wide receivers coach. "Nothing was happening out there."

"Between doing media and working out, being that secluded didn't allow for the experience we wanted," said Derrick Mayes, the wide receiver. "We went out a few times, but it was all kind of lame."

There were other issues, too. Without Rison, the Packers were a significantly more businesslike team than they had been. "We were overly analytical," said Darius Holland, the defensive lineman. "Sometimes you just have to play without so much conversation." There were fewer trash talkers; expletive hurlers; dynamos anxious to kick ass and tell you all about it. Everything felt official, structured. "We weren't the same," said Haskell. "No Andre, no Keith Jackson, no Sean Jones, no Desmond Howard. And Edgar Bennett was injured that season, so we didn't have a key running back. We were good. But we weren't as good." Holmgren was less communicative and unwilling to laugh at himself. He was more critical, oftentimes irrationally so. Early on in his career at Green Bay, he stressed loyalty and sincerity. Now, something had changed.

One incident, in particular, crippled the Packers more than the coaches probably ever knew. Now in his second season with Green Bay, Don Beebe — the veteran wide receiver — had struggled throughout the post-season with a strained left hamstring that caused him to miss the match-ups against Tampa Bay and San Francisco. In the week after the NFC Championship Game, Beebe practiced every day, and assured Holmgren he'd be ready for the Super Bowl. When the team reached San Diego, Holmgren called Beebe in for a meeting. "I'm gonna cut to the chase," the coach said. "We're not dressing you."

Beebe was flabbergasted. "What?" he said. "I fought back to make it here. I told you I'd be ready . . ."

Holmgren explained that the team was adding Ronnie Anderson — a rookie free agent out of Allegheny College who had yet to appear in a game — to the roster. "We're doing it because we don't want to lose Ron-nie as a free agent," Holmgren said. "It's nothing you've done."

Beebe felt the anger rise through his body. All those extra hours in the weight room, with the trainers, sprinting, lifting, stretching. "Mike," he said, "that's a flat-out lie, and you know it. I deserve better than this. Why aren't you dressing me?"

Holmgren shrugged. "That's all I can tell you," he said. "I'm sorry."

Beebe stormed out. He never learned, for a fact, why he was deacti-vated (though others in the organization insist Wolf was never a fan and didn't want him in the game — an idea Wolf denied), but he retreated to his room and stewed for an hour. His roommate, a receiver named Bill Schroeder, walked in. When Beebe told him the news, he lost it. "That's such bullshit," he said. "That's not how you treat people."

Word spread. Teammates knew how hard Beebe worked. He was a be-loved grinder who brought savvy and experience and integrity to a rela-tively green wide receiver corps. Anderson, meanwhile, was a marginal NFL talent — "I loved Ronnie," said Beebe, "but he was not going to play in the league."* At that moment, something inside the Green Bay locker room changed. Coaches spoke of "family" all the time. *We're a family. Together, as a family, we can overcome. Don't forget your brothers.* But, as

---

* Anderson was cut at the end of training camp in 1998.

Don Beebe illustrated, it was nonsense. "Stuff like that opens your eyes," said Beebe. "It opens everyone's eyes."

It hardly helped that no one seemed to take Denver particularly seriously. Many of the players — Favre included — were drinking and partying the nights away, either inside the resort or somewhere downtown. "The way some of the guys handled preparation that week was awful," said John Michels, a second-year offensive lineman. "If you were a Packer you knew about Max McGee, and how hung over he was before the first Super Bowl. Well, it seemed like our guys were trying to replicate that. Our mentality wasn't the same as it had been in New Orleans. It was very disappointing."

Favre was a split personality. On the practice field — determined, focused. With his guy pals — a teenager seeking out dirty fun. With his family and friends — loving, kind, decent. During the 1995 season, Favre had struck up a kinship with Peter King, the *Sports Illustrated* football writer who came to Green Bay to profile the young quarterback. King was immediately mesmerized by Favre — "one of the most unique and interesting athletes I've ever covered," he said. In particular King was moved to near tears by a moment from a Friday during the '95 regular season, when the Packers staff held a 41st birthday party for Leo Yelle, the developmentally disabled man who worked in the mailroom and whose name Brett used to check into hotels. Practice had ended, and all the players were invited to attend. Only one did. "Not a single coach, staffer, player came, but Brett was there," said King. "He probably spent an hour at the party, and he was really present. The secretaries who put the party on were crying. It was beautiful."

Now, more than two years later, Favre and King were tight enough to start a tradition. If the writer was covering the Packers that week, he and Favre would share a Friday-night dinner. "It began with a win, so Brett saw it as good luck," said King. "They kept on winning, we kept eating together." King would be covering the Super Bowl, so, naturally, Favre insisted they dine. He called the writer and said, "There's gonna be 19 of us. Can you find somewhere we can eat in San Diego?" Then, a pause. "Do me a favor. Can you find a girl you might know, around Brittany's age? Maybe 9 or 10? She'd hate it, being the only kid at a dinner with all the adults."

King is from New Jersey. He was a writer who spent the majority of his time in press boxes and locker rooms. He knew no 10-year-old girls in

San Diego. However, this was no ordinary request. When you're covering the Super Bowl for *Sports Illustrated,* and the league MVP wants to dine, you find a way to dine. So King called Dan Squiller, his closest friend dating back to their days at Ohio University, and asked whether his daughter Brooke (age: 10) would enjoy eating with Brett Favre two nights before the Super Bowl.

Come again?

"My best friend was Annalisa, and her birthday party was the same day," said Brooke, who is now an attorney. "I wasn't a Packers fan, but I sort of knew who Brett Favre was. I mean, I knew he was important and famous. For a kid, how do you pass this up?"

They ate at George's, a fancy La Jolla restaurant. Brooke was terrified. She wore a new lime-green dress, just as bright as Favre's neon-orange T-shirt. The quarterback complimented her on the wardrobe choice.

"Hey, Brooke," Favre said, "what'd you do in school today?"

"Studied Spanish, I guess. Lots of Spanish," said Brooke, who attended a bilingual magnet school. "Everybody's talking about the Super Bowl, though."

"What do you want to do with your life?" he said.

"Be a marine biologist, I think."

"You have a boyfriend?" he said.

Brooke's cheeks turned bright red. "I actually had two boyfriends at the time," she said. "But I denied it, and everyone laughed because it was so obviously a lie."

The evening was wonderful ("A top-five life moment," Brooke said). Brooke thought Deanna Favre was beautiful. She found Brittney to be charming. As the evening came to an end, Brooke asked King for a coin. He dug a penny from his pocket, and she proceeded to kiss it, then hand it to the quarterback of the Green Bay Packers. "This is for good luck," she told him. "In the Super Bowl."

According to pretty much everyone, the Denver Broncos were in San Diego to serve as Packer roadkill. By Sunday, the betting line had increased to two touchdowns, and only one major football writer — Adam Schefter of the *Denver Post* — predicted a Broncos triumph. "I was around that team a lot," he said. "And they were good. People didn't seem to see that." It hardly helped Denver's cause that the AFC had lost 13 straight Super Bowls. Its teams were considered soft, passive, weak.

"But that was nonsense," said Terrell Davis, Denver's star halfback. "We were built like an NFC team. Everyone talked about John Elway, and rightly so — he's a legend, a great man, everything. But, really, we were a team that ran the ball and played physical defense. There was nothing flamboyant about us."

In the week leading up to the game, the Broncos were everything the Packers were not — focused, happy, relaxed. Just as Favre liked to dine with King as a regular good-luck charm, Davis had his own weekly ritual. Every Wednesday or Thursday he would check in with Ray Crockett, the Broncos' standout cornerback, and ask how he felt about the week's defensive game plan. "Sometimes Ray would say, 'It's some raw bullshit. I don't like it,' and I knew we were in trouble," said Davis. "But he was convinced we were gonna beat up Green Bay."

Sports Illustrated's Michael Silver spent the week following the Broncos, and he developed a rapport with Mike Shanahan, the head coach. During an off-the-record sit-down, Shanahan told the writer, "Just between you and me, we're going to win the game. With all this hype Green Bay's getting, the whole AFC inferiority thing, how Denver has played in the Super Bowl and how the Packers played against the 49ers, everybody will be stroking them. It will all work in our favor." Each morning in San Diego, Shanahan devoted 45 minutes to finding disparaging articles about his team and meticulously clipping them from the newspapers. On Saturday night, he presented the players with one derogatory story after another.

The game was slated to commence at 6:30 p.m. eastern time, on a manicured field with the air warmed to a delightful 60 degrees. Shortly before kickoff, when the teams were introduced, enormous banners featuring the likenesses of Favre and Elway were unfurled. Up in a Qualcomm Stadium luxury suite, Bonita and Irvin Favre beamed. "The two of them looked at each other and I saw pride across their faces," said Mark Kelly, a family friend. "I wish I had a camera, because it was a look of, 'All that hard work paid off.' It was beautiful."

As opposed to New Orleans, where Packers fans outnumbered Patriots fans by a solid 10:1 ratio, the divide in San Diego was fairly even. When Favre trotted out to the field for the opening series, he received a standing ovation from half the crowd. Moments later, when he beat Denver's blitz to hit Antonio Freeman with a 22-yard bullet for a touchdown, the roar was loud — but hardly volcanic. "No one said it was over on our sideline," Favre recalled, "but in the back of our minds everyone was thinking that this might be one of those 52–17 deals like Dallas and Buffalo a few years back." Five minutes later, though, Denver countered with Davis's 1-yard end zone plunge to tie the game, and an equally loud sound overtook the stands. "You could tell pretty early this wasn't going to be a repeat, where we controlled everything," said Michels. "The Broncos were a lot better than the Patriots."

Toward the end of the first quarter, Davis was leg-whipped by Santana Dotson, the Packers' enormous lineman, and slammed his head into the ground. The blow was firm and direct, and Davis knew trouble was likely. Beginning when he was seven and growing up in a small house on Florence Street in (of all places) San Diego, Davis suffered from crippling migraines that could last as briefly as an hour or as long as a few days. The first one occurred as he was waiting in a parking lot for his mother to pick him up from Pop Warner. "I was seeing things in pieces, looking at players on the field but I could no longer see them," he said. "I could barely find my way to the car, it was so bad." The headaches followed. "I wanted to kill myself," he said. "It was that bad — I actually wanted to commit suicide. And it lasted until the next morning."

On the morning of the Super Bowl, Davis had somehow forgotten to ingest Indocin, the preventative migraine medicine he used before every game, in a timely manner. "I took it right before introductions, which wasn't enough time," he said. "It didn't kick in." When a whistle marked the conclusion of the first quarter, Davis's vision went out. "I could see nothing clearly," he recalled. "Not the colorful Super Bowl XXXII banners hanging all around Qualcomm, not the Bronco trainers trying to fend off my migraine, not my teammates asking me if I was alright. All I saw was a kaleidoscope of pain."

The second quarter resumed with the Broncos sitting on the Green Bay 1-yard line. Shanahan knew Davis was living his own private hell, but begged him to return to the field for the upcoming play, a quarterback keeper after a fake handoff. "If you're not in there," Shanahan said, "they won't believe we're going to run the ball."

Davis could barely see. But he could hear. When the ball was snapped, he charged straight ahead and plunged into Green Bay's Bernardo Harris, a blob of white, green, and gold, as Elway snuck into the end zone.

Davis retreated to the sideline and vomited. In all the hype of returning home to play in his first Super Bowl, Davis spent the remainder of the half on the bench, and the Broncos entered halftime with a 17–14 lead. The pain finally cleared, and he returned for the third quarter, and promptly fumbled on his first touch. The turnover resulted in a 27-yard field goal from Green Bay's Ryan Longwell. The game was tied at 17.

The Denver defense was strong. Against the Patriots in Super Bowl XXXI, Favre enjoyed endless hours of sitting in the pocket, waiting for receivers. This time, the Broncos disguised blitzes and coverage schemes. Steve Atwater, an All-Pro safety, was unstoppable, at one point destroying Favre with a backside blitz that caused him to fumble. "We found out how good they really were," said Bob Kuberski, the Packers' defensive tackle. "They were anything but pushovers." Denver scored on a short Davis run to hold a 24–17 lead at the end of the third quarter, but Green Bay again bounced back, and Favre's 13-yard dart to Freeman in the corner of the end zone resulted in another tie. With 13 minutes remaining, fans were witnessing one of the all-time great Super Bowls.

As the game wore on, Denver's offensive linemen retreated to the sideline to report that Green Bay's defense seemed exhausted. Reggie White, the greatest pass rusher on the planet, had torn his hamstring earlier in the week, missed two days of practice, then returned to explain to his dumbfounded teammates that God had healed him. The religious Packers players found this inspiring. The others were skeptical. "I don't give a shit what he's saying," Wayne Simmons, the linebacker, said in the locker room, "God don't reattach hamstrings." He was right. By the third quarter White was a Division III lineman in No. 92 clothing, leaning and pushing with no trace of power. His stat line for the game: one tackle. The team's second-best lineman, Gilbert Brown, wasn't hurt, but also turned in a mediocre performance. "I had Gilbert [as a rookie] in Minnesota," said John Teerlinck, Denver's defensive line coach. "We let him go because he was unwilling to work. He was a lazy player. You saw it in the Super Bowl."

"He was lying down out there," said Tom Nalen, Denver's center. "We thought he was hurt, but he was just tired."

Holmgren had to place his hopes in Gabe Wilkins, a fourth-year defensive tackle whose six-foot-five, 304-pound frame made him as easy to move as a fire hydrant. The year had been a breakout one for the former Gardner-Webb standout, who recorded a career-high 50 total tackles and five and a half sacks. Wilkins, however, was in the final year of his contract and playing on a slightly injured right knee. "He changed his mentality," said Travis Jervey, the reserve running back. "I sat and watched him argue with coaches on the sideline, screaming, 'Shit! I'm not ruining my knee for this!'" Jervey couldn't believe it. He turned to a teammate and said, 'Holy shit, Gabe basically said, Fuck it. I'm not staying in.'"

"If you ask Gabe today, hopefully he's man enough to admit he didn't step up," said Kuberski. "We needed him, because we were battered and out of breath."

Shanahan recognized a wounded opponent. Denver ran 20 offensive plays over three fourth-quarter possessions. Twelve were handoffs to Terrell Davis (two were nullified because of penalties), who gained 51 yards and carried the Broncos to the Green Bay 1-yard line with the score tied and 1:47 remaining. By now, the Packers defense was a pile of slop — huffing, puffing, hands atop knees. "They were all totally exhausted," said Teerlinck. "The field was super wet, super soft, and super slow. We always substituted players to keep everyone fresh. Green Bay did not." Steve Bono, the smart backup quarterback, noticed time ticking away and the Packers down to only two time-outs. He ran to Holmgren and screamed, "Let them score! Let them score!"

On the next play, Davis took the ball from Elway and the seas parted. As he walked into the end zone, the Bronco players leapt into the air, fists pumping, screaming, hollering, exulting. "So much for the push-over AFC," said Davis. "That was put to rest." With Jason Elam's extra point, the Broncos led 31–24. There was 1:45 remaining. "Too much time to give Brett," said Chamberlain. "Way, way too much time." Favre began to warm up along the sideline, and Freeman returned the kickoff to the Packers 30.

This was the type of moment Brett Favre embraced. He wanted the ball late, with the stadium packed and the lights bright and everything on the line. On first down, he threw a screen to Dorsey Levens, who scampered 22 yards to the Broncos 48. The next play was another screen to Levens, who was immediately tackled for no gain. There was 1:11 left, and the Packers called a time-out. "I don't think anyone on our team didn't believe we were about to win the Super Bowl," said Michels. "Brett's marching us down the field, they can't really stop us." The next two passes went to Levens, who gained a combined 17 yards. It was now second and 6 from the Denver 31. The Packers needed a touchdown to tie.

Favre dropped back and fired a pass up the middle to Freeman, who dropped a catchable ball. His next throw, on third and 6, reached Robert

Brooks at the same moment Atwater bulldozed the receiver. Incomplete. A time-out was called. The clock read 32 seconds. Favre walked the cocky walk and talked the cocky talk. Inside, though, he was doubtful. "I didn't give up," he recalled. "Believe me, I wanted it worse than anything. But they had played well in those situations all day long and I didn't think it'd be any different now."

The play call arrived from the sideline — "All Hook." Derrick Mayes, the wide receiver, lined up wide left and ran a square out route. Freeman, standing in the left slot, and Brooks, wide right, ran hooks. And Mark Chmura, Favre's close friend, lined up across from John Mobley, the Broncos' excellent linebacker. "When I came to the line I could see that they were going to blitz," Favre recalled. "Which means I had to pick a side. You don't have time to look all over the field."

Of the four options, the one Favre trusted least was Mayes, whose flair for making acrobatic catches in practice was offset by an injury-ravaged body. Favre didn't have many pet peeves, but one was teammates who couldn't stay on the field. Mayes was always hurt.

This time, as Favre took the snap from Frank Winters, Mayes ran the perfect route, darting through the secondary and into the end zone, where he stood *all alone.* "Uncovered," he said. "Nobody near me." Maybe it was the hugeness of the moment, or his mistrust of Mayes, or a simple misread, but Favre failed to spot the receiver. What he did see was Chmura — tall, strong, dependable — 8 yards away. Favre threw the ball his way, and as the tight end crossed the middle he seemed in perfect position to make the catch. At the last moment, however, Mobley — running along with Chmura — stretched his arms and knocked the ball to the ground.

Game over.

The Broncos sideline turned into a New Year's Eve bash. The Packers sideline turned into a funeral procession. Mayes fell to his knees. Super Bowl glory had been one throw away. Everything would have changed had Favre found him in the rear of the end zone. "We fucking lost," Mayes said. "How? All of a sudden you hear nothing but crickets, and you feel like the lowest thing on earth."

"I played with Cleveland one season when we went 3-13. That was awful. but I'd rather go 3-13 than lose in the Super Bowl," said Holland, the defensive lineman. "It's the ultimate insult, the worst feeling you can possibly have on the earth. You're inches away, and you get nothing."

Favre met with Elway on the field, hugged and congratulated his friendly rival. "I know you feel bad and everything," Elway said. "But imagine what I've been through to get where I am right now." Favre smiled and retreated to the gloom of the locker room, where he greeted the inevitable onslaught of reporters. King let his peers ask their questions before approaching for his own one-on-one. Favre was pulling off his uniform when King reached his locker. The quarterback removed both socks, then ripped a piece of tape off his ankle and snatched a small object from the sticky side. "Here," Favre said. "Give this back to Brooke if you see her, and make sure to thank her. I'm sure it's good luck to her. It just wasn't for me."

He handed King the penny.

18

SOMETHING ABOUT

O N NOVEMBER 13, 1997, six members of the New England Patriots headed to Boston for an Everclear concert at the Paradise Rock Club. Among those in attendance were Scott Zolak, the backup quarterback, Max Lane, an offensive tackle, and Drew Bledsoe, the team's star and leader.

At the time, Bledsoe was in the running for the NFL's best — and most coveted by those seeking celebrity endorsers — quarterback. He was tall, strong, handsome, successful. "Drew had it all going for him," said Terry Glenn, a New England wide receiver. "He was the package."

Toward the end of the show, the Patriots players gathered on the rear of the stage and, one by one, took dives into a crowded mosh pit. When Bledsoe jumped, he allegedly landed atop Tameeka Messier, a 23-year-old Maynard, Massachusetts, woman who, as a result of the evening's happenings, underwent surgery on her neck and spinal column to treat various injuries. Predictably, Messier filed a lawsuit against Bledsoe and the nation's newspapers and sports radio programs had a field day.

A couple of days after the incident, Bledsoe called Bobby and Peter Farrelly, the sibling directors of two of the country's biggest comedy hits, *Dumb and Dumber* and *Kingpin*. They had recently cast Bledsoe in a small role in their upcoming film, and were scheduled to begin work in a few weeks. "I can't come and do your movie in Miami," Bledsoe said. "If they find out I did a movie after that they're going to run me out of town."

The Farrellys immediately turned to their second choice, San Francisco quarterback Steve Young. They sent him a copy of the script, and he failed to read more than a few paragraphs without laughing. There was, however, the issue of Young's faith. "That's the funniest script I've ever read," he told them. "But I cannot do it, because if I do it, it's R-rated and I know all the Mormon kids will be sneaking in and I wouldn't feel good about that."

This is how Brett Favre came to play himself (aka: Pack Man) in *There's Something About Mary.*

The Farrellys called, asked if he'd like to spend a few days in Florida filming a small role. Money was offered, but Favre requested it be donated to charity. "We had a meeting before Brett got there, and the one thing he asked for was no autograph requests," said Bradley Thomas, the producer. "So we told the 250 people on the crew not to ask Brett to sign anything." When Favre entered his trailer, he was greeted by a box filled with 100 footballs and a black Sharpie. "He signed every one," said Thomas. "I loved him from that moment. You could not have had a more likeable, fun, cool athlete fill that part."

Though he had appeared in a handful of commercials, Favre's acting debut came just a year earlier, when he played a janitor in *Reggie's Prayer,* a brutal here-and-gone film starring Reggie White as "Reggie Knox," a retired football star turned high school history teacher.* The Farrellys never inquired whether Favre could act, because, really, it didn't matter. "He was somebody the audience would like and admire," said Thomas. "That's what was most important."

Favre spent three days on set, filming what he figured would be a funny-yet-forgettable two-minute scene for a film that starred, among other A-listers, Ben Stiller, Cameron Diaz, and Matt Dillon. He uttered five pieces of dialogue ("Hi, Mary,"; "I'm in town to play the Dolphins, you dumbass"; "That's right, Mary. You know I'll always be true to you"; "Thank you"; and "God, Mary, I've missed you"), each one as wooden as dry oak, and gave the experience little thought. One line from the film, in particular, resonated. After Stiller's character exits a room to allow Favre and Diaz to resume a romantic relationship, he walks down a sidewalk, mourning his loss by hysterically crying. Diaz chases him down and assures him he's her true love. To which Stiller replies, "But what about Brett *Fahvra?*"

There's Something About Mary opened in theaters on July 15, 1998, to

---

* The film also featured Pat Morita, Roosevelt Grier, and MC Hammer. Which means, while it was poorly received and minimally viewed, it remains the finest film to ever feature Pat Morita, Roosevelt Grier, and MC Hammer.

packed houses and glowing reviews. It grossed $176 million in the United States and $369 million worldwide. Seventeen members of Favre's family drove to a theater in Gulfport, Mississippi, to see their kin on the big screen. "When Brett comes out, the people behind us are heckling that he needs to stick to football," said Brandi, his sister. "They didn't know who we were, but we were all cracking up because we knew how bad it was."

Inside the Green Bay locker room, Favre took tremendous grief over his limited acting chops. Teammates ridiculed his intonation, his stiffness. Sean Jensen, the longtime NFL writer, was there one Friday after practice when a player said to Favre, "Wow, Brett, you're pretty brutal in *Something About Mary*. It looks like you got no acting lessons."

Favre, owner of one of the game's great senses of humor, looked the teammate over. "Oh, yeah," he said, "how many movies have you sucked in?"

The cinematic breakthrough was only one nugget in an eventful few months for Favre, who skipped out on the Pro Bowl (his knee was bothering him), cooperated in an undercover autograph sting involving two men forging his signature (Rex Valenti wound up serving 60 days in prison and paying a $5,000 fine), watched Green Bay name a street Brett Favre Pass, signed on to have Treat Entertainment sell a six-and-a-half-inch Brett Favre action figure, and took batting practice with the Milwaukee Brewers. He also became part owner of Dale Jarrett's NASCAR Busch Grand National team and played some pretty bad football.

Actually, "bad" might be a stretch. But for all the magic of the past two seasons, the 1998 Packers and Favre were both merely good. His positive numbers again jumped off the page (4,212 yards, 23 touchdowns), but so did 23 interceptions and Mike Holmgren's ever-rising blood pressure. Favre slogged through the worst three-game stretch of his career, throwing back-to-back-to-back three-interception outings against the Panthers, Vikings, and Lions. There would be no fourth-straight MVP trophy. "It's a little surprising," an exasperated Holmgren said. "He's still making some great plays, but it reminds me a little of 1993, when he was trying to make *every* play." In front of the media, Holmgren mildly admonished his quarterback, urging him to stop trying to play like Superman. Behind closed doors, he was near apoplectic. What happened to the player he'd groomed?

The quarterback had his own questions about Holmgren. By now, the coach seemed somewhat checked out. At one time he loved the small quaintness of Green Bay, but after six full years it wore thin. Holmgren didn't like seeing fans standing in his driveway, photographing his home, asking for autographs every time he stopped for gas or a Pepsi. "He was quieter than he'd been in the past, not as outgoing," recalled Bob Harlan, the team president. "He'd get on the team plane and kind of be by himself. There was a different demeanor. It seemed to me that he knew it was about to end for him in Green Bay."

Holmgren and Ron Wolf no longer spoke regularly — two powerful men, two large egos, two drifting ships. Even as the Packers wrapped the season with an 11-5 mark, there was little belief inside the building that a third Super Bowl run was at hand. They were no match for the rival Vikings, who went 15-1 to take the NFC Central, and yet another first-round playoff meeting at San Francisco did not bode well. Indeed, the 49ers toppled the Packers, 30–27, on a 25-yard touchdown pass from Young to Terrell Owens with eight seconds remaining, and the string of Super Bowls came to an end.

Shortly thereafter, Holmgren agreed to an eight-year, $32-million contract to become the coach and general manager of the Seattle Seahawks. His replacement, former Eagles coach Ray Rhodes, figured to bring in his own staff, his own changes. This was presumed to be the biggest challenge Brett Favre would have to face.

People had no idea.

It is impossible to know what impact Brett Favre's problematic drinking and womanizing had on his on-field performance over the previous few years — if there was any impact at all. He was still an elite NFL quarterback, one of the game's two or three best. But by the aftermath of the 1998 season, Deanna Favre had had enough.

Following a lengthy in vitro fertilization struggle, she was pregnant for the second time and hopeful that, with another child on the way, her husband might finally behave responsibly. Yet it was not Brett's way. Deanna heard the rumors, found the scraps of paper (with numbers jotted down) in his pockets, knew the names of his preferred clubs and beverages. "I was even more depressed than I'd been when Brett was popping pills," she recalled. "At least then I hadn't been pregnant. Now, here I was, carrying the child we had worked so hard to conceive, yet Brett seemed to care more about partying with his friends than being a husband and father."

There were lies on top of lies. One weekend Brett told Deanna he was going camping. Instead, he was at a bar. He insisted there were no other women — but there were many, spread across the map. Brett's younger brother Jeff got married, and at the wedding reception Brett said to Deanna, "Don't let me drink!"

She agreed, then said, "You have to help me, too. You can't hide this stuff from me. This had to be a 50-50 deal, and you have to do your part."

A few hours later, with an exhausted and pregnant Deanna ready for bed, Brett told her he was going to drive to Biloxi with a bunch of the guests — but that he wouldn't drink. "You shouldn't go," she told him. "You know what you're going to do." He ignored her, left, and didn't return until the next morning. It was the final straw for a wounded woman. She gathered Brett's belongings, placed them in the courtyard of their house, and reached out to a divorce attorney. Brett pleaded for another chance. "If you're not going to quit drinking, you can leave," she told him. "I'm not going down that road again. I'm done. Brett, I love you to death. We have been together since we were little kids. We have been through a lot together. I was with you before you started drinking, and I want to be with you after you stop drinking. But I would like for you to be alive through this."

During the conversation, the phone rang. It was the divorce attorney. With Brett within earshot, Deanna assured him she was ready to end her marriage. She hung up and told Brett he had two choices: leave or suffer the public humiliation of a 911 call. Bus Cook, his agent, came by to pick him up. The two left the house, and Brett asked Cook not to drive him to a hotel, but to the airport.

He would be returning to the Menninger Clinic in Topeka, Kansas.

This time, the rehabilitation was not for Vicodin, but alcoholism. There would be no press conference and no brave declarations of self-improvement. The Packers told no one. It wasn't brave, it was embarrassing. He'd been through this once before, and afterward told everyone the demons were kicked. In truth, the Packers organization knew Favre had been living a lie, and did everything it could to hide their moneymaker. One writer recalled having seen Favre drinking at a bar after a game, then receiving a call later that night from a team PR person. "I heard you ran into Favre," the representative said. "You know it was nonalcoholic beer, right? It wasn't a real beer."

The label on the bottle had read MILLER.

The exact Menninger check-in date was April 1, 1999, and he traveled via chartered plane. The pilot didn't know he'd be flying the famed Brett Favre until he arrived at the airport, and even spent 20 minutes chatting with his passenger before realizing — holy crap! — that's Brett Favre. The flight was quiet and heartbreaking, with the quarterback wondering what his life had become. Upon arriving and checking back in, Favre was happy to see the familiar smile of Kerry Collins, the New Orleans Saints quarterback whose alcoholism had led to great public shame. "For the first time in a long time, I started to take a look at myself as a person," Collins said of rehab, "and tried to find out what I was all about and what was wrong, and what I needed to do for myself."

During his time back in Menninger, Favre, too, made personal discoveries. Any of the joy he gained from a night out was crushed the following morning, when he inevitably felt guilty, alone, pathetic. He thought a lot about what it meant to be a husband and a father, and also about the hell alcohol brought to his life. For all the fun, the joy, the action, and adventure, he came home to darkness and secrecy. On the football field, Favre was bravado and guts. His legendary trash-talking exchanges with Tampa Bay's Warren Sapp were catnip to NFL Films — the smaller quarterback giving it to the behemoth defensive lineman, a sly grin accompanying every insult ("You fat piece of shit . . ."). Off it, though, he was wayward. Favre knew he needed to change, what with a second child on the way (a daughter, Breleigh Ann, would be born five weeks premature — but healthy — on July 13) and a wife with one foot out the door. He was turning 30 in October; no longer the kid in the locker room. Almost all of the guys he came up with were gone. The bars remained fun, but he couldn't keep up as he once did. Favre was still the life of a party. But the parties no longer went until 2:00 a.m. Many of his friends had settled down — marriages, kids, mortgages, family vacations to theme parks. It all seemed simultaneously appealing and terrifying. He was growing up without fully committing himself to growing up. LeRoy Butler called Favre "Peter Pan" for his eternal boyishness. But, he was learning, immortality is mere myth. You grow. You change. You evolve.

So Brett Favre stopped drinking.

He was done. Kaput. Over. No more beer, no more liquor, no more wine (not that he drank much wine). He returned from Kansas after a couple of weeks determined that he would never go back to alcohol. "I don't want 15 years to go by and be looked at as a goofball bum who could still throw touchdown passes and defy the odds," he said. "And I don't want to be remembered as just being a good football player. I want to be remembered as a good family man, too. At times I haven't been that.

"In this job, guys drink beer," he told ESPN's Chris Mortensen. "The linemen go out and drink beer after the game. I went to drink beer. Yeah, I've done all those things, but [now] I can't wait to get home."

Brett Favre hasn't had a drink in 17 years.

Were there ever a season where alcohol could have come in handy, it was 1999.

Training camp commenced on July 26 with Favre still in Mississippi alongside Deanna and their new daughter. He arrived six days late, 30 pounds lighter than the previous year, and a sight for sore eyes to Rhodes and his staff.

Throughout his first few weeks, all the new-coach platitudes were applied to Rhodes. Unlike the power-hungry Holmgren, Rhodes — the first African American head coach in team history — was relaxed and refreshing and open and direct and compassionate. He would joke with players, pull youngsters aside and offer tidbits of wisdom. "He came to you like a man and would be totally honest," said Basil Mitchell, a Packers running back. "He'd lay out expectations and expect you to meet them."

Rhodes had played running back at Texas Christian and wide receiver at Tulsa, then enjoyed a solid pro career with the New York Giants and San Francisco 49ers from 1974 to 1980. Rhodes spent four years (1995–98) as the head coach in Philadelphia, and following two straight 10-6 seasons he was the most beloved man in the city. Unfortunately for Rhodes, optimism faded, two subpar seasons followed, and he was fired by the Eagles after going 3-13 in 1998. Wolf first broached his name midway through the '98 season, when Holmgren was clearly preparing to leave Wisconsin. The Packers' GM felt his team needed more toughness. Everyone who Wolf confided in believed Rhodes was the perfect man for the job. "I thought he would bring something back," said Wolf. "An attitude we sort of lost."

Maybe it would have worked. *Maybe*. In winning all four preseason contests, the Packers were a popular Super Bowl pick and a clear-cut divisional favorite. (In the Acclaim Sports' NFL Quarterback Club 2000 simulation of the season, the Packers demolished the Jets in the Super

Bowl, 47–16.) But in an August 23 exhibition game against the Broncos in Madison, Wisconsin, Favre was rolling right when — while releasing a pass — he banged his right thumb on the helmet of John Mobley, the blitzing linebacker. "I knew it was bad right away," he said later. "I was scared it was broken. It felt like someone slashed my hand with a knife."

Afterward, Favre said the injury was merely a bruise, and that nobody had to worry about him missing time. "It's all right," he insisted two days later. "Just sore." Yet his thumb wasn't merely bruised — it was mangled. Late in the season, a *Milwaukee Journal Sentinel* writer was granted a close look. He described the knuckle on his right thumb appearing to be dramatically larger than the knuckle on his left, and the area near the joint also significantly swollen. Wrote the scribe: "When Favre extended both thumbs out with his fingers clenched, he showed that he can't bend the right thumb back as far as the left one."

The malady remained a tightly kept secret. Throughout his Super Bowl appearances and multiple MVP trophies, Favre never forgot how he received his break: Don Majkowski's injury. He played with a sense of insecurity and lingering fears that, with one missed snap, his job could vanish. Favre believed himself to be the best quarterback on the planet. But that wasn't enough to survive in the NFL. He had to be the toughest, too. The Packers' backups were Matt Hasselbeck and Aaron Brooks, both young, raw, and promising.* Though never a jerk to either man, Favre hardly went out of his way to groom them. "Brett made himself pretty clear," said Brooks, a rookie out of the University of Virginia. "He was like, 'I'm gonna teach you some things, but I'm not going to teach you to take my job.' I did my learning from afar, just watching."

"Brett was not a teacher," said Hasselbeck. "I love him. He's great. And I should have been paying them money for the honor of sitting in the meeting room and hearing them talk quarterbacking. But back then it was, 'Hey, he's going to win us a Super Bowl, and you'll get a ring, too. In the meantime, shut up and listen and learn what you can.'"

Because no one knew Favre was crippled, no one cut the Packers (or Rhodes) a break when they struggled. On November 1, in a Monday-

---

* Hasselbeck (Seattle) and Brooks (New Orleans) both became Pro Bowl quarterbacks after leaving Green Bay.

night clash against Holmgren and the visiting Seahawks, Favre tied an NFL record for quarterbacks by starting his 116th straight game — a marvelous achievement dampened by a pitiful 27–7 setback that dropped Green Bay to 4-3. The Packers lost to Chicago the following week, then suffered a 27–13 beatdown at the hands of Dallas on November 14. The loss was particularly galling, in that the Cowboys were without their three injured superstars — Troy Aikman, Emmitt Smith, and Michael Irvin. Jason Garrett started at quarterback, and his controlled showing (13-of-23, 199 yards, two touchdowns) was far more pleasing to the eye than Favre's wildness and unpredictability (he completed 26 of 50 passes for one touchdown and two picks). From Favre's second season on, Packers fans came to see the playoffs as an inevitability. The team qualified for six straight years. Now, however, Green Bay was 4-5 and sinking quickly. *Sports Illustrated* even featured the team on the cover of its September 27 issue with an accompanying headline, BOTTOMS UP. Wolf, the man who considered Rhodes the solution to the franchise's fortunes, was bewildered by his coach. Where was the emotion? The passion? Mostly, where was the discipline? Many of the team's practice rituals reminded Wolf of the dreaded Lindy Infante era. Jerry Parins, the team's longtime chief of security, was hearing more and more weird things about Rhodes's behavior, so he did some investigating. "Ray was going out to the casino, and he'd stay there until 3, 4 in the morning," Parins said. "Then people would call me and say, 'Your head coach is in the casino.' Everything that year turned relaxed, and the players knew what they could get away with. I love Ray, but he lost control."

Two days after the Cowboys setback, Brandi Favre was arrested for shoplifting clothing from a Dillard's department store at the Edgewater Mall in Biloxi. It was Brett's sister's second high-profile arrest in three years, and while the two siblings weren't overwhelmingly close, the headlines (BRETT FAVRE'S SISTER CHARGED WITH SHOPLIFTING) were bountiful and humiliating. "Whenever something happened to anyone in the family, it always went back to Brett," said Bonita Favre, his mother. "It was never fair. And why should people have their lives exposed just because they might be related to a famous athlete?" Despite the distraction (Favre refused to comment to the press on his sister), Favre led the Packers to three straight wins (over the Lions, 49ers, and Bears), and on December 12 they faced the Panthers at Lambeau. With a win, the 7-5

Packers would close in on a playoff spot and continue to fight Tampa Bay and Minnesota for the NFC Central title. Lowly Carolina was not merely 5-7, but a warm-weather team. The temperature in Lambeau was expected to hit 35 degrees by the one o'clock kickoff. This was thought to be a pretty clear triumph.

The teams battled back and forth, with Green Bay's porous defense allowing Steve Beuerlein to complete 29 of 42 passes for 373 yards and three touchdowns. "Some of their guys were so wide open, you could almost underhand them the ball." said Butler, the safety. "It's beyond me how we could play this bad at home." Though far from perfect, Favre was solid, hitting on 26 of 38 attempts for 302 yards, two touchdowns, and an interception. His arm was as strong as ever, his accuracy sharp. "That's the amazing thing," said Hasselbeck. "Even with a thumb that most guys don't play with, he was special."

With four minutes remaining in the final quarter, Green Bay fullback William Henderson plunged into the end zone from a yard away, putting the Packers in the lead, 31–27. The Panthers immediately marched back down the field, and with 45 seconds to play, Beuerlein hit tight end Wesley Walls with a pass that brought the team to the Packers 5. It was now fourth down, and the clock was ticking . . . ticking . . . ticking. Green Bay held three time-outs, and as the time continued to dwindle Favre screamed for Rhodes to use one. "What are we doing?" he yelled. "What are we doing?" On the game's final play, the plodding Beuerlein somehow charged through the middle and into the end zone. A silent crowd of 59,869 sat in disbelief as the Panthers celebrated a 33–31 victory. Green Bay had dropped an unfathomable three of four home games, and afterward a morose Rhodes admitted his mistake. "I'm miffed at myself about it," he said. "I don't know how much time I could have left our offense, but I was hoping to at least leave them something, and I didn't get that part done."

In the days that followed, Favre and his teammates spoke of a broken organization, and Wolf steeled himself to make yet another coaching change. It was an awkward and uncomfortable thing — firing the first African American coach after a sliver of a chance, with a marred quarterback and an aged roster — but Wolf felt he had little choice. "It didn't work," he said. "Sometimes you just accept that you made a bad choice and correct it."

Favre's statistics (22 touchdowns, 23 interceptions, 4,091 yards) were some of the worst of his career as a starter, and questions arose as to whether he was about to slip into inevitable decline. He was 30, hurt, and despondent. His quarterback rating was 74.7, ranking him 25th in the NFL.

Life wasn't a movie, after all.

19

CHEWED UP

O N APRIL 9, 2000, in the aftermath of the Waukesha Catholic Memorial High School senior prom, Jamie Gessert held a party at her house at 1809 East Bristlecone Drive in Hartland, Wisconsin.

On the surface, this was no different than the hundreds of other postprom bashes that take place across the United States. A bunch of kids, laughter, some food, some alcohol, drinking games, hooking up.

The Gesserts lived in an affluent Milwaukee neighborhood, filled with large brick houses and $70,000 vehicles and adorned with elaborate walkways and swimming pools. Jamie's father, Robert Gessert, was the successful 43-year-old owner of a Milwaukee medical marketing firm, and earlier in the evening he and his wife allegedly went out to dinner with their neighbors — a woman named Lynda and her husband, Packers tight end Mark Chmura.

The party had been largely unattended by adults. Then, at approximately 3:30 in the morning, Chmura arrived. He later explained he thought it would be "nice" to surprise the high schoolers (many of whom played football) with a pop-in. He was surrounded by the teens, who clamored for autographs and pictures, and tried impressing the attendees by prank-calling his Packers teammates. According to a complaint later filed, Chmura lathered in the adulation, then called out, "You call this a party? Where's the alcohol?" The high schoolers, according to the complaint, exposed glasses of liquid they had been purposefully hiding. Chmura allegedly kicked off a game called, "the drinking Ping-Pong," whereby the loser chugs after a missed point. The complaint stated that he appeared to be "really drunk."

At 4:30 a.m., Robert Gessert announced, according to the complaint, that it was "hot-tub time," and when several of the young women said they lacked swimsuits, he replied by saying, "No problem" — underwear would be perfectly fine. A handful of the females entered the tub, one of whom had worked as a babysitter for the Chmuras' two children. When, according to the complaint, a teen started to vomit, the hot tub cleared out.

According to the babysitter, who was 17, this is when Chmura lured her into a bathroom, locked the door, removed her jeans and underwear, and forced her into sexual intercourse.

The following day, after the teen and her mother contacted local police, both Chmura and Gessert were arrested at their homes and held in Waukesha County Jail for 12 hours before posting $5,000 bail. Chmura issued a statement insisting he was "not guilty," and looked forward to the day "when the public hears the rest of the story."

Less than two months later, he was released by the Packers.

When the news of Chmura's alleged rape broke, the dialogue among many who knew Favre well went thusly . . .

Thought: Was Brett there?

Reply: No.

Thought: Brett *could* have been there.

Reply: Yup.

Much like Favre, Chmura's image didn't fully match reality. In the unabashedly conservative Brown County (which included Green Bay, De Pere, as well as 22 towns and villages), he had been held in high esteem ever since, after the Super Bowl XXXI title, he refused to accompany the Packers on the requisite White House visit because he objected to President Bill Clinton's affair with Monica Lewinsky. Chmura was a vocal supporter of Republican Bob Dole's 1996 presidential run, was staunchly pro-life, and once told *The Compass*, the newspaper of the Catholic Diocese of Green Bay, "Today's society puts athletes on a pedestal whether we want it or not. I would not want my kids to grow up to be like Dennis Rodman or Charles Barkley."

Meanwhile, Chmura, Favre, and Frank Winters were three of the state's most prominent night lifers — drinking, dancing, partying their way from Green Bay to Milwaukee to Madison. They exercised questionable judgment, relying on the passions of Packers loyalists not to talk about seeing them out and doing . . . everything. Anything. Could Favre have been the one at the prom party, engaging inappropriately with a slew of teenagers? Saying things he shouldn't have said? Doing what many referred to as "dumb shit"? It wasn't hard to imagine. Like Favre, Chmura was known to embrace the action and, according to the *New York Daily News,* "made it no secret that he liked young, pretty women."

"Mark was the most selective of the three, but when they went out it was to screw," said a friend of the three men. "There wasn't any ambiguity about it."

That's why, as Deanna Favre fought to have her husband distance himself from his alcoholic, playboy ways, she urged him to shed friends like Chmura. Which he did—beginning with the arrest. In the days and weeks after Chmura's name had been dragged through the dirt and ridiculed by the nation's newspaper columnists and talk show hosts, a long line of former teammates and coaches called to offer encouragement and support. It was the lowest span of his life. Chmura was out of work, out of career options, the target of headline writers' cruel jokes. For 10 months, through rumors, jury selection, sparring among lawyers in the newspapers, and, ultimately, a trial that resulted with all charges of third-degree sexual assault and child enticement being dropped, Chmura waited for the call from Brett Favre that never came.

"He's a selfish guy," Chmura said years later. "He's a very selfish guy. And what people don't know, I'm not going to say this to throw the guy under the bus, but this is a guy from my arrest to my acquittal never called me one time."

"I'm trying to give him space," Favre explained when asked. "I can't imagine what he's going through. Several of the guys have called. When the time's right, I will try to call him."

He did not.

It was an awful way to begin a fresh season, one that brought the hope of yet another new head coach (Mike Sherman, who had been the team's tight ends coach from 1997–98, then spent 1999 as the Seattle offensive coordinator under Mike Holmgren), yet felt suffocated by a pronounced darkness. On July 30, on the same day it was announced that Brett Favre's Steakhouse would be closing its doors in Milwaukee because of dwindling business (Favre was a co-owner), a man entered the eatery, threatened employees with a knife, and ran off with several hundred dollars. A couple of weeks after that, Favre reported to camp. Usually, even if he were not in the mood to report, he put on a good face, a boyish smile, and regaled the media with stories of Mississippi summers. Not this time. "Football is a job [now], and it wasn't always like that," he said. "I knew it was a business, but it's a lot of work now. I still enjoy it, and I wouldn't want to do anything else, but it's not like it used to be."

Aside from Chmura's downfall and the demise of his restaurant and the still relatively new (and not particularly easy to maintain) sobriety, Favre had reason for moodiness. Though he was happy to see Rhodes leave, the hiring of Sherman was hardly a birthday present. Green Bay's new coach made clear from early on that his quarterback needed to change. Along with Tom Rossley, the new offensive coordinator, Sherman dedicated himself to adjusting Favre's approach. It had now been two straight seasons of high interception totals, and the videos told the story of a man throwing blindfolded off the wrong foot with a gambler's sense of risk. Specifically, the coaches wanted Favre to alter his decision-making process, to read plays more deliberately and freelance less.

This was, to a quarterback who prided himself upon thinking things up on the fly, sour milk.

"If the quarterback doesn't believe in what you're doing, it's a struggle," said Trent Miles, an offensive quality-control assistant in 2000. "You have to be on the same page, speak the same language. Otherwise, it's hard."

The truth is, opposing defenses felt as if they were beginning to figure Brett Favre out. It started in the weeks leading up to Super Bowl XXXII, when John Teerlinck, the Broncos' defensive line coach, presented his players with a PhD-level course on destroying Brett Favre. A onetime San Diego Chargers defensive lineman, Teerlinck had been coaching in the NFL since 1989. His two obsessions were trash talk and quarterback annihilation. Along the sidelines, Teerlinck — a mountainous man with short brown hair and a vocabulary dominated by "shits" and "fucks" — took pride in barking, screaming, cursing at the opposing team's signal callers. In the lead-up to a game against the Los Angeles Rams in 1992, Teerlinck (at the time Minnesota's defensive line coach) walked up to Jim Everett, the opposing quarterback, and hollered, "You better tell Mike Pagel [the Rams backup] to be ready, because you're not gonna finish this game! We're gonna knock your ass out!"

"Hey, screw you," Everett replied.

"OK, Jim," Teerlinck replied. "Just be careful along our sideline."

In the second quarter, Everett ran out of bounds and into a sea of Vikings. "Hey, Jim, I'm right here!" Teerlinck screamed. "You fucking pussy!

I'm right here!" Everett fired the football at Teerlinck's face, splitting open his chin and receiving a 15-yard unsportsmanlike conduct penalty. Teerlinck, blood everywhere, sneered giddily. "I hated Everett," he said. "He had no guts."

Teerlinck did not hate Brett Favre. In many regards, he loved him. The coach would sling trash toward the Packers quarterback, and be greeted either with a laugh, a smile, or some version of "You still talking, you fat fuck?" To Teerlinck, Favre was everything a team wanted in a leader. "You couldn't rattle him," he said. "He was so damn good. Usually we were figuring out how to rattle players. But it didn't work. You hit him and he got up. Hit him again, he got up even faster. He was what I like to call a wild horse rider. They'd make a mistake, but to hell with it — the next play they'd bounce right back."

If Favre was the NFL's Moby Dick, Teerlinck was Captain Ahab. Before the Super Bowl, Teerlinck spent his days and nights charting every Favre game tape he could uncover. "I had 523 passes of his on one VHS tape," he said. His binder was stuffed with charts, diagrams, notes, reminders. Some of the things he highlighted:

- **Favre doesn't have a quick release:** "Teams thought he did, because he threw so fucking hard," Teerlinck said. "But he didn't. So don't think the ball is out of his hand as soon as he cocks his arm. Go after him."
- **Be alert on the hard count:** "He hard-counted mainly on first down, and he did it really well," Teerlinck said. "Don't jump on first down."
- **When under pressure, Favre relies on the stiff arm more than any other quarterback in the league:** "So when you go for the tackle, aim low," Teerlinck said. "I'm not saying you hit his knees, but I'm saying he's strong enough to push you away from his arm. So take out the legs."
- **Dick, Balls, Muff:** "Every quarterback in the league had language they used for the snap," he said. "[San Francisco's] Elvis Grbac was 'Gilligan, Skipper, Thurston,' [Buffalo's] Jim Kelly was 'Oscar, Noah, Preakness.' Brett was unique. If he screamed, 'Dick! Dick!' the snap was on one. 'Balls!' was on two, 'Muff!' on three. He was a different kind of guy."
- **Steer Favre toward Zone No. 3:** "We organized the pocket in four zones," Teerlinck said. "Left, middle, middle, center. If you could

keep Brett in the third zone, right center, and get some pressure on him, he forced a lot of balls, made a ton of mistakes. So you don't just rush him, you rush him and corner him."

- **Ignore the Green Bay running game:** "Insignificant," he said. "Not very good, not very imaginative. You stop Brett, you win. So let them run, hope they run."

- **Brett Favre will never give up on a play:** "It's a quality, but also a curse," Teerlinck said. "He made some amazing, improbable throws, but he also forced stuff. So you have to make sure — make 100 percent certain — your defensive backs never stop coverage. Even if it looks like Brett's down. Even if he *is* down. Don't stop covering. Because a lot of times he'd throw it, and if you're there you have a 50-50 chance of intercepting."

The short-term result of Teerlinck's Super Bowl preparation was Denver's first championship. The long-term result was mass copycatting. The tape of Bronco pass rushers harassing Favre became must-see material, as did the vision of Denver cornerbacks glued to the receivers until the blowing of a whistle. "You can't master Brett Favre," said Teerlinck. "But if you do everything right, you might be able to frustrate the hell out of him."

Sherman saw much of what Teerlinck saw — a quarterback slow to adjust to a league adjusting to a quarterback. "You can't argue that Brett did lots of stupid stuff," said Bob Slowik, the Packers' defensive backs coach. "A hook-shot throw, a behind-the-back throw. Mike wanted to rein that in." Sherman tried to impress upon Favre the importance of poise, of patience. He never called his quarterback out in front of teammates, but one-on-one urged better judgment. The coach was neither warm nor fuzzy. Directness trumped empathy. "He would really challenge guys to step up," said Josh Bidwell, the Packers punter. "He had a way of getting to you, in a good way. You wanted to succeed for him."

"People thought Mike came in and let Brett do whatever he wanted," said LeRoy Butler. "That's bullshit. Mike had high standards."

Much like the Ray Rhodes Packers, the Mike Sherman Packers were sloppy, disorganized, subpar. They opened with losses to the Jets and Bills, followed by winning two of three before coming to Detroit for an October 8 game against the perennially mediocre Lions. By late in the third quarter Detroit was ahead 31–9, and Favre threw three interceptions and fumbled twice, noting afterward, with a hapless sigh, "It may be like this all year. Who knows?" Much of the blame fell upon tackles Mike Wahle and Mark Tauscher, who allowed Detroit's standout defensive ends, Tracy Scoggins and Robert Porcher, to repeatedly hit Favre. But the quarterback seemed befuddled, confused. The Lions followed the Denver game plan to a tee, and it worked. Favre had two fourth-quarter touchdown throws to cut the score to 31–24, but with 1:37 remaining tossed a perfect pass to Lions safety Kurt Schulz. Wrote Mitch Albom in the *Detroit Free Press:* "Because I like Brett Favre, as a guy and as a quarterback, I almost felt bad for him at the end of Sunday's game, surrounded by Lions, looking desperately downfield, forcing a bad pass and watching it land in the arms of the wrong guy to choke a would-be miracle. Well, I said 'almost.' In the end, I choose to feel about Favre's fate the way I did about eating crocodile down in Australia: It's payback. Eat or be eaten."

Favre never fully took to Sherman's plan, but — even as a year of hope turned ugly — he maintained his sense of humor. Late in the season, with the playoffs a longshot and morale low, the Packers traveled to Minnesota to battle the Vikings at the Metrodome. In the week leading up to the game, Darrell Bevell, the quarterbacks coach, impressed upon Favre the importance of ball control and limited turnovers. "During the quarterback meetings Brett would chew tobacco," said Danny Wuerffel, the former Heisman Trophy winner who spent the season as the third-stringer behind Favre and Matt Hasselbeck. "He always asked me if I wanted some, and I never took him up on it." Before kickoff Wuerffel told Favre, "If you throw more touchdowns than interceptions, I'll dip with you Monday."

Favre cackled, and even told members of the media about the deal. "So the game's going on," said Wuerffel, "and they talk about Danny Wuerffel possibly dipping tobacco." His wife, Jessica, was watching at home. "I had a lot to answer for," he said. The Packers won, 33–28, and Favre passed for three touchdowns . . . and no interceptions.

"I dipped," Wuerffel said. "Brett loved it."

Green Bay finished 9-7 and missed the playoffs for the second straight season, and much blame went to Favre. His interceptions fell to 16, but his touchdown passes also dropped, to a mere 20. Along with the sophistication of opposing defenses, some of the statistical passing decline had to do with the emergence of Ahman Green, the third-year halfback who compiled 1,175 rushing yards and 13 total touchdowns. It hardly helped that his wide receiver corps was, by NFL standards, subpar. "He played with a bunch of No. 2 and No. 3 wideouts," said Teerlinck. "He fooled people into thinking they were better than they actually were."

What went unspoken (and, for many, unknown) was that, yet again, Favre was playing when other men would have sat. In the third quarter of the November 12 game at Tampa Bay, he was plowed into the turf by Warren Sapp, the powerful defensive tackle. Favre's left ankle made a crunching sound, and both tackler and victim presumed it to be broken. He was replaced by Hasselbeck, and everyone on the Green Bay staff figured he would miss at least one Sunday, and perhaps the remainder of the season. So much for his consecutive-start streak, now at 135 games. So much for indestructability. So much for . . .

He started the next week against Indianapolis.

"His ankle was red and blue," said Frank Novak, the special teams coach. "On the plane the team doctor told us not to count on him that week. OK, so Hasselbeck takes snaps with the first team. On Wednesday, Brett jogged out to the field, moved Hasselbeck out of the huddle, and took the snaps." For the new staff, it was Jesus walking across water. Name an NFL quarterback — any NFL quarterback — and he would not have even *attempted* such a return. Jeff Garcia of the 49ers? No way. Troy Aikman in Dallas? Unlikely. The Vikings' Daunte Culpepper? The Redskins' Brad Johnson? The Rams' Kurt Warner? No, no, no. Favre was no longer using Vicodin, so the pain that once vanished beneath a large dosage of pills lingered for hours, days, weeks. But he was forever his father's son — the kid who wasn't allowed to cry or moan or lie on the ground after absorbing a big hit. You got up and played. You *always* got up and played. This was not merely a self-expectation. Favre demanded ruggedness from others. Novak fondly recalled a game against the Broncos when Bill Romanowski, the famously dirty and vocal linebacker, took a bad hit and struggled to rise off the field. "Brett's screaming at him — 'Hey, you big pussy! Stay in the fucking game! What kind of leader are you!'" Novak said. "I mean, sweet Jesus, he was tough.

"People didn't get it that year. We were not a very good team. We were in transition. They blamed Brett. Blame Brett? He was the only reason we were able to go 9-7. Without him, we win five, maybe six.

"He was everything to us."

20
BIG IRV

ALTHOUGH MIKE SHERMAN'S debut as the Green Bay head coach was a disappointment, his next two years — back-to-back 12-4 seasons — restored glory to the franchise.

This was wonderful for Brett Favre.

This was even more wonderful for Irv Favre.

From the time his son debuted with the Packers in 1992, Big Irv was a regular presence around the team. Much of this was due to Mark Kelly, a Pewaukee, Wisconsin–based financial consultant and die-hard Green Bay fan. One time, early in Brett's career, Kelly found himself alone at the lobby bar of the Packers' team hotel. He turned to a man sitting nearby to ask, "Hey, what are you doing here?"

"My son plays for the Packers," he replied.

"Well," replied Kelly, "who's your son?"

"Brett Favre," Irv said. "The quarterback."

They talked for a bit, parted ways, but ran into one another at various games. Phone numbers were exchanged, and before the 1995 season Kelly called to ask if he would be seeing Irv at the opener — Rams vs. Packers at Lambeau Field. "Nah," said Irv. "I don't have enough money for the airfare."

"You don't have enough money?" Kelly said. "Isn't Brett your son?"

Irv explained that he hated asking for favors or handouts. The next day, Kelly called again. He had accumulated thousands of frequent-flier miles and wanted to fly Irv and Bonita from Mississippi to Wisconsin for the game. That Sunday, Kelly's cell phone rang as he was driving to the stadium.

"Hey, it's Irv. Where are you gonna be watching from?"

"From my seats," he said. "That's what people do."

Irv wouldn't have it. "I talked to Brett, and you're gonna watch the game from the suite with us," he said. "I insist."

From that day forward, Irv Favre and Mark Kelly were inseparable. Kelly would pick Irv up at Milwaukee's General Mitchell International Airport on a Saturday afternoon and take him to Brett Favre's Steakhouse. They'd eat and drink for hours, then Kelly drove Irv to his son's home in Green Bay. The next morning Irv and Kelly would join Brett at the Packers' team chapel service and drive with him to the stadium. "We'd enter where the players enter, go up the elevator, go to our suite," Kelly said. "I like to think Irv was my best friend, and he was mine."

Many of the players' parents attended games. None were Irv Favre. First, he was easily recognizable, what with his large head, his gruff voice, his flattop, his guffaw, his swagger. Second, he went places others weren't allowed. He was the only father to spend considerable time inside the Packers' locker room, the only parent all the players knew by name. Third, he became a celebrity, not nearly as famous as his son, but far more recognizable than, say, Tyrone Davis or Tony Fisher. He did local commercials, and signed an endorsement deal with Ticket King, a ticket brokerage firm in Milwaukee. "Irv was everywhere," wrote Les Carpenter of the *Seattle Times*. "Irv was at the Packers' bus when it arrived at games, his No. 4 jersey stretching wide across the waist. Irv was at the hotels, in the hallways, outside pregame dinners. When Green Bay got Brett Favre, it got his father, too." As the years passed, Irv Favre spent an increased amount of time in Green Bay during the season. Sometimes Bonita would come, sometimes she wouldn't. He would often stay at the Hilton, just down the block from Lambeau, and if one wanted to meet him, to hear stories and down beers, all they had to do was wander from one Green Bay bar to the other. If Irv wasn't at the Stadium View, he was at the Sideline Sports Bar. Or the local Brett Favre's Steakhouse. Or wherever the drinks were cold and the audiences large. "Irv liked his Budweiser," said Jerry Watson, the Stadium View owner. "He would be here any time, day or night. He loved being Irv Favre. But what he really loved was being Brett Favre's father."

When Irv Favre entered a bar or restaurant, he made it clear to anyone within earshot that his son was — *oh, you might have heard of him* — Brett Favre. He held court, counted the attendees, answered question after question with a child's enthusiasm, be it asked the first time or the

10,000th time. "He lathered it in," said Maggie Mahoney, the manager of Brett Favre's Steakhouse. "Fans wanted access to Brett. His dad was access." Irv also wanted you to buy him a beer. Or 12. Bottle, please. "Irv sold a lot of Budweiser for me," said Watson. "But he wasn't paying for it." Back in 1997, 11 months after the Packers won Super Bowl XXXI, Irv called Kelly on Christmas morning, his voice overcome by glee. "You're never gonna guess what Brett got me as a present," he said. "It's a real Super Bowl ring, just like the players have!" On the inner portion of the ring Brett had THANKS DAD engraved. Irv Favre wore the diamond-encrusted jewelry piece like a peacock wears its feathers. For years, he had been a big fish in a small pond—Mississippi high school coach and teacher. Ho-hum. Now, he was important. Mark and Irv liked the hamburgers and French fries at the Penguin Drive-In in Manitowoc, Wisconsin, and stopped there often. One time the friends were sitting at the counter when Mark spotted two men staring at Irv's ring and chatting amongst themselves. Finally . . .

That's a nice ring.

"Thanks," Irv said.

Is it a Super Bowl ring?

"Aw, yeah," Irv said. "It is."

Did you play?

"No, my son plays."

Cool. Who's your son?

"Brett Favre, the quarterback."

WHAT!?!? Your son is . . .

"He tried appearing modest, and he was always friendly," said Kelly. "But Irv definitely lived his life through Brett. I remember another time we were somewhere, about to leave, kind of bored, and the person on the PA said, 'We want to welcome Brett Favre's father, who is here with us today!' Irv looked at me, kind of smiled and said, 'Maybe we should stay . . .'"

In 1999, Bill Michaels, a Cincinnati-based radio personality, was hired by Milwaukee's WTMJ to come to Wisconsin and handle the pre- and postgame Packer shows for the station. He had never been to Green Bay, and didn't fully appreciate the fierce protectionism of the fan base until, during an early broadcast, he mildly criticized Brett Favre. The reaction was intense: *Who the hell was this outsider to rip No. 4? What did he know? Go back to Cincinnati!* To Michaels's surprise, the Packer loyalist who had no problem with the take was Irv. "He never was one who would pick and choose words," said Michaels. "If Brett threw a bad pass he'd say, 'That pass sucked. He shouldn't have thrown it.' There was no agenda. He didn't care what people would think, or even what Brett thought."

Michaels's on-air partner was Brian Noble, the former Green Bay linebacker, and one day he invited Irv to sit in on a segment during the postgame show. He was funny, folksy, smart. "He pulled no punches," Michaels said. "People ate it up."

Irv was asked to return for the next home game and, again, it went over magnificently. He soon became a regular, and in 2001 was formally named a cohost for the postgame show. For nearly three seasons he brought a unique perspective to broadcasts. Sometimes he said things that irritated the Packers and/or his son ("Nobody in that locker room wants Cris Carter," he suggested when there was talk of adding the wide receiver), oftentimes he was insightful, relying upon the knowledge gleaned from decades on a sideline. He was always either tipsy or fully intoxicated. "Irv loved Budweiser, but Lambeau Field served Miller," said Michaels. "So he would have Budweiser brought in, and he would have a couple. And if the game was going bad he would have more than a couple."

The radio station enforced some rules. First, Irv could not start drinking until the second half. Second, Irv was not allowed to place his beer bottles on the table, which was visible to those passing by. The station forked over the $5 to buy Irv an enormous coffee mug, into which he would pour his beer. "We had a girl named Paula who worked for us for years, and she was our server," said Michaels. "She always knew what we drank—she got me Sprite, Brian tea or water, and Irv his mug of beer." One season, close to Christmas, Paula traveled to see family, and a temporary assistant filled in. "I heard everyone gets a drink!" she said to the hosts, then handed off the Sprite, the tea, the mug.

The countdown to the show began. The intro music started to play. The engineer shouted, "Mics are hot!" Michaels spoke—"Good evening. The Green Bay Packers got a win . . ."

"Who put this goddamn coffee in my coffee!" Irv shouted.

"The whole broadcast stopped," said Michaels. "Everyone in the live audience is looking at Irv. He's smiling. Brian has just lost it—he's cracking up. I'm cracking up."

"I swear to God, every time he was on the radio he was hammered from a day of drinking," said Rob Reischel of the *Milwaukee Journal Sentinel*. "He'd slam Brett and it'd be so funny."

The 2001 and 2002 Packers were Irv Favre's glory years. His son was the rejuvenated hero, back from the near-dead and throwing the deep ball better than anyone in the league. He tossed 32 touchdowns in 2001, another 27 in 2002, and led his team to the playoffs both seasons. Some of what Sherman said sunk in — he was making smarter decisions, willing to let a play go. Some of it was an improved cast of characters — Donald Driver, a seventh-round draft pick out of Alcorn State in 1999, emerged as a legitimate No. 1 target; Ahman Green continued to slice through defenses; Bubba Franks was a top-tier tight end. Much of it was simply an elite quarterback playing great football.

The better his son played, the bigger Irv Favre became. When the postgame show wrapped, he would sign autographs by the dozens. Often fans waited to share a moment of his time. To offer a word. To pick his brain. A persona was created, and Wisconsin bought in: Irv Favre, the lovable lug with the heart of gold. Irv Favre, the good ol' Mississippi boy who created a football legend. Irv Favre, the man Brett Favre was fortunate enough to call Dad. Everyone could use a father like Big Irv, gruff yet supportive, quirky yet indispensible.

It was true, too. Some of it. Sort of. Irvin Favre was, indeed, a lug from Mississippi, and Kelly vividly recalled the quarterback and his father engaging in vicious fart battles during long drives. "Two funny, cool guys," Kelly said. "They didn't take themselves too seriously." But, as is the case with most people, a complexity lingered beneath the surface. The son was the father and the father was the son. Though Irv was never diagnosed as an alcoholic, he was an unrepentant drinker whose dependence on alcohol went far beyond the occasional beer. Stories abound of an intoxicated Irv Favre falling asleep with his head slumped atop a wood bar; of him saying inappropriate things, *doing* inappropriate things. This, too, was a commonality between Green Bay's two favorite Favres. While Irv passed himself off as cuddly, he was a prolific womanizer who, by the time Brett reached NFL stardom, treated his marriage to Bonita as much mutual living arrangement as a bond forged by commitment. His children respected their father, but bristled at the way their mother (a remarkable woman who held the family together during hard times) was treated as a side dish. To Irv, young women weren't merely young women. They were *sweetie, honey, sugar, babe.* And they were potential (though, with his age and looks, unlikely) sexual partners. "He was a pinch-the-ass type, absolutely," said Mahoney. "One time he was at the bar and these two girls were hanging all over him — 'Oh, that's Brett's dad!' And Bonita was four stools down from him and Brandi was sitting next to Bonita. And Irv had plenty to drink and he said to one of the girls, 'Think you can give me a blowjob?' The girls giggled and Brandi piped in and said, 'Daddy, Mommy's *right* here!' I don't think Bonita gave a shit. She just looked the other way, like, 'I don't care.'"

A waitress at one of the more popular Green Bay bars recalled the evening Irv offered her $100 for sex. When she declined, he upped the ante to $200. "He tried to pay me off, right there," she said. "I said, 'Do I have w-h-o-r-e written across my forehead?'"

One time, when the Packers played in San Francisco, Irv was in Brett's hotel room when the phone rang. His son had stepped out, so Irv answered. A young woman was on the line, searching for the quarterback. "This is his daddy," Irv said. "I taught him everything he knows. You bring that sweet little pussy over to the apartment and I'll fuck it real good."

She showed up later, clad in leather — looking for Brett.

"I think Irv hit on women because he was aging a bit and looking for acceptance," Kelly said. "We'd drive, and Irv would say, 'When women get older they don't want it anymore.' That was a disappointment to him, and it probably led him to straying."

Irv's father, Alvin Favre, hadn't been faithful to his wife, and his father's father probably hadn't been faithful to his wife. Infidelity seemed to come naturally to Favre men. Brett's came accompanied by guilt. Irv's generally did not. "Love was a complicated thing with Irv," said Kelly. "He never received affection from his dad, and he didn't give much affection to his kids."

Brett Favre's two favorite nonfootball activities were hunting and golfing. Though each endeavor used its own unique instruments, both brought him a similar peace of mind.

Favre began hunting as a boy in Mississippi, using a pellet gun to shoot squirrels, rabbits, birds. On occasion, he and his pals would saunter around the property, aiming at stray dogs and cats. This sounds cruel. And, truly, it is cruel. But it was also what one did in rural Mississippi, between the ages of 8 and 15. "The boys all had BB guns," said Bonita

Favre. "I can't tell you how many daisies I bought over the years that'd get shot up." As Brett grew in stature, he acquired more equipment and more friends who liked to traverse the woods. What Green Bay lacked in nightlife it made up for with nearby hunting options. Favre and his pals traveled near and far, often at the invite of Packer die-hards eager to host the great quarterback. Because fame is magnetic and fame plus success plus charisma is übermagnetic, Favre was feted with free rifles, free gear, free lodging. A hunting TV show once offered Favre $450,000 to go on three expeditions. He declined. "I used to take Brett on the Menominee Indian reservation about 55 miles from Green Bay, just so he could shoot buck," said Jerry Parins, the team's longtime head of security. "He'd use a bow and arrow, and was always looking for that trophy deer. I'm sure we broke some reservation rules about hunting, but you know what was special? The following Tuesday, on the team's day off, we'd drive back up to the reservation and he'd go to the school and they'd have an assembly and Brett would go in, talk to the kids, touch them, hand out stuff."

Unlike hunting, Favre's devotion to golf came after he arrived in Green Bay and, in particular, after he returned from his first stint at Menninger. "He really needed an outlet to pass the time when he got out of that," said Ryan Longwell, the Packers kicker. "Brett and I would play once or twice a week during the season." He advanced from duffer to a near-scratch golfer, and went through a stretch of devoting all of his free time to hitting small white balls into slightly larger holes. The golf course became his refuge.

That's why, on the late afternoon of Sunday, December 21, 2003, Brett Favre found himself on the greens of the golf course near the Packers' hotel in Berkeley, California. He, along with Longwell, backup quarterback Doug Pederson, and punter Josh Bidwell, was getting in a quick nine holes the day before Green Bay would meet Oakland on *Monday Night Football*. "There was no one else around," Longwell said. "It was just the four of us."

Because he is the type of man who forgets his wallet and loses his keys, Favre did not have his cell phone with him. Pederson, however, did, and when it rang he was surprised to hear the voice of Deanna Favre.

"Hey Doug, it's Deanna," she said. "Is Brett with you?"

"He's nearby," he said. "Is everything OK?"

"No," she said. "Not really."

Ever since arriving as a little-known journeyman free agent before the 1996 season, Pederson had shared a bond with Favre over quarter-backing, hunting, Southern sensibilities. He starred at Northeast Louisiana, a Division I-AA powerhouse, then bounced around from the World League of American Football to NFL training camps before landing in Wisconsin. He was the perfect backup for the territorial Favre — good enough to fill in, but lacking the skill set to ever be considered a genuine threat.

Deanna told Pederson the worst news imaginable: earlier that day, Irv Favre, age 58, had died.

"What?"

"Brett's father is dead."

The backup quarterback — face ashen — handed the phone to his friend.

"Brett, honey . . ."

The shock arrived first, followed by the sobbing and pained breaths. "It was crushing," said Longwell. The toughest man anyone knew had lost the toughest man anyone knew. The sun was shining, the temperature was in the high 60s. There was not a cloud in the sky. On the following day his team (8-6 and in the thick of the playoff race) would be playing the biggest game of the season on national television. It was the stuff Brett Favre *lived* for. Silencing a riotous stadium. Picking apart an eager secondary. Jogging off the field, finger pointed skyward. Glory.

And now — heartbreak. Brett asked Deanna to fly to California, then he put Pederson back on the line with his wife. "Please comfort him and pray for him," Deanna said, "while I try and find a flight out there."

The details of what happened trickled in. At approximately 5:23 p.m., while driving his pickup truck along Highway 603 near Kiln, Irv Favre swerved off the road and into a ditch. A woman named Leslie Stevens was directly behind him in her vehicle. She saw the accident, pulled to the side, and rushed toward the scene. "I got out to see who it was, and I recognized him as being Brett's daddy," said Stevens, who worked at an area motel. "He had a pulse, he was breathing. But he wasn't talking." Others joined her, and someone called 911. Irv was rushed to Hancock Medical Center.

He was pronounced dead at 6:15 p.m. The cause wasn't the automobile impact, but a heart attack he suffered while driving. "The news was so shocking that at first it didn't register," Deanna recalled. "Brett's dad was only 58 — way too young to die. It just didn't seem right."

Over the course of her 38-year marriage, Bonita repeatedly implored Irv to take better care of himself, to eat healthier, to have regular check-ups. Both Irv and Bonita were pack-a-day cigarette smokers, and Irv's diet often seemed to consist of anything layered in grease topped with more grease. Following the autopsy, a doctor told Bonita that Irv had suf-fered a pair of previous heart attacks over the past two years, but — he said — "your husband blew us off."

When the Associated Press story hit the wires, the reaction was quick and predictable. Across Wisconsin and Mississippi, there were outpour-ings of affection, of loss, of compassion. Columnists and analysts lined up to pay homage to a person who served as a model father and hus-band. Wrote Thomas Rozwadowski in the *Green Bay Press-Gazette*: "If you spent 10 minutes with Irvin Favre, you might as well have known him for 10 years."

This was true for many. But inside the family, the death was more con-fusing. Yes, Irvin Favre was beloved. But he was also the cause of tre-mendous pain. Through recent years the family had learned more and more about his infidelity, and the stories were ugly. It wasn't so much that he strayed — Brett, his brothers, and sister were well aware their father was no Ward Cleaver. And, truly, how could Brett condemn a man for moral transgressions? Yet it was a repeated slap in the face to Bonita, who put up a positive front and protected the image of a man who deserved no protection. Every year Irv's birthday gift to his wife was money, ac-companied by the words "Buy what you want." Sometimes he purchased greeting cards. Usually he reached into a drawer for a card he had given two . . . three . . . four years earlier. It was exasperating and belittling and, worst of all, selfish.

He was, however, also the only father Brett Favre ever knew. And for all the moments the son longed for unattainable affection, Irv Favre was the one who taught him football, toughness, resiliency. He was there for the good times and the hard times, and the insufferable barstool bragging Irv besieged upon others was fueled by pride. So when he learned of his dad's death, Brett refused to focus on the flaws. Instead, he was overcome by the idea of never again hearing his old man's gruff voice.

After hanging up with her husband, Deanna called David Thomason, a pilot and family friend who handled private travel for the Favres. He ar-ranged for a plane that would take her from Green Bay to Oakland, with a 4:00 a.m. arrival time. Meanwhile, Mike Sherman — who was now both the coach and general manager — reached out to Favre and urged him to do what was best for the family. If he wanted to skip the Oakland game, it was completely acceptable.

Brett called his mother. He asked whether he should come home or face the Raiders. "It's your choice," she said. "Whatever you do, I support." When Favre returned to the Claremont, the team hotel, he was greeted in his room by Father Jim Baraniak, the team's Catholic chaplain and a man the quarterback loved. He knelt on the floor alongside Favre, who sat on the bed. "It wasn't to be in a prayerful stance," Baraniak said. "It was so we could be more eye to eye." They spent the next 40 minutes discussing the loss of a parent. The feeling of emptiness. The burn of abandonment. "When we focus on our personal loss, it's terrible," the priest said. "But when we focus upon what someone else gains, it's beautiful. Your father is in heaven now, with Jesus. That's to be celebrated."

Favre was crying. "I believe you," he said. "But it hurts."

He decided to play against the Raiders, but wavered. Would he be able to think about first downs and slant routes when all his focus was upon his father? Maybe, just maybe, he should take this one off. "How can I go on?" he asked Baraniak. "I don't know if I can do this."

"Brett," Baraniak replied, "nobody expects you to do this."

When he finally left the room, the priest was convinced Brett would miss his first start in 11 years. "He seemed prepared to leave," Baraniak said. "Like that's what he was going to do."

Moments later, there was a knock on the door. It was Donald Driver, the standout wide receiver. The men hugged for what felt like an hour. "You know, Donald," Favre said, "I never told Dad I loved him."

The Packers were scheduled to hold a team meeting that evening in one of the hotel's ballrooms. Sherman didn't expect his quarterback to attend, but there he was, standing in the hallway. "He asked if he could speak to the team," Sherman said. By now, word had spread. All 53 players knew of Big Irv's passing. When Favre entered, he was greeted by a library-like silence. "You could hear a pin drop," said Ray Sherman, the wide receivers coach. "I mean, nobody made a sound."

"You could see how broken up he was," said Mark Tauscher, the offensive lineman. "It was more than just football."

Mike Sherman took his place at the front of the room. Everyone was seated. "Brett," he said, "would like to say a few words."

Favre stood. He was wearing a T-shirt, shorts, sandals. He cleared his throat and wiped his eyes. Marco Rivera, the burly offensive lineman, couldn't look at Favre's face. Others also kept their eyes on the floor. Grief owned the room. "By now y'all know what happened with my dad," Favre said in his familiarly soft drawl. There was pausing. Tears. More pausing. "And I appreciate Coach Sherman giving me the option not to play. I really do." Pause. "I loved my dad. I love football. I love you guys. I grew up playing baseball for my dad, and I grew up playing football for my dad. It's all I know. It's my life. I'm playing this game because I've invested too much in the game, in you, in this team, not to play. If you ever doubted my commitment to this team, never doubt it again."

He sat down, crumbling into his seat.

"I still get goosebumps thinking about it," said John Bonamego, the special teams coordinator. "Talk about a moment . . ."

The meeting concluded with Longwell leading the room in prayer. Many of the Packers knew similar loss. Rob Davis, the long snapper, was a senior at Shippensburg when his mother Reba died of a heart attack at age 51. Nick Luchey, the fullback, was a Miami freshman when his dad James succumbed to cancer. "Hey, Brett, as a man you're going to be OK," Luchey said to him. "It's hard to lose a parent, but everything your dad put into you stays."

Favre barely slept. When Deanna finally reached the Claremont, they hugged for, in her words, "what felt like forever." He had spent the majority of their marriage wounding his wife in many of the same ways Irv had wounded *his* wife. Through addiction, infidelity, indifference, he utilized every method to crush a marriage. Yet Deanna Favre remained loyal and faithful, and now she was here, by his side.

"I just — I just can't imagine never seeing Dad again," he said.

"Your dad was so proud of you, Brett," Deanna said. "He came to every one of your college games and has watched all of your pro games. Do you think he'd want you to sit out tomorrow? I'm convinced he would have wanted you to play."

On Monday morning Favre woke up tired but resolute. Save for a difficult phone conversation with his sister Brandi ("Brett lost it," she recalled. "And then I started to cry"), he felt determined. He would play, and he would play well. The day was treated like any other game day. Breakfast, a few meetings. Then, about four and a half hours before the 6:05 kickoff, the Packers left the hotel in Berkeley. "I remember sitting on the team bus, waiting to go to the stadium," said Bob Harlan, the team president.

"Brett and Deanna come out of the lobby, and he has his arm around her, and they looked more like they were on the way to a funeral, not the Oakland Coliseum."

There was little of the usual pregame banter and none of the jokes. Favre dressed quietly alongside Pederson and Craig Nall, the two reserve quarterbacks, and his mind was focused upon his father. Normally Favre spent the time before games thinking about his opponent, his worries, the obstacles he might face. He was never an overwhelmingly deep ponderer of life's issues, but his brain broke down football games well before they actually happened. Now, looking into an unfamiliar metal locker with some hangers and a small shelf, Favre could only see his dad; could only hear his voice. The Raiders? Hell, they could have been the Mahopac High School freshman team. The evening wasn't about overcoming Oakland. No, it was about living up to a standard set by a man no longer walking the earth. Under normal circumstances Favre would devote a good deal of time to warming up, stretching, tossing the ball. This time, he walked into the field just 45 minutes before kickoff, and his pregame throws were wild and uninspired. He looked down at his hands, which were shaking. He could barely breathe.

The Packers were 8-6, and trailed the Vikings by half a game in the NFC Central. The playoffs were far from a certainty. But none of that mattered. "You didn't talk to Brett right then," said Kevin Barry, the offensive tackle. "You let him be, but you knew you'd play your heart out for him."

The Oakland Coliseum has long been a dump. Granted, not when it opened in 1966 as the home of the Raiders, and not when Major League Baseball's Athletics relocated to California from Kansas City two years later. But over the decades, as newer stadiums debuted across America, the Coliseum steadily devolved from modern to moldy, from upbeat to barely upright.

With that progressive decay came an attitude. Whether the Raiders go 16-0 or 0-16, the team's fans show up for home games ready to bark. They paint their faces silver and black, add shoulder pads and breast plates to their outfits, make certain opposing players feel like they're about to engage in gang warfare. The stadium's south end zone is known as the Black Hole, and it is the worst place on earth. "Batteries, chicken bones, coins, you name it," Jets center Kevin Mawae once said of the items he dodged while playing the Raiders. "I've had it all." Through the years, Raiders fans have engaged in some awful behaviors. Fights. Shankings. Beatings. Drunken brawls straight out of a *Mad Max* sequence. They are — along with Philadelphia — the league's most vicious loyalists.

On the evening of Monday, December 22, however, they did something spontaneous, out of character, and remarkable. In the moments before the game, 10 of the 11 offensive starters for the Packers were introduced and (of course) booed. The last man was Favre, and as he ran onto the field and through a tunnel of teammates, the 62,298 people in attendance stood and applauded. It wasn't uproarious, or overwhelming. It was (gasp) respectful. "Amazing," Favre later said. "It was almost God's way of saying, 'See? There is compassion in this world.'"

For a quarterback whose mind wasn't on the game ("He was a dishrag," said *Sports Illustrated*'s Peter King), the Raiders were an ideal opponent. One season earlier, they had shocked the AFC by going 11-5 and reaching the Super Bowl behind a rookie head coach, Bill Callahan. Now the organization was an ode to dysfunction — a 4-10 record, a wannabe tough-guy coach whom no one listened to, a roster of disinterested and/or arrogant kids and worn-down has-beens. "It was very dark," said Chuck Bresnahan, the Oakland defensive coordinator. "We quit as a team. I hate to say that, but we hit a point midway through the year and it was no longer important to everyone. Players' cars were leaving the stadium almost as soon as the final gun went off."

"We were a mess," said Derrick Gibson, a Raiders safety. "Nobody bought in, nobody respected what we were doing."

Oakland's weaknesses were plentiful, but none more pronounced than the secondary. Put simply, teams that liked to pass owned the Raiders and, in particular, owned Phillip Buchanon, the second-year cornerback from Miami. That's why, even with a distracted Favre, the game plan was simple: attack through the air.

"Brett," said Paris Lenon, the Packers linebacker, "carved those boys up like a turkey."

Immediately before player introductions, Donald Driver called his fellow wide receivers together and said, "Listen, anything he throws we catch. I don't care what it is. Behind us, over our head. If we have to get on a ladder, jump on the guy's shoulder, we're gonna catch the ball." The grieving quarterback sent a message when, on the Packers' third play, he hoisted a magnificent 47-yard bomb over Buchanon to receiver Robert

Ferguson. Two snaps later, he looped a rainbow over Gibson's head and into the arms of tight end Wesley Walls in the rear of the end zone. Favre pointed toward the sky, then at Deanna in a box near the top of the stadium. He and Walls hugged, and one could all but see Big Irv hovering atop a cloud, preparing to ask his son why the ball wasn't delivered a second or two earlier. "Sometimes in special circumstances, you make special plays," Walls said. "I think it's fair to say we were inspired by Irv." Favre completed his opening nine throws for 183 yards and two touchdowns. It was part accuracy, part determination, part . . . otherworldliness.

Four minutes after the Walls connection, Favre eluded the pass rush, rolled right, caught Buchanon twisting in the wrong direction, and hit receiver Javon Walker with a 23-yard touchdown rocket. "It was the worst game I ever played," said Buchanon. "The worst. I didn't do anything well, it was on national TV, I got lit up multiple times. Much respect to Brett, because he earned it. But I was brutal."

The greatest — and most divine — moment occurred midway through the second quarter, with Green Bay leading 17–7 and driving yet again. On first and 10 from the Raiders 43, Favre faked a handoff to Najeh Davenport, drifted right, and felt linebacker Napoleon Harris bearing down. He stepped and threw one of his trademark *what-the-hell-did-you-do-that-for?* bombs into the end zone, where Walker was blanketed by Buchanon and free safety Anthony Dorsett. Somehow, the wide receiver leapt skyward, extended his arms, and — in front of the two defensive backs — cradled the football for a score. It was the sort of throw a receiver catches 1 of 100 times. Again, Big Irv was somewhere. He had to be, right? Said Al Michaels, calling the game for ABC: "You bring this script to a studio and they throw it out. I mean, this is like fantasy." In sports, much is often done to overhype a moment. Excessive adjectives, descriptions that aren't quite right. But no extra oomph was needed here. Nobody could believe what they were witnessing. Favre completed 22 of 30 passes for 399 yards, four touchdowns, and no interceptions. That Green Bay won, 41–7, was an afterthought. The night belonged to Brett Favre and his father. Up and down the Packers sideline, teammates were in tears. "It was amazing, astonishing, otherworldly," said Michaels. "I can tell you, my father had died and it's what they call the sinking spell feeling. You looked at Brett on the sideline, and he was having sinking spells. But somehow, some way, he would wrap it up and get back on the field."

As the fourth quarter began, the *Monday Night Football* television crew concerned itself with arranging an on-field postgame interview with Favre. They were told beforehand that the quarterback would not speak. The words meant nothing. This was a special game, and it needed to be conveyed properly. Lisa Guerrero was in her first year as *Monday Night Football*'s sideline reporter. With the clock running down, she stood on the Green Bay sideline, angling for an opening. "He came near me to get some water," she said. "I was standing right there and I said, 'Brett, please, after the game, can I get one minute?'"

Favre looked at Guerrero, whom he knew from past interviews. "OK," he said.

"Promise?" she said.

"Yeah," he replied.

Guerrero informed one of the team's media relations representatives, who was simultaneously furious and powerless. As soon as the final gun sounded, Guerrero dashed toward Favre's side. She cleared her throat, looked into the camera and spoke the words that had first entered her mind moments earlier. "It's one thing to play with a broken thumb," she said, "but another thing altogether to play with a broken heart . . ."

21

HEIR APPARENT

I N THE LEAD-UP to the 2004 NFL draft, the decision makers within the Green Bay Packers front office collectively agreed that it was time to think about selecting a quarterback.

Despite the magic of Favre's night against the Raiders, yet another season concluded with disappointment. This time, late in the fourth quarter of a second-round playoff game at Philadelphia, Eagles quarterback Donovan McNabb completed a fourth-and-26 pass to wide receiver Freddie Mitchell, keeping his team alive when hope seemed dead. Then, after the contest went into overtime, Favre lofted an indescribably bad pass that was intercepted by Eagles safety Brian Dawkins. Philadelphia won, 20–17, and Green Bay was once again devastated. "That game was a funeral," said Na'il Diggs, the Packers linebacker. "Our funeral as a team."

In the weeks that followed, a battered Favre, now 34 and with 208 consecutive starts in the record book, broached the subject of his possible retirement. The topic had first been mentioned back in 2001, when he signed a lifetime contract that ran through 2010 and, it was believed, would result in him playing out his days as a Packer. Then in November 2002, he was pressed by Fox Sports' Terry Bradshaw for specifics on any retirement plans. "You are going to finish this season out and you are going to play next year," Bradshaw said — as much question as statement.

"As far as I know," Favre said, "I'm playing next year."

Now, with the loss of his father and the Philadelphia crusher still fresh, Favre again discussed the end, though in vague terms that resolved little. "The talk gets old and repetitive," wrote Dave Lubach in the *Sheboygan Press*. "I personally don't care to hear anything about it until he comes to the decision."

Hence, the commitment to draft a potential replacement.

Having won 10 games, the Packers — selecting 25th overall — knew they were in no position to land either of the year's two best college quarterbacks, Eli Manning of Ole Miss and Philip Rivers of North Carolina State. They also presumed Ben Roethlisberger of Miami (Ohio) would be long gone.* There was, however, one signal caller who both caught their fancy and seemed to be within reach. His name was Jonathan Paul "J.P." Losman. Back in 1999, after being named a *Parade* All-American at Venice High School in Los Angeles, Losman enrolled early at UCLA, so he could set himself up to win the starting quarterback job as a true freshman. When that didn't pan out (a shock only to the cocky newcomer), Losman transferred to Tulane University in New Orleans. He started two seasons for the Green Wave and emerged as a star. Like Favre, he had swagger, a strong arm, and boundless enthusiasm. That's why, in the weeks leading up to the draft, the Packers asked Favre if he would host Losman at his Mississippi home for some bonding time. "It was two or three days of awesomeness," said Losman. "It was a whirlwind of meeting people, hanging out, doing a little throwing. On that trip he gave me the best advice anyone had ever given me. He said, 'You can't be the best if you're hurt. So the number one thing is to take care of your body and don't allow anyone to take your reps at practice.'" Though he never mentioned it to the Packers, Favre found Losman insufferable. "Brett told me when J.P. got there he didn't even shake his hand," said Craig Nall. "He just picked up a football and fired it into a net."

By the time the April 24 NFL draft rolled around, the Green Bay plan was set. Losman said the Packers assured him, should he be available, he would be their selection. "It was just a matter of waiting," he said. "I was thrilled." The draft, though, is as predictable as a Tijuana cockfight. After using the 13th selection to take wide receiver Lee Evans, Buffalo traded into the 22nd slot, three ahead of the Packers, and nabbed Losman. "I still don't get it," said Sam Wyche, the Bills' quarterbacks coach. "I filed a full scouting report on J.P., and he had thin fingers, thin calves, and when he didn't see the primary receiver, he tucked the ball and ran. I said we shouldn't touch him." The Packers didn't agree. A collective groan could be heard in the Green Bay draft room. Losman, too, was crest-

* The Packers were correct. Manning was drafted first overall, Rivers fourth, Roethlisberger 11th.

fallen. Instead of learning from the great Brett Favre, he'd be learning from a weathered Drew Bledsoe and the journeyman Shane Matthews. "I think about how my career could have been," said Losman, who lasted seven undistinguished years. "Learning from Brett, seeing how he handled things."

Without Losman, the Packers settled on another year of Doug Pederson and Craig Nall as the backups, as well as another year of good yet ultimately unfulfilling football. Green Bay again went 10-6 in 2004, and again lost in the playoffs (this time in an ugly 31–17 setback to the Vikings in the wild card game). The season was ultimately forgettable, but also quite annoying. For the first time since he entered the league, Favre seemed to be taking near-daily questions about his retirement. Or, as a *Winston-Salem Journal* headline read, FAVRE IS ALWAYS ASKED WHEN HE'LL HANG IT UP. Perhaps, had he simply said, "I'm not retiring" the inquisition would have ceased. But Favre didn't. Instead, he postured, mumbled, projected, rambled. "Favre's refusal to retire retirement talk is not a good sign," columnist Mike Woods wrote in the *Appleton Post-Crescent*. There was something about the speculation that Favre appeared to enjoy. Which was strange, in that Favre wasn't one to chase headlines. He never ran from the media, but he also never seemed to openly crave the spotlight. Now, he was craving it.

In August he promised Rick Gosselin of the *Dallas Morning News* that he would never — absolutely never — play for another franchise. "I wouldn't do it," he said. "If it comes down to that, I'll just go home." A few weeks later, he told a handful of reporters, "I have been through a lot. Most people would think that makes it easier. I don't know that it makes it any easier, and I don't know if it makes it any tougher." Shortly thereafter, the Associated Press ran a piece headlined, FAVRE'S KINDERGARTNER WANTS HER DADDY TO QUIT. For some inexplicable reason, Favre asked Breleigh, now five, whether he should continue to be a quarterback, and — for some even greater inexplicable reason — chose to share the dialogue with the media. "I said, 'If I quit playing, there's no more football, there's no more games, no more cheering,'" Favre said. "She said, 'No, I'm ready for you to do that.'"

It was the story of the up-and-down season. Would Favre keep playing? Would Favre retire? Favre aggravated an injury to his nonthrowing shoulder in a game against the Colts — would that impact his decision? Favre joined Dan Marino and John Elway as the third member of the

4,000 completion club — would that impact his decision? A poll showed Wisconsinites viewed Favre more favorably than either of the 2004 presidential candidates, incumbent George W. Bush and Senator John Kerry. Would *that* impact his decision?

Finally, something happened that *actually* carried the weight to affect his future. During a routine August self-examination, Deanna Favre discovered a BB-sized lump between her right armpit and her breast. She paid it little mind, but two months later her gynecologist checked the growth and suggested — just to be safe — she see Dr. Lyle Henry at Columbia St. Mary's Hospital in Milwaukee. She underwent a biopsy, then had to wait a day to learn the result. "Brett called my cell phone every hour, wanting to know if I knew anything," she recalled. "When he called around three or four in the afternoon I told him they were doing the biopsy, but I was sure it'd be fine, no big deal."

The following afternoon, shortly after 12:00, Deanna's cell phone rang. The date was October 14, and Brett was at the practice facility preparing for the Lions; Breleigh was at school (Brittany, the oldest daughter, chose to stay in Mississippi for the entire year and attend high school there). Deanna picked up, and heard Dr. Henry's voice. "Dear," he said stoically, "the biopsy shows that you do, in fact, have breast cancer."

She couldn't breathe. Just eight days earlier her 24-year-old brother, Casey Tynes, was killed in an ATV accident. Now this. Moments later the phone rang again. This time, it was Brett. "Did you hear anything?" he asked.

Deanna couldn't speak. "Oh, God," he said, and mumbled something about coming home ASAP. Then, without prompting, he spoke aloud to God.

"[It] would have to suffice," she recalled. "I was too numb to pray."

Eleven days later, on October 26, the Favres released the news to the media. Deanna would undergo a lumpectomy and chemotherapy and radiation treatments, but was expected to make a full recovery. The next few months showed Deanna (and the nation) Brett Favre at his best. Not as a football player, but as a human being. Here was a man, who once seemed more committed to alcohol, drugs, and infidelity than to anything else, riding an exercise bike at the team facility while reading cancer brochures; a man reviewing the options, speaking with the doctors, trying to stay emotionally strong for his daughters as his wife went through hell. "He really studied it," Deanna recalled. "He began to look things up and kept telling me what the experts said about various treatment options." This was not the way Brett had been raised to be a man. In Big Irv's household, the women worried about health and wellness and anything touching the emotions. Yet here he was, hands-on and vulnerable. Thanks to three months of chemo and six weeks of radiation, Deanna made a full recovery, and she regularly credited her husband's support. On December 7, five days before a game against Detroit, Favre showed up for practice and removed his hat. His hair — brown and wavy just a day earlier — was now mowed into a crew cut. He didn't announce it, or draw attention. But when a reporter noticed and asked, "Why'd you do that?" Favre smiled.

"I'm gradually cutting it down," he said, "so I can be like my wife."

"Look, it was cool," said Dylan Tomlinson, who covered the Packers for Gannett Wisconsin Newspapers. "Really nice. But I think journalists make a mistake when they buy everything. My editor at the time asked me to write a piece about Brett Favre, the family man. I said, 'You're joking, right? After all he's done to that woman over the years. Sorry, but I don't write fiction.'"

Because J.P. Losman and his skinny fingers and erratic decision-making abilities were resting on an icy bench in western New York, the 2004 campaign concluded with the Packers *still* feeling the need to find an eventual successor for Favre.

Throughout his 13 seasons in Green Bay, an endless stream of quarterbacks had come and gone. Once, when Mark Brunell rose from the bench in 1994, there was a (relatively slim) possibility of Favre being replaced. Otherwise, every signal caller brought to town was there solely to provide support. Through the years, the men signed to back Favre had been a mixed bag of seasoned veterans (Ken O'Brien, Jim McMahon, David Klingler, Steve Bono, Tim Couch) and unspectacular yet useful youngsters (Ty Detmer, Doug Pederson, Craig Nall). Some, like Detmer and Pederson, turned into lifelong friends. Others, like O'Brien and Couch, arrived and departed with barely a shadow. "When you signed with Green Bay, there was no false illusion you were there to fight Brett for a job," said Akili Smith, the Bengals' first-round pick in 1999, who attended camp with the Packers four years later. "He wasn't just the team and he wasn't just the city. He was the state. You just wanted to hang on and hold a clipboard."

Favre was 35 by the time the season concluded, on January 9, 2005, with the wild card defeat to the Vikings (he played terribly, throwing four interceptions), and the long run, coupled with Deanna's illness, had beaten him down. After the game, he was asked about retirement and again hemmed and hawed. *Maybe. Possibly. I'll pray on it. I think so. I think no.* Michael Hunt of the *Milwaukee Journal Sentinel* became the first local scribe to push for Favre to hang it up, noting that the league's second-oldest starting quarterback had to ask himself, "What motivation would [I] have to play a 14th season with a slipping organization?" Donald Driver, the veteran wide receiver and Favre's friend, told the *Arizona Republic,* "I think he's had enough. I really do."

Favre *felt* the call of retirement. The team wasn't the same anymore. He was the oldest Packer by two years, and struggled to relate with the modern era of me-me-me football players. Where was Reggie White? Where was Jim McMahon? LeRoy Butler? Frank Winters?* The new kids were largely about highlights, headlines, attention. The locker room had once been a place of laughter and jokes and farts and stink bombs. Over the years, everything quieted. The younger Packers spent their time with headphones in their ears, listening to their own tunes while drowning out the world. No one went out after games. There was Xbox to play.

As a greener man Favre had bounded from one corner of the room to the other, absorbing the flavors, the lingo. Now, fed up and no longer fully engaged, he chose to change with the coaching staff, in their isolated dressing area to the side. If he drove to the stadium, Favre parked his Ford F-150 in its own private area and walked in through a back entrance. When Mike Sherman came to Green Bay before the 2000 season, he envisioned working with Favre in the way Bill Walsh and Joe Montana did in San Francisco — a two-headed offensive football juggernaut. But Sherman lacked Walsh's strength, and over the years he allowed Favre increased liberties. If he wanted to miss a practice? OK. Arrive a bit late for a meeting? Fine. Dress away from the teammates? No biggie.

Perhaps that's why, when the Packers hired Ted Thompson as the new general manager that January, more than a few Green Bay executives hoped he would start by encouraging Favre to fade into the Mississippi sunset. A linebacker with the Houston Oilers in the late 1970s and early

---

* White died of a heart attack in 2004; Favre served as a pallbearer at his funeral. McMahon, Butler, and Winters had retired.

'80s, Thompson was a seemingly humorless man who had spent five seasons as Seattle's vice president of operations and, before that, seven years
in Green Bay heading the pro personnel department. Bob Harlan, the
team president, initially promoted Sherman to coach *and* general manager when Ron Wolf left before the 2001 season. "I wanted cohesion for
the franchise," he said. Harlan, however, was never comfortable with such
a consolidation of power, and grew increasingly concerned as Sherman
blew high draft picks on busts and floundered in drawing free agents.
"The burden changed him as a person," Harlan said. "He became very
quiet, he ignored everybody. He would get on the airplane on Saturdays,
put on earphones, and not talk to anybody. I made a mistake in giving
Mike both jobs. It was too much." So now Thompson was the GM, Sherman back to serving merely as the head coach.

With the (admittedly large) exception of Thompson's presence, the
lead-up to the 2005 draft was similar to a year earlier. Once again Green
Bay wanted a quarterback, but knew the two best available players (Utah's
Alex Smith and California's Aaron Rodgers) would be distant memories
once their slot (24th overall) arrived. Much of the attention turned to
Charlie Frye, the Akron quarterback who gained national respect (and
more than a few Favre comparisons) by starting nine games with a broken thumb on his throwing hand in 2002. Were he still available at No.
24, the Packers were likely to pounce.

The draft unfolded unpredictably. Smith and Rodgers were widely
considered a coin flip. One quarterback would go first, the other shortly
thereafter. Both were big, strong, accurate, smart. Smith was quiet; Rodgers, confident. When the day arrived and the Utah senior was selected
No. 1 overall, nobody was particularly shocked. ESPN's Ron Jaworski said
the 49ers made the right call, that "the delta" between Smith and Rodgers
was "significant."

But what followed — *strange*. Three running backs, three wide receivers, and three cornerbacks rounded out the Top 10. Sitting behind the
stage in the green room at the Javits Center in New York City, Rodgers
waited . . . waited . . . waited. He wore a blue pinstriped suit, a maroon tie,
his hair closely cropped. At times the ESPN cameras caught his drooping
expression. While waiting for San Diego to use its 12th pick, ESPN's Suzy
Kolber sat alongside Rodgers and asked, "A couple of weeks ago, Aaron,
you were the clear-cut No. 1. What's changed over that time?" Forcing a
smile, Rodgers said, "I wish I could tell you." He was embarrassed, and

the grin failed to mask dismay. "You start questioning everything," he later said. "From where you worked out to how hard you worked." The Dolphins had lacked a standout starting quarterback since Dan Marino's retirement in 1999 — and they took a running back, Auburn's Ronnie Brown, second. Tampa Bay's starting quarterback was the mediocre Brian Griese — and they selected a halfback, Auburn's Cadillac Williams, fifth. Arizona's starting quarterback was the forgettable Josh McCown — and they selected a cornerback, Miami's Antrel Rolle, eighth. One by one, franchises that were thought to need a quarterback let Rodgers sit and wait. In hindsight, much of it had to do with a cold-footed reaction to negative scouting reports. Shortly before the draft, for example, a scout for an NFC team told Pete Dougherty of the *Green Bay Press-Gazette* that he would pass on Rodgers. "I just think Aaron's the product of being on a good team," the scout said. "He's got a good running back who takes a lot of the pressure off him, they throw a lot of screens and dump balls. I see Utah winning because of Alex Smith, he's the one that does it. I don't think Cal was winning because of Aaron Rodgers." Jaworski repeatedly cited Rodgers's "blemishes," and said he did not project well to the NFL. There was also the matter of finances. First-round draft choices are expensive, and first-round quarterbacks tend to be *very* expensive. Of the 21 teams selecting ahead of Green Bay (the Cowboys and Vikings possessed two first-round picks), 12 were about to take a quarterback salary cap hit in excess of $2.4 million for 2005.

So Aaron Rodgers dropped.

And dropped.

And dropped.

A decade earlier Tom Rossley, the Packers' offensive coordinator, had been the head coach at Southern Methodist. His quarterbacks coach was George Cortez, who now held the same position at Cal. One day, weeks before the draft, Cortez called Rossley and begged him to come and watch Rodgers throw. "You need to see this guy," he said. Rossley hadn't planned on scouting Rodgers, because he was certain he wouldn't be available for the Packers. But, out of friendship, he made the trip. "He worked out for an hour, and every ball he threw was caught," Rossley said. "I watched [former Ravens quarterback] Kyle Boller's Cal workout, and he got on his knees at the 50 and threw one over the goalpost. It was amazing — and Aaron's workout eclipsed that. I told Ted, 'This guy Rodgers is special.'"

When the Oakland Raiders grabbed a Nebraska cornerback named

Fabian Washington with the 23rd selection, Thompson knew immediately whom the Packers would take. "About three or four days before the draft," he said, "I was convinced that the best thing to do, if he got to us, was draft Aaron Rodgers." Finally, approximately five hours after Smith went No. 1, Rodgers's cell phone rang. It was Thompson — "How do you feel about coming to Green Bay?"

Before rising to walk onto the stage and shake Commissioner Paul Tagliabue's hand, Rodgers was grabbed by Merton Hanks, a former Pro Bowl defensive back now employed by the NFL. Back in 1991 he'd lasted into the fifth round before being picked by San Francisco. "I played my whole career with a chip on my shoulder," Hanks whispered. "You should do the same."

Indeed.

"It wasn't the easiest day," Rodgers said. "But I'm just so excited about being able to go to a team that wants me, and to learn from the greatest quarterback of our day right now. And I couldn't be happier with what next year, and the years to come, will look like. Being a Packer."

Later that day, Rodgers spoke via conference call with the Green Bay media. He handled himself perfectly, especially when asked about the incumbent.

"You know," he said, "I don't think you can ever replace a legend."

A couple of weeks after the draft, Dylan Tomlinson of Gannett Wisconsin Newspapers was sent 90 miles northwest of Sacramento to Chico, California, to visit with Aaron Rodgers for a profile.

Tomlinson had been on the Packers beat since 2003, and Brett Favre was far from his favorite player. He found the quarterback to be phony, arrogant, thin-skinned. He hated how the team's notoriously protective PR staff served as Favre's personal brick wall, and laughed as rival journalists left offerings at the Shrine of Brett. Through the years, Tomlinson had heard dozens of rumors about Favre's infidelity and drunkenness, yet felt constrained by the bonds of local Packer love to write anything. "People felt loyal to Brett, because in Green Bay he was a football god," Tomlinson said. "But, just being honest, I couldn't stand him."

Rodgers, on the other hand, immediately impressed the scribe. Though just 21, he was clearly more intelligent and probing than Favre. Rodgers scored a 1310 on the SATs and graduated Pleasant Valley High with an A- average.

Because he played quarterback for an off-the-map high school in an off-the-map nugget of California, Rodgers — who threw for 4,421 yards in two seasons as a prep starter — received no Division I scholarship offers. The University of Illinois invited him for a visit, but merely extended a walk-on opportunity. He enrolled at Butte College in nearby Oroville, California, starred on the football field ("No one on the team understood why he was there," said Shaun Bodiford, a Butte wide receiver), and finished with two spectacular years at Cal. After the Golden Bears lost to Texas Tech in the Holiday Bowl, Rodgers declared himself eligible for the NFL draft.

Tomlinson loved Rodgers's openness. He was laid-back and casual and happy to show the reporter around his home. At one point during their day together, Tomlinson asked Rodgers what people had told him about Brett Favre.

"Not much," Rodgers said. "I really don't know what to expect."

Tomlinson felt pangs of sympathy for the kid. "Honestly," the writer said, "I think he'll torment the hell out of you. Knowing how insecure he is, I think he'll give you a lot of shit."

Rodgers and Favre finally met on June 2, when the Packers held a seven-practice organized team activity camp. Now merely a head coach (and a disgruntled one at that), Sherman allowed Favre to skip the workouts, but that didn't mean he would not attend. In fact, that morning, Favre was alone, sitting in the team cafeteria and reading a newspaper, when Rodgers saw him in person for the first time. The new quarterback approached the old quarterback and uttered what will forever go down as the worst introductory line in the history of professional sports.

"Good morning, Grandpa!"

Silence.

Rodgers surely recognized the mistake as soon as the words escaped his lips. But there was no taking it back. "Brett couldn't believe that," said Craig Nall, the backup quarterback. "It was like, '*Grandpa?* Who the hell are you?'"

When asked by reporters about meeting the legend, Rodgers failed to mention the foible. At the time, some in the media tried selling the story of the superstar assisting the newbie. In truth, it was reminiscent of 1951 spring training with the New York Yankees, when a 19-year-old rookie named Mickey Mantle tried to ingratiate himself with the 36-year-old icon Joe DiMaggio, only to be rebuffed. "My contract doesn't say I have to get Aaron Rodgers ready to play," Favre told ESPN. "Now hopefully he watches me and gets something from that."

From that first day, Favre did nothing to help Rodgers and much to hurt and ridicule him. With Doug Pederson now retired, Nall served as Favre's primary sidekick, and the two Southern boys talked about Rodgers like two bullies mocking a math club nerd. Not that the newcomer made it particularly difficult. "Very cocky, very arrogant," said Nall. "That's how he came off. Like a rookie who knew everything."

"Somebody must have told Aaron he was brought in to replace Brett, because that's how he acted," said Najeh Davenport, the veteran running back. "Maybe his agent or someone convinced him he was important, because he walked around like he was the next best thing."

Many of the Packers participated in a summer charity softball game in nearby Appleton. In his first at bat, Rodgers clubbed a home run and skipped and hopped around the bases. "He was jumping on the heels of the guy in front of him," said Ben Steele, a Packers tight end. "You could tell the guys were not happy. They expected him to be shy and quiet and not try to outshine Brett Favre, the legend. It bothered me. It bothered a lot of us."

Sean McHugh, a Packers tight end, said Rodgers was a nice kid with "California swag." Which wasn't the same as Mississippi or Green Bay swag. During that opening camp, then training camp two months later, Rodgers liked to brag about the 35 he scored on the Wonderlic, a test used by NFL teams to assess the aptitude of prospective employees. One day in a quarterbacks meeting he said, "Brett, what did you get on it?"

"I have no idea," he replied.

"I do," Rodgers said. "I looked it up. You got a 22."

When the meeting concluded, Rodgers exited the room first, followed by Darrell Bevell, the quarterbacks coach, then Favre and Nall. "Fucking Wonderlic score," Favre mumbled. "Do you believe that shit? I run circles around his ass."

Rodgers made it a point to sit in the front row of team meetings and raise his hand to answer every question from the coaches. He was smart and studious, and it all went over like a bowl of maggot-coated oatmeal. Eventually Driver, the veteran receiver and Favre's close friend, pulled the youngster aside and said, bluntly, "Aaron, we get it. You're smart. Now shut the fuck up."

Rodgers listened to Driver for all of four seconds. During drills, he refused to let a play end sans resolution. Were he, for example, flushed from the pocket, a coach might blow the whistle for a restart. Rodgers, though, kept moving, kept running, kept looking. "He was super competitive, and he would not let the defense win," said Ruvell Martin, a rookie wide receiver from Saginaw Valley State. "He didn't care that it was just the scout team. He wanted to win whether it was polite or not." Oftentimes, after completing a pass against the defense *in practice,* Rodgers let loose an inane celebratory dance, where he slid his right foot forward while pretending to roll dice with his right hand. After enough gazes of disbelief from Favre and Co., Bevell pulled the kid aside and said, "You've been on the football field before. Act like it."

By virtue of his status as the heir apparent, Favre would not have taken to Rodgers had he been a kid from Southern Miss with a wad of tobacco in his cheek. But Rodgers was confident and cool and tone-deaf. Favre offered little (well, no) advice, but the kid wasn't exactly seeking out the information. He seemed to believe he was not only ready for the NFL, but ready to lead the Packers. Before long an unspoken yet clear divide formed in camp. The veterans viewed Rodgers as an unwelcomed intruder. ("I was friends with Craig Nall and [quarterback] J.T. O'Sullivan," said Steele. "And they were like, 'Why'd we draft this guy? He's not even good.' Which was laughable — he was real good.") The younger players felt his sense of urgency, and responded. Favre was of a bygone era; Rodgers was now. Favre had "his" guys. Rodgers just threw the ball. When he arrived in camp, Chris Samp, a rookie free agent wide receiver from Winona State, couldn't wait to work with his hero, ol' No. 4. "He was such a disappointment to me," said Samp. "If it was his turn in the quarterback rotation and he saw me at wide receiver, he'd wave Rodgers in instead of throwing to me. Just because I was no one. It wasn't just me. He had favorites.

"I looked up to him. But if I had to run a 12-yard route, he'd wing the ball even before I got to the cut. Then he'd throw his hands up. I'd come back and say, 'What am I doing wrong?' He'd say, 'Forget it. I'm not looking at you.' He was a jerk. To me. To Aaron."

Rodgers's presence clearly irked and threatened Favre, and the relationship (or lack thereof) dominated much of training camp. Rob Demovsky, who covered the team for the *Green Bay Press-Gazette*, asked

Rodgers whether he had hung out with Favre. "Seriously," Rodgers said, "I don't even have his number."

When Bonita Favre initially heard of Hurricane Katrina approaching the Gulf Coast, she shrugged. In the long Hancock County history of the Favre family, there had been nearly as many wind and rain assaults as there had been births and deaths. Thirty-six years earlier, Hurricane Camille had battered the Favre household, and it was thought to be the Genghis Khan of storms. "The worst one ever," she said. "But we didn't get water inside."

Bonita lived in a lovely house at the end of Irvin Farve Road, and approximately 100 yards away her 87-year-old mother, Izella French (Mee Maw) resided in a double-wide trailer. The property also held a pool house, an old barn, a henhouse, and a residence that Karen (Irv's sister) called home. Brett had purchased the adjoining 50 acres, and Scott was building a house on the land. His two palomino ponies roamed nearby. Everything would be fine. There were a handful of water bottles in Bonita's refrigerator. Some Cokes and Diet Cokes. Her white Cadillac had about half a tank of gas. "At first," said Bonita, "I wasn't concerned. Just at first."

Katrina hit on the morning of August 29, and the blow was neither gradual nor cushioned. It was a nuclear bomb. Brett was in Green Bay, preparing his soon-to-be-36-year-old body for the season opener against Detroit, and a slew of relatives and friends (20 in total) were inside Bonita's house on the family homestead, boarding the windows. There was no panic and minimal fear. "We turned it into a big party," said Dylan Favre, Brett's nephew, who was 13 at the time. "Because you can't really do much, can't go anywhere. So we all stayed in the house and ate."

At 6:30 a.m., the winds whistled — "not a big deal," said Dylan. "But we're watching for water coming over the hill in front of the house. And it starts getting closer." Nobody panicked. The water advanced closer and closer to the house. And closer. And closer. It reached the front door, and trickled through the crack. "Even then," said Dylan, "we were like, 'Well, we'll have to replace the floor.'" Then — *whoosh!* The water broke through the entranceway, rose from shin level to waist level to chin level. People screamed. Cried. A family friend was there with her two small dogs. "My God!" she yelled. "The dogs! The dogs! What about the dogs!"

Scott Favre, who shared Brett's calm under pressure, momentarily flipped. "We're about to die," he screamed, "and you're worried about your little dogs?" The children were placed in the attic. Mee Maw — orange life preserver wrapped around her neck — was floating, surreally, through the house, along with clouds of brown water and clumped masses of feces from the now-broken sewage. The refrigerator bobbed past. Chairs and cabinets, too. About 200 yards from the front door, Bonita had a boat, and Scott and Jeff (Brett's brother, Dylan's father) swam toward it, hoping it could be used as an escape. No go — they returned, defeated. "I was crying," said Dylan. "I was telling my dad, 'Please let me out of here! I'll take my chances holding on to a tree before I die in this house!' I looked out the back window and thought, *This really might be the last time I'm alive.*"

In Wisconsin, Brett watched the storm unfold on TV. Deanna and the girls were at their home in Hattiesburg, and all three were fine. He repeatedly tried calling Bonita, but the phone lines were dead. He knew it was bad, but couldn't have realized the utter terror ripping its way through his childhood home. When the water finally started to recede, Scott led a mass swimming exodus from the main house to the pool house, about 50 yards away. Jeff placed Mee Maw on his shoulder. She was intoxicated and waterlogged, and as they swam she vomited atop her grandson. "The pool house was just a little room with one bed," Dylan said. "We got there, took our clothes off — everything was so gross. And there were a bunch of shirts up there. We put them on, slept on the floor. All of us."

When they woke the next morning, the wind had died and the water returned to its place of origin. The wreckage was a scene from the worst disaster movie. The path from Bonita's house to civilization was a mile-long trek along Irvin Farve Road, only it was blocked by downed trees. "We had no food, no water," said Dylan. "I'm in eighth grade and my Uncle David hands me a pistol, because there's looting over water, food."

The Favres managed to break through and were able to secure provisions. All told, 238 people died along the Gulf Coast of the state. "We didn't lose anyone," said Brandi Favre. "That's the most important thing."

Like Brett, Brandi was away from home, living in Nixa, Missouri. She couldn't reach the family and — by virtue of having lost her cell phone and all its stored numbers two days earlier — couldn't reach Brett. She dialed the number for the Packers' front office and told the receptionist that she was Brandi Favre, Brett's sister, and this was an emergency.

Ma'am, we hear this kind of thing all the time . . .

"Please," Brandi said. "Do me a favor, go out there to practice and tell him his sister Brandi needs him to call ASAP. Here's my number."

Five minutes later, her phone rang. "Have you heard anything?" Brett said, his voice panicked.

"No," said Brandi. "Have you?"

"No."

Had their family survived? Perished? They had no idea. "It's 2005 and I can't get in touch," Brett told reporters. "When I turn on the TV it's never anything positive. I'd like to have at least an answer." The night following the storm he barely slept. "I had nightmares the whole time," he said.

That afternoon Bonita and the others made their way to nearby Diamondhead. She saw a man talking on a cell phone, and pleaded. "Sir, I'm Brett Favre's mother and I want to let him know I'm alive! Please!"

Moments later, she heard Brett's voice. It had been 30 hours since they last spoke.

"Mom, are you . . ."

"We're OK," she said. "But we've lost everything."

One day later, the Packers traveled to Nashville for their final preseason game, and Sherman granted Favre permission to drive a truck filled with supplies to his home turf. He wound up staying with the team (most of the roads to the Gulf Coast remained undrivable), but hired someone to deliver goods to his state. His foundation, the Brett Favre Fourward Foundation, raised $189,000 in donations for the recovery effort. Favre conducted a series of interviews, including one with *Good Morning America*'s Robin Roberts (also a Mississippi native) that was equal parts poignant and heartbreaking. It wasn't famous television host and famous quarterback, but two products of a decimated state. "The people down there right now have nothing," he said. "My family has only the clothes that they had on during the hurricane. . . . Send satellite phones, you know, send something people can eat right away, send something they can drink — right away, something that will enable them to get power. There's no gas. There's no diesel down there. And so, whatever they can give, obviously, is much appreciated. But it's stuff that they need right away. I mean, there's no way to get food. There's no way to cook it . . ."

When Favre eventually returned home, his mother insisted he see all the devastation, to which he replied, "Well, I've watched it all on TV."

"No," she said. "Not like this."

They took a slow drive. Where once there was something, now there was nothing. "You couldn't find a landmark," said Bonita. "We didn't know where to turn to take my mother to the hospital, because there was nothing where it used to be. My house was ruined. Forty years of my life, gone. It was heartbreaking, but you realize things aren't important. Especially when you're that close to losing your family."

Lessons of perspective generally last in sports about as long as fumble-prone free agent halfbacks. You learn, you digest, and then you move on and return to the normalcy of your existence.

With the long and arduous Katrina recovery slowly kicking into gear and his family members safe, Brett Favre was able to return to focusing on quarterbacking the Green Bay Packers. The problem, though, was that the Green Bay Packers didn't seem ready for him. With a young roster featuring 11 rookies, the year was destined to be a struggle. The team opened at Detroit, and the 17–3 loss was as bad as it sounds (Favre tossed two interceptions). They then dropped the next three to start 0-4 for the first time in 17 years. Before long, experts were suggesting a quarterback change. On the HBO series *Inside the NFL,* analyst Cris Collinsworth, one of the game's most respected voices, said, "If this Packer team is sitting there at 2-8, the last six games absolutely have to go to Aaron Rodgers."

Favre's play was inconsistent. His treatment of Rodgers was not. Shortly before the opening game, Sherman announced that Nall — a locker room favorite of the veterans — would be demoted to third-string quarterback in favor of the rookie. This was not well received, and rightly believed to be more about draft status than readiness. The morning after the news, Nall arrived at the facility with a copy of an image someone had e-mailed him, featuring a person in a shirt reading ALL DADDY WANTED WAS A BLOW JOB. Pepper Burruss, the team trainer, told Nall to bring it to his office, found a photograph of Rodgers from draft day, snipped off his head, affixed it to the body in the picture, and laminated the newly mastered image onto a T-shirt. The garment was passed to Brett in the team meeting, and he could not stop laughing. It was handed to Bevell and, lastly, to Rodgers. "He looked at it for 10 seconds and dropped it to the floor," said Nall. "There was this awkward tension in the room." When the meeting ended, Nall apologized to Rodgers, but advised him to relax. "You're a first-round pick, Aaron," he said. "You have to expect to be poked at a bit."

If that was bad, what happened weeks later was significantly worse. Every so often the team placed varied items on a locker room table for the players to sign. Most were donated to charity. On this particular day one of the things to be autographed was a replica Packers helmet. Favre eyed it, turned to Nall, and said, "You know what would be funny? If we put someone's real helmet out there." The next morning Rodgers arrived at the facility and could not locate his helmet. He looked, asked around — nothing. Most of his teammates were in on the joke and chuckling to themselves. Chad Clifton, an offensive tackle, told Rodgers that the marketing staff needed him to sign the items on the table. Rodgers grabbed a pen and, without knowing, scribbled "Aaron Rodgers" in black Sharpie on his own helmet, which was covered with signatures. He walked onto the field still searching for his headgear. An equipment staffer finally brought him the one covered in ink. "Aaron," he said, "this is yours . . ."

Rodgers wanted to vanish. "He had to wear it all practice," said Nall. "To his credit, he took it well."

Not true. When the workout ended, Rodgers retreated to his locker. Tomlinson, the reporter, approached. "He was about to cry," Tomlinson said. "He was devastated. It was pure humiliation, and that Favre did it made it 100 times worse."

"Aaron does not have a kind word to say about Brett," said a friend of Rodgers. "Nothing even slightly kind. He was always a dick to him."

It was never-ending. Rodgers was the butt of jokes — some that he heard, many that he did not. A rumor circulated around the locker room that he was gay, based upon the fact that — unlike many of his teammates — he wasn't one to brag about his penis size or his endless string of sexual conquests. Favre sought out Rodgers's weaknesses (a bad throw, a clumsy scramble) and took a selfish pleasure in noting them. The problem, however, was that they were tough to find. Rodgers was Favre's equal when it came to arm strength, and he was already, as a rookie, a far better decision maker. He read defenses like a 12-year veteran and stayed in the pocket without cowering.

Rodgers only appeared in three games, but as the season progressed and the Packers faltered, it felt like a changing of the guard was near. In a humiliating 21–14 loss at Cincinnati on October 30, Favre was intercepted five times. Seven weeks later, he hit on a mere 14 of 29 attempts (with two interceptions) as the Ravens smothered Green Bay, 48–3. That game, played on Monday night, included John Madden, Favre's most vocal public supporter through the years, speaking as if the quarterback were a mouse surrounded by a gaggle of alley cats. "Do something!" he pleaded. "You have to compete. You have to fight." Rodgers entered the game late and took a beating. "He got annihilated," said Tom Silverstein of the *Milwaukee Journal Sentinel.* "Favre just stood on the sideline, a parka on, and he never went over and talked to Aaron. I asked Rodgers afterward if he was surprised Brett didn't offer any help. He didn't know what to say."

All told, Favre's 20 touchdown passes were marred by 29 interceptions. When the final whistle blew on a horrific 4-12 campaign, it was presumed (rightly) that Mike Sherman would be fired and (wrongly) that Favre would retire to a life of tractor rides and hunting trips. Before the gear was packed and the flights arranged, Rodgers had one last exchange with Tomlinson, the reporter who, months earlier, warned him about the ensuing nightmare.

"What you told me about Brett," Rodgers said. "You were 100 percent right."

22

McCARTHYISM

I N THE WANING DAYS of the 2005 season, when hope was dead and criticism strong, Brett Favre suggested that, should Mike Sherman be fired as head coach of the Green Bay Packers, he would likely retire.

This threat seemed to be a serious one. He would turn 37 during the upcoming season, and the idea of adjusting to a new coaching staff wasn't exactly appealing.

Plus, there was the whole Aaron Rodgers thing. Though Favre was loath to admit it, the kid could flat-out play. This wasn't Matt Hasselbeck (who was excellent) or even Mark Brunell (also excellent). No, this was a quarterback who felt like a future superstar. "By then Aaron's arm was stronger than Brett's," said Jerron Wishom, the defensive back. "Though you couldn't say that out loud."

On January 2, 2006, Ted Thompson fired a coach who went 57-39 and won three division titles in six seasons. He did so without consulting his quarterback, or even giving him a heads-up. Ten days later, Sherman's replacement was named, and once again Favre had no involvement with the decision.

Not that Favre had anything bad to say about Mike McCarthy. It's just that . . . *Mike McCarthy?* Really? Of all the available coaching candidates, Thompson picked a guy who, at age 42, was only five years older than the quarterback. A guy whose playing career peaked after a few years as a tight end at Baker University.* A guy whose NFL track record was, at best, a mixed bag. McCarthy and Favre actually worked together seven

---

* Baker University is in Baldwin City, Kansas. Mike McCarthy isn't its only famous alum. Baker also brought the world Andrew Cherng, founder of Panda Express.

years earlier, when he was the quarterbacks coach under Ray Rhodes. And while they coexisted well, the season was a mess. McCarthy served as the 49ers' offensive coordinator in 2005, and the unit ranked last in the NFL in total yards. Mike Nolan, San Francisco's head coach, defended his protégée, but the words rang hollow. McCarthy's number one task had been to guide Alex Smith, the rookie quarterback he urged the team to draft first overall (over, ahem, Aaron Rodgers), and the product was atrocious. Smith started seven games, and threw one touchdown and 11 interceptions. In a results-driven business, McCarthy could not have done a worse job.

Now, not only was he being introduced as the new coach, but he was clearly hired with Rodgers in mind. As Don Pierson rightly noted in the following day's *Chicago Tribune,* "How [McCarthy] relates to last year's first-round Packers' draft choice, Aaron Rodgers, is more important to the Packers than whether the 36-year-old Favre decides to return."

In public, Favre applauded the hiring, and said all the requisite kind words about McCarthy. But he was insulted over not being consulted. For years, the organization measured every move with Brett Favre in mind. How would the locker room dynamic work between him and Reggie White? Was he OK with Andre Rison? What did he think of Mike Sherman as the next head coach? But those days were over. Shortly before the concluding game of the 2005 season, he complained to the *Wisconsin State Journal* that the Packers lacked the guts to explain their plans to him. "They don't know how to tell Brett Favre, 'We want to go in a different direction,'" he said. In fact, Green Bay wasn't fearful of consulting Favre — Thompson simply didn't feel the need.

Was he OK with Favre standing behind center for another season or two? Sure — even though the organization would save $10 million should he not return. But the garbage and drama that accompanied the whole production was exasperating. On January 26, McCarthy and Thompson made the 100-mile drive from Mobile, Alabama (they were in town scouting the Senior Bowl), to Hattiesburg to visit Favre and gauge his thoughts for 2006. They left after a couple of hours, both certain he would return. Then, in an interview that aired on ESPN three days later, Favre said, "If I had to pick right now and make a decision, I would say I'm not coming back."

In mid-February, Bob Harlan told the *Green Bay Press-Gazette* that it would be lovely for Favre to fill the organization in by March 1. On (of all the dates) February 28, Favre conducted yet another interview with ESPN, and said he was anxious to observe what free-agency moves the franchise made in the coming weeks. "It's a little bit of a waiting game," he said from Homestead, Florida, where he was taking (to the team's surprise and dismay) NASCAR driving lessons. Those close to Favre insisted the indecision had nothing to do with ego and everything to do with legitimate uncertainty. That was ludicrous. "He turned into a prima donna, no question about it," said Dylan Tomlinson, the Gannett Wisconsin football writer. "He liked the attention that came with this all."

The NFL meetings were held in Lake Buena Vista, Florida, in late March, and reporters hovered around Thompson and McCarthy while they walked the halls of the Hyatt Grand Cypress resort. For the first time, the rookie head coach suggested he *required* an answer ("It needs to be real soon") — but shortly thereafter Thompson said to ESPN that the deadline for Favre's $3 million roster bonus (which was April 1) was being pushed back. During this time, Green Bay was wooing Marc Boerigter, a free agent wide receiver who played four seasons with Kansas City. Boerigter asked Reggie McKenzie, the Packers' director of pro personnel, whether Favre was returning. "He's *always* coming back," McKenzie said with a sigh. "He loves playing this up every year, but we know he's coming back."

Favre scheduled a news conference to be held on April 8 at his charity golf tournament in Tunica, Mississippi, then — surprise! — offered the shocking words, "No change. I don't know, once again. I don't know why you guys wasted a trip down here." It was maddening, and when a TRADE BRETT! billboard went up along a road in Janesville, Wisconsin, a surprisingly large number of people supported the sentiment. Later, Favre uttered a quote that stuck to him like body odor: "What are they going to do," he told a reporter, "cut me?"

Finally, on April 25, Favre confirmed to the team that he would be returning for what was presumed to be a farewell season. The news was celebrated by most of Green Bay, if not by Thompson, McCarthy, and Rodgers. "Given the choice, you always take a guy like Brett on your team," said Wishom. "He's a veteran who has won a Super Bowl."

Green Bay opened its first training camp under McCarthy on Friday, July 28, at the fields across from Lambeau. Favre, who attended offseason workouts to help learn the new terminology of McCarthy's version of the West Coast offense, arrived on time and in shape. His arm was still strong, but he lacked proper insoles for his game shoes. One day, a member of the training staff approached Dave Tollefson, a rookie defensive lineman selected out of Northwest Missouri State with a seventh-round pick, and noted that he and Favre both wore size 15.

"That's interesting," Tollefson said drolly.

"Yeah," the man said. "You need to break in Brett's cleats and insoles. He doesn't like doing it himself."

Tollefson thought this to be a joke, until he was handed the footgear. Favre spent most of camp wearing tennis shoes as the newcomer wore *his* shoes. "It was strange," Tollefson said. "But as a rookie, are you kidding me? I'll break in Brett Favre's jockstrap if that's what's asked."

With Nall gone to the Buffalo Bills, Favre tried to be more accepting of Rodgers. Did he go out of his way to help him? No. But the ridiculing ceased and the dialogue opened. "I thought our relationship really got strong," Rodgers told ESPN's Jeremy Schaap. "He realized I was in his corner."

Compared to Sherman, who by the end of his tenure was stoic and guarded, McCarthy was an ocean mist. He was funny, engaging, open. Favre quickly declared the 2006 Packers to be the most talented team he had yet to play for, and a bounce returned to his step. He was introduced to a rookie free-agent fullback from North Dakota State named A.J. Cooper, and from that moment on referred to him only as Fargo. A wide receiver named Carlyle Holiday was signed as a free agent and Favre nicknamed him Doc. During drills one day, Boerigter ran a curl route and Favre fired the ball, high and hard. The free agent receiver leapt, and the pigskin exploded into his right middle finger. "I thought I broke it," Boerigter said. "So I went in afterward for the X-ray and there was just a little crack in it." Favre entered to see how he was doing. "Did I break it?" he asked.

"Yeah," replied Boerigter. "But just a small piece."

"Fuck, I'm getting old," said Favre. "I used to shatter those things."

Both men laughed.

"He was terrific," said Shaun Bodiford, a free agent wide receiver. "My first day there I was running at full tilt, trying to impress everyone. Favre came over to me and said, 'One, we all know you're fast; two, welcome to the team; three, you're here for a reason.' I've played with quarterbacks who will have nothing to do with you. Brett went out of his way to be helpful."

Unfortunately for Favre, his assessment of the team's talent level was incorrect. Green Bay struggled throughout the season, the by-product of yet another so-so year from its quarterback (18 touchdowns, 18 interceptions, 3,885 yards), a thin wide receiver corps, an offensive line that did very little, and Thompson's rebuilding efforts. In a late-November contest against New England, Favre — starting his record 251st straight game — suffered a right elbow injury before halftime, and Rodgers was thrust onto the stage for his first significant action. The results were appalling: 12 passes, four completions, 32 yards, three sacks, no command or feel. The Patriots won, 35-0, and a humbled McCarthy optimistically called the debacle "a great test."

Overall, the Packers ranked 22nd in offense, and scored 10 or fewer points in 6 of 16 games. Once thought to be the master of returning his team from the dead (his career included 35 come-from-behind wins), Favre was now flailing in fourth quarters. Things got so bad that, after a rare Week 10 victory over Minnesota, sports editor Dave DeLand of the *St. Cloud Times* suggested — *purely as ludicrous fantasy* — that Brett Favre would make a wonderful Viking. "Tell me you wouldn't take him right now," he wrote beneath the headline FAVRE WOULD LOOK GREAT IN PURPLE. "In a perfect world, that's what we'd be watching today."

Like that would ever happen.

In the last game of the 2006 season, the Packers secured an 8-8 record with a meaningless 26-7 win over Chicago. As a sign of respect, McCarthy removed Favre in the fourth quarter, and he was saluted with a standing ovation from the Bears players. Afterward, he choked up during a TV interview and said, "It's tough. It's tough. I'm going to miss these guys and miss the game."

When Favre entered the NFL 15 years earlier, snark and ridicule weren't big parts of the sports media landscape. Sure, every so often a newspaper columnist might rip you. But overall, coverage was straightforward. Deadspin.com, a relatively new entity on the sports media landscape (and one more drawn to the social pratfalls of athletes than on-field results), was not an outlet prone to sentimentality or cliché. In Green Bay, journalists often behaved as if the quarterback's decisions were Christlike in importance. Not Deadspin. Wrote Will Leitch, the site's editor: "How can we tell he's not done with us yet? Well, first off, he's Brett Favre. He was back to his old 'will he or won't he?' games with the media last

night, refusing to take questions after the game, which is something media types typically hate, unless they're Brett Favre. But why go out and answer the same 'hey, Brett, we know this is the 47,000th time we've asked
this, but, uh, so . . . next year, we were wondering . . .' questions when
you can just ignore them and get everyone talking about you even more
through the next week?"

The piece was pitch-perfect, and prophetic. Ten days after the Bears
game, Favre said he was planning on returning. Fourteen days after that,
he said he was uncertain, but didn't want to "drag this out." Finally, on
February 2, Favre told Al Jones of the *Biloxi Sun-Herald* that, yes, he
would grace the Packers with another season of quarterbacking. "We
have a good nucleus of young players," he said. "I am so excited about
coming back."

Thompson and McCarthy were ready to move forward with Rodgers,
yet Favre was an icon. To dump him, or trade him, would bring the wrath
of 95 percent of Wisconsin — which just so happened to be the source of
an enormous chunk of the team's revenue. Hence, the Packers issued a
lukewarm statement from Thompson, expressing moderate delight (or
tolerance) with the news. Noted Mike Hart of the *Milwaukee Journal Sentinel*: "That was probably chosen over the more candid, 'Why doesn't he
just &%$#@!! retire already!?'"

So how did Favre thank the organization that allowed him a 16th
season? First, by ripping Thompson in an interview with WMC-TV of
Memphis for failing to acquire Randy Moss,* the eccentric star wide receiver who was dealt by the Raiders to New England. "The last thing I
want to do is start anything," Favre said — before starting something. Second, by announcing he would skip the team's mandatory minicamp to attend his daughter's high school graduation ceremony.

Third . . . by playing some of the most masterful football of his career.

It's perhaps the greatest mystery of many Brett Favre mysteries. How
does a 38-year-old quarterback coming off two straight subpar seasons,
with a hatred of the general manager, an indifference toward the head

---

* In an interview with Tom Silverstein of the *Milwaukee Journal Sentinel*, Moss explained
why he didn't wind up a Packer: "It was like they were telling me that they're going to
take a chance on me, but if you do come here these are the things you have to work out:
'Be on your best behavior; Donald Driver is the top receiver here so don't come in there
trying to step on his toes.' Things like that."

coach, and a young hotshot nipping at his heels, engage upon the ultimate revival? Answer: *By just playing.* Once the season began, Favre stopped worrying about Thompson, about no Randy Moss, about retirement. He performed with the boyish enthusiasm of yesteryear, and didn't seem to mind that he was now surrounded by teammates who were elementary school students when he starred at Southern Miss. Over the past few years, young Packers tiptoed around Favre, hoping to spend more time with Rodgers, their contemporary. Favre often seemed in a rush, unapproachable. He had his guys, and if you weren't one of them, skedaddle. In 2007, that appeared to change. Green Bay opened with four straight victories, highlighted by back-to-back 30-point outbursts against the Giants and Chargers. In the San Diego win, a 31–24 home thriller, the injury-depleted offense started DeShawn Wynn, a rookie seventh-round draft pick, at halfback. Wynn and Favre had exchanged approximately 17 words in their time together, but now they found themselves standing side by side in a shotgun set. "I was on his left, and he changed the play from a pass to a quarterback sprint to the right," Wynn said. "But he didn't give me the time to move over." Wynn, in his third NFL game, screamed toward Favre, in his 264th: "Move me over! Brett, move me over!" Favre took the snap, rolled right, and found himself met by half the Charger defense. "Brett! Brett! Brett!" Wynn yelled. Without making eye contact, Favre fired the ball left to the rookie, who scampered for a 22-yard gain. "Brett ran at me, jumped on my back, hugging me," Wynn said. "It was awesome." In the locker room afterward, Favre admitted to reporters that he didn't know Wynn's name. "God, he was cool," said Wynn. "He'd be eating a Snickers bar in practice, he would come over, offer some to us."

Even without Moss, Green Bay featured its best wide receiver corps in years. Donald Driver, Favre's closest friend on the team, was now in his ninth season and as good as ever. Greg Jennings was in his second year and had a playmaker's skill-set. Koren Robinson possessed Andre Rison–level talent (but also Andre Rison–level inconsistency). Because Ahman Green, the standout halfback, left for Houston as a free agent, McCarthy needed Favre to throw, and throw, and throw. Which sounded wonderful to the quarterback. At the Vikings on September 30, Favre surpassed Dan Marino as the NFL's all-time leader in touchdown passes, connecting with Jennings on a third-and-7 slant from the Minnesota 16. The play was quintessential by-the-seat-of-his-pants Favre. Jennings was supposed to run an 8-yard hitch, but when Favre read blitz he called an audible. Donald Lee, the tight end, failed to hear his quarterback because of the crowd noise. With the clock running down, Favre sprinted toward Lee, told him the instructions, sprinted back behind center, took the snap with a second remaining, watched Jennings bolt past cornerback Marcus McCauley, and hit him in stride. Touchdown. Record. Favre lifted Jennings off the ground as if he were a bag of sugar. He was mobbed by teammates as a message from Marino played on the Metrodome scoreboard, The Packers won 23–16, and Favre was giddy. "It was everything I thought it would be," he said. "Everything."

So was the season. On the one hand, Favre would never again be the same guy he had been as a kid quarterback, bopping around the room and spitting out hip-hop lyrics. "As I've grown older I've become more of a loner," he said. "I used to thrive on that adrenaline. I never wanted it to end." Media access nearly vanished; his once joyfully meandering answers to questions were replaced with a simple yes or no. He hid in side rooms. Stayed out of sight. When, at year's end, the Pro Football Writers of America gave Favre their Good Guy Award, local media members laughed. "I thought it was bullshit," said Greg Bedard, who covered the team for the *Milwaukee Journal Sentinel*. "My first week of training camp I introduced myself to him and said, 'See you around this year.' He couldn't have been nicer. The next time I saw him in the locker room during media availability was the playoffs, when he held court for the national media. I watched that and thought, 'You must be fucking kidding me.'"

And yet Favre was happy, especially when Ryan Grant, a nobody running back acquired from the Giants for a low draft pick, emerged as Green's second coming. Grant was everything Favre liked in a runner — tough, hardened, not one to choose the sideline over contact. He ran for 956 yards and eight touchdowns, and knew he had arrived late in the season, when on an otherwise forgettable Thursday morning, Gordon "Red" Batty, the equipment manager, tapped him on the shoulder and said, "R.G., what are you doing for lunch after practice?"

"Cafeteria," he said. "Like I always do."

"Nah," Batty said. "Go to the back."

Grant retreated to a private section of the locker room, where once a week Favre brought in a luxury chef to cater a gourmet spread. "Hey, Ryan, grab a plate," Favre said. "Come back here and get yourself some food." Grant was equal parts euphoric and bewildered. "It was really cool of him to accept me," he said. "But I also understand why there were mixed feelings about Brett. He didn't change with us. He didn't shower with us. And it's not like you need to shower next to Brett Favre. But why is he on his own? This is a team sport, no?"

"He didn't spend much time with us," said Wynn. "But on the practice field he was amazing. And we won. That's what's most important."

On December 30, Green Bay wrapped a marvelous season with a 34–13 slaying of the Lions. The 13-3 record resulted in an NFC North title, a second seed in the playoffs, and a first-round bye. Favre's 4,155 passing yards were his best in nine years, and he cut his interceptions to 15 while raising his touchdown throws to 28. His 66.5 completion percentage was a career-best. "He literally eliminated [mistakes] from his game," said Tom Coughlin, the Giants' coach. "I haven't really seen anything like that for quite some time."

In the lead-up to the playoffs, *Sports Illustrated* named Favre its 54th Sportsman of the Year. The magazine's editors did not select Favre because he was the NFL's best quarterback (New England's Tom Brady threw 50 touchdowns, and his 117.2 passer rating was far superior to Favre's 95.7). No, they cited his "perseverance and his passion," and pointed specifically to a Week 13 game at Dallas, during which — on a single play — Favre separated his left shoulder *and* took a helmet to his right elbow, that resulted in numbness on two fingers. "To no one's surprise," Alan Shipnuck wrote, "Favre said he expected he would not miss a game."

Against Oakland the following week, Favre started his 270th straight contest. The Packers won. He threw for 266 yards and two touchdowns, including an 80-yard bomb to Jennings.

It looked to be terrific fun.

On the afternoon of Sunday, January 13, in what increasingly felt like a dream season, the Green Bay Packers were handed a gift. One day earlier, they slaughtered the overmatched Seattle Seahawks, 42–20, to reach the NFC title game, where they were expected to meet the top-ranked Dallas Cowboys at Texas Stadium.

Then, against all odds (literally, the Cowboys were favored by a touchdown), the subpar Giants pulled out a 21–17 stunner, thereby assuring the Packers home-field advantage for the chance to reach Super Bowl XLII. In the season's second week, Green Bay destroyed New York, 35–13, at Giants Stadium. It was presumed this matchup would end similarly. "In a nutshell," wrote Todd Finkelmeyer of the *Capital Times,* "the Packers have a significantly better offense than New York, a marginally better defense than the nicked-up Giants and special teams units which have shown the ability to make the big play. Add in the home-field, home-weather advantage, and this is the Packers' to lose."

The game began at 5:42 p.m., with a temperature of 1 below. A sellout crowd of 72,740 filed in for what was being called Ice Bowl II. On the New York sideline, defensive lineman Michael Strahan gathered his teammates for a pep talk. "All you hear is Brett Favre this, Brett Favre that!" he bellowed. "The past is the fucking past! This is the present!" Favre, who by now was as much Wisconsin as Mississippi, looked miserably cold, primarily because he was miserably cold. He wore long white sleeves and a black stocking over his head and neck. At 25, the chills had rarely bothered him. He could not say the same at 38. Favre was also experiencing nerve issues in his throwing arm. The more frigid the temperatures, the more difficult the follow-through on throws.

With five minutes remaining in the third quarter, the Packers took a 17–13 lead on Favre's 12-yard pass to Donald Lee. On the next drive, New York's Ahmad Bradshaw ran for a 4-yard touchdown, but Green Bay tied the score at 20 with Mason Crosby's 37-yard field goal. When New York's Lawrence Tynes missed a 43-yard field goal attempt with 6:49 remaining in the fourth quarter, all felt aligned. When he missed another one, this time 36 yards with 4 seconds in regulation, all felt arranged. "Everything was right there for us," said Will Blackmon, the Green Bay cornerback. "The Giants were coming with the expectation of losing, and they were right to have that. There was no reason to think we don't pull that out. Plus, we had Brett. I mean, think about it. We had Brett Favre."

The game went into overtime, and the Packers won the toss and received the ball. Along the sideline, cornerback Aaron Rouse walked man to man, screaming, "Let's go! Right here! Let's go!" Larry McCarren, the Packers Radio color commentator, leaned toward the microphone and said, "It's Favre time. Here . . . comes . . . Brett."

The Giants had a fierce pass rush and a strong linebacking corps, but the Packers knew they could throw on the defensive backs—and especially Corey Webster, a third-year corner out of LSU. "I don't think they realized how good Corey was," said Dave Tollefson, the former Packers defensive lineman now playing for New York. "Maybe his statistics weren't amazing, but he made everything look so easy. He could make a mistake and correct himself very quickly."

On the second play of the extra period, Favre grabbed the snap at the Packers 28 and dropped far back into the pocket. With defensive end Osi Umenyiora charging from the blind side, Favre took two small hops and launched a pass toward Driver 20 yards down the field. It was the quarterback at his best (powerful arm) and worst (boneheaded decision), and Webster jumped the route, corralled the interception, and ran it back 9 yards. Lambeau went dead. "I just didn't throw it outside enough," Favre explained. "Just didn't get it out far enough." It was, by all measures, a horrible pass.

Four plays later, Tynes hit a 47-yard field goal and the Giants escaped with a 23–20 shocker. Favre was devastated. His shoulders slumped beneath a green Packers parka, he shuffled off the field, suddenly feeling all 38 years on his body. "That's no way for Favre to go out," wrote Barry Wilner of the Associated Press. The fans were watching the end of something they would never again witness. Through the crisp, biting air, that much was clear. In the locker room afterward, there was no peppiness, optimism, hope. Favre simply wanted to wallow.

"I didn't rise up to the occasion," he said. "I have in the past. So my emotions aren't good. I know I expect more out of myself. I know it's part of the game but it's very disappointing."

Brett Favre was ready to retire from the NFL.

The Green Bay Packers are as storied as any franchise in NFL history. Yet of all their superstars, no player approaches the legendary status of Brett Favre. © *Jim Biever*

Brett Favre and Reggie White spending some quiet time alone during a commercial shoot in the mid-1990s. Though very different people, the two teammates formed a tight bond that lasted until White's 2004 death. *© David Thomason*

Brett, with "Big Irv" in 1998, always credited his father with much of his football success. As Brett excelled, Irv basked in the limelight.
© Jim Biever

Brett Favre (second from left) and his older brother, Scott Favre (second from right), shared loves of football, golf, beer, and hijinks. Later, they also shared tragedy. © David Thomason

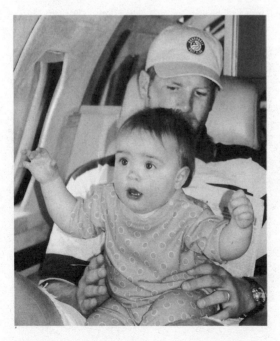

Brett, here with younger daughter Breleigh, was a loving yet distracted father during his days in Green Bay. © David Thomason

Although Brett's friends have varying opinions of Deanna Favre, no one can deny the hell the quarterback-husband put his wife through. © *Jim Biever*

Though he came to think of Green Bay as a second home, Favre relished simple days back in the yard in Mississippi.
© *Jim Biever*

Days after his father died in 2003, Brett Favre returned to the field for a Monday Night Football game at Oakland. He performed brilliantly — and refused to hide his emotions afterward during a locker room speech. © *Jim Biever*

While far from a vocal leader, Favre could use his words to motivate from time to time. Here, before a game against the Vikings, he stands and delivers. © *Jim Biever*

Favre joking around with two of his favorite targets, wide receivers Donald Driver (left) and Greg Jennings. © *Jim Biever*

After the Packers used a first-round pick to select quarterback Aaron Rodgers from California, Brett Favre dedicated himself to making the newcomer miserable. © *Jim Biever*

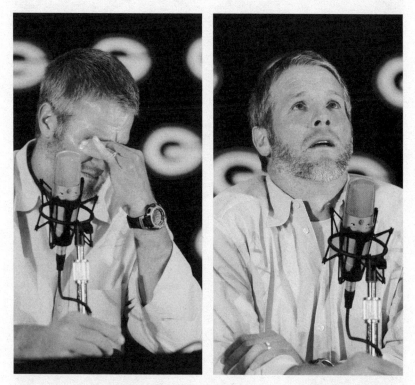

One of Brett Favre's seemingly endless retirement announcements — but this one, in 2008, was for real. Sort of. Kind of. Actually, no. He was a New York Jet months later. © *Jim Biever*

There was no more upsetting sight for Packers fans than Brett Favre in Minnesota Viking duds. To many, it was borderline treason. © *Jim Biever*

23

SOAP

WHAT THE HELL *am I doing?*

Those were the words circulating through Brett Favre's mind, over and over and over again. For half a decade, he had been alluding to retirement as if it were a decision akin to canceling a magazine subscription, or upgrading from economy to midsize rental car. In his heart, deep down, Favre mostly knew he wouldn't be hanging up his uniform. He simply liked the attention, the buzz, the speculation. He mentioned the *R* word, and members of the media spun round and round. It was fun and relatively harmless, and even put a little pressure on the organization to upgrade the roster.

But this . . .

This was different.

On the morning of Thursday, March 6, 2008, Brett Favre found himself sitting on a stage inside the Legends Club in the Lambeau Field Atrium.

He was wearing a collared shirt (a collared shirt!?). He was in a chair, before a table. There was a microphone. It was silver. There was a green backdrop with a bunch of the trademarked Packer logos. About 100 or so members of the media sat across from him. They had been urged to arrive on time. Brett Favre would, at long last, be retiring.

What the hell am I doing here?

He began to speak. Slowly. Softly. In the huddle, he had power and command. Here, he appeared to be shrunken. Small. "It seems like yesterday we were all here. Well, I think we all know why I'm here. First of all, sorry I'm late. But I am officially retiring from the NFL and the Green Bay Packers, and as much as I've thought about what I would say, and how . . ."

Pause.

Deep breath.

What the hell am I doing here?

"I promised I wouldn't get emotional."

Long pause.

A gaze downward.

A wipe of the nose.

What the hell am I doing here?

Deep breaths.

"It's never easy." Deep breath. "You know, it's funny. I've watched hundreds of players retire . . . and you wonder what that would be like . . . you think you're prepared . . ."

What the hell am I doing here?

A tear began to stream down his left cheek. Two tears. No one else in the room dared say a word. The Packers were an organization of legends. Bart Starr. Jim Taylor. Paul Hornung. Vince Lombardi. Most of all, Brett Favre. "But I was telling Deanna on the way over here, God has blessed me with so many great things. Ability, wonderful family. And as I was flying up here today I thought about so many different things and how I wanted to say some of the things that I felt like I need to say, but He gave me an opportunity to use my abilities, and I seized that opportunity." A lengthy pause. "I thank Him for that."

Many in attendance had covered Favre through the highs and lows. They arrived with justified skepticism — another year, another Favre retirement. Clearly, this was not another Favre retirement. This *was* Favre's retirement. "It's been everything I thought it would be, and then some," he said. Tears. Breaths. Tears. "And it's hard to leave. You think you're prepared for it. I know there's been comments and issues in the press lately about why I'm leaving, whether or not the Packers did enough, whether or not Ted and Mike tried to convince me to stay. None of those things have anything to do with me retiring, and that's from the heart. I've given everything I possibly can give to this organization, to the game of football . . .

. . . and I don't think I have anything left to give."

Wait. Stop. Hold it. Did Brett Favre just say "think"? Because there's a difference between "I don't have anything left to give" and "I don't *think* I have anything left to give."

What the hell am I doing here?

"I know I can play, but I don't think I want to. And that's really what it comes down to . . ."

Again, the "think." Did Brett Favre not want to play, or *think* he did not want to play?

He continued.

"Fishing for different answers and what ifs and will he come back and things like that, what matters is it's been a great career for me, and it's over. As hard as that is for me to say, it's over. There's only one way for me to play the game, and that's 100 percent. Mike and I had that conversation the other night, and I will wonder if I made the wrong decision. I'm sure on Sundays, I will say I could be doing that, I should be doing that . . ."

By the time the press conference concluded and Favre had sniffled and sighed and paused his way through 10 gut-wrenching minutes, a good number of those in attendance thought the whole show reeked of ma-larkey. Not that Favre was lying. It was just that, when superstar athletes hold retirement announcements, they are almost always decisive and ad-amant. From Kareem Abdul-Jabbar and Julius Erving to Mike Schmidt and Wayne Gretzky, the words "I'm done" do not tend to find themselves attached to an "I think." Perhaps that's why, when it was time to open the floor to questions, the first one was whether Favre just might change his mind.

"I think last year and the year before I was tired and it took a while but I came back," America's newest retiree replied. "Something told me this time not to come back. It took a while once again. Once again, I won-dered if it was the right decision. But I think in my situation, and I had this conversation with Mike and Ted, that it's a unique situation in that at 17 years I had one of the better years in my career, the team had a great year, everything seems to be going great, the team wants me back, I still can play, for the most part everyone would think I would be back, would want me back. That's a unique situation going into an 18th season. There's no guarantees next year, personally and as a team, and I'm well aware of that. It's a tough business and last year and the year before I questioned whether or not I should come back because I didn't play at a high-enough level. Other people questioned that. I really didn't question my commit-ment. I just wondered, 'Could I not play anymore?' I know I can play. But this year, and this is not the first year but it really to me and Deanna was more noticeable, the stress part of it. It's demanding. It always has been, but I think as I've gotten older I'm much more aware of that. I'm much more aware of how hard it is to win in this league and to play at a high level. I'm not up to the challenge anymore. I can play, but I'm not up to the challenge. You can't just show up and play for three hours on Sunday. If you could, there'd be a lot more people doing it and they'd be doing it for a lot longer. I have way too much pride, I expect a lot out of myself, and if I cannot do those things 100 percent, then I can't play."

Translation: Who the hell knows?

Later that day, Favre flew home to Mississippi, to the house he and Deanna had built on 465 acres in Sumrall. They returned to Sam, the chocolate lab; to lots of turkey and deer to hunt; to mowing the lawn and riding his tractor and swimming in the pool and watching the ducks swim in the two ponds. The estate encapsulated all he had endured. The concussions, the sprains, the breaks. This is why — so the Favres would forever live in comfort.

What the hell am I doing here?

It was a mistake. Deep down, he knew. Favre was certain the Packers wanted him to retire. Green Bay didn't use a first-round pick on Aaron Rodgers to merely have him leave without ever really playing. The future *needed* to be now. Thompson never uttered those words, but his actions and mannerisms screamed them. Even when, in February, the general manager called Favre from the league's annual scouting combine to say he was welcome to return. Those were mere words. Brett felt it, Deanna felt it. They were no longer wanted by the organization they had carried for nearly two decades. But, when asked what he planned on doing with his life, Favre shrugged. "Nothing," he told a reporter.

Nothing?

What the hell am I doing here?

When Willie Mays retired from the majors in 1973, he observed that "growing old is just a helpless hurt." Favre didn't feel old. He could still launch a football, could still roam the pocket. When Barry Sanders left the Detroit Lions at age 31 after the 1998 season, he said his desire to exit the game "is greater than my desire to remain in it." Favre didn't desire to exit the game. He wanted Sundays in front of 70,000 fans. He wanted the smell of the locker room, the feel of a new pair of cleats. He was a football player.

Mark Murphy, the Packers' new president, announced 12 days later that the team would retire Favre's No. 4 during a game in the upcoming season. "I would say it's a no-brainer," he said. But, truly, it was more than a no-brainer. There was fear (justified fear) that Favre would once again bring forth his inner Jason Voorhees and return from the dead. The more official his retirement felt, the less likely *Friday the 13th: Green Bay Edition* would come to pass.

In the spring of 2008, few sports writers possessed the chops of Sam Farmer.

The veteran *Los Angeles Times* scribe had emerged in journalism as the Oakland Raiders beat writer for the *San Jose Mercury News,* and now was in his eighth year covering the NFL for the *Times.* His reputation as a reporter was unblemished. When Farmer broke news, you knew it was legitimate.

A couple of weeks after Favre's press conference, Farmer started hearing things. "I was told from a couple of sources that Bus Cook had been kicking the tires on Brett coming back," said Farmer. "I was told he was taking the temperature, like, 'What if this were to happen . . .'"

On April 4, the headline FAVRE RETIRED? MAYBE NOT appeared on the newspaper's website. According to Farmer, Cook "had quietly inquired with teams about their interest in trading for the three-time NFL most valuable player. The sources did not indicate whether Favre knew of the inquiries." Favre, it turns out, had asked James Campen, the team's offensive line coach, whether the Packers might take him back. Farmer reached out to Cook, who denied the account and added, "He's retired, period, point blank."

In the coming days, Farmer's work was condemned by many in the mainstream media. When reached by *Sports Illustrated*'s website, Favre insisted, "That's the last thing I'm thinking about." And then — "I suppose anything could happen. How will I feel in months? Who knows?"

Um . . .

A few days later, Favre told Al Jones of the *Biloxi Sun-Herald* that should the Packers reach out to him, he could — theoretically — reconsider. "It would be hard to pass up," he said. "I guess." He called a return "tempting."

Um . . .

The organization responded in the best way it could, by announcing that not only would Favre's number be retired in 2008, but it would be retired in one of the first four home contests. A few days later, the team finalized September 8 — the season opener against Minnesota — as Brett Favre's special day. Terrific times awaited, Murphy insisted. The quarterback was a Packer for life, and the jersey thing should happen as soon as possible. "To me," Murphy said wistfully, "he's made a decision to retire."

At the Packers' facility, meanwhile, the players spent late May going through the drills of organized team activities. On May 21, Rodgers arrived, only to look 10 feet away from his stool and see Favre's locker still intact, complete with a FAVRE 4 nameplate and his old shoulder pads dangling from a hook. "No. 4, he's not here," said Donald Driver. "But he's here in spirit."

One day in early June, Peter King was washing his golden retriever, Bailey, in the driveway of his New Jersey home. His phone rang — it was Favre. "Peter, can I ask you a question?" Favre said. "An off-the-record one?"

"Of course," King said.

"Well, what would you think if I came back?" Favre asked.

"Really?" said King. "Are you sure you want to?"

"Pretty sure," Favre said.

"Well," King said, "I guess it depends where you'd be coming back to."

"My preference is to stay in the [NFC North], because I know the teams," he said. "My first choices would be Minnesota or Chicago."

King was thunderstruck. "Brett," he said, "if you do that, Packer fans will be pissed off. If you wanna play somewhere else, a few will be pissed. But Chicago or Minnesota? Little kids will tear down their Brett Favre posters and burn them."

Three months after Farmer's initial Favre-might-return report was discredited by the quarterback, his agent, and much of the sports media world, ESPN ran a piece that said the quarterback told McCarthy he had "an itch" to play. By pure coincidence, the story ran on the same day *Sports Illustrated* pre-released an upcoming Rodgers profile, in which he said, "I don't feel I need to sell myself to the fans. They need to get on board or keep their mouths shut."

This was *not* going well for the Packers — and it became significantly worse on July 11, when Favre officially asked the team to release his rights so that he could make a comeback with another organization. Two things, both unforeseeable a mere few months earlier, were now officially undeniable:

1. Brett Favre would be playing in the NFL in 2008.
2. Brett Favre was declaring war on the Green Bay Packers.

Except, really, it wasn't the Green Bay Packers, but Ted Thompson. One of the league's worst-kept secrets through the years had been the quarterback's contempt for his team's general manager. Favre didn't like the way the Packers drafted. He didn't like the way the Packers approached free agents. But most of all, he didn't like how Thompson addressed him as he would any other player. There was never an ounce of special treatment, or extra consideration, or even the type of check-in-and-see-what-you-think courtesy phone calls Jerry Jones paid Tony Romo in Dallas, Robert Kraft paid Tom Brady with the Patriots. All the perks Favre enjoyed (the private space, the back-entrance parking, the weekly catered meal) were by-products of the Mike Sherman era. Thompson wasn't going to yank them away, but he felt no need to add on. In his mind, Favre was a great player — but great players come and go. Plus, for a guy long known as being low maintenance, Favre sure was high maintenance. Were he 25 and entering his prime, perhaps the demands would be digestible. But Thompson saw no reason to bow down to a player approaching 40 — especially one who hadn't sniffed a Super Bowl in a decade.

Favre's two mouthpieces at this time were Al Jones, the *Biloxi Sun-Herald* reporter who protected and defended a man he also covered, and Scott Favre, his older brother. On the day Brett Favre requested his independence, Scott Favre explained to Jones's readers, "Why wouldn't he want a release? [The Packers] have moved on. By not saying anything, it says a lot. If they wanted him back, they could have said, 'If you want to come back, we want you back.' Why would he want to go back if he's not wanted? You tell me?"

Wrote Jones: "I could not agree more . . . it was only a matter of time before the bomb was dropped and from my standpoint, the reason for the explosion around the NFL falls on the shoulders of . . . Ted Thompson."

It was insanity. Favre decided to retire, and the Packers had a talented young quarterback ready to take over. Favre held a press conference, insisting he was done. Favre denied he was returning, then denied again and again and again. And this was now . . . *Ted Thompson's fault?* "Ted was the kind of guy who believes all your loyalty has to be toward the team," said Tom Silverstein, the *Milwaukee Journal Sentinel* writer. "Favre was a distraction, but Ted refused to let him dictate how things went. Favre took exception to that. But Ted was pretty much right."

Behind the scenes, Bus Cook was working the phones, working the media, supplying information as an "anonymous source close to Favre." According to the "anonymous source close to Favre," the quarterback's feelings were hurt. Also according to an "anonymous source close to Favre," he was spending time at Oak Grove High School near his home doing "core-oriented workouts." Translation: he was ready to play. Generally speaking, those who covered Favre trusted Cook as they would a rattlesnake in the bunny coop. He was your typical fast-talking agent, spewing the side of the story that helped his client. He was notorious for only returning phone calls when it met his needs. Among his detractors was Bonita Favre, Brett's mother, who neither believed nor particularly liked Cook.

On July 8, Thompson, Favre, and Cook spoke via conference call, and it wasn't pretty. Favre wanted to return — period. The Packers wanted him retired. There was no wiggle room, and the hostility was palpable. Three days later, Cook sent a formal letter to the organization, requesting Favre's unconditional contractual release — "with no strings attached." According to an anonymous source (aka: Bus Cook), Favre did not desire a trade, because he wanted to decide where he would play next. "Why would he want to play where he's not wanted?" Scott Favre told Lori Nickel of the *Journal Sentinel*, repeating what he'd told Al Jones. "The Packers have moved on, so why wouldn't he?"

The letter was greeted inside the Green Bay offices with a mixture of incredulity and derision. *Sure, we'll just let our legendary quarterback go sign wherever he wants. That's a wonderful idea . . .*

Training camp was scheduled to begin in two weeks, and nobody knew how this would end. The day after the conference call, Thompson conducted a series of damage-control interviews, telling reporters that Favre could possibly return to the team, but as Rodgers's backup. It sounded silly, but he was sincere. Thompson made certain to avoid ripping the old quarterback, walking the tightrope between *We admire him* and *This is a nightmare*. Even within the facilities, behind closed doors, Thompson remained respectful of Favre. He, too, had once been an NFL player, and remembered the emotions that accompanied retirement from the Houston Oilers in 1984. He wasn't enjoying Favre's indecision. But he understood. "Ted gets as vilified as anyone, but he never said one bad word about Brett," said Jason Wied, the team's general counsel at the time. "Not one bad word. Ever."

Life was a daily soap opera, starring Favre as the jilted lover and Thompson as the heartless villain. On July 13, 100 Packers fans held a pro-Favre rally outside Lambeau Field, chanting "We want Brett!" and holding FAVRE FOR PRESIDENT signs.* Newspaper columnists across the country made their pitches to Favre. David Whitley of the *Orlando Sentinel* penned a piece headlined HEY, BRETT! WE'D LOVE TO SEE YOU BECOME A BUC. Bob Matthews of the *Rochester Democrat and Chronicle* stepped forward with FAVRE PLAYING FOR BILLS ISN'T SUCH A CRAZY IDEA. Cam Inman, a *Contra Costa Times* columnist, gave the hometown 49ers and Raiders a push with DO US A FAVOR, FAVRE: COME TO BAY AREA. The day of the rally, Favre appeared on Fox News for an exclusive (and weird) two-part interview with Greta Van Susteren, during which he repeatedly bashed Thompson for, among other things, failing to acquire Randy Moss and for refusing to interview Steve Mariucci, his old offensive coordinator, for the head coaching position that ultimately went to McCarthy. He added that he was tempted to show up at Green Bay's training camp, simply to call the team's "bluff." Less than 24 hours later, another pro-Favre rally was held, this one in the parking lot of the Wisconsin State Fair in Milwaukee. Thirty people attended.

The Packers filed tampering charges against the Vikings, who by now were communicating with Cook about Favre coming to Minnesota. (The Vikings refuted the charges, but they were lying. There was regular contact between the team and the agent — "That is undeniable," said Wied.) Green Bay then hired Ari Fleischer, the former press secretary to President George W. Bush, to handle Favre backlash. On the night of Saturday, July 19, Favre came to Lambeau Field to induct Frank Winters, his friend and longtime center, into the team's Hall of Fame. He spoke for three minutes, noting that Green Bay is "a special place. There's a lot of tradition."

Favre then walked off the stage and ducked out a side door.

· · ·

---

* It can be noted here that Favre rarely voted, and would probably be an awful presidential candidate.

The back-and-forth continued. The rumors flew. On the same day the *New York Post* published a story insisting Favre would remain retired, the *Minneapolis Star Tribune* ran a piece suggesting Favre would wind up a Viking. Favre agreed to not report to camp with the other Packers — but that didn't mean he would permanently stay away. An exasperated Murphy traveled to Mississippi on July 30 and — without Thompson or McCarthy's knowledge — offered Favre a 10-year, $20 million deal *not* to play football. Favre's people immediately leaked the information to select members of the national sports media. "His solution," Favre wrote in a text to ESPN's Ed Werder, "although awkward and unsettling for most, may be the best in the end."

Finally, the NFL stepped in. Roger Goodell, the league's commissioner, decreed that either Favre and the Packers come to some sort of agreement by Monday, August 4, or he would take action. "I think we have to force it," Goodell said. "It's come to the point where there needs to be some decisions made."

That Sunday, the Packers reluctantly agreed their old quarterback could return and battle Rodgers. Brett, Deanna, and Bus Cook boarded a plane later that day to fly from Hattiesburg to Green Bay. In a few hours the team would host the annual Family Night scrimmage at Lambeau, and Murphy told Favre via phone that he could walk onto the field for a wave to the crowd. As the three flew north to Austin Straubel International Airport, however, the Packers decided to withdraw the invite. Favre could sit in a Lambeau luxury box, but that would be all. He was *not* happy.

Before leaving Mississippi, Favre's handlers called some supporters in Green Bay to leak the news of his arrival, and to make certain there would be a swarm of adoring die-hards at the airport. Hence, as Favre and Co. exited the aircraft, myriad fans and TV cameras braved a soft rain to greet them with loud cheers. Favre, dressed in a black T-shirt and cargo shorts, a backpack slung over his shoulder, smiled and waved with his right hand high in the air. It was all prearranged. "The goal was to pressure the Packers," said a Favre friend. "Brett doesn't get told no by anybody." Around that same time at Lambeau Field, Rodgers — playing in the Family Night scrimmage — was being booed. His crime? Not wearing No. 4.

Favre had a four-hour meeting with McCarthy at the stadium. Members of the media presumed the discussion concerned how he would fit in with the 2008 Packers. It was nothing of the sort. Instead, Favre let loose. He was furious with the organization, furious with Thompson, furious with their unwillingness to let him sign with the Vikings. He didn't want to back up Aaron Rodgers, or even have a competition with Aaron Rodgers. He had given 16 seasons to the organization. Wasn't that worth something? The following morning McCarthy told the media that Favre was not "in the right mindset" to play for Green Bay.

"We agreed to disagree," McCarthy said. "We stood on opposite sides of the fence on a number of issues, and I respect the way he feels. But the one thing that I was looking for out of that conversation [was], was he ready and committed to play football for the Green Bay Packers? And his answer frankly throughout the conversation [indicated] that's not where he was. So with that, we didn't really move ahead. I had a list of questions for him to answer. I had questions that I felt were important for him to answer. I had questions for him from the locker room, from his teammates . . . I don't want to speak for him, but based on where he is [and] the path that it took to get to this [point], he wasn't in the right mindset to play here."

In other words, it was over. But not before one last meeting.

The following morning, Thompson, Murphy, Wied, and Russ Ball, the team's contract negotiator, drove to the Favre household to meet with Brett, Deanna, and Cook. There was no confusion over the purpose. This wasn't to keep Brett Favre a Packer. It was to be rid of him. As the four men entered through the front door, the tension was cheesecake-thick. Brett made them wait. He was dressed in a ratty T-shirt and a pair of shorts. They sat down in a living room. No food or drinks. Just talk. "I wanna go to Minnesota," Favre said — and the frowns spoke volumes.

"Look, Brett, we have a lot of respect for you," Thompson said. "But we have to do what's best for the Green Bay Packers. You playing for Minnesota — that won't happen."

Favre was not happy. "My blood was boiling," he told the NFL Network. "I was not good enough to play there, but I was too good to play against them."

He took a different approach. The Lions were in the NFC North, but were never a threat to the Packers.

"How about Detroit?" he asked. "I could play there."

Silence. "No," Thompson said. "We won't trade you there." More silence. "But how about Tampa?"

Favre didn't hate the idea. The Buccaneers' head coach was Jon Gruden, the former Mike Holmgren assistant. Their quarterbacks, Jeff Garcia and Brian Griese, were ordinary. He could wear flip-flops and shorts without the fear of frostbite. "I dunno," Favre said. "Not my first choice. I dunno."

"The funniest thing was watching Bus Cook," said one of the attendees. "His face was red, he looked absolutely beaten down. He was clearly tired, and he couldn't do right for his client for the first time in their relationship together."

The meeting lasted an hour. There was no resolution, just awkward handshakes. "It was the worst two hours of my life," said Wied.

Where would Brett Favre wind up? Nobody knew.

On the evening of July 3, 2008, a month before the Favre-Packer divorce became official, Adam Schefter, an on-air reporter with the NFL Network, was eating dinner at La Ginestra, the Italian bistro near his home in Glen Cove, New York. "I had the branzino," he said. While there, he bumped into Mike Tannenbaum, the general manager of the New York Jets and a man he had known for some time.

With the draft having passed two months ago and opening day two months away, the NFL landscape was dominated by all things Brett Favre. Where would he go? When would he go? How would he go? "We started talking about it," said Schefter. "And I remember laying out to him how the Favre scenario would turn out." To his credit, Schefter was never one to get caught up in the day-to-day frenzy of sports. He capably took the long view, and in this case he had some strong opinions. "People are missing the point on Favre," he told Tannenbaum. "They're talking about him getting released, but there's no way that happens. The Packers aren't just going to let him sign with whoever he wants."

Schefter had thought much about possible landing spots for the quarterback, and only two teams made any sense. "It's Tampa Bay," he said, "and it's you." The Jets were coming off a nightmarish 4-12 season. Their starting quarterback, Chad Pennington, missed one game with a high ankle sprain, then was benched for Kellen Clemens, a subpar backup. Pennington had been one of the team's four first-round picks in 2000, but repeated injuries and a weak throwing arm made him an option with limited returns.

"Adam first brought the Favre idea to my attention," said Tannenbaum. "And I definitely thought, 'This is a pretty unique thing.'"

In the aftermath of the meeting at Favre's house, the consensus was that the Tampa Bay Buccaneers were about to have themselves a new quarterback. Brett, Deanna, and Bus Cook left Green Bay for Hattiesburg on the afternoon of Wednesday, August 6, with expectations that by the time the plane landed, the Bucs would likely wrap a deal. "I was sure we had Brett Favre," said Gruden. The Packers did not want players, only picks. Thompson and John Schneider, the Packers' director of football operations, were in regular contact with Bruce Allen, Tampa's general manager, as well as Tannenbaum. In fact, the Packers had first contacted the Jets — as well as 20 other teams — on July 17 with the message that Favre was on the trading block. A week later, when camp commenced, Tannenbaum called Pennington and Clemens into his office out of professional courtesy, but assured both players it was merely rumor. Now, with only two organizations in the running, "merely rumor" was "potentially enormous acquisition." Woody Johnson, the team owner, met with Tannenbaum, head coach Eric Mangini, and Brian Schottenheimer, the offensive coordinator, after a practice to discuss whether Favre could succeed in New York. "For me," said Schottenheimer, "it was a no-brainer."

Tannenbaum spoke with Favre on Monday night, and presented him with the 20-minute sales pitch of his life. "Look, you won't be practicing in Times Square," he said. "The only time you'll see a big building, Brett, is when you want to see one, I promise you. It's not what you think it is. In terms of where we're gonna be is rural New Jersey. There are a lot of good people here . . . We have four first-round picks on the offensive line . . . You can make your own judgment. I think Green Bay has good skill players, but so do we. I feel like we have a good team . . . you give us an opportunity to make it better."

He and Cook had two phone conversations, but Tannenbaum knew Favre was not feeling New York. The agent literally said, "Mike, he does not like you guys. He feels more comfortable in Tampa Bay." That same day Deanna reached out to a member of the Packers board of directors, begging him to intervene and make certain a Jets deal would not happen. When the man said there was nothing he could do, Deanna turned noticeably upset. "It was craziness," said a family friend. "Nobody knew what would happen. Deanna tried the whole 'Brett has been so loyal to the organization' thing, and everyone was fed up and sick of it." The Buccaneers were willing to surrender a third-round draft pick and, if the Packers so desired, Griese. Green Bay liked what the Jets were offering—a conditional fourth-round pick that would rise in value with different milestones. Should the team reach the Super Bowl, New York would owe the Packers a first-rounder. Thompson and Murphy also preferred Favre leave the NFC.

Finally, late Wednesday night, Thompson, Schneider, and Tannenbaum reached an agreement. Woody Johnson, the billionaire owner of the franchise, was at a movie with family in the Hamptons when his cell phone rang. He excused himself from the theater and took the call. It was Tannenbaum. "Woody, we're ready to go," he said. "I think Brett is gonna come, but I can't be 100 percent sure he's going to show up. And if he doesn't, and we make this trade, you and I are going to be on the back page of the tabloids next to a headline that says, THE TWO DUMBEST MEN IN THE HISTORY OF NEW YORK SPORTS."

There was also an uncomfortable catch: because of salary-cap restrictions, the Jets would have to simultaneously cut a big contract while adding the $12.7 million Favre was owed. The obvious move was to shed Pennington's $6 million. "Which means if we cut Chad and Brett doesn't come, we're left with Kellen Clemens," Tannenbaum told the owner.

Johnson listened, thought for a few seconds. "OK," he said. "Go ahead and let's do it."

Tannenbaum called Schneider and Thompson to confirm the exchange: a draft pick for Brett Favre. It was approximately 11:00 p.m. eastern standard time. "Ted," he said, "we're gonna do it."

"Sign those trade papers right now," Thompson replied.

"Done," he said. "Signed."

At 11:15 p.m., Brett Favre was the property of the New York Jets. Tannenbaum, sitting at his desk in the team's offices, started to scream. *"Yesssssss! Yesssssss! Brett Favre! Yesssssss!"* Thompson, sitting at his desk in the team's offices, took a deep breath. Thank God that was over with.

The Jets, of course, had no idea whether Favre would actually come to New York. After completing the swap, Tannenbaum dialed the number for Cook. "Bus," he said, "I've got an update for you."

"Brett's not really sure what he wants to do," Cook said.

"Well, just let Brett know he's a New York Jet," Tannenbaum said. "We just traded for him."

"You did what?" Cook yelled. "You're a crazy bastard. I told you I don't know if he's coming. This was not smart."

"Listen, I just want to talk to him," Tannenbaum said. "I have a great story to tell. We're going to put him in a great situation to be successful. We're excited to have him."

"Lemme call you back," Cook said.

The next 20 minutes were the longest of Tannenbaum's life. When his cell finally rang, Cook kept it short. "OK," he said. "Brett will talk to you." Moments later, Favre called.

"Hey, Brett," said Tannenbaum.

"Hey, Mike," Favre replied. "What's the dress code?"

Mangini, the Jets coach, was a stickler for rules. Members of the team were required to travel in sport coats and ties.

"What do you want it to be?" Tannenbaum said.

"I don't like wearing coats and ties," Favre said.

Tannenbaum laughed. "What size waist do you have, Brett?" he asked.

"I'm a 38," Favre replied.

"Look," Tannenbaum said, "you tell me you're coming and I'll have a custom-made pair of size 38 camouflage hunting pants that I'm gonna make mandatory on every one of our away trips."

With that line, the tension melted. Tannenbaum had Favre converse with Mangini, and the chat went well. By the time the GM next spoke with the quarterback, the outlook shifted. It was no longer whether he would join the Jets. "We're gonna come down and get you," Tannenbaum said. "We're gonna stand shoulder to shoulder with you, and we're gonna do great things together."

"Alright," Favre said. "Get those pants and come on down."

Tannenbaum hung up and fired off the most excited e-mail of his life. It was sent to Bruce Speight, the team's media relations director, and read: "I have great FUCKING NEWS! CALL ME! GREAT NEWS!!!!!!!!!!!"

At 12:36 a.m., the organization sent out a press release that began, "The New York Jets have acquired QB Brett Favre from the Green Bay Packers . . ."

By the time Tannenbaum returned to his Roslyn, Long Island, home from the Jets' facility, it was three o'clock Thursday morning. Just a few hours earlier, Tannenbaum told his wife, Michelle, that it wasn't looking good. Now, he entered the bedroom and shook her from a deep sleep. "Hey, Michelle! Hey, Michelle!"

"Huh . . . what . . . huh?"

"We got Brett Favre!" he said again.

"What do I wear?" she mumbled.

"Um, I don't know," he said. "But we have to go get him."

Michelle woke up and changed from pajamas to a pantsuit. Within two hours, the Tannenbaums, accompanied by Dave Szott, the Jets' player-development director, found themselves at Republic Airport in Farmingdale, Long Island, boarding Johnson's twin-jet Cessna Citation. "This sure beats JetBlue," Michelle said. At 5:54 a.m., the plane lifted off for Hattiesburg. Mike Tannenbaum slept the entire two-hour journey. They were met by a limo, which took the crew to Cook's office. En route, Tannenbaum texted Favre, asking what sort of dip he liked. "Copenhagen," Favre replied.

In the name of a strong first impression, Tannenbaum had the car stop so he could grab Favre a tin.

Cook drove the three-person Jets convoy to the Favre household. They were shown in by Deanna and asked to make themselves comfortable as Favre prepared to leave. For the next 90 minutes, they waited, and waited, and waited. The Tannenbaums were in the process of constructing a house, and Michelle spent much of the time perusing the Favre's palatial kitchen. "Michelle, this is Brett Favre's house," he said. "You married a front-office executive, not a quarterback. Keep that in mind."

Tannenbaum checked his phone. He chatted with Szott. He paced. Mostly he sweated. He first started working for the Jets in 1997, and through the years he'd seen his fair share of sure things devolve into near misses. When Favre finally came down, he looked at the threesome and said, "Hey, lemme show you guys around the property!"

Glub.

"I'm thinking, *The last thing I want you to do is show me around the property — I just want to get you to New York*," said Tannenbaum. "But that would not have gone over so well."

Following the tour, the fivesome (Szott, the Tannenbaums, and Brett and Deanna) took a limo back to the airport. There were several TV reporters waiting outside, so Tannenbaum handed Favre a Jets baseball cap. "Brett, put this on," he said.

Deanna grinned awkwardly. "You're gonna break a lot of hearts," she said, "when you get out of this car."

On the flight to Morristown Muni Airport in New Jersey, the women and Szott sat in the rear of the plane, Tannenbaum and Favre in front. Brett was talking when, suddenly, the Jets' general manager fell asleep, then stirred awake, then fell asleep again. "I was just dead tired," he said.

Favre laughed and asked Tannenbaum, "Am I boring you?" The quiet time was actually torturous for Brett Favre. *How did this all happen? Was it a good thing or a bad thing? Maybe I should have just stayed retired.* Deanna could see the concern across her husband's face. "Hey," she said. "Whether you're here one year, two years, five weeks, whatever, you've got to be committed."

He nodded.

After finally landing, the group took a helicopter to Johnson's farm in Bedminster, New Jersey. Favre and the Jets owner spent several hours together, discussing everything from football to hunting. "That was a pivotal part of everything," said Tannenbaum. "Having them start off on the right foot."

The Jets were in Cleveland for the preseason opener against the Browns, and Tannenbaum and Favre, along with Johnson, Clay Hampton, the senior director of operations, and Matt Higgins, the executive vice president for business operations, flew to join the team (Deanna returned to Mississippi). Favre had grown accustomed to the beats and rhythms of Green Bay. From the little (where to grab a bottle of water) to the big (the playbook), Favre knew the Packers like he knew the contours of his own hands. Now, within a matter of hours, everything had changed. He was a Jet? The idea itself felt out of body. Thomas Jones was a Jet. Kerry Rhodes was a Jet. Chad Pennington was a Jet. But Brett Favre? It didn't sound right.

There was also the matter of the now-released Pennington, who could not have been more beloved by teammates and coaches. "He was the best," said Brad Smith, a wide receiver. "Chad was the kind of guy who had the guys to his house, who was all about hard work, togetherness." Some of New York's players first heard of the Favre trade as they arrived at Cleveland Browns Stadium. They were also learning of Pennington's expatriation — their longtime quarterback was nowhere to be found. He had checked out of the Cleveland Marriott and flown back to New York. "I loved Chad," said Chansi Stuckey, a wide receiver. "He was a great guy. But this was Brett Favre. It's like, Carmelo Anthony is amazing. But if you have a chance to get Michael Jordan, you take it . . ."

Favre arrived at the stadium roughly 45 minutes before kickoff. He introduced himself to as many Jets as he could, and took a moment to meet Nick Mangold, the standout center. "My hands are gonna be tickling your balls," he said, and Mangold let out a hearty chuckle. Fullback Tony Richardson, 36 and in his 14th NFL season, extended his hand. "I'm so happy you're here, Brett," he said. "Because now I'm no longer the oldest guy."

A hastily arranged press conference was held in the bowels of the facility. There were 150 reporters, and Favre sat between Tannenbaum and Johnson. "It was manic," said Peter King. "It was very intense and people were pushing, jockeying for position, trying to get near him." Favre held up his new kelly-green No. 4 Jets jersey and grinned for the cameras. He was wearing a gray T-shirt and white baseball cap with a green *NY* stitched in. His face was covered by weeks' old stubble, and he looked both tired and mildly confused. First, Johnson spoke. Then Tannenbaum conveyed his appreciation for Pennington and his excitement about Favre. Finally, the new quarterback of the New York Jets took his turn. "To a certain degree, I really don't know what I'm getting into," he said. "And I'm talking about from a team standpoint. What can I do in a short amount of time to get this team where we wanna go and get myself ready. It doesn't matter what city it's in. I'm here for one reason — not to do commercials and Broadway and all those things. I'm here to help the Jets win. And that's why they got me. So . . . no offense to you guys . . . ladies, but the sooner I can get to that, the better."

Before the session concluded, Favre admitted that he would have preferred to be a Bear or a Viking. "Maybe that was a little bit of vindictive nature, or whatever, competitive nature, whatever," he said. "I think in the end, that was probably the wrong motive."

After 20 or so minutes, Favre walked onto the field. He had a headset strapped over his cap, a play sheet in his right hand. He played catch for a few moments with Cortez Robinson, the equipment assistant, and spent much of the game alongside Clemens and Bubba Franks, the tight end who had played with him for eight seasons in Green Bay. "It's a new system for him," said Clemens, "so I'd give him the play and Bubba served as a translator."

The Jets beat the Browns, 24–20, and the ideal schedule would have Favre flying back to New York with his teammates.* That was changed, however, when the office of Michael Bloomberg, New York City's mayor, requested the new quarterback come to City Hall for an official wel-

---

* New York's star that night was Brett Ratliff, a fringe quarterback who threw two touchdown passes. The lead to the ensuing ESPN.com story was, "A new quarterback named Brett threw two long touchdown passes for the New York Jets."

come. Favre was told of the plan by Higgins and seemed agreeable. So he, Johnson, Tannenbaum, and Higgins took the owner's private flight back to New York City. The Jets booked two rooms at a midtown hotel, and Favre and Tannenbaum arrived at approximately 3:00 a.m. Neither one had packed extra clothing, so four hours later there was a knock on the door. It was a man holding a large box filled with garments. "We've now spent, like, 28 straight hours together, I hadn't slept in two days, and we're rummaging through shirts and boxers," said Tannenbaum. "I paused for a second and thought, *I'm sharing boxers with Brett Favre. What is going on here?*" Favre settled on a powder-blue short-sleeve golf shirt, khakis, and his old sneakers. Tannenbaum stuck with what he had been wearing for the past few days (slacks, dress shirt), but went with a new pair of underwear.

"In hindsight it was too much on Brett," he said. "When the mayor wants to meet it's hard to say no. But we should have waited."

Together they took a town car to City Hall and entered the Blue Room, where they were met by Johnson, Bloomberg, and a monsoon of reporters of all stripes. "Just like home," Favre cracked. What followed was an ode to awkwardness. Though a popular mayor, Bloomberg was both small (five feet eight) and a noted sports ignoramus.* Standing behind a podium, with Favre sitting to his left, Bloomberg read from a sheet of paper filled with prepared notes. "You are joining a team that won the Super Bowl with a quarterback named Broadway Joe," Bloomberg said. "Now Broadway Brett has a nice ring to it, and . . . here's something to make the name official." He stepped back, turned around, bent at the waist, and handed Favre a green-and-white BROADWAY street sign, not unlike those peddled at Times Square storefronts for $5.99. "This is your very own street sign," he said, then approached Favre. They initially posed with the quarterback in his chair, but Favre rose after the mayor softly snapped, "You better stand up and do this." Of the 8,000 awkward and uncomfortable moments of Brett Favre's life, this had to rank first. He was wearing clothes that were not his, standing in a city he barely knew, next to a mayor he had never heard of, accepting a street sign that would surely wind up in either a trash bin or a Jets intern's man cave.

Before Favre left, the mayor also presented him with a $4 MetroCard

---

* Wrote Michael J. Lewis, the veteran newspaper scribe: "Only Ted Kennedy knew less about sports than Bloomberg."

("If you had picked a higher number," he joked, "you would've gotten more money on it."), a bunch of cheesecakes, a copy of his book, and an empty key ring.

An empty key ring?

"You win the Super Bowl," Bloomberg said, "and I promise you will get a key."

Not that there was any pressure.

24

J-E-T-S

THE PROFESSIONAL FOOTBALL franchise that would ultimately be known as the New York Jets came into existence in 1959, when the Titans of New York (as they were initially named) were chartered into the new American Football League.

The debut season soon followed, and the team went 7-7 behind the mediocre quarterbacking of Al Dorow, whose 26 touchdowns were offset by 26 interceptions. Dorow was an interesting case—a journeyman who bounced from Washington to Philadelphia, then spent two years in the Canadian Football League before joining New York. After tossing 19 touchdowns and a league-high 30 interceptions in 1961, he never again played for the organization. Few seemed to notice.

Four years later, a cocky kid from the University of Alabama named Joe Namath arrived in the Big Apple, and before long he was not only the talk of the city, but the most celebrated football player in America. Namath spent 12 years quarterbacking the Jets, and in 1969 he gained eternal fame for guaranteeing a victory over the heavily favored Baltimore Colts in Super Bowl III, then delivering. That triumph, the AFL's first over the NFL, forever changed professional football.

As far as quarterbacks go, that was pretty much it for the Jets.

Oh, there have been some other OK players. Richard Todd took the team to the 1982 AFC title game, then threw five interceptions in a muddy loss at Miami. Ken O'Brien started for seven seasons in the 1980s and early 1990s, and even made a pair of Pro Bowls. Boomer Esiason and Vinny Testaverde had their moments, Ray Lucas and Chad Pennington had theirs. Overall, though, the Jets' quarterbacking history begins and ends with Namath.

Perhaps that's why, when the Favre trade was consummated, the team's loyalists responded as if they each individually won the $100 million lottery. Joe Namath had been a transcendent star who carried a team and a league. But Brett Favre was the embodiment of toughness. Now he was a Jet.

"It was madness," said Rich Cimini, the beat writer for the *New York Daily News*. "Total madness."

Favre made his Jets debut on the afternoon of Saturday, August 9, when he arrived at Hofstra University, home to the team's training camp, a few hours before the scheduled 1:20 practice. On a good day, 2,000 spectators attended practices. On this day, there were 10,500. On a good day, 30 credentialed media members might show. On this day, there were more than 100. The NFL's website broke a sales record by peddling 3,200 Brett Favre Jet jerseys in a 24-hour span.

He walked onto the field wearing a familiar red No. 4, and received a thunderous standing ovation. Bruce Springsteen's "Glory Days" blared from the PA system. One day earlier, the rival Miami Dolphins signed Pennington to take over as the starting quarterback, and Jets officials worried whether there would be some fan backlash. There was none.

Eric Mangini, the Jets' coach, and offensive coordinator Brian Schottenheimer devoted themselves to making Favre's transition as seamless as possible. Pennington's game was predicated upon slants and quick hits. He was a soft thrower with a sniper's accuracy, so New York's receivers were used to getting the ball quickly and generating yardage via their legs. Favre was the opposite — big arm, deep routes, speed, and power. "On that first day we found 15–20 plays he was really comfortable with, and we started to build the system around those," Schottenheimer said. "We had certain plays with certain names, and we changed those for Brett to things he already knew." Favre was a crossword junkie, so Brian Daboll, the quarterbacks coach, created a book of puzzles that involved the team's plays and left it at the quarterback's locker.

For New York's pass catchers, the major adjustment wasn't verbal, but physical. Although their quarterback was about to turn 39, with 69,350 college and NFL yards on his right arm, he still threw one of the hardest balls in the league. "It was eye opening," said Chris Baker, the tight end. "I'll never forget one of the first balls he threw to me — it curved in the air. I've never seen that before or since."

In particular, Favre sought out Laveranues Coles, the team's ninth-year wide receiver and Pennington's closest friend on the Jets. When he learned of the quarterback change, Coles fell into a deep funk. He and Pennington had been drafted together in 2000, and developed a genuine kinship. Coles was a moody locker room figure, but Pennington seemed to understand him. "Laveranues was a lone ranger," said Chansi Stuckey, a wide receiver. "He wasn't easy to know."

On their first day together, Favre tried breaking the ice. "I heard you're not talking to the media," he said. "I understand you don't want to say anything good about me. That's OK."

"It's not that," Coles said. "It's not that."

"Look," Favre said. "I'm not here to take Chad's spot, or to replace him."

Only he *was* here to take Chad's spot. On repeated occasions, Favre praised Pennington in the media, and expressed empathy for Coles's plight. "I think he'll realize, if he doesn't already, that I'm an easygoing guy, easy to work with," Favre said. "You drop a ball, so what? I throw bad passes. We're in this together."

It was an uphill battle. Favre looked terrible on his first day, and confessed to thinking, on multiple occasions, that perhaps this was a mistake. "There were times in practice I was wondering if I made the right move," he told Gary Myers of the *Daily News* — and the words rubbed many wrongly. "I think everybody on the team was excited to play with a legend," said kicker Jay Feely, then in his eighth season. "But I don't think the legend was very excited to play with us."

Favre made his first start 10 days after the trade, jogging onto the field at Giants Stadium for a preseason clash with the Redskins. A whopping 76,132 fans stood and cheered, and Favre later noted that he "had some feelings that I haven't felt in 17 years." On his first play, he took a three-step drop and rocketed an 11-yard completion to Jerricho Cotchery. The ball looked as if it had been fired from a bazooka, and as Cotchery bounded to his feet the crowd roared. Favre played the first two series, went 5 of 6 for 48 yards and a 4-yard touchdown pass to Dustin Keller, the rookie tight end. Afterward, he seemed happy for the first time since the arrival. "I feel like I'm a Jet, I do," he said. "Does that sound a little awkward or funny? Maybe a little bit. Believe me, I feel very comfortable here."

The Jets were scheduled to kick off at Miami (and Pennington) on September 7, and Favre used the three weeks to adjust. He and Deanna put their 3,000-square-foot Ashwaubenon, Wisconsin, house on the market for $475,000 while renting a home in Morristown, New Jersey, an 11-minute drive from the team's Florham Park headquarters and facilities. Breleigh, now 9, enrolled in school (her older sister, Brittany, was at college), and Deanna tried grasping the intricacies of the New Jersey Turnpike.

One thing that became clear to teammates was that Favre wasn't here to socialize and make friends. Just like Green Bay, the Jets gave Favre both a regular stall in the locker room and a back office (with a team-supplied desktop computer) where he could keep to himself. This was a request made by Bus Cook, Favre's agent, and granted by an organization willing to do whatever necessary to placate a star. It was not well received. Behind their quarterback's back, members of the Jets mumbled about unfair treatment, about a diva quarterback, about a revised definition of "team." "I never actually saw Brett at his locker," said Hank Poteat, a cornerback. "He'd come into the locker room, but then he'd go back to his area. I don't know if he was trying to get away from the media or keep his distance. But we never saw him."

Said a veteran Jet: "I don't think Brett wanted to be anyone's friend, or be around there with us. If he had to talk to the media he'd come in the locker room for those 30 minutes, but then he'd be gone. Not once did he ask anyone to dinner, did he spend real time with people."

It presented an ugly contrast to Pennington, who considered the other Jets his brothers. As the opener approached, Coles spoke at length to some teammates about what was lost, not gained. Pennington was a Jet, Favre merely a rent-a-Jet. Pennington played because he loved his guys and wanted to do right for them. Favre was a larger-than-life deity brought here as a mercenary. Yes, he was a legend with a strong arm. But he was a *Green Bay Packers* legend with a strong arm. Local newspapers reported that Favre was "voted" a team captain — an untrue notion put forth by the organization. "We all knew what that was about," said Thomas Jones, the star halfback. "It was because, how do you bring Brett Favre in and not make him a captain? But me and Laveranues were the captains of that offense.

"One thing I'll say in Brett's defense: he was almost 40. Why would you expect him to hang with a bunch of 25-year-olds? Should the NFL be about the team? Yes. But it's not. The people making the most money are made the most comfortable, and Brett was making a ton of money. Most of us understood what it was."

The Jets–Dolphins rivalry dated back to the days of Namath and Bob Griese, and it had been many things to many players. Heated. Intense. Rough. Dirty. Never before, though, had it been so awkward. "I think it's disrespectful, and I'd be doing a disservice to my teammates, if I made this about me and wanting to beat the Jets," Pennington said during the lead-up. "But I would be remiss to say there are no emotions at all."

Too classy to publically vent, Pennington didn't say what was on his mind. Which was that he felt betrayed. Pennington had given everything to the Jets; fought through injuries for the Jets; provided stability for a franchise that generally lacked it. Then he was kicked to the curb like a bag of trash. "I hurt for Chad," said Jones. "But it's a business. Sooner or later, we all learn it the hard way."

Kickoff was scheduled for one o'clock, with 65,859 fans packed into Dolphin Stadium for what was surely one of the most heavily hyped contests featuring clubs that combined to win five games a season earlier (Miami had gone 1-15). With the arrival of Pennington, as well as a new head coach in Tony Sparano, the Dolphins featured genuine optimism for the first time in years. The Jets, meanwhile, hoped to be Super Bowl contenders.

The temperature was 88, but the heat index made it feel like 110. Pennington looked weird in his turquoise-and-orange No. 10 jersey, as did Favre in his green-and-white No. 4. The Jets received the ball after the Dolphins opened with an unsuccessful possession, and Favre's first official pass as a Jet was a 5-yard completion to Coles along the sideline. Later in the quarter, New York faced a first and 10 from their 44-yard line. Favre executed a masterful fake handoff to Jones, which caused cornerback André Goodman to mistakenly charge forward. The quarterback dropped back, waited, waited, waited—and uncorked a majestic rainbow of a bomb that sailed over Goodman and hit a wide-open Cotchery at the Dolphins 10. He ran into the end zone, and Favre couldn't contain his jubilation. He pointed his finger skyward, charged toward Richardson, and leapt into his arms. The Jets led, 7–0, on a throw Chad Pennington *never* could have completed. "Our coaches told us all week, 'Just keep running,'" Cotchery said afterward. "'We promise he won't overthrow you.'"

Favre wasn't done. In the second quarter, the Jets faced a fourth and 13 from the Miami 22. Mike Nugent, the kicker, was suffering through a thigh injury, so Mangini kept the offense on the field. Facing a five-man rush, Favre took the snap from the shotgun and drifted back. Defensive tackle Randy Starks broke through the line and seemed to have the quarterback in his grasp — until, somehow, Favre switched the football from his left hand to his right, stepped up, planted his feet, and launched a pass toward the end zone just as two Miami defenders slammed him to the ground.

Down the field, Stuckey, a second-year player of little note, found himself alone and crossing pay dirt. "I wasn't even in the progression," Stuckey said. "But I saw him start to scramble, then disappear, then roll out, then throw it as hard as he could. So I just got open. It was an amazing throw, because it wasn't just an accident. He knew what he was doing."

Stuckey leapt to catch the ball between three defenders and fell in for the score. It was the first touchdown of his career.

New York triumphed, 20–14, and while it wasn't Favre's best career performance, Phil Simms, calling the game for CBS, rightly termed it "borderline magnificent." He completed 15 of 22 passes for 194 yards and two touchdowns. There were no interceptions, no boneheaded mistakes. Pennington, too, performed capably, but the difference between Favre's AIM-4 Sidewinder missile and Pennington's peashooter was clear. The New York Jets were well armed.

Of course, ever since Namath's heyday the team had a certain Murphy's Law quality, and here was no exception. Favre Fever gripped the region, and then the team proceeded to lose two straight. The first, a 19–10 setback against rival New England, was painful yet digestible. The second, a 48–29 flogging at San Diego on *Monday Night Football,* was not. Favre had never lost to the Chargers and, a season earlier, threw for 369 yards and three touchdowns in a Green Bay triumph. But now, for the first time in three games, he looked old and out of sorts. San Diego sacked him three times, intercepted him twice. Mangini had been ripped in the press for an overly conservative game plan. (Wrote the *New York Post*'s Steve Serby: "Take the shackles off . . . let him wing it, let him sling it, let him bring it.") He opened it up against the Chargers, and the result was disastrous. After the game Favre was seen limping down a hallway, his left ankle heavily wrapped in an ACE bandage. He had rolled it in the third quarter, and now the consecutive-start streak, 256 strong, seemed to be in jeopardy. "I will be alright," he said afterward — but nobody could be sure.

That week, Favre limped through much of practice. He spent considerable hours on the sideline, as Clemens took an increased share of reps. Two days before the Sunday kickoff against Arizona he was listed as "questionable" in the injury report, and split his time with the media talking about the ankle and Cardinals quarterback Kurt Warner, a two-time league MVP who attended camp with the Packers in 1994 as a free agent out of Northern Iowa. "There are guys that come and go," Favre recalled. "He was one of them."

Now Warner was bringing one of the NFL's top offenses to Giants Stadium. Through three games, the 2-1 Cardinals scored 71 points, and the wide receiver tandem of Larry Fitzgerald and Anquan Boldin seemed unstoppable. "It was hard to be overly positive," said Kerry Rhodes, the Jets' free safety. "It was like living through an experiment that wasn't working out."

Boom!

The first lightning bolt came early in the second quarter. On third and goal from the 12, with 14:50 left, Favre (decked out in the unattractive blue-and-yellow New York Titans throwbacks) dropped back and waited for Coles to sprint down the field and cut through the end zone. The quarterback stepped forward in the pocket, hopped, and threw a strike to the wide receiver, who beat two defenders for the ball. It could not have been thrown any harder.

New York took a 14–0 lead on Darrelle Revis's 32-yard interception return, then, midway through the second quarter, Favre and Coles hit again. This time, on a first and 10 from the Arizona 34, the quarterback faked a screen, watched defensive back Eric Green bite, and found a wide-open Coles all alone near the end zone. The normally stoic receiver did an electric dance before being hugged and hoisted by Favre. It was now 21–0. A Feely field goal shortly thereafter made it 24–0, and with 10 seconds left in the half, Favre completed yet another touchdown pass to Coles — this one a perfectly thrown 2-yard fade into the corner of the end zone. Score: 31–0.

When they found one another on the sideline, Coles handed the ball to Favre — a small gesture that carried great weight. Even Coles could admit Favre brought an electricity Pennington never had. "He deserved it," Coles said. "It meant a lot for me to give the football to a legend."

New York won, 56–35, and Favre's six touchdown passes marked a career high and tied Namath's team record. Toward the end of the game, he

walked up and down the sideline, shaking hands, extending congratulations. The postgame locker room was a land of giddiness. "I enjoy being
here," Favre said. "I don't know where we go from here. I hope we continue to go up. But it's been fun."

New York's players were learning what to expect from Favre: strong
throws, tons of on-field enthusiasm, limited locker room interaction.
Also, to their universal delight, he served as a buffer between the team
and Mangini.

Now in his third year with New York, the 37-year-old head coach
had begun to wear out his welcome. Back in 2006, when he took over
and guided the team to the playoffs, fans and the media nicknamed him
"Mangenius." A longtime assistant to Bill Belichick in New England,
Mangini shared his former boss's rigidity and attention to detail — attributes when you're winning, liabilities when a team goes 4-12, as the Jets
did in 2007. Although it's a stretch to say Mangini was intimidated by
Favre, he never seemed fully comfortable in his presence. He also surely
felt some of his authority diminish with the quarterback's arrival. That
dress code Mangini had brought to New York from New England? Gone
— thanks to Favre's hatred of suit and tie, all the players and staffers were
presented with travel-appropriate Jets sweat suits. That run-first, ball-
control offensive he preferred? Scrapped — Woody Johnson wasn't paying $12 million to have his quarterback hand off to Thomas Jones and
Leon Washington 45 times per Sunday. The cold-weather practices that
Mangini felt built character and toughness? Um, no. Favre hated workouts, and he especially hated workouts when the temperature dipped below 50 degrees. The team's new digs included a 100-yard indoor facility,
and Favre insisted it was the best option. What was Mangini supposed to
do? Have his prehistoric quarterback live uncomfortably?

Following the Arizona victory, the Jets had their bye week, for most
teams a laid-back period of limited hitting. Yet Mangini insisted the Jets
practice in pads, which made no one happy. "You don't want to be doing that stuff during that week," said Richardson. "It's unnecessary." Favre
wasn't feeling it. He practiced lazily, tossed three interceptions, fumbled
a few exchanges from Mangold. The coach held another full-pad practice the next day, and before it commenced he called Favre into his office.
"Brett, how'd you feel about practice yesterday?" Mangini asked.

"It was fine," Favre replied.

"No," said Mangini. "It wasn't fine. It was bullshit. I don't know what the hell you thought you were doing, but . . ."

When the brief meeting ended, Mangini spotted Richardson. "Tony, how do you feel?"

"I feel good, Coach," he said.

"Yeah, you should feel good," Mangini said. "Because you didn't fucking block anyone."

Richardson was in his 14th NFL season, Favre his 18th. Afterward, they sat together and reviewed, in the fullback's words, "how bullshit that was."

"It was tone-deafness," Richardson said. "Eric needed to know better."

He didn't, but it mattered little. This was no longer his team. It belonged to Favre, and he behaved as he pleased, practiced when he pleased, approached Sundays as he pleased. After the first four games, he led the NFL with 12 touchdown passes and a 70.2 completion percentage, making him new king of the city. Mangini could bark, yell, curse, swear, and what difference did it make? Favre was still Favre. "It kind of unraveled a little," said Rhodes. "Because you can't build yourself as someone who treats everyone equally, then not treat everyone equally. It's a quick way to lose respect."

The Jets returned to action with a home game against the woeful Cincinnati Bengals, and one moment spoke volumes. Leading 20–14 late in the fourth quarter, New York found itself on the Bengals 1-yard line. Schottenheimer sent in the play—a simple handoff to Jones. "So we come out of the huddle, and Brett forgets which way I'm going," Jones said. "He's standing behind center and he turns around and points to my left. And I'm thinking, *What the fuck are you doing, man?*" Jones nodded, and the Cincinnati linebackers shifted toward their right. When the ball was snapped, Favre handed off to the halfback, and he jumped over the linemen to score. On the sideline, Jones grabbed Favre and said with a laugh, "Man, you're gonna get me killed out there."

"Nah," Favre said, grinning, "you'll be all right."

"Then he smacked me on the ass," Jones said. "He didn't know all the plays. Or probably even most of the plays. And he wasn't that big, or even that strong. His legs were surprisingly skinny. He was pretty slow. But he was just one of those unique players who makes things happen."

The Jets topped the Bengals, 26–14, and captured four of the next five, including a thrilling 34–31 overtime win at the hated Patriots. On November 23, in what was billed as the biggest game of the 12-week-old NFL season, New York was scheduled to travel to Tennessee and confront the 10-0 Titans. Led by the resurgent play of quarterback Kerry Collins (who was in rehab with Favre nine years earlier) and a defense that allowed but 13.1 points per game, Tennessee was justifiably favored by 5½ points, and the younger Jets had reason to be uptight.

Favre, however, wouldn't allow it. That week in practice he was his loosey-goofy self. During one break in the action, he approached Mike Bloomgren, an assistant coach. "Hey, Mike," he said, "do you have any fillings?"

Bloomgren opened his mouth and the quarterback filled it with a handful of pellets from the field. "With Brett," Bloomgren said, "you had to always be watching out."

Eric Barton, one of the team's better linebackers, ran over a goose with his car, and expressed regret to teammates. The next day, upon arriving at the facility, Barton found a dead wild turkey draped over his locker. Favre snuck an air horn into meetings and blew it randomly — and obnoxiously — during conversations. He had a black rubber snake that he liked to place at the bottom of buckets of equipment. "Whenever someone wasn't paying attention, he'd throw it at their feet," said Meghan Gilmore, who worked in media relations. "Throw it in their locker."

"One day it's snowing outside, and Eric takes us out to practice," said Rhodes. "I'm out there early, and I hear someone charging up behind me." It was Favre, who dumped a pile of snow atop the safety's head.

His greatest — and worst — takedown was directed toward Jimmy Raye, the team's 62-year-old running backs coach. A walking football history museum, Raye was one of Division I's first African American quarterbacks at Michigan State and went on to a distinguished coaching/mentoring career that lasted more than 40 years. Of all the people on New York's staff, he was the one not to mess with.

One day, during a practice, Raye was standing on the outdoor field. Because he had recently undergone back surgery, he walked slowly and had limited range of motion. Favre either didn't know or didn't care, because he approached from behind and yanked Raye's pants to his ankles. As the entire roster howled, Raye struggled to pull them back up. The laughter failed to conceal the unspeakable meanness of the act. "I wasn't pissed," said Raye. "Really, I wasn't. It was a little bit . . . I don't know. I didn't love it, but it was what Brett did. He spared no one."

The Jets arrived in Nashville as loose as they had been all season. Mangini was marginalized, Favre was rolling, the team was 7–3. What followed was a breezy 34–13 victory, in which Favre threw two more touchdown passes and halfback Leon Washington ran for two scores. New York outgained Tennessee, 409 yards to 281, and the players left the stadium as certifiable favorites to represent the AFC in the Super Bowl. "It was our high-water mark," said Tannenbaum. "To beat that team in Tennessee, and to do it handily. I'd been through a lot of ups and downs, and I knew there was a lot of wood to chop. But was I feeling confident? Yes, I was."

Then, Brett Favre's arm fell off.

OK, it didn't literally detach from his body. There were no reports of Brett Favre's severed limb. But something was wrong. First notice actually came a few weeks earlier, when an AFC scout anonymously told Steve Serby of the *New York Post* that Favre was throwing the ball "funny." The words were largely dismissed, because to the naked eye his passes against Tennessee looked crisp and on point. "He made a throw in practice, and I saw him grab his arm," said Baker. "I had good relations with our training staff, so I asked. They told me he had a tear, but that he could still do stuff. It'd just come and go." The following week the Denver Broncos visited Giants Stadium, and their 6-5 record and porous defense suggested another win for football's hottest team.

In the lead-up to the game, more than a few football writers took a moment to compare Favre and the Jets with Aaron Rodgers and the Packers. Green Bay was 5-6, and their young quarterback had played poorly in back-to-back losses. Tom Oates of the *Wisconsin State Journal* penned a piece headlined WRONG PLAY, and explained that the Packers would certainly be better with Favre. In the *Marshfield (Wis.) News-Herald*, D. J. Slater found one fan after another who longed for Favre's return. "The Jets have a solid chance of making the Super Bowl," one interviewee wailed. "That should have been us."

The Jets were favored by 8, but as they warmed up beforehand, Favre didn't seem quite right. His right arm was a mess. After the season, he would learn the cause: a partially torn biceps tendon. "It was raining, and he was having trouble gripping the ball," said Bloomgren. "The whole game, he was never really on point." Favre completed 23 of 43 passes for 247 yards and no touchdowns. He hung tough in the pocket, took a ton of hits, yet passes that soared earlier in the season now merely traveled.

"It was obvious," said Ty Law, a Jets cornerback. "He didn't have the Favre *zing*." New York lost 34–17, fell the next week to San Francisco, somehow snuck past Buffalo ("Honestly, we got lucky," said Andy Dickerson, an assistant coach) and, on December 21, headed to Seattle for what was suddenly a must-win meeting against Mike Holmgren's 3-11 Seahawks. In the days leading up to the game, Favre surprised the coaching staff and his teammates by volunteering to run the Jets' scout team offense. "He felt like he knew Holmgren better than anyone," said Dickerson, "and that he could show us what they'd do. It was really unselfish."

The Seahawks started a young backup quarterback named Seneca Wallace, and clearing 20 points tended to be a struggle. They were thin in all areas, ranked last in the league in passing yards allowed (260.9 per game), and projected into an easy win for the Jets.

It was cold (31 degrees) and snowy in Seattle. New York scored first on a 20-yard field goal from Feely — then did nothing. Favre's arm was gone. Sometimes, he winced. Other times, his follow-through seemed shortened. Mostly, he started looking more like Pennington, less like a legend. Yet for reasons neither man has ever fully explained, neither Schottenheimer nor Mangini altered the offense. In Jones and Washington, the Jets had two explosive running backs. Against Seattle, they combined for only 20 carries. Favre, meanwhile, launched 31 passes, completing 18. "We knew he was hurt," said Baker. "He was still functioning, but he wasn't himself."

"He just couldn't do it," said Feely. "He tried. But his balls were going 15 yards wide, 15 yards short. It wasn't there."

By Seattle, Favre was experiencing numbness in his fingers and shooting pains up and down his right arm. He never complained. "He's the toughest guy to ever play the sport," said Schottenheimer. "I saw him take some hellacious shots that season and get right back up. He had a hard time at some points. But you never had to worry about him not answering the bell."

New York lost 13–3, as Favre underthrew one pass after another. His 19 interceptions now led the league, and it was the fourth straight game where his passer rating was below 62. The defeat dropped the team to 9-6. "Brett was bad," said Baker. "Really bad." Immediately afterward, Favre's hand was noticeably discolored from frostbite. "I don't have all the answers," he said with a shrug. He spoke briefly and softly, before dressing and heading with the team to the airport. The Jets spent the ensuing two hours sitting on the runway waiting for the weather to clear.

"If you want a low point," said Schottenheimer, "there you go."

By now, Favre had already made up his mind that he would not be spending another year with the Jets. He was annoyed by Mangini, felt disconnected from most of his teammates and generally out of sorts. He was bored and frustrated, and never fully accepted that he could possibly be a long-term Jet. "It wasn't right for him," said Bonita Favre. "You had to drive forever to get anywhere. There were no straight roads from one point to another." When asked about his future, he was noncommittal, and insisted it was possible he'd return. But that was untrue. "He wasn't really made to play in New York," said Jeff Favre, his brother. "He's a small-town guy. That was a bad fit. It wasn't a bad place. But it wasn't really him."

If life is truly a poem, as the writer Steve Maraboli once observed, the final week of the NFL season was Chad Pennington's sonnet on revenge. The Dolphins were coming to Giants Stadium, and with a 10-5 record not only were they headed toward the playoffs, but stood in position to both clinch the AFC East and knock the Jets out (New York needed a win, plus a loss by either New England or Baltimore). Because his name was Pennington (not Favre) and because he played in South Florida (not New York), Miami's quarterback reveled as the season's best-kept secret. His 96.4 passer rating was second in the league to San Diego's Philip Rivers, and his 17 touchdowns and seven interceptions were far preferable to Favre's 21–19. Dave Goldberg of the Associated Press even wrote an impassioned piece supporting Pennington's MVP candidacy. Over the last four games, on the other hand, Favre had one touchdown and six interceptions. He finally admitted the day before Christmas that something was wrong with the arm — "I don't know," he said. "Just knowing my body, there may be something." Interestingly, the drama of the past few seasons (will he or won't he return?) didn't dominate headlines in New York — primarily because it didn't much matter. Favre looked to be shot. Would the Jets even want him to return? Hard to say.

Pennington once again insisted the game was nothing personal, and no one believed him. It *was* personal — not against the Jets quarterback (who he actually liked), but the Jets organization. "You don't think he wanted that one?" said Rhodes. "I mean, come on."

Giants Stadium was sold out, with 79,454 fans enjoying an unseasonably pleasurable 64-degree afternoon. But there was little oomph and even less zest. This was a team rolling off a cliff. As the *Daily News's* Ohm Youngmisuk rightly observed, "the magic disappeared." Before kickoff, Favre gathered his teammates in a sideline huddle and offered up a lame and uninspired pep talk. With hands together in the center of a circle, he said, somewhat flatly, "If it works out, it works out. If it doesn't, it doesn't. All you can do is give your best. OK? Love you guys!"

Jim Valvano he was not.

To Favre's credit, the game was close. To his discredit, it wasn't really his doing. Midway through the first quarter, with neither team yet on the scoreboard, Favre threw a pass down the left sideline that sailed over Washington's head and into the arms of cornerback André Goodman. The cameras flashed to Mangini, whose lips were easy to read: *Why would we do that?*

Late in the second quarter Favre struck again. He dropped back from the New York 30, did a little pirouette, tossed a screen in Jones's direction, then watched in horror as a defensive lineman named Phillip Merling plucked it from the air, bowled over the old quarterback, and rambled in for the touchdown and a 14–6 Miami advantage. Favre walked off the field wincing and holding his arm.

New York scored on a Washington run to take a brief 17–14 lead, but the day belonged to Pennington. He hit tight end Anthony Fasano on a 20-yard scoring strike to go up 21–17, and a late Dan Carpenter field goal upped the final score to 24–17. As he jogged off the field and into the joyful visiting locker room, Pennington was grabbed by cornerback Jason Allen. "Get your hat, boy!" Allen screamed. "Go get your hat." It was a gray division title cap being distributed by the equipment staffers.

The Miami Dolphins, led by a discard, were AFC East champions.

The New York Jets, led by a quarterback who changed the dress code, were done.

One day later, Favre underwent an MRI on his right shoulder, which would reveal the tear. He was asked about returning, and uttered the familiar "I don't know yet" refrain that would not be tolerated in New York as it had been for so long in Green Bay.

"If he wants to come back and if he can put in his time for the whole year, that's fine with me," Rhodes said. "If he's not going to be committed to it and not want to be here the whole time, it's going to be tough for everybody. I'm just saying — if he's going to come back, don't string it out."

Within three days, Brett Favre was out of his New Jersey home and back in Mississippi. "I was hoping he'd stick with us," said Tannenbaum. "I really was."

It was wishful thinking. Brett Favre had bigger plans.

25

A NORSE GOD

THROUGHOUT THE LONG and storied history of American sport, revenge has served as a motivating factor for countless professional athletes. You've been traded, you've been released, you've been disrespected in one way or another, and now you crave payback.

Think about it. When Tom Seaver was shipped from the Mets to the Reds in 1977, he returned to New York and stuck it to his old team, striking out 11 and surrendering one run over six innings. When Joe Montana faced the 49ers for the first time as a Kansas City Chief, he played every down as if it were life or death. Wayne Gretzky tallied two assists for the Los Angeles Kings against the Edmonton Oilers, Reggie Jackson — California Angel — went deep against the New York Yankees in his return to the Big Apple.

When Brett Favre finished his season with the Jets, he, too, sought revenge. The feeling had lingered for a year, ever since Ted Thompson and the Green Bay Packers disrespected him, first by pressuring his retirement, then by giving away his job, then by not welcoming him back, and finally by shipping him off to New York.

Although it's probably a stretch to say Favre *hated* the Packers, he abhorred Thompson in the way one abhors an abusive boss or unfaithful lover.

He loathed Ted Thompson.

He wanted retribution.

What better way than joining the franchise's greatest rival?

Of course, Favre first needed to do his little self-indulgent jig. On February 11, 2009, Bus Cook told the Jets his client was officially retiring.

Then, in late April, speculation surfaced that Favre was considering a return with the Minnesota Vikings. Then Cook told several journalists that — *seriously!* — Brett Favre was done. Then, in early May, Vikings coach Brad Childress was scheduled to fly to Mississippi to talk with Favre. But then the trip was canceled. Then rescheduled. Then canceled again. On June 5, Cook told the Associated Press that Favre was — *seriously, seriously!* — done, and there were no changes in his plans. That same day Childress, attending a community event, said he wasn't even thinking about Favre, and that the Vikings quarterbacks were Tarvaris Jackson and Sage Rosenfels. Within 72 hours, ESPN reported that Favre underwent arthroscopic surgery on his throwing shoulder with the intention of returning for a 19th season. Cook neither confirmed nor denied the operation — even though he knew, with absolute certainty, that Favre spent a day with Dr. James Andrews, under sedation, having his right arm repaired. On June 9, the *Green Bay Press-Gazette* reported that Favre's family booked 25 to 30 rooms at the Midway Motor Lodge near Lambeau Field for the weekend of November 1, when the Vikings were scheduled to visit Green Bay. On June 15, in an interview with HBO, Favre admitted that playing with the Vikings "makes perfect sense," and referred to the team as "we." He explained that while he and Childress had yet to speak, Eric Sugarman, the Minnesota trainer, visited Mississippi to show him some exercises related to rehabbing the arm.

This went on.

And on.

And on.

And on.

On July 19 Jared Allen, Minnesota's star defensive end, told the *Chicago Tribune* that his patience was wearing thin — "Let's either get it done and get moving on with it or let it go." On July 20, Childress said he'd watched video of Favre, throwing with a high school team in Mississippi, and his motion "looked fine." On July 23, ESPN's Ed Werder reported Brett Favre was wavering, but would decide shortly. On (also) July 23, ESPN's Rachel Nichols reported that Brett Favre's family and friends hoped he would make up his mind. A handful of Vikings — Allen and halfback Adrian Peterson among them — reached out to Favre, thereby irking Jackson and Rosenfels. Finally, on July 28, Favre called Childress and told him that he would stay retired. "It was the hardest decision I ever made," he told

ESPN. "I didn't feel like physically I could play at a level that was accept-able. I would like to thank everyone, including the Packers, Jets, and Vi-kings — but, most importantly, the fans."

End of story. He. Was. Not. Coming. Back.

On the afternoon of Sunday, August 16, Childress, now three weeks into training camp at Minnesota State University–Mankato, met with his quarterbacks in a small room inside the complex. Along with Jackson, a fourth-year pro from Alabama State, and Rosenfels, a veteran acquired from Houston to challenge for the job, two other players were present. John David Booty, the Vikings' 2008 fifth-round draft choice out of USC, sat in one chair. Sean Glennon, an undrafted rookie free agent from Vir-ginia Tech, sat in another. Rumors of Favre had once again started up, and the head coach wanted to put his quarterbacks at ease. "Brett's not coming," Childress told the group. "Just so all of you know, there has been a lot said and a lot of talk. But it's not happening. He's not coming."

Though Jackson and Rosenfels both felt relief, it was particularly great news for Booty and Glennon, who were fighting for a third-string/prac-tice-squad gig. The following afternoon, Glennon — having just com-pleted a workout — was sitting in the players' lounge, watching tennis on a nearby TV. Rick Spielman, the team's vice president of player personnel, tapped him on the shoulder. "Hey, Sean," he said. "Come up to talk."

This couldn't be good.

"I'm just gonna be blunt," Spielman said. "We're signing Brett, and un-fortunately we have to clear a roster spot. After some deliberation you're the odd man out. We appreciate everything you've done. If a roster spot opens, we might call . . ."

"Football," Glennon said, "is a cold-blooded business."

Less than 24 hours later, on the morning of Tuesday, August 18, Booty reported to the facility, walked up to his locker, and did a double take. Dangling from a hook was a No. 9 jersey — not the No. 4 he wore throughout camp. "It wasn't like I was married to No. 4 or anything," he said. "But the way it was all handled was wrong. First, Brad gave us his word that Brett wasn't coming. Second, you don't even say anything? You just change my number? It's a business, I get that. But we were being told something totally different than what was going on behind closed doors. It was slimy."

On Monday morning — after assuring the quarterbacks they need not worry — Childress placed a final call to Mississippi, urging the veteran to join the team. A two-year, $25 million contract was waiting for his signature. "I can be persistent at times," Childress said later. "I just felt like it was a small window that we had to reconsider adding him potentially to our football team." Later in the day, Cook told Spielman that, yes, Brett Favre would join the Vikings, and that the team could expect him to report shortly. Hence, on the morning of Tuesday, August 18, Brad Childress stepped into his black Escalade and made the 20-minute drive to Mankato Regional Airport, where, at approximately 11:20 a.m., the private plane belonging to Vikings owner Zygi Wilf arrived with a nearly 40-year-old quarterback savior in tow. By now word had leaked that Favre was a Viking, and a news helicopter tracked the Escalade as Childress and Favre drove to the facility. Many of the Vikings watched in bemusement, joking about "our own O.J. chase." Visanthe Shiancoe, Minnesota's veteran tight end, referred to the coverage as "Favre-a-palooza."

When the car reached the facility, madness broke out. Purple-and-yellow-clad fans stormed the street to greet the Escalade, then stormed the training-camp property. Wrote Chip Scoggins of the *Minneapolis Star Tribune:* "In a sight fitting the moment, a person dressed in a full parrot costume walked along the street, carrying a sign advertisement."

"It was like we were welcoming a UN ambassador, or some high government official," said Ben Leber, a Vikings linebacker. "But it was just ol' Brett."

Roughly two hours later, Favre — wearing Booty's No. 4 — jogged onto the field for his first practice as a Viking. This was Vince Neil joining Van Halen. Or, if that's too mild, this was Luke Skywalker joining Darth Vader. In Green Bay, many players have done many bad things through the decades, only to be forgiven. Key drops. Missed tackles. Drug abuse. Robbery. Even sexual assault. But none had gone out of his way to purposefully enlist as a Minnesota Viking. "It was hard to digest," said Bob Harlan, the former Packers president. "Of all the teams, of all the players . . ."

Favre introduced himself to the other quarterbacks, to the wide receivers, to the running backs, to his linemen. "It was weird," said Bryant McKinnie, the veteran offensive tackle. "This was Brett Favre, the Packer I'm supposed to hate. And he's wearing purple." Some faces Favre recognized, many he did not. One of the initial reasons Favre considered Minnesota was because the offensive coordinator, Darrell Bevell, had been his quarterbacks coach for six seasons in Green Bay. They exchanged a warm greeting, then Favre turned to Kevin Rogers, the team's quarter-backs coach.

"I'm Kevin," Rogers said.

"I know who you are," Favre replied. "Great to be working with you."

"It was very flattering," said Rogers. "He was happy, upbeat, enthusias-tic. He could not have made a better first impression."

Though Jackson was liked by teammates and Rosenfels had earned respect, there was little awkwardness about Favre being handed the job. Ever since Daunte Culpepper's breathtaking 39-touchdown 2004 season, the Vikings had been searching for a capable quarterback. The outreach included such nonluminaries as a faded Brad Johnson, an incapable Brooks Bollinger, a battered Kelly Holcomb, an ordinary Gus Frerotte. "We needed somebody with a truly proven track record," said Jim Hue-ber, the assistant offensive line coach. "We needed a difference maker, a guy who had been around the block but had something left in the tank. We had a lot of talent, but we were missing that one thing."

When he joined the Jets, Favre liked what surrounded him. When he joined the Vikings, Favre *loved* it. As a child, Favre took to watching Chi-cago's Walter Payton, a fellow Mississippian and the game's best running back. Peterson, just 24, was a Sweetness reincarnate who ran for 1,760 yards and 10 touchdowns in 2008. The wide receivers were equally stu-pendous. On one side Favre would be throwing to Sidney Rice, a six-foot-four, 200-pound picture of grace and fluidity. On the other, he had the team's latest first-round pick, a 21-year-old speedster from Florida named Percy Harvin. "The two of them were unreal," said Leber. "Sidney had this pep in his step that Brett gave him, and he made some catches I'd never seen. And Percy — he wasn't that big, but he ran with so much power, and he did things in space that humans don't do." Toss in a soft-handed tight end (Shiancoe) and a veteran offensive line with multiple Pro Bowlers, and the Viking roster was special.

Favre adapted quickly. He was back in the NFC North, back with Bev-ell, back to a part of the country that reflected (and resembled) his Mis-sissippi upbringing. One day Favre asked Childress for permission to ad-dress the team. With everyone seated, he stood and apologized for the offseason indecision. He said he shouldn't have waited so long; said it was unfair to Jackson and Rosenfels and the coaching staff. The words only took five minutes, but they were perfectly received. "He talked about the quality team and the chemistry we already have," said Antoine Winfield,

the cornerback, "and how he wants to be a part of that." Favre seemed
to learn from the mistakes of New York, where he walled off too many
teammates. This time, there was no requesting a private changing space
or a back office. He made himself accessible to the media and chatted
with teammates as if they were long-lost pals (a rocking chair was playfully placed in front of his locker). Perhaps it was an old quarterback realizing the end was near, or maybe he was simply comfortable and happy
to be a Viking. Whatever the case, it went over brilliantly.

Three days after his signing, Favre debuted in a home exhibition game,
starting against the Chiefs and generating a standing ovation (and thousands of camera flashes) as he jogged onto the Metrodome turf. He performed poorly (1 for 4, four yards) and lasted only two series before a
Kansas City linebacker named Corey Mayes slammed him into the turf.
Favre was able to walk off, but there were no shortages of deep breaths
along the Minnesota sideline.

He played three quarters the next week at Houston, and this time made
more of an impression. First, he was a solid 13 of 18 for 142 yards while
suffering through the pain of a cracked rib. Second, he threw a nasty —
and outrageously illegal — crackback block to the knees of Texans safety
Eugene Wilson, which infuriated the opposing defense but inspired the
Vikings. If their ancient quarterback was willing to do whatever it took,
how could the Vikings play at half speed? "His teammates loved him immediately," said Sean Jensen, who covered the Vikings for the *St. Paul
Pioneer Press*. "I've been around a lot of alpha males, and none were as
beloved as Brett Favre. He didn't throw his status and money around, he
didn't act better than anyone."

Off the field, he adjusted quickly. Tony Richardson, Favre's fullback
with the Jets, still owned a house from his two seasons as a Viking, and he
rented it to the quarterback. He went on a few hunting trips with teammates, took Deanna and Breleigh to see *Grease* and a Miley Cyrus concert. The kid who used to party like every day was New Year's Eve was
now a man in bed by 10:00 p.m. "I'll bring film home and I'll watch it," he
said, "and 9 o'clock will come, and I'll decide to watch a little TV.

"Now I go home and help my daughter with homework. I have studying to do myself. I really don't do anything. My wife and our 10-year-old
love it here, so it's been good."

The Vikings opened at Cleveland on September 13, and Favre could
barely contain his excitement. Under Childress (a longtime NFL offen-

sive coordinator) and Bevell, he was back running the exact version of
the West Coast offense that had made him millions in Green Bay. Only
now he found himself surrounded by the type of skill players who rarely
seemed to materialize with Mike Sherman and Ted Thompson. The perpetually awful Browns packed 70,560 fans into their stadium, and Minnesota dominated. It wasn't vintage Favre, or even interesting Favre, but
Peterson ran for 180 yards and three touchdowns, Favre chipped in 14
completions on 21 attempts, and the Vikings won, 34–20. The quarterback's 270th straight start generated one real highlight — after throwing
a 6-yard touchdown pass to Harvin, he charged into the end zone and
tackled the rookie (who was four when Favre made his NFL debut). "You
don't find too many players who still love the game," Harvin said. "For
him to be that old — he's got a daughter my age — and still have a love for
the game . . . he's by himself."

Peterson added another 92 rushing yards the next week in a 27–13 vic-
tory against Detroit, and Favre threw for 155 yards and two touchdowns.
It was early, but some in the media were beginning to wonder whether
Favre would do much besides handing off.

Finally, against the 49ers in the third week, something clicked. It was
Favre's first regular-season home game as a Viking, and for most of the afternoon the performance had fans wondering whether Tarvaris Jackson
should be playing. Favre made a handful of bad throws, and two or three
awful ones. San Francisco led 14–13 at the break. He was hit, and hit hard;
Minnesota's first five series of the second half resulted in three punts, an
interception, and a turnover in downs. When 49ers quarterback Shaun
Hill connected with tight end Vernon Davis on a 20-yard touchdown
pass with 8:12 remaining in the game, the Vikings trailed 24–20, and the
normally loud Metrodome went silent.

Minnesota got the ball back with 89 seconds remaining. Before the offense returned to the field, Bevell said to Favre, "We're going to have to
start throwing it."

The plays came quickly. On first down, Favre hit Shiancoe in the right
flat for 12 yards. He followed with a 9-yarder to Rice, an incomplete duck,
and another 5-yard completion to Harvin, which placed the Vikings on
their own 46. Favre spiked the ball with exactly one minute left, then
missed Rice on a 44-yard lob that landed out of bounds. One play later,
Harvin found a gap in the defense and snagged a 15-yard completion.
Another spike, a 7-yard pass to wide receiver Bernard Berrian, and now,

with 12 seconds remaining and the football sitting on San Francisco's 32, Bevell called for "All go": Two wide receivers to the right, two wide receivers to the left, all heading toward the end zone.

Favre stood in the shotgun, with halfback Chester Taylor directly to his right. When the ball was snapped, Favre pump-faked to his left, then rolled the opposite direction. San Francisco's Justin Smith, an elite pass rusher, came charging, and Taylor briefly walled him off to the side. Favre kept rolling, did some sort of Sugar Ray Leonard bolo punch motion with his right arm, readied to throw, and launched the ball just as Manny Lawson, a linebacker, hammered him from the blind side. The pass was a blur through the air, but as it neared the end zone one couldn't help but watch Greg Lewis, a six-foot, 180-pound wide receiver who had recently been signed as a free agent. He was crossing the paint, one step ahead of strong safety Mark Roman, one and a half steps ahead of free safety Dashon Goldson. Lewis soared through the air and somehow pinned the ball to his chest, landed with both feet inbounds, and fell to the ground. Paul Allen, broadcasting the game for KFAN radio in Minneapolis, offered up the best call of his career . . .

> "He gets away from the pressure . . . fires to the end zooooooone . . . it's caught! It's Greg Lewis! Touchdown! Oh my heavens! Greg Lewis, welcome to Minnesota! Oh! My! Heavens! Greg Lewis's first catch has given the Minnesota Vikings an improbable victory! No flags on the field. Brett Favre! Greg Lewis! How do you like that?"

The stadium's 63,398 fans went berserk. The 27–24 win wasn't only amazing, it was Favre-esque. He was brought to Minnesota to win in ways other Vikings quarterbacks had been unable to. Now, with the team 3-0, he had done it.

"Bottom line was that Favre makes plays when he needs to make plays," said Takeo Spikes, the 49ers linebacker. "That's just who he is."

When members of an NFL team are first presented with the schedule for the upcoming season, they immediately look for "their" games. This doesn't always mean what one might think. A "their" game isn't necessarily one against an archrival, à la Steelers–Ravens or Cowboys–Giants. No, a "their" game could be one against your best friend from college, or against a defensive tackle who tried ripping your knee out a year earlier. It could be a chance to exact revenge against a coach who did you wrong, or blanket the wide receiver who burned you for 180 yards and three scores back in the day.

For Brett Favre, there were two "their" games.

- Green Bay at Minnesota.
- Minnesota at Green Bay.

The first meeting would be held in Week 4 on Monday night, and the regional hype reached a Super Bowl level. In both cities, the narratives were intense, harsh, Shakespearean. Favre was either the new hero or the betraying brother. In Minnesota, he was a Norse god. In Wisconsin, he was a traitor. Nick Barnett, the Packers linebacker, tried to explain the bruised feelings of his team's fan base, noting, "They were in love with Brett Favre and he dumped them and went with another chick. So they're a little heartbroken." Perhaps a better representation of the mood came from a restaurant, Milwaukee Burger Co., that organized a celebratory burning of Favre memorabilia. Regrettably, Rick Merryfield, the Eau Claire deputy fire chief, deemed the torching illegal, so the eatery instead lit aflame a single Favre jersey and donated the hundreds of other used Favre items to Goodwill.

Aaron Rodgers, Green Bay's quarterback, was asked twice in a media session whether he and Favre had conversed since the Viking signing, and his answer (two variations of "I think that's between him and I. I don't think that has relevance to the game") spoke volumes about a nonrelationship and Rodgers's genuine contempt for his predecessor. *Call him?* Why would he call someone who treated him like dog excrement? Favre said revenge had nothing to do with his existence as a Viking. "Never was motivated for that reason," he said — and it was ludicrous. He was motivated for that *very* reason. Nobody explained it better than Curtis Martin, the former New York Jets halfback who was asked by ESPN what it was like to play against a former team for the first time. "I would want to annihilate Green Bay," he said. "I would want to stomp on their heads and crush them if I were Brett Favre."

Exactly.

The game was a dandy. When the captains came to midfield, Favre and Rodgers found themselves face-to-face for the first time since the end of the 2007 season. The exchange was quick — "Good luck. You, too" — and uncomfortable.

On the first offensive series of the evening, Rodgers, who by now was beginning to exert himself as a top-level NFL quarterback, marched the Packers 50 yards down the field, only to fumble the ball away on a sack by Allen and Brian Robison. When Favre stepped into the huddle for his first crack, the stadium — filled with 63,846 people — sounded like an airport runway. He drove the Vikings to the Green Bay 1-yard line, and — *backpedaling, backpedaling* — hit Shiancoe with a pass for the score, and the 7–0 lead. What followed was a boxing match between two free-swinging sluggers. Rodgers started to scramble, pulled up, and chucked a jump toss to tight end Jermichael Finley for a 62-yard score — *Bam!* Favre looked left, pumped, swiveled his head to the right, and hit Rice for a 14-yard strike — *Pop!* Clay Matthews, the Packers linebacker, ripped the ball from Peterson's hands and returned it 42 yards — *Wham!* Peterson pounded the ball across the line from a yard out — *Smack!* At halftime, it was 21–14, Vikings, and the home locker room was overflowing with confidence. "Favre came out on fire," said Peterson. "Me personally, I definitely wanted the game for Brett. I could see it in his eyes."

Allen and the Vikings' defensive line made Rodgers's life miserable, while Favre enjoyed long stretches of uninterrupted pocket time. He hit Berrian for a 31-yard score early in the third quarter, and an Allen safety 18 minutes later gave Minnesota a 30–14 advantage. Green Bay came back late, but it wasn't enough. The Vikings walked off the field with a 30–23 victory, a 4-0 record, and a belief that they were the best team in football. "I was about as nervous as I've ever been before a game," said Favre, who would turn 40 in five days. "I had church about 3 o'clock, and I was throwing all kinds of prayers out there."

Four weeks later, Favre learned that his nerves had yet to hit a peak. Now 7-1, the Vikings traveled to Wisconsin for the return of the fallen icon, and the scene was ugly. "I thought after the first game, 'OK, butterflies are gone, I've kind of gotten back to reality,'" he said. "'Lambeau is gonna be easy.' Wrong."

If an outsider spends enough time in Green Bay, he inevitably comes to see the region's denizens as folksy, kind, good-natured. People will ask about your hat and your children and whether you have any room left for pie. It's an inexpensive place to live and a difficult one to leave. "We're a tight community," said Jim Schmitt, Green Bay's mayor since 2003. "It's a family-oriented world here." When Favre joined the Vikings, people felt punctured. "For almost 20 years," read an editorial in the *Waterloo (Ontario) Chronicle,* "Brett Favre was like a member of every Wisconsin family." Mark Sinclair, a bartender from Barron, Wisconsin, has three Favre tattoos on his body. He felt punctured. David Kinsaul, a correctional probation officer from Madison, named his twin sons Brett and Favre. He felt punctured. Jim Doyle, Wisconsin's governor from 2003 to 2011, felt punctured. "You're talking about very strong feelings," Doyle said. "Very, very strong."

The lead-up was labeled "Favre Week" in Green Bay. The local convention and visitor bureau held a contest soliciting the best ways to "welcome" Favre back—and within two days they received 1,600 e-mails.* On Tuesday, Schmitt temporarily changed the name of Minnesota Avenue to Aaron Rodgers Drive. Titletown Brewing Company offered up a new menu item, waffle fries, to remind diners of Favre's interminable hedging. Schmitt encouraged people to wear flip-flops to work on Friday. There was a heavily attended Favre funeral procession that went from the Lambeau Field parking lot, past Brett Favre's Steakhouse, and to a bar, Tom, Dick & Harry's. The event included an open casket (holding a dummy wearing flip-flops, Wrangler jeans, and a Vikings jersey and helmet) and three hearses—"one to carry Brett's body, one to carry Brett's ego, and another to carry Brett away from here before he changes his mind and decides he didn't want to be dead after all," explained Len Nelson, a local radio personality. Favre once had a street named for him, and before the game a civic-minded resident covered the *P* on Brett Favre Pass. "It's almost like divorcing your wife," explained LeRoy Butler, the former Packer, "and marrying her sister."

That the matchup was a battle for NFC North supremacy (Green Bay was 4-2) took a backseat to the story line. Favre, preparing at the Vikings' facility in Eden Prairie, Minnesota, understood. "If you're a true Packers fan, you want the Packers to win," he said. "If you're a Brett Favre fan this week, you obviously don't want me to win. Or you hope the guy does well, but hope that the Packers go all the way."

---

* The best suggestion by far was to hold a halftime ceremony and retire the No. 4 jersey in honor of Chuck Fusina, a backup quarterback who, as No. 4, threw 32 passes in seven games for the 1986 Packers.

Something like that.

The whole thing was disorienting. The Vikings stayed at the Paper Valley Hotel in Appleton, about 30 miles south of Green Bay. Favre knew of the hotel, but had never been there. When the bus arrived at Lambeau, Favre steeled himself for the negativity. But even with nearly two decades of NFL service, there was no way he could have prepared. "I didn't think it would be a good reception," he said. "And it was worse than that." Minutes before the start of the 3:15 p.m. game, the Vikings jogged onto the field, one by one, sometimes two by two. The booing from the 71,213 spectators was loud, as it would be for any contest against a heated rival. As soon as Favre emerged from the tunnel, though, the tone . . . feel . . . texture . . . throatiness changed. As if by script, he was the last Viking to appear. There's rote booing, and there's I-would-prefer-for-you-to-be-stabbed-in-the-kidney booing. It wasn't, *We want you to lose.* It was, *We want you dead.* "It's by far the worst I've ever felt," Favre said. "Ever."

Among some of the longtime Packer executives and employees, this was not a joyful occasion. Bob Harlan, the team's former president, could barely watch. Jerry Parins, the longtime head of security, hated everything about it. He saw Favre wink playfully toward teammates during his reception, but didn't buy it. "He's human," Parins said. "He can say it didn't hurt, but I know it did. It had to."

When the game finally began, it was predictably physical and fierce. It was also, to the horror of locals, a blowout. The Vikings jumped out to a 17–3 lead, and when Favre found Harvin crossing the field and hit him for a 51-yard touchdown early in the third quarter, the 24–3 margin symbolized a Packer fan's worst nightmare. Not only was Favre winning, but he was behaving like a six-year-old, jumping and laughing and pumping his fists. When he was Green Bay's six-year-old, this was fine. But now it just seemed obnoxious and wrongheaded. "He wanted us in Lambeau," said Greg Jennings, the Packers wide receiver. "He knew everything. Every check our defense made, he knew it all. He was calling our blitzes before they were happening. And he picked us apart."

When all looked dead, the game turned fascinating. The Packers answered with a 26-yard Mason Crosby field goal, recovered a fumble on the kickoff, scored on a 16-yard touchdown pass from Rodgers to Spencer Havner and *another* Rodgers-Havner hookup — this one for 5 yards. Suddenly, with 1:57 left in the third quarter, the Minnesota advantage was down to 24–20.

"I don't know if I could play any better," Favre said—but he had to. Following the second Havner score, Harvin returned the kickoff 48 yards, and moments later Favre, facing third and goal, rolled right and tossed a 2-yard touchdown pass to tight end Jeff Dugan. It was 31–20, and the crowd again hushed. With 11 minutes remaining, Rodgers scrambled for 35 yards and completed a 10-yard touchdown pass to Jennings, slicing the margin to 31–26. Favre was masterful. Rodgers was masterful. There was no bad quarterback here, no goat. Green Bay's Crosby missed a 51-yard field goal try midway through that fourth that would have cut the lead to 2, and on the Vikings' next possession Favre found Berrian for a 16-yard game-sealing touchdown.

The final score was 38–26, and Favre could not have been more re-lieved. Green Bay gave the Methuselah quarterback all that it had, and he'd emerged stronger than ever. In two games against his old club, he had seven touchdowns and no interceptions. His team was in first place, and Brett Favre was at the top of his game.

From the outside looking in, this was turning into the perfect season. The Lambeau triumph began a four-game victorious streak for Minnesota, including back-to-back games of 35 and 36 points against Seattle and Chicago, respectively. Favre was, once again, one of the best quarterbacks in football, and he surely had to be the happiest 40-year-old in America.

But he wasn't.

It's not that Favre was miserable, or itching to retire yet again, or re-gretting the move to Minnesota. Nope, he simply could not stomach Brad Childress. Which didn't actually make Favre unique. Of the 32 NFL head coaches in 2009, it would be impossible for any to be less liked than the one in Minnesota. "He was my least favorite coach in all of college, high school, the NFL," said one veteran Viking, who requested anonym-ity. "He didn't know how to treat people, how to talk to people. From the secretaries to the assistant coaches to the players, he didn't show respect."

"Brad was probably a little delusional when it came to thinking he could dictate everything about a player's life," said Sean Jensen, the *St. Paul Pioneer Press* beat writer. "That was him—a dictator-type coach. But when guys are making five times more money than you, it doesn't work."

One-on-one, away from football, Childress could be charming, warm, engaging. He was well read and well informed, a psychology major at

Eastern Illinois University with a taste for Shakespeare. Before coming to Minnesota, he spent seven years as an Eagles assistant — the last three as offensive coordinator. There were few, if any, known complaints.

When he was hired to guide the Vikings in 2006, however, Childress was told the organization needed discipline and seriousness. The 2005 season had been pocked by a humiliating scandal, in which 17 members of the team were involved in a yacht sex party than involved prostitutes and photographs and police charges. Mike Tice, the coach at the time, was a lovely man, but hardly instilled fear. "Brad was willing to do things players didn't like," said Scoggins. "He wasn't afraid." His most infamous move came during his rookie season, when Childress cut a wide receiver named Marcus Robinson on Christmas Eve. "That," said Jensen, "is cold."

It wasn't the frostiness that bothered Favre, but Childress's need to be involved in every facet of every detail of the offense. Bevell was a mastermind who had the quarterback's trust, but Childress refused to simply let his offensive coordinator handle the offense. He was particularly awful to Rogers, the quarterbacks coach, and demeaned him in front of players. "Childress just treated him like shit," said the anonymous Viking. "Like he didn't matter."

In his need to control everything at all moments, Childress struggled with Favre's tendency to audible out of plays. Having come up under Mike Holmgren, Favre had the green light to see the field, observe the defense, and, if need be, change things. That's how he played for 16 years in Green Bay and 1 in New York. But Minnesota's boss hated two things: audibles and players who were bigger than the team. "Brad was not a good game coach," said Chris Kluwe, the punter. "Great at personnel, but under him the sidelines were chaotic, you had guys all over screaming. And Brad wanted his plays to be what were called, not Brett's."

Although he had been hailed as an offensive innovator with the Eagles, Childress did not actually call the plays in Philadelphia. Favre and his teammates knew this to be true, and their respect for his offensive smarts was nonexistent. Behind Childress's back Favre would mock the coach's knowledge and judgment — and with just cause. "Brett's mind goes beyond strict execution of how plays are drawn up and techniques are designed," Rosenfels, the backup, recalled. "He goes by feel and creates to get what he wants, instead of doing everything by the book. Most coaches cringe at that."

Although he insisted otherwise, Childress never seemed to fully trust

Favre. He nearly replaced him with Jackson during a rough stretch in the home game against the Packers, then again in a November 15 win over the Lions. At Childress's urging, Minnesota traded for Pittsburgh's second-round pick in the 2006 draft to select the strong-armed but obscure Jackson, and his performance had been underwhelming. Childress still believed in the 26-year-old, or at least felt the need to believe. "He always thought he could rehab Tarvaris," said Judd Zulgad, a *Minneapolis Star Tribune* football writer. "But he just wasn't that good."

The tension bubbled to the surface in a Week 15 matchup at Carolina, during which Favre and the offense performed miserably. The Vikings led 7–6 at halftime, and Childress ripped into the unit, cursing and saying it was "laughable" that they viewed themselves as Super Bowl contenders. He also decided to insert Jackson, then changed his mind. Favre hadn't had a coach yell at him like this since his father, and it didn't sit well. According to Jensen, in the second half Favre "apparently pushed his coach over the edge" when he checked out of a handoff to Peterson, dropped back to pass, and was sacked for a 5-yard loss. Cameras caught coach and quarterback arguing on the sideline, though they failed to catch an even more engrossing scene in the locker room. Following the 26–7 setback, a livid Childress chewed Favre out, and demanded the quarterback begin listening to the selected plays.

Favre didn't agree and didn't plan on changing. He had the support of his teammates, one of whom told the *Chicago Tribune,* "If [Childress] just manages and doesn't meddle, we have a chance to win the Super Bowl." After losing three of five games near season's end, the team capped things off with a 44–7 shellacking of the New York Giants, during which Favre threw four touchdown passes and Shiancoe had seven catches for 94 yards. When the final whistle blew, the Vikings were 12-4 and champions of the NFC North. Favre's statistics (33 touchdowns, seven interceptions, 4,202 yards) were some of the best of his career, and the team entered the playoffs as the NFC's No. 2 seed, only behind the 13-3 New Orleans Saints.

"That was OK," said Eric Frampton, a Vikings safety. "Because we were better than the Saints. We knew it, they knew it. We were the best team in football."

Were there any doubt about this, it seemed to be eradicated on January 17, when the Cowboys came to the Metrodome for the NFC divisional-round playoff game. At 11-5, Dallas was a worthy NFC East champion. Wade Phillips, the head coach, was a defensive mastermind who

planned on attacking Favre with a series of blitz packages. It was a logical strategy — strong-armed 40-year-old quarterbacks had certain skills,
but eluding a rush and staying healthy weren't two of them. Never much
of a pregame trash talker, Favre called the Cowboys "the hottest team in
the league right now," and paid special homage to their three imposing
defensive linemen, Anthony Spencer, Jay Ratliff, and DeMarcus Ware.
He then noted (uncharacteristically) that he expected to be having another press conference the following week about the NFC Championship
game. "If that doesn't happen," he said, "to me, it will be a shock."

Gerald Sensabaugh, a Dallas safety, took the statement as foolishness.
"We'd have to beat ourselves to lose," he said. "The way we are playing
right now, I don't think we can be beat."

The game was ugly. Or beautiful. Depends on one's vantage point. The
Vikings were favored by 2½, and it was far too little. The final score was
34–3, Minnesota. Favre completed 15 of 24 passes for 234 yards, including three touchdowns to Rice. In the fourth quarter, with 1:55 remaining,
Favre threw an 11-yard scoring pass to Shiancoe. It brought the home
crowd to its feet — a capper on one of the great days in the franchise's
48-year history. The Cowboys defenders, on the other hand, were livid.
As Favre walked off the field, he was berated by Keith Brooking, a Dallas
linebacker. "That's bullshit!" he screamed. "That's such fucking bullshit!

"One day you'll get yours, Brett!"

26

A SAINTLY BEATING

O N S E P T E M B E R 8, 2008, a year before Brett Favre would join the organization, the Minnesota Vikings traveled to Lambeau Field to face the Green Bay Packers. Aside from being Aaron Rodgers's debut as a starter, the game was noteworthy for its physicality and aggressiveness. In the first half alone, the teams combined for 12 penalties for 86 yards. It was a sloppy, messy, nasty affair, and in the days and weeks following the Packers' 24–19 win, Minnesota's coaches stewed. After watching the tape, they were convinced that Nick Barnett, Green Bay's outstanding linebacker, had gone out of his way to injure Adrian Peterson, the Vikings halfback.*

The rival franchises played again nine weeks later, and three days before kickoff a Minnesota coach stood up in a team meeting, mentioned Barnett by name, and said, "I will give $500 to anyone who takes this motherfucker out of the game."

This was hardly a shocking move in the Vikings' locker room, where piles of money were regularly collected — then distributed as rewards — for injuring opposing stars. "It was part of the culture," said Artis Hicks, a Minnesota offensive lineman. "If you hurt someone special, you get the money. There was a bottom line, and I think we all bought in: you're

---

* I asked Barnett about this privately via social media. He wrote: "I never went out of my way to hurt anyone. I play at 1 speed — hard as fuck! It doesn't surprise me at all. I was in Puerto Rico that offseason and ended up running into [Viking running back] Michael Bennett and he was surprised about how chill I was. He said that they hated me over there because of how I played. So it wouldn't surprise me if their coach would do something so classless as to pay someone to hurt me. I never was offered money to hurt anyone. I played football where the object is to be as physical as possible."

there to win, and if taking out the other team's best player helps you win, hey, it's nothing personal. Just business."

Although the Barnett affair occurred in 2008, Hicks insists the Vikings were no different a year later, when Brett Favre was quarterback. He recalled no one on the team complaining or arguing with the approach. "This isn't a game or culture for the fainthearted," Hicks said. "You bleed, you suffer, you sacrifice, and if need be, you try and knock people out. It's the NFL."

Following the win over Dallas, the Vikings weren't thinking about injuring opposing players, or taking someone out. That type of talk was often reserved for meetings with the league's more aggressive teams; black-and-blue franchises like Green Bay, Chicago, and Pittsburgh.

Not the New Orleans Saints.

The NFC Championship game would be held on January 24, 2010, in the Crescent City, and while the Vikings certainly preferred a home contest, this was the next-best scenario. Minnesota's coaches and players watched film of the Saints and came away both confident and surprisingly unimpressed. In compiling a 13-3 record, New Orleans relied on a high-flying offense that, behind quarterback Drew Brees and a gaggle of dangerous wide receivers, led the NFL in total yards and touchdowns. One week earlier they advanced to the title game by whooping the Arizona Cardinals, 45–14. It was the 10th time in 17 contests that New Orleans put up at least 30 points. "They scored and they scored quickly," said Leslie Frazier, the Minnesota defensive coordinator. "You had to be ready."

It was on the other side of the ball, though, where the Saints struggled. Gregg Williams, New Orleans's defensive coordinator, was known as one of the sport's great masterminds, and his ability to mix and disguise blitz packages became something of a calling card. Yet in 2009 the Saints ranked 20th in total defense, and their 35 sacks were just the 15th most in the league. Not one player accumulated 90 tackles, and only one (defensive end Will Smith) eclipsed 10 sacks. Darren Sharper, the 34-year-old free safety, led the Saints with nine interceptions, but Favre's former Green Bay teammate was a risk taker who — on tape — missed nearly as many tackles as he made. A couple of days before the game Favre was asked about Williams's group, and while he made certain to sound impressed, he wasn't particularly concerned. The Cowboys had a defense. Look how that turned out.

There were lots of marvelous narratives for the press to spend a week lapping up. Favre was the 40-year-old man returning to the region where he was raised watching Archie Manning and the Saints. New Orleans, as a city, was still recovering from Hurricane Katrina, and a Super Bowl trip would do wonders for the region. Could the Vikings handle the noise inside the Louisiana Superdome? Could the Saints stop Peterson, the game's best running back?

One thing that went undiscussed: Williams's plan to handle Favre. In a way, it's sort of surprising. For all the talk of the quarterback's experience, no one asked Williams or his defensive players what — in hindsight — seems to be a perfectly sensible inquiry: *At his advanced age, will you try and be more physically dominant than usual?*

New Orleans knew the Vikings were dangerous. They also knew it would be a lot easier stopping Favre than Peterson. So the goal was, simply, to beat the snot out of the quarterback. To hit him and hit him and hit him some more. To wear him down and wipe him out. To cause him to limp and cause him to bleed. "Make him pick his old ass up — that was our plan," said Anthony Hargrove, a Saints defensive lineman. "Make Brett keep getting off the ground, and hope at some point he just said, 'This is too much. I'm not getting up this time. I quit.'"

Favre was about to start his 309th straight game. He was as likely to quit as the French Quarter was to go dry. But Williams's men would try. Much like the Vikings, Saints players operated a reward system for hurting and incapacitating opposing stars. "It wasn't a bounty, where you name one guy and offer money for him," said Hargrove. "It was incentives for good plays, hard hits, changing the game. We all put in, and maybe you could get $100, $200, $500. That's what it was."

Would taking out Brett Favre be lucrative?

"There's a brotherhood in football," said Hargrove. "You never want to end anyone's career. But at the same time, we have incentives . . ."

Of the 39 NFC Championship games played before 2010, few could match this one for excitement, energy, intrigue. The Vikings scored first on a 19-yard Peterson run, and the Saints fired back with a 38-yard pass from Brees to Pierre Thomas. The Vikings made it 14–7 on Favre's 5-yard pass to Rice, the Saints tied the score at 14 on a 9-yarder from Brees to Devery Henderson. For fans in the stands, or fans viewing at home, it was everything you could hope for from a football game.

For Favre's family members and friends, however, it was unwatchable.

By one count, Favre was unnecessarily/gratuitously hit 13 times. Many were awful. Some were horrible. Two, in particular, were borderline criminal. In the first quarter, Favre handed off to Percy Harvin on a jet sweep. The ball was out of his hands, and Harvin had taken five full steps in the opposite direction when — *Pop!* — defensive end Bobby McCray (all six feet six, 260 pounds of him) pulverized an unsuspecting Favre into the turf. Later in the game, with 13 minutes gone in the third quarter, Favre dropped back to pass when McCray swarmed from the right and linebacker Remi Ayodele from straight ahead. Almost simultaneously, McCray dove into Favre's knees while Ayodele bent him backward like a soggy slice of bread, then rolled atop his listless corpse. Favre hobbled to the sideline, favoring his left ankle. Hargrove later said that after running off the field, Ayodele yelled, "Gimme my money!"*

Jeff Favre, Brett's younger brother, and Brandi Favre, his sister, were sitting in the Superdome, observing the beating, hands covering eyes, when they rose and left. They had attended plenty of games where Favre was the enemy. That was fine. But here, inside the Superdome, it felt more like a bullfight than a football game. The matadors were the Saints, the weakened bull was Favre. The fans wanted blood. "Jeff and I got a cab and watched the rest from the hotel on TV," Brandi said. "They were out to kill him. I knew they were trying to kill him. I've seen a lot of football, and that wasn't normal. It was disgusting."

"They were destroying him," said Scott Favre. "The Saints — they still rub me the wrong way from that game."

"It was inexcusable," said David Peterson, Favre's cousin. "I couldn't believe what I was seeing."

In some ways, it was Favre's lowest moment as a professional football player. In many ways, it was his greatest. The hits kept coming, and Favre kept standing up, brushing himself off, returning. The Saints pass rushers were bigger than the quarterback, more powerful than the quarterback, younger than the quarterback. But they weren't tougher than the quarterback. "He took every shot they had," said Pat Morris, the Vikings' offensive line coach. "And he didn't flinch once."

The Vikings were right — they were the better team. Faster, stronger, significantly more athletic. The Vikings won the possession and yardage

---

* Ayodele disputed this account via Twitter, writing, "I said NOTHING nobody on the team did I'm still trying to figure out this bounty what's he talking bout?"

battles — Peterson rushed for 122 yards and Minnesota gained 475 overall. But they also made lots of mistakes. Favre threw two interceptions (he was 28 of 46 for the game, with 310 yards and a touchdown); there were six total fumbles. It was ugly execution. "The football turned seemingly slick," wrote Jim Souhan of the *Star Tribune*, "as Andouille sausage plucked from a bowl of gumbo."

And yet, after driving the Vikings to a 28–28 tie with 4:58 remaining, Favre had a chance for the win. Minnesota's defense held the Saints' offense to plays, and with 2:37 left in the fourth the Vikings started at their own 21. They had three time-outs. Two Peterson runs gained little, but on third and 8 Favre found Bernard Berrian for 10. The Vikings used their first time-out, and Favre returned to the field and hit Rice with a 20-yard bullet. The New Orleans defense looked winded.

On first and 10 from the Saints 47, Chester Taylor took a handoff and rumbled 14 yards to the Saints 33. New Orleans called its final time-out, and along the sideline Ryan Longwell, one of the league's best kickers, was preparing to hit the field goal that would take the Vikings to their first Super Bowl since 1977. There was now 1:06 left, and two runs — one by Taylor, one by Peterson — gained nothing. Minnesota called its second time-out with 19 seconds left, and it was third and 10 from the Saints 33. Longwell peeked at the field between kicks into a net. From here, the field goal would be 50 yards — not out of question, but a bit long for his range.

Then, stupidity. On the sideline Eric Bieniemy, the running backs coach, could be seen wildly waving his arms, trying to get someone — anyone — off the field. Minnesota accidentally had 12 offensive players in the huddle, which resulted in a 5-yard penalty that pushed the team back to the 38. The Vikings' two requirements were clear: move a bit closer to give Longwell his best possible shot, and don't — *under any circumstance* — turn over the football.

The play call was unremarkable: A short throw to Berrian in the flat. Favre lined up behind center. Peterson stood 5 yards to his rear, Berrian jogged in motion, right to left, then back toward the right. Sidney Rice was lined up in the right slot, tight end Visanthe Shiancoe in the left slot. It was a collection of Minnesota's best weapons on the field for the season's most important play. The stadium noise was deafening. Seats vibrated from the decibels. Favre dropped back and rolled to the right. Berrian — who was not fully trusted by his quarterback — was never alone, but Shiancoe immediately turned around at the 35, where he was wide open.

Favre either didn't see him or didn't feel comfortable with the throw. He did, however, spot Rice crisscrossing the middle of the field near the New Orleans 23. With his body moving hard to the right, Favre reared back and fired to Rice, who was running leftward. The first person to see the pass was Tracy Porter, the speedy Saints cornerback. As the ball came closer and closer, Porter stepped in front of a lunging Rice, caught the football, and returned it to the Saints 47. "I did happen to read his eyes," Porter said. "He was looking at Rice the whole time." Favre dropped his head in disgust. There were seven seconds remaining.

Paul Allen, the Vikings' radio voice, was incredulous — and screaming like a madman. "Why do you even ponder passing? You can take a knee and try a 56-yard field goal! This is not Detroit, man! This is the Super Bowl!"

New Orleans won 31–28 on a 40-yard Garrett Hartley field goal in overtime, and as the city celebrated its first conference title, Favre's pain was as deep physically as it was emotionally. He could barely walk. His legs and torso were covered with black-and-blue craters. "Favre was pounded like a gavel, twisted like an Auntie Anne's pretzel," wrote Gene Wojciechowski of ESPN.com. "You should have seen him sitting in front of that locker immediately after the loss. Red welts on his left arm. Blood on his upper right shoulder. A puffy left wrist. A raw gash on the same wrist. A swollen left ankle. A tender right thigh and lower back . . . He was 40 at kickoff. He was 60 at the final whistle."

"He looked like Joe Frazier after having gone 15 rounds with Muhammad Ali," said Peter King. "There were three or four roughing-the-passer penalties that were never called, and he paid a big price in pain."

Favre admitted, in hindsight, that he should have run the ball (there was room), though his scrambling days were the stuff of yesteryear and his ankle the size of a baby panda.

One by one, teammates stopped by to pay their respects. Rice hugged him for a solid 30 seconds. Peterson whispered something into his ear. "I appreciate you," Favre replied softly. Harvin approached, wrapped his arms around the old quarterback. The eyes of both men were red and watery.

In the months that followed, much was written about what would become known as Bountygate — Williams's alleged system of paying his players to hurt opponents. Sean Payton, the New Orleans head coach, was suspended for an entire season, and the team's general manager, as well as Williams and assistant coach Joe Vitt, also faced temporary bans. The organization was fined $500,000 and forced two forfeit draft selections, and four players were suspended for their involvement. It was one of the biggest scandals in the 90-year history of the NFL.

For the league's 1,600 or so players, however, it was much ado about nothing. Yes, a curtain had been pulled back on life in professional football. But the majority of veterans greeted the news with a shrug. Thomas Jones, Favre's halfback with the Jets, found himself laughing at the uninformed ramblings from people making outside assessments. "What would make you think someone who is not in that environment would even have the slight idea of what we're feeling, what we're thinking?" he said. "It's like the military. Those people who come back from Iraq — they look the same. But they're not the same. In football, if I knock the shit out of somebody and he wasn't looking, that means I'm a nasty guy. I'm gonna get a positive grade for being nasty. You're not in your right state of mind. All you're thinking is, 'If I don't knock the shit out of him, he's gonna knock the shit out of me.' If a dude pushes me in the back and I'm not looking, I'm fucking pissed. Pissed. So the next time I get a chance to fucking do something, I'm doing it. You've seen *Braveheart*? *Braveheart* is exactly what football is. The scene where the Irish and the English are all running toward each other, and they clash, and it's all individual little fucking battles.

"If you're in a playoff game you know what the stakes are . . . what you've put into getting here, and you're not like, 'I'm not gonna knock this guy out because I care about him.' No, you want to intimidate the fuck out of him. Because I want him to be scared, so I have a better chance to win so I can win the Super Bowl and get my $50,000 bonus. You're not thinking about someone's well-being. You're doing whatever it takes."

Favre initially avoided talking about the scandal. He finally sat down for an interview with the NFL Network, and said he was neither upset nor haunted. Football, Favre said, is a rough and ugly game, played by rough and ugly people. "My feeling, and I mean this wholeheartedly, is I don't care," he later told ESPN. "What bothers me is we didn't win the game. They didn't take me out of the game. They came close . . . [but] I'm not gonna sit the last three minutes. I'm gonna go out there with bones sticking out of my skin and finish it."

· · ·

And that should have been that. Brett Favre played valiantly, took a beating, and lost. He made an ill-advised throw, but part of his charm was the ill-advised throws. You don't become a gunslinger by dumping passes off to halfbacks. You take shots, and sometimes they don't work.

"He had nothing to be ashamed of," said Childress. "Without Brett, there's no way we go that far."

So, again, that should have been that. And, truly, that *was* that. For the first time, Favre was genuinely committed to retirement. Deanna was encouraging it. So were his other Mississippi family members. Hell, on April 2, 2010, he became a grandfather when Brittany, now 21, gave birth to a seven-pound, seven-ounce boy named Parker Brett. There were things other than football in life, and Favre, nearing his 41st birthday, was prepared to move forward.

But then — dammit — the begging commenced. On August 16 three veteran Vikings (Jared Allen, Steve Hutchinson, and Ryan Longwell) were flown by the organization to Hattiesburg on team owner Zygi Wilf's 10-seat, Dassault-Breguet Falcon 50 jet to try and persuade Brett Favre to return for a 20th NFL season. "We told him how much all the guys loved playing with him and that we would love to do it again," said Hutchinson, a Pro Bowl offensive guard. "We also told him that if he didn't want to do it, then congratulations, you deserve it; you've had an incredible career. But we've got to know one way or another."

They spent the night at Favre's house, grilling steaks, touring the property, weighing the pros and cons. The players knew Favre didn't love playing for Childress, but assured him the coach was a marginalized presence. The offense didn't belong to Brad Childress. It belonged to Brett Favre. "We spilled our guts," Longwell said.

The next day Favre agreed to come back, and he returned with his three teammates aboard Wilf's jet to rejoin the Vikings and chase a Super Bowl. He said all the right things to the media about being excited and refreshed. But, deep down, this wasn't right. Favre had always been drawn by his love for football. Now, he was being drawn by the guilt of not wanting to disappoint teammates.

It resulted in one of the worst years of his life.

First, the Vikings had peaked. Favre expressed brashness in the lead-up to the September 9 opener at (of all teams) New Orleans, saying that, "I feel as confident as I did this time last year — maybe even more confident." It was terribly misplaced. Minnesota was one of the NFL's older teams, and whatever magic was present in 2009 no longer existed. They lost 14–9 to the Saints in a game as dispiriting as it was boring, and Favre (who went 15 of 27 for 171 yards, a touchdown, and an interception) tossed repeated inaccurate passes. The next week was even worse — a 14–10 home setback against the mediocre Dolphins, followed by a victory against lowly Detroit and the bye week.

Second, there was Brett Favre's penis. Yes, you have read that correctly: *Brett Favre's penis*. On August 4, 2010, Deadspin.com, the popular sports-gossip website, ran the headline BRETT FAVRE ONCE SENT ME COCK SHOTS: NOT A LOVE STORY. The accompanying piece, written by A. J. Daulerio, told the alleged saga of Jenn Sterger, a former in-house side-line reporter for the New York Jets best known for being the sexy Florida State football fan who wound up posing for *Playboy* and *Maxim*. Accord-ing to the Deadspin article, when Favre was playing for the Jets he repeat-edly hit on her via voice messages, then texted a photograph of his penis. Wrote Daulerio: "And it happened multiple times. In fact, Sterger claims that, in one of the photos Favre allegedly sent her, he's masturbating — while wearing a pair of Crocs. In another photo, Favre is holding his penis while wearing the wristwatch he wore during his first teary-eyed retirement press conference."

Although the story received a fair amount of attention, it was largely marginalized. Deadspin was eyed skeptically by mainstream media out-lets, and this felt more like juvenile yellow nonsense than legitimate ma-terial. That changed, though, on the morning of October 7. The Vikings were scheduled to play the Jets on *Monday Night Football* in four days, marking Favre's first time facing his old team, and Deadspin celebrated the return with another Daulerio offering, headlined BRETT FAVRE'S CELLPHONE SEDUCTION OF JENN STERGER. Unlike the previous arti-cle, this one was accompanied by a video that presented a timeline of the Favre–Sterger nonrelationship, plus audio recordings of two cell phone messages the quarterback left for the reporter, as well as three penis pic-tures — confirmed by a friend to be the official member of Brett Favre.* A whopping 6.2 million people viewed the segment, and when asked for

---

* According to Deadspin, the material was supplied by a third party, not Sterger. The website paid $12,000 for the photographs and voice messages.

comment Favre neither confirmed nor denied the account's accuracy. "I'm not getting into that," he said. "I've got my hands full with the Jets."

The story was gossipy and juvenile. Mostly, it was pathetic. A mere six months earlier, Favre had become a grandfather. Not only was Sterger just five years older than Brittany, but she bore a striking resemblance to a young Deanna Tynes. The NFL issued a statement saying it would review the Deadspin report, and the Jets directed all questions to a public relations firm. Daulerio was 100 percent certain of the content. He said one former Packers player looked at the images and said, "I showered next to Brett for years. That's *his* dick."

Favre was lost as to how to handle the situation. According to a family friend, when the initial Deadspin report broke in August, he told Deanna that it was nonsense. Once the photographs and voice messages surfaced, there was no denying the truth. Favre attempted to come up with excuses, alibis, explanations — but there were none. That was his voice and his penis and his hand holding his penis. "That whole experience was the lowest I'd ever seen him," said a friend. "It was just so humiliating."

Shortly after the story ran, Deanna appeared on *Good Morning America* to promote a new book. Robin Roberts told her beforehand that, journalistically, she had to ask about the photographs. "I can tell you that obviously, I'm a woman of faith," Deanna said on the air. "Faith has got me through many difficult struggles and it will get me through this one. I'm handling this through faith, Robin."

Off camera, Deanna Favre was devastated. She had stood by her husband through drug addiction, through serial infidelity. He had grown and matured, she believed, from a wannabe frat boy to a responsible adult, and she genuinely thought their relationship to be one that, through hard times, was stronger than ever.

And now millions of people were looking at his penis.

"You could see the hurt on Brett, and I'm sure that extended to his entire family," said Ben Leber, the Vikings linebacker. "He came back when he probably really didn't want to, we weren't a good team — and then he had the Sterger stuff. At his core, you could tell he was hurting. But there wasn't anything we could do."

Much like the way Magic Johnson's 1991 HIV announcement caused professional athletes to reconsider their sexual habits, the Favre images hit home throughout NFL locker rooms. "Dick pics" (as they're colloquially known) were an increasingly normal way for players to hit on women. "If anything, what that story did for me was make me a dick merchant," said Daulerio. "Anyone who had a photo of a celebrity dick seemed to send it my way."

A couple of days after the article came out, Favre again asked Childress to let him speak to the team. This time, without getting into specifics, he apologized for the distraction. "It wasn't helpful, that scandal," said Childress. "He was really bothered by that, and he was focused on trying to save his marriage. I mean, we're going to New York City right after it comes out, the worst place for him to be."

The Vikings fell to the Jets, 29–20, then lost four of their next six games to kill any hopes of a return to the playoffs. If the sexting scandal was the biggest problem of the awful season, a close second was the Favre-influenced acquisition of wide receiver Randy Moss from the New England Patriots. Ever since he was a Packer, Favre had been itching to play with Moss, who spent the first 12 years of his career becoming one of the most dominant players in NFL history and simultaneously establishing a reputation as a moody, selfish dog. Moss was a Viking from 1998 until 2004, and Favre begged Rick Spielman, the vice president of player personnel, to bring him back. When New England accepted the offer of a third-round pick, Moss was again in Minnesota. "This is an exciting move," Favre raved. "It's rare you get to play with a future Hall of Famer."

That giddiness lasted for a solid two days. Moss met with Childress, assured him he had matured and, at age 33, was appreciative of what it meant to be a Viking. "I was thinking, 'This can be really great,'" said Childress. "He seems really happy. Boy, was I wrong about that one."

Most Fridays following practices the team furnished a meal catered by various local establishments. On the afternoon of Friday, October 29, Moss entered the locker room, took a plate, and loaded up on the chicken, pasta, and ribs prepared by Tinucci's Restaurant and Catering. "What the fuck!" Moss yelled. "Who ordered this crap? I wouldn't feed this to my dog!"

According to Gus Tinucci, co-owner of the business, Favre gave Moss a stare of utter contempt. "If Favre would have had a ball, he would have beaned him right in the head," Tinucci said. "Favre looked at him like, 'Are you kidding me?'"

When Moss wasn't complaining about the food, he was complaining — with Favre — about the coach. Neither man liked or respected Childress, and both believed the team would be better served without him.

They routinely compared notes, laughed about his incompetence, itched for the moment he would be gone. One day, when Vikings owner Zygi Wilf walked through the locker room, Moss looked at him and hissed, "You need to get rid of the fucking coach." Wilf was horrified. What happened to the glory of 2009? Where was his Super Bowl contender? "Randy destroyed our team," said one Viking. "He just destroyed us."

Following a 28–18 loss to the Patriots, Moss used the postgame as an opportunity to take to the podium and question Childress's decision making while praising his former coach, Bill Belichick. He was released a day later, but then, on November 22, Childress was fired and replaced by Leslie Frazier, the defensive coordinator. Nothing helped. The Vikings fell at home to the Packers, 31–3, on November 21, and as Favre played terribly, Aaron Rodgers lit up the Minnesota defense. Three weeks later, in a perfectly symbolic moment, the Metrodome's inflated roof collapsed during a snowstorm, and the Giants–Vikings game was moved to Detroit's Ford Field. Favre was recovering from a sprained right shoulder, and Bernard Berrian tweeted, "Joke goin round is Gods Tryin to preserve Bretts streak record."

Alas, it was not to be. Frazier placed Favre on the inactive list, and his streak of 297 consecutive starts came to an end. Because the Vikings were terrible and Favre was in the midst of his worst season, the conclusion of his record run failed to garner the sort of attention Cal Ripken Jr. generated in 1998 when he sat after 2,632 straight games. It was, largely, a footnote to the weirdness of a Vikings home game played in Michigan. "The whole thing is bizarre," said Pete Bercich, the team's radio analyst. Favre stood on the sideline, wearing a wool Vikings cap, watching the action, advising Jackson in yet another defeat. "None of it seemed right," said Jensen. "You hate seeing legends go out like that."

No. What you hate is seeing legends go out as Favre did a week later, when he returned for a home game against the Chicago Bears. He had initially been ruled out, and a rookie, Joe Webb, was named the starter. But come December 20, Favre somehow jogged out onto the field at the University of Minnesota's TCF Bank Stadium in full pads and uniform, ready to begin a new streak. By now the Vikings were 5-8, and there was no logical reason for a battered, fossilized quarterback to continue. Yet pride had been Brett Favre's signature for so long, and now it was his weakness. Chicago jumped out to an early lead, and was up 10-7 when, with 11:32 left in the second quarter, the Vikings faced third and 4 from the Bears 48. Immediately before the play Julius Peppers, the star pass rusher, sprinted to the sideline with an injury. His backup, a rookie from Northwestern named Corey Wootton, wasn't paying attention, and the team had to burn a time-out. Rod Marinelli, the Bears' defensive coordinator, lit into Wootton. "Get the fuck on the field," he snarled, "and make something happen!"

When play resumed, the six-foot-seven, 280-pound Wootton read the count perfectly, bulldozed over left tackle Bryant McKinnie, grabbed Favre (who took the snap from the shotgun), twirled him around like a dishrag, and slammed his body — and head — into the frozen ground. It was Wootton's first career sack, and he leapt up, pumped his fists, and started to celebrate before looking back. The quarterback was motionless. "Favre's lying there in pain," Wootton said. "I was immediately disappointed. It's never been my goal to hurt people. And Brett Favre — there was nobody I admired more. So, no, sacking him didn't make me feel good."

Said Mike Tirico, calling the game for ESPN, "You wonder if that will be the play that ends Brett Favre's career."

There wasn't much wondering — it *was* the play that ended Brett Favre's career. Eric Sugarman, the Vikings trainer, leaned over the downed quarterback and said, "Come with me."

"Why are the Bears here?" Favre replied as he rose. His first two steps were toward the Chicago sideline. In the locker room he showered, ate a hot dog, and sipped from a cup of hot chocolate. He was diagnosed with a concussion, and deactivated for the last two games. His final statistics (11 touchdowns, 19 interceptions) accurately depicted his play. "It's a terrible way to end," said Frazier. "I wanted him to have one last moment, where he could come onto the field, have the fans show their appreciation, get that final round of applause. But there wasn't really a final round of applause. He got hurt, he left, it ended."

A pause.

"With athletes, that's sort of how it goes," Frazier said. "It ends ugly. Even for gunslingers."

AFTERWORD

BACK IN 2010, when Brett Favre took his last NFL snap, a presumption among many was that the 41-year-old quarterback would struggle with retirement. There was a reason, the thinking went, that he kept coming back, then coming back again, and again, and again. Playing football was a lifeline for him, and without the action he would be lost.

Yet one person who saw things differently was Scott Favre, Brett's older brother. That final miserable season as a Viking, he believes, was as important as the Super Bowls. "Had he not played that year, he always would have thought, 'What would have happened had I gone back?'" Scott Favre said. "It didn't work out, and that sealed the deal for him. He was like, 'It's time to retire. I'm ready. I'm tired. I'm done.' He needed an ending, and had he not played, people would have said, 'Man, the Vikings could have won a Super Bowl with you.' That would have eaten at him. But that last year was terrible. He needed terrible to be able to walk away."

As with many athletes, once the vanishing act began, it progressed quickly. Favre had no desire to serve as an announcer, or a studio analyst, or to walk the sidelines as somebody's quarterbacks coach. He didn't want to be a Packers ambassador, or a Vikings ambassador, or work in the front office as some sort of player personnel guru. Even at the end of his career, with graying hair and a worn-down body, Favre remained the kid in sandals, shorts, and a T-shirt, three days' worth of scruff covering his cheeks. He knew an off-the-field job would likely entail either meeting regularly with the press or wearing some sort of suit-tie-slacks combo. No, thank you. Furthermore, he had little desire to be put in the position of criticizing players. In 2011 he made some disparaging comments about Aaron Rodgers, and they went off like a stink bomb. Nobody enjoys hearing old fogies tell youngsters how to do their jobs. Favre realized this quickly.

Truly, what he genuinely aspired to do was nothing — or at least his version of nothing. Initially, he sat around the house and ate. Then ate some more. And a little more. He gained 25 pounds in his first year away from the game, following the well-worn path of thousands of ex-jocks no longer obligated to daily workouts. He entered a 5K race in 2011, walked most of the course, and finished in 48 minutes (by comparison, an in-his-prime Alberto Salazar could have lapped him three and a half times in that span). It was an embarrassing eye-opener, one that resulted in the old quarterback taking up running and cycling. On family trips, he began to rise at the crack of dawn to go for an anonymous trot along city streets and country trails. No, it didn't have the intensity of a fourth and 7 against the Bears. But he didn't want that.

At home, away from helmets and pads, Favre seemed to realize how much football had taken from his family. Brittany, his 22-year-old daughter, was now Brittany Favre-Mallion — married to a British man, Alex (who knew nothing about the NFL), and attending Loyola University's College of Law, and his grandson Parker turned 1 in April. Breleigh, meanwhile, was emerging as one of Mississippi's elite youth volleyball players (in 2012 she would make the Oak Grove High varsity team as an eighth grader). Throughout his career, Brett appeared, disappeared, attended, missed, appeared for a few minutes. He would be interviewed about his kids, and speak as a proud papa, but Deanna (and Deanna's mother, Ann Byrd, who lives in a separate home on the property), did most of the child rearing. Brett sorta knew how to change diapers and warm bottles and cook family dinners — but it had never been a regular thing, because football called.

Now, for the first time, football didn't call. So, along with the exercising, he did what people do when they own a rural 465-acre estate. He mowed the lawn, pulled out the shrubs, took care of the house, raked the sand volleyball court. He would hunt a bit, fish a bit, golf a bit. He planned family vacations and traveled with Deanna as she competed in myriad triathlons. "He's a very good husband now," said David Thomason, Favre's longtime colleague. "I think Brett learned a lot about being a good family guy from all those years away. He wants to make these days count."

On the opening Sunday of the 2011 NFL season, the Vikings were playing at San Diego. Donovan McNabb, the longtime Philadelphia Eagle, was the new starting quarterback. Favre was outside when Deanna called him in for kickoff. He sat in front of a large flat-screen television and watched, more bored than engrossed. When it ended he returned to what he had been doing. Ho-hum. No biggie. Wrote Greg Bishop in *Sports Illustrated,* "He woke up Monday morning free of soreness." It was, Favre had to admit, absolutely delightful. He didn't miss the game one iota.

Then, in the summer of 2013, a strange twist. Favre lives down the road from Oak Grove High, the school both his daughters attended. In fact, throughout the final years of his playing career, he would prepare for training camp by working out with the varsity football team. The head coach, an affable man named Nevil Barr, loved having Favre around. Now, with the season but a few months away, Barr was in a pickle. His offensive coordinator, Tim Held, and the offensive line coach, Bob Bird, shared the Warriors' play-calling duties, but both recently left. On a whim, Barr called Favre and asked if he would consider joining the staff.

"I think I could maybe do that," he replied.

"Oh, I *know* you could," said Barr.

"Well, what's my salary gonna be?" Favre said with a chuckle.

"We'll pay you absolutely nothing," Barr said.

"Lemme get this straight," Favre said. "You want me to come every day for no pay *and* come in on Sundays for film work?"

"Yeah," Barr replied.

"OK," Favre said. "I'll do it."

"He was fantastic," said Barr. "He obviously knows more about football than most of us can dream of, but that wasn't it. It was how he related with the kids, and got to know them. It was special."

Barr insists it's no coincidence that the 13-1 Warriors had one of the state's highest-scoring offenses, and wound up winning the Mississippi Class 6A championship game. Favre showed up for work every day, never made a big deal about himself, flashed nary an ounce of ego or entitlement. He was "Brett" or "Coach" — never "Mr. Favre" — and his play calling was inventive and funky. Whereas once there was Antonio Freeman and Ahman Green, now there were spindly high school kids with pimply faces and cracking voices. He loved it.

"There was one game where we were playing another team and he said to me, 'Take the snap, look that way, and [wide receiver] Logan Scott is gonna be wide open and all alone,'" said Kirk McCarty, the Oak Grove quarterback. "I probably didn't believe him, but I got the ball, looked at Logan — and there he was, uncovered. Brett just knew this stuff, and he communicated it."

That October, midway through the Warriors' schedule, the St. Louis Rams lost Sam Bradford, their starting quarterback, to season-ending knee surgery. The team reached out to Bus Cook to see if Favre would consider coming out of retirement. The offer was relayed, and the old quarterback greeted it with derisive laughter. "It's flattering," Favre said. "But you know there's no way I'm going to do that."

He continued to coach, devoting two seasons to the school before deciding enough was enough. Breleigh was traveling more and more for volleyball, and he wanted to watch as much as possible. "That's hard to argue with," said Barr. "Brett just needed to be a dad."

Because Favre was rarely heard from on a national level (save for the random TV commercial), it was during his high school coaching run that word began to circulate about his declining health and, specifically, potentially impaired memory. The NFL was in the midst of what seemed to be a concussion epidemic, and a nonstop stream of former players were suing the league for damages. Though unspoken, the feelings on Brett Favre could be stated in a single sentence: *What man took more hits?* During a 2013 radio interview Favre was asked about his memory, and the response made instant headlines. "I don't remember my daughter playing soccer, youth soccer, one summer," he said. "I don't remember that." He went on to admit that he was terrified by how his brain might function years down the road, and added that he was uncertain whether he'd want his grandchildren to play football. Favre told *Sports Illustrated* that, at times, he misplaced his keys, or couldn't remember where he left his sunglasses.

Favre has not undergone any sort of testing, and since the interview has felt no noticeable decline in memory capacity. In fact, those who deal with Favre on a regular basis insist he is sharp and lucid. Thomason said he sees little change. "Brett's still very quick," he said. "I'm not saying the hits haven't impacted him. Maybe they have. But I can't always remember where I left my keys, either."

The one thing that has perplexed many colleagues (and former colleagues) is his major post-NFL business move. During his heyday, Favre relied on Cook's savvy and decision-making abilities to steer him in the right direction. And, indeed, even those who dislike the pushy Mississippi agent (there are many) concede he genuinely served his client well. Favre earned millions in endorsement opportunities, including a long-standing relationship with Wrangler that made him the face of the blue jeans manufacturer. (Favre practiced good money management and remains quite wealthy.)

Three years ago, however, in a decision that left friends and family members scratching their heads, Favre joined the board of directors of Sqor Sports, a Twitter-like social media site created to connect athletes with fans. "The success to date has been awesome, and I think the sky is the limit with Sqor," Favre said at the time. "I am excited to be joining the Board of Directors and looking forward to contributing in any way that I can to help the company succeed." Before long, Sqor was handling Favre's Twitter account (and botching basic football facts), peddling bewildering T-shirts and glossy photographs (featuring a bearded Brett Favre looking like a cross between Santa Claus and Charles Manson) and helping arrange his endorsements. Cook, once the puppeteer behind Favre, Inc., found himself in the cold as his star client began popping up in cheesy low-rent TV advertisements for items like nasal-hair extractors and knee supports. *Hey, I'm Brett Favre! And I got my groom back with Micro Touch!* One of the products he promoted was a topical pain cream called Rx Pro. Favre also invested in the parent company, World Health Industries. "I can speak volumes on pain and narcotics use," Favre raved to SiriusXM's Bruce Murray in 2013. Rx Pro, he added, "is a safe way to treat some of your ailments. It even works with cramps, stomach pain . . . It's just endless what will happen with this product and this company." The ointment, he insisted, would "revolutionize" sports recovery.

By 2016, years after Favre's initial investment, World Health Industries was being investigated by the Justice Department for alleged healthcare fraud. The cream apparently did nothing.

Much of his postretirement revenue went to Sqor. In interviews, he would almost always wear a Sqor T-shirt, yet never seemed to be able to explain what, exactly, Sqor does. As of early 2016, Sqor Sports had a mere 13,900 Twitter followers and was not making inroads into the sports media landscape. "I think Brett wanted to do something on his own, and that's commendable," said a friend. "But nobody has been able to figure this one out. He hasn't made money from Sqor, they control his image, and Bus doesn't understand why he stopped listening to him. It's a head-scratcher, but he thinks it's going to make him billions of dollars.

"He already has millions, so, really, there's no big harm. But it's kind of fucked up."

On the evening of June 20, 2015, nearly five years after Brett Favre took his final NFL snap, Kenny Chesney and Jason Aldean held a concert at Lambeau Field.

For a neck of the woods that loves country music and lacks nonfootball excitement, this was a huge deal. A sellout crowd of nearly 53,000 people packed the stadium, and stayed for four hours as three opening acts, then the co-headliners, brought forth one song after another. It was, Piet Levy of the *Milwaukee Journal Sentinel* wrote, "almost as good as a Packers Super Bowl victory." Everyone seemed to win. The fans experienced musical bliss, the city's restaurants and hotels filled up, the Packers generated $1 million to host the gig.

There was just one problem: the following day, the once-pristine field looked as if it had been attacked by a ruthless swarm of mutant grass-eating pig monsters. Where once there was green, now there was mud. Some team officials were so horrified they insisted Lambeau would never again be home to a concert.

One month later, the Packers hosted Favre's highly anticipated return to Green Bay. Ever since the trade to the Jets, relations between the quarterback and the organization had been, at best, hostile. Favre still resented the Packers for not allowing him to return and fight Aaron Rodgers for the job. The Packers resented Favre for retiring 106 times and turning what should have been a smooth resolution into war. Now, though, with the passing of years, the organization — as well as local fans — seemed willing to forgive the greatest player in franchise history for the crime of ending his career as a Minnesota Viking. Over the weekend days of July 18 and 19, Favre was celebrated with the retiring of his No. 4 and an induction into the team's Hall of Fame. There was a signing at a local bar, a heavily attended press conference, a magnificent banquet inside the Lambeau Field Atrium (tickets, which went for $180, sold out quickly). Bonita Favre was in attendance, as were about 30 former Packer teammates. In a moment that will go down in city lore, Favre excused himself from the event to walk out into the stadium, where 67,000 fans paid $4 a pop to watch on the large screen. As soon as the icon appeared, everyone rose and gave him a standing ovation. Favre — joined by his family — was overcome by emotion and reduced to tears. "One of the coolest things I've ever seen," said Lance Allan, a Milwaukee sports anchor who conducted a quick Q&A with Favre on the field. "If you didn't have chills, you're not human."

It was outstanding and magical and wonderful and as memorable as anything many had ever witnessed. But for the Favre family (and specifically Brett and Deanna), it was tainted. On the following afternoon Favre would play in Brett Favre's Legends Game, a flag football showdown between a team of former Packers stars and a squad of onetime NFL "greats." (Sage Rosenfels was one of the quarterbacks. "Greats" was pushing it.) The beauty, as Brett had envisioned things, was that it would allow Green Bay's cherished quarterback to throw his final passes inside Lambeau Field while rightly wearing the green and gold. Then, finally, he could walk off into the sunset as a Packer, and all would be right.

Or not.

According to the Packers, the Chesney-Aldean concert was enough for fragile Lambeau to handle, and a flag football game (even one played a full month later) would *really* be enough. So, magical moments be damned, Favre was told he and his pals would have to do their thing 135 miles to the south at Camp Randall Stadium, home to the Wisconsin Badgers. A group of Favre family friends committed themselves to making sure the game would wind up sold out — "to show the Packers how dumb they were," one said. Tickets ran between $34 and $55. On the big day, the 80,321-seat stadium was about 70 percent empty, and while it was somewhat amusing (and even a bit nostalgic) watching Favre once again launch passes to Javon Walker and Andre Rison, one could hear the grunts of has-been heroes echoing off vacant plastic seats.

It was the sound of old men playing a young man's sport.

It was also the sound of one last slap to Brett Favre's face.

On the afternoon of Saturday, February 6, 2016, the 46 members of the Pro Football Hall of Fame committee gathered inside a room in San Francisco to determine the worthiness of 15 modern-era finalists. As is often the case, the debating — oft-heated, oft-exasperating — went on interminably. For example, in regards to Eddie DeBartolo Jr., the former San Francisco 49ers' owner, committee members argued for 50 minutes and 33 seconds about whether he was great for the game, good for the game, or awful for the game. There were shouts, squeals, supportive exclamations, and dismissive shrugs. Finally, because life must go on and bath-

room breaks taken, DeBartolo was granted a spot in Canton. Even those
opposed were relieved to reach a resolution.

Because Hall of Fame enshrinement is an inexact art, few sail in
smoothly. With 15,934 receiving yards and 153 touchdowns, Terrell Owens, the former 49ers and Cowboys pass catcher, was a statistical no-
brainer to reach the Hall on his first try. Instead, he was rejected. Kevin
Greene, a pass-rushing linebacker who last played in 1999, seemed forgotten by time and a near certainty to be rejected. He was voted in.

Such is how it went. One name after another came to the floor, and
one name after another was argued and argued and argued and argued
and . . .

Save Brett Favre.

When the legendary quarterback's name was brought forth, the debate lasted for either six or nine seconds (depending on whom you believe). Actually, there was no debate. Literally none. Just as, one month
earlier, Ken Griffey Jr. had entered the Baseball Hall of Fame sans issue,
Favre was perhaps the easiest choice the committee ever faced. Was he a
winner? Yes — two Super Bowl appearances. Was he a good teammate?
For most of his career, the best. A leader? Undeniably. Talented? Excep-
tionally so. Statistically successful? Pre–Peyton Manning, Favre was the
NFL's all-time leader in passing yards and touchdowns. Durable? Well,
321 straight starts don't lie. Sure, he stuck around too long. And sure, he
had an ego. But were those true crimes, most of America's sports superstars would never sniff a Hall of Fame.

What Brett Favre offered, more than anything, was a never-before-
seen merging of toughness, recklessness, skill, and joy. Without much
debate, there have been better quarterbacks in NFL history. Joe Montana
and Terry Bradshaw were bigger winners; Johnny Unitas and John Elway
were more savvy; Roger Staubach and Steve Young were more mobile.
Even though he has only been the Packers starter since 2008, Aaron Rodgers is — in many measures — a far superior player to Favre. He's more
accurate, a better decision maker. Rodgers rarely throws into double coverage; *never* throws into triple coverage. If you had to pick the man who
represents the perfectly groomed and modeled modern quarterback, and
the choice was either Favre or Rodgers, well, there's no choice at all. Rodgers wins.

But that's just it — Favre was never perfect. He mangled plays, threw
off the wrong foot, made the sloppy read, misjudged, and miscalculated.

He brought Packers fans to tears nearly as often as he brought them to euphoria. He was a show — drama, comedy, heartbreak, giddiness. You wanted to watch, but you couldn't watch. At least not without peeking through your fingers, afraid of what might unfold.

Ultimately, that unpredictability will be Brett Favre's lasting legacy, long after the numbers have faded and the Hall of Fame bust has collected dust. For all the importance we place upon athletic events, they are — come day's end — mere entertainment. In Green Bay, Wisconsin, where the winters are long and the snow piles are deep and the values of hard work and doggedness are treasured, who was ever more entertaining than Brett Favre? He was neither pretty nor predictable, flawless nor family-friendly. He was an addict, he was an alcoholic, he was a womanizer, selfish, unfaithful to his wife, unfaithful to his most loyal fans. In short, he was flawed. Just as you're flawed. Just as I'm flawed.

But, on those magical moments atop an ice-coated field, he could throw the football far into the Wisconsin sky . . .

. . . and you never quite knew where it would wind up.

ACKNOWLEDGMENTS

On a muggy Mississippi evening in the summer of 2014, I was driving along the backroads from Kiln to Diamondhead when, out of giddiness, I called my wife.

"I had such a great day," I told her. "I just spent four hours with Brett Favre's mom and sister."

"You what?" the wife asked.

"I was at their house," I said. "They're just the friendliest people imaginable. I was even given some scrapbooks to borrow."

A pause.

"Don't you think that's weird?" the wife said.

"How so?" I replied.

"Brett Favre hasn't talked to you," she said. "But his family has?"

"No," I said. "That's not weird at all."

"Really?" she said

"Really," I said.

"OK," she said. "Imagine someone is doing a book on you, and you don't talk. Wouldn't you find it strange if your parents and brothers then spent time with the author?"

Eh, she had a point. She also didn't have a point. Because unless you know the Favres, and know Hancock County, Mississippi, it's hard to grasp the idea of people being so open, so welcoming, so accommodating—circumstances be damned. But that's Bonita Favre, as well as her children, her cousins, her friends. You talk because someone took the time to show up and ask questions. You talk because you have stories to tell and anecdotes to share.

You talk because you like to talk.

I cannot overstate my affection for the Favre family. They knew from the start that I wasn't visiting to write an ode to Brett, but an explanation of Brett. I hope this book validates their willingness to share.

Writing a book is a nightmare. This is my seventh published work, and each one includes that six-word sentence. You rarely sleep, you dig, you chase, you face great rejection, you doubt, then doubt again and again. I shouldn't complain, because being a full-time author is actually the best gig in the world. But it can — and has — driven a guy quite insane.

That being said, the insanity is a collective lunacy. Back when I agreed to write *Gunslinger* for Houghton Mifflin Harcourt, my friend Jon Wertheim, the excellent *Sports Illustrated* writer, said, "Are you doing it with Susan?"

"Yup," I said.

"She's the absolute best," he replied.

This was no lie. Susan Canavan is everything you'd want in an editor, which is to say she was supportive, inventive, smart, and quirky.

In Michael J. Lewis I'm gifted with the best proofreader in the business, and Casey Angle is the Bubba Franks of fact-checkers. David Black, my agent, has had a tough run these past two years, but his resiliency and doggedness are beyond inspiring. Jack Cassidy was a terrific new edition to the squad, Jeff Ash has my vote for mayor of Green Bay, and Melissa Dobson is the 8:30 p.m. goddess of the red pen. I can't say enough about Stanley Herz, my Yugoslavian spell-checker, Frank Zaccheo, purveyor of freaks, and Brant Beaupre, friend, website designer, and former Burger King superstar. The endless late-night struggles were made bearable by chats and reassurances with a collective of wonderful friends, including Elizabeth Newman, Gary Miller, Jeanne Beaupre, Matthew Walker, Bev Oden, Mirin Fader, Paul Ercolino, Russ Edmondson, Andrew Dallos, Donna Massaro, Amy Bass, Nick Mirto, Davis Webb, Amy Fabry, Patrick McShan, Russ Bengtson, Carrie Ferguson, John Degl, Jeff Bidwell, Daniel Paisner, Nick Greenizan, Gary Rind, Mike Brandyberry, Matt Butler, Robert O'Neill, Yaron Weitzman, Steven (Bionic) Azrak, and Paul, my son's doll, who speaks in a deep voice and stares at me quite awkwardly. Throughout my travels to Mississippi and Green Bay, I was repeatedly assisted by intelligent, eager people thrilled to help. They included E. W. Suarez of the Biloxi Public Library, Ty Stewart at Southern Miss, Zachary Stipe of the Florida State sports information staff, Mary Jane Herber of the Brown County Central Library, Philip Klein from Klein Investigations and Consulting, E. J. Borghetti, the media relations director at the University of Pittsburgh, Holly Borga of the Green Bay Packers Hall of Fame, Christopher Dunaway from Tulane University, and Matty Goldman of MLB Daily Dish. Big props to Ashley Brouwer for her John Jefferson hunt, Maggie Mahoney for steakhouse tips, Alexandra Makal for being Milwaukee's finest bartender, Justin Duplain for the tutoring, and Wanda Cooper for being Wanda Cooper. In Noel Besuzzi, I found both an unparalleled photographer and a wonderful spirit.

I wound up interviewing 573 people for this book, and while it's too high a number to thank folks individually, I hope this work meets your expectations and standards. Special happy emojis to William Browning, Lori Nickel, Sean Jensen, Peter King, Greg Bedard, Greg Bishop, Rich Cimini, Jenny Xu, Kyle Cousineau, Adam Czech, A.J. Daulerio, Rob Demovsky, Pete Dougherty, Sam Farmer, Roy Firestone, Lisa Guerrero, Al Michaels, Brenda Heathcock, Al Jones, David Maraniss, Jeremy Schaap, Adam Schefter, Steve Serby, Tom Silverstein, Dylan Tomlinson, Billy Watkins, Judd Zulgad, Charles Burton, Drew Malley, Joe Sweeney, Craig Nall, Ryan Grant, Na'il Diggs, Mark Brunell, John Teerlinck, LeRoy Butler, Mike Tannenbaum, Leon Washington, Artis Hicks, and Brad Childress for going above and beyond. Oh, and nothing but genuine love and admiration for Dylan Favre, Xavier Favre, and Brianna McLeod — the prides of Martin, Tennessee.

I'd like to thank a family filled with people who never want to hear another word about Brett Favre. Jordan and Isaiah Williams are my sons from another father, Leah Guggenheimer smells like teen spirit, Laura and Rodney Cole always encourage an extra helping of dessert, and Norma Shapiro, my wife's 96-year-old grandmother, is a daily ode to the power of positive thinking. Congrats to Jessica Guggenheimer and Chris Berman on the wedding — nothing says "I love you, honey!" like 500 copies of a Brett Favre biography (preferably purchased during the first week of availability).

My parents, Stan and Joan Pearlman, know nothing about football (a repeated quote from my mother: "I keep trying to tell my friends who you're writing about. Is his name Brent Ferry or Brent Favor?") and everything about support. My daughter Casey Marta is blessed with the flutter of a butterfly and the smile of an angel (she and 33 will be quite happy together), and my son Emmett is the king of Lynn Cain and '80s NFL highlight videos. When a 9-year-old Jewish kid longs for Billy Sims's 1981 Afro, you know he's special. There is no more noble human than Richard Guggenheimer, my father-in-law.

I've now been married 14 years, and if I'd known an engagement ring could also snag a fantastic proofreader and life/career adviser, I'd have proposed much earlier. Without Catherine Pearlman, I'm a lonely sack of crap talking to myself in the corner of a Starbucks.

Instead, I'm a happy sack of crap talking to myself in the corner of a Starbucks.

I couldn't ask for more.

Lastly, I'd like to thank Brett Favre — who didn't speak for this project, but who provided me with enough oohs and aahs to fill 1,000 pages. To his credit, Brett sent me a lengthy text explaining why he decided not to talk, and was perfectly cordial and polite during the process. I've never felt it a man or woman's obligation to cooperate with an author, and Favre is no exception.

Ultimately, it matters not. His legacy is secure.

He's the Gunslinger.

NOTES

1. Beginning

page

6 *in 1970 guided the school to the state baseball championship:* Doug Barber, "Favre's Father Dies; Family Urges QB to Play Tonight," *Jackson (Miss.) Clarion-Ledger,* December 22, 2003.

7 *"He's a big one, Bonita":* Brett Favre, with Chris Havel, *Favre: For the Record* (New York: Doubleday, 1997), p. 89.

2. Childhood

9 *Perhaps the nervousness had to do with an incident:* Bonita Favre, "A Mother's Story," in Brett Favre and Bonita Favre, with Chris Havel, *Favre* (New York: Rugged Land, 2004), p. 191.

"Irv was up on the roof one day doing some stuff at the house": Gary D'Amato, "Favre Was Toughened by Brothers, Dad," *Milwaukee Journal Sentinel,* September 10, 2005.

"When Mom went into town to go shopping": *Favre: For the Record,* pp. 86–87.

10 *"The roads used to have numbers down there":* Curt Brown, "Out of Nowhere," *Minneapolis Star Tribune,* December 20, 1992.

The family owned four dogs — a collie named Fluffy: Favre: For the Record, p. 85.

"Alligators don't eat a dog right away": Brett Favre, interview by Kevin Cook, *Playboy,* November 1, 1997.

"It got so dark [in the house] you couldn't see": Ibid.

11 *"He went out one morning, all bundled up":* Steve Cameron, *Brett Favre: Huck Finn Grows Up* (Indianapolis, Ind.: Masters Press, 1997), p. 61.

"Our family was always familiar with alligators": Brett Favre interview, *Playboy.*

12 *"I wish I had a nickel":* John Glennon, in *The Brett Favre Story: From the Kiln to Green Bay; the Story of America's Quaterback as Told by Family, Friends, and the Hometown Sportswriters Who Know Him Best,* edited by Kate Magandy (Biloxi, Miss.: Sun-Herald, 2008), p. 25.

Once, Brett accidentally shot Scott in the face: Favre: For the Record, p. 85.

13 *It could be a stick from the yard. Or a belt or black rubber hose:* Brett Favre interview, *Playboy.*

14 *"You could go out there and say it was just a game; that second place":* Irv Favre, "Competitiveness," in Brett Favre and Bonita Favre, *Favre,* pp. 177–80.

16 *"Jeff had to run through us":* Favre: For the Record, p. 95.
    When Brett Favre was a year old: Ibid., pp. 94–95.
    Along with coaching the teams at Hancock North Central: John Bialas, "Joe Graham 119 Takes Second Step," *Biloxi (Miss.) Sun-Herald,* August 5, 1975.
    Big Irv served as the manager: Mike Woten, in *The Brett Favre Story,* ed. Magandy, p. 118.

17 *"Jeff came to me at the age of three":* Bonita Favre, "A Mother's Story," p. 193.
    "I saw the catcher adjusting his cup": Brett Favre interview, *Playboy.*
    But many white families greeted the inevitability: Joan Howard and Robert Howard, *Many Faces of Change: Kiln, Mississippi* (Spartanburg, S.C.: Reprint Company, 1976), p. 23.

18 *In one game, he struck out 15 hitters:* Cameron, *Brett Favre: Huck Finn Grows Up,* p. 61.

19 *"I'm sitting there in full uniform":* Favre: For the Record, pp. 99–101.

3. High School

22 *"He was big and could run":* Irv Favre, "Competitiveness," p. 180.

28 *"[Irvin] Favre's Hawks lost most of their skill players":* Brenda Heathcock, "Three Local Bouts to Open High School Football Season," *Sea Coast Echo* (Bay St. Louis, Miss.), September 6, 1984.
    His season could be summed up: Brenda Heathcock, "Hawks Shut Down Vancleave," *Sea Coast Echo* (Bay St. Louis, Miss.), October 21, 1984.
    "I've been told that I first met Brett": Deanna Favre, with Angela Hunt, *Don't Bet Against Me!: Beating the Odds Against Breast Cancer and in Life* (Carol Stream, Ill: Tyndale, 2007), p. 12.

29 *"Realizing that I wasn't going to get any relief":* Ibid., p. 13.

30 *"At one point Brett's hand brushed against mine":* Ibid., pp. 13–15.
    Their first official date was a dance in nearby Dedeaux: Rachel A. Koestler-Grack, *Football Superstars: Brett Favre* (New York: Checkmark, 2008), p. 31.
    "Deanna and I talked nonstop every night": Favre: For the Record, pp. 106–7.
    Their dates weren't typical dates: Deanna Favre, *Don't Bet Against Me!,* pp. 16–19.

32 *"I did all kinds of things I wasn't supposed to":* Steve Cameron, "You Just Had to Know Favre's Mom and Dad," *Merced (Calif.) Sun-Star,* September 24, 2007.

34 *"He'd write letters to his own players":* Favre: For the Record, p. 101.
    The Hawks gained 342 yards of total offense in a 32–7 crushing of St. Stanislaus: Brenda Heathcock, "High-Powered Hawk Offense Pounds Rocks," *Sea Coast Echo* (Bay St. Louis, Miss.), October 6, 1985.

then scored six touchdowns on 350 total yards: Brenda Heathcock, "Hawks Sting St. Martin Yellow Jackets, 39–6," *Sea Coast Echo* (Bay St. Louis, Miss.), October 13, 1985.

"I remember after one game": Doug Barber, in *The Brett Favre Story*, ed. Magandy, p. 16.

In one game, he rifled a touchdown pass to Tommy Lull: *Favre: For the Record*, p. 103.

35 *In a 14–6 Hawks loss at Stone County High*: Randy Ponder, "Cats Down Hawks, 14–6," *Sea Coast Echo* (Bay St. Louis, Miss.), September 22, 1985.

"I guess we didn't want it bad enough": Brenda Heathcock, "Long Beach Grabs Win from Hancock," *Sea Coast Echo* (Bay St. Louis, Miss.), October 20, 1985.

The most egregious setback came on November 20: Brenda Heathcock, "Strong Play by Hawks in Second Quarter Comes Up Short, 24–22," *Sea Coast Echo* (Bay St. Louis, Miss.), November 21, 1985.

As he walked off the field: Cassie King, "Birth of Daughter Induces Beebe to Play," *Washington Post*, November 9, 1996.

4. Varsity Blues

36 *On page 110 of his very own autobiography*: *Favre: For the Record*, p. 110.

37 *Pearl River College's starting quarterback*: Amy Webb, "Favre Alone Among River's Returning Offensive Starters," *Sea Coast Echo* (Bay St. Louis, Miss.), August 14, 1986.

"You watch," he'd say: *Favre: For the Record*, p. 107.

three years of high school with perfect attendance: Richard J. Brenner, *Deion Sanders & Brett Favre* (Syosset, NY: East End Publishing, 1996), p. 52.

Granted, in the Sea Coast Echo *football preview*: Brenda Heathcock, "Hawks List No. 1 Goal: District 4A Championship," *Sea Coast Echo* (Bay St. Louis, Miss.), September 4, 1986.

38 *Burton compiled touchdown runs of 43, 58, and 55 yards*: Brenda Heathcock, "Hancock Wins Opener, 20–7," *Sea Coast Echo* (Bay St. Louis, Miss.), September 5, 1986.

He completed two, for zero yards: Sonya T. Rath, "Hawks' Burton Runs Over Eagles," *Picayune (Miss.) Item*, September 5, 1986.

The Picayune Item, *another local newspaper*: Keith Clingan, "Carriere Showdown Caps First Friday," *Picayune (Miss.) Item*, September 5, 1986.

40 *During his senior year, a classmate*: *Favre: For the Record*, p. 105.

McHale had been hired by Keith Daniels: Mark McHale, with Brett Favre and Tim Stephens, *10 to 4* (Macon, GA: Indigo Publishing, 2007), pp. 9–20.

42 *He started out throwing*: Ibid., p. 20.

43 *On the first play of the second quarter*: Brenda Heathcock, "Hawks Score in Final Seconds, Defeat Long Beach in Thriller," *Sea Coast Echo* (Bay St. Louis, Miss.), October 19, 1986.

"Don't worry, big brother": Cameron, *Brett Favre: Huck Finn Grows Up*, p. 78.

44 *"He assured me"*: McHale, *10 to 4*, p. 22.

    But Burton slipped through a seam: Brenda Heathcock, "Hawks Come Back to Defeat District Rival," *Sea Coast Echo* (Bay St. Louis, Miss.), October 26, 1986.

45 *"Did you get a chance to look at the tapes?"*: McHale, *10 to 4*, p. 29.

46 *Mickey Joseph from Marrero, Louisiana*: "The Top 100 College Football Prospects," *Los Angeles Times*, February 10, 1987.

5. College-Bound

50 *"I think Coach Carmody thought"*: McHale, *10 to 4*, p. 53.

    Favre kept things simple: Chuck Culpepper, "Trip to the Favre Side Seemed a Super Idea," *Lexington (Ky.) Herald-Leader*, January 27, 1997.

    "The defensive staff observed the players in the morning": McHale, *10 to 4*, p. 56.

51 *Whereas Favre was clocked at 5.0 seconds in the 40-yard dash*: Don Hudson, "Unknown Favre Soaring for Golden Eagles," *Jackson (Miss.) Clarion-Ledger*, September 2, 1987.

    "Michael fit what they were trying to do": McHale, *10 to 4*, p. 59.

    "No," White replied. "Let's not do that just yet": Ibid., p. 57.

52 *"When I first came here, I was depressed"*: Chuck Bennett, in Sports Collectors Digest, *Favre: The Total Package*, ed. Paul Kennedy (Iola, Wis.: Krause Publications: 2008), p. 16.

53 *"He split my hands open a couple of times"*: Ibid.

54 *McHale later wrote of what transpired*: McHale, *10 to 4*, pp. 62–64.

55 *"detailed organization and the ability to sustain long hours of hard work"*: University of Southern Mississippi, 1987 football media guide, p. 7.

    "Coach, I don't know how he can be ready": McHale, *10 to 4*, p. 65.

56 *In particular, much scrutiny was heaped upon Young*: Doug Barber, "Golden Eagles Engage Alabama in a Turf War," *Biloxi (Miss.) Sun-Herald*, September 4, 1987.

57 *"Freshman Brett Favre of Hancock North Central"*: Ibid.

    "I thought Ailrick did a good job": Doug Barber, "Young Washed by Tide," *Biloxi (Miss.) Sun-Herald*, September 7, 1987.

58 *"It was exciting to be on the sideline"*: Doug Barber, "USM Likes Favre on Offense," *Biloxi (Miss.) Sun-Herald*, September 15, 1987.

    Because Vann Hall had three separate: Sports Collectors Digest, *Favre: The Total Package*, p. 16.

    "Sometimes the coaches would ask me to try and calm [Brett] down a little": "Shoot, I'll Tell Ya'll a Story 'Bout Brett," MSNBC.com, January 24, 1997.

59 *After a couple of weeks, though, Favre tired of Anderson*: *Favre: For the Record*, p. 116.

60 *"Six bucks a case"*: Ibid., p. 114.

61 *"We sat there and just got drunk, drunk, drunk"*: Gary D'Amato, "Favre Caught On Quickly in College," *Milwaukee Journal Sentinel*, September 17, 2005.

    "We," coach Mack Brown said at the time, "have firepower": Doug Barber, "USM

Prepares for Tulane Aerial Attack," *Biloxi (Miss.) Sun-Herald,* September 18, 1987.

62   *"[Tulane] had scouted us well against Alabama and they were shutting us down":*
Sports Collectors Digest, *Favre: The Total Package,* p. 16.

"All I could think of was how much trouble our quarterbacks": McHale, *10 to 4,* p. 71.

63   *"He went over to the wall and bent over and ralphed":* D'Amato, "Favre Caught On Quickly."

64   *On first and 10 from the Southern Miss 21:* Doug Barber, "Favre Leads USM Rally," *Biloxi (Miss.) Sun-Herald,* September 20, 1987.

65   *"My problem," Favre recalled:* McHale, *10 to 4,* p. 74.

6. The Man

68   *The plays White introduced were relatively simple:* Koestler-Grack, *Football Superstars: Brett Favre,* p. 43.

Then, on the morning of September 23, 1987: "Favre Earns Starting Job for USM Against Texas A&M," *Biloxi (Miss.) Sun-Herald,* September 23, 1987.

69   *"Did Southern leave its receivers in Hattiesburg?":* Dick Lightsey, "Dropped Passes Was USM Disease," *Biloxi (Miss.) Sun-Herald,* September 27, 1987.

"Favre ran 40 yards under duress": Doug Barber, "Favre Proves He Is No Fluke," *Biloxi (Miss.) Sun-Herald,* September 28, 1987.

71   *Barber, the* Sun-Herald's *excellent beat writer, called it "a nuking":* Doug Barber, "USM Levels Louisville," *Biloxi (Miss.) Sun-Herald,* October 4, 1987.

When the Golden Eagles took a 24–0 first-quarter lead: Ibid.

The next week Southern Miss hosted No. 6 Florida State: Doug Barber, "No. 6 FSU Humiliates Eagles, 61–10," *Biloxi (Miss.) Sun-Herald,* October 11, 1987.

72   *"We got to a point where I could see we had stagnated":* Doug Barber, "Young's Heroics Revive Southern," *Biloxi (Miss.) Sun-Herald,* October 18, 1987.

73   *She had been experiencing slight vaginal bleeding:* Deanna Favre, *Don't Bet Against Me!,* p. 21.

74   *"I just blurted it out":* Favre: For the Record, p. 119.

75   *At age 40, the new head coach had been something of a surprising hire:* Bobby Hall, "Hallman Making a Splash," *Memphis (Tenn.) Commercial Appeal,* October 28, 1988.

78   *"USM is a football team that's fun to watch":* Chuck Abadie, "It's Time USM Get Recognized," *Hattiesburg (Miss.) American,* October 16, 1988.

79   *The Tigers boasted college football's top-ranked defense:* Charles Goldberg, "Auburn to Honor 1988 Team Saturday Night," Auburntigers.com, September 5, 2013.

Before 73,787 die-hards: "No. 9 Auburn Tuned Up for the Southeastern Conference," United Press International, November 5, 1988.

80   *She weighed seven pounds, two ounces:* Deanna Favre, *Don't Bet Against Me!,* pp. 22–23.

81   *"We agreed to love our daughter"*: Brett Favre interview, *Playboy*.
     As Brett was living life as the big man on the Southern Miss campus: Deanna
     Favre, *Don't Bet Against Me!*, pp. 24–25.

82   *"We've sort of broke up right now"*: Billy Watkins, "USM's Favre: From Fifth
     String to Fantastic," *Jackson (Miss.) Clarion-Ledger*, August 27, 1989.

7. Legend

85   *Within days, Bennett ordered*: Arnold Van, "USM Starting Heisman Campaign
     for Favre," *Hattiesburg (Miss.) American*, April 14, 1989.
     A CNN anchor held one of the bumper stickers: Sports Collectors Digest, *Favre:
     The Total Package*, p. 21.

86   *"When you talk about the top players in the country"*: Van Arnold, "Eagles
     Should Soar Again with Favre's Golden Wing," *Hattiesburg (Miss.) American*,
     August 27, 1989.

88   *"our entire athletic department budget was only $2.7 million"*: Rick Cleveland,
     "Survival Proves Difficult for USM," *Jackson (Miss.) Clarion-Ledger*, April 26,
     1989.

89   *"Players were sweating as they put on their shoulder pads"*: McHale, *10 to 4*, p. 77.

91   *"I just figured that FSU would be jamming down"*: Cameron, *Brett Favre: Huck
     Finn Grows Up*, p. 101.

92   *Chris Ryals, his closest friend on the team*: Cameron, *Brett Favre, Huck Finn
     Grows Up*, pp. 101–2.
     A few days earlier, a Sports Illustrated *writer had arrived*: Leigh Montville,
     "The Kid from Kiln," *Sports Illustrated*, August 23, 1993.

93   *It was filled with laughter, shouting, relief*: Favre: For the Record, p. 122.

94   *The first time Favre worked out for an NFL scout*: Bruce Feldman, *The QB: The
     Making of Modern Quarterbacks* (New York: Crown Archetype, 2014), p. 32.

95   *Favre dropped back 11 steps*: Chuck Abadie, "Hail Darryl! USM Wins, 16–10,"
     Hattiesburg (Miss.) American, October 15, 1989.
     Did the university's Heisman campaign pay off?: Robert McG Thomas, "Hous-
     ton's Ware Wins Heisman," *New York Times*, December 3, 1989.

8. Near Death

97   *In 1997 Brett told Steve Cameron, author of*: Cameron, *Brett Favre: Huck Finn
     Grows Up*, p. 108.
     In 2007 he told Mark McHale: McHale, *10 to 4*, p. 87.
     In his 1997 autobiography, he also failed to mention: Favre: For the Record, p. 123.
     When asked about the accident by Russ Brown: Russ Brown, "Southern Miss'
     Favre Has Had Toughest Road Trip," *Louisville (Ky.) Courier-Journal*, Septem-
     ber 27, 1990.

98   *"they'd been repairing the road and I forgot it"*: Furman Bisher, "The Battling
     QB from Dogpatch," *Atlanta Journal-Constitution*, August 18, 1991.

"Hell, yeah, you're gonna be alright": Len Pasquarelli, "Falcons' Search for a Backup QB Leads to a Backwoods Town for One," *Atlanta Journal-Constitution*, May 21, 1991.

99   *"I remember Scott screaming at me, 'Are you alright?'"*: McHale, *10 to 4*, p. 87.

"I had one of those concussions": Brett Favre interview, *Playboy*.

"I screamed with every bump we hit": McHale, *10 to 4*, p. 87.

Staff writer Robert Wilson: Robert Wilson, "Favre Hurt in Wreck," *Jackson (Miss.) Clarion-Ledger*, July 16, 1990.

Two days later, a piece from Billy Watkins: Billy Watkins, "Favre Should Recover for '90 Season," *Jackson (Miss.) Clarion-Ledger*, July 17, 1990.

100   *Willie Morris's landmark book*: Morris, *The Courting of Marcus Dupree* (New York: Doubleday, 1983).

McHale visited a couple of days after: McHale, *10 to 4*, pp. 82–83.

101   *"His liver is still bleeding, and we're watching that"*: Watkins, "Favre Should Recover."

One day later, Favre guaranteed his return: Slim Smith, "Favre Promises, 'I'll Be Back,'" *Biloxi (Miss.) Sun-Herald*, July 18, 1990.

"Screw that," Favre said. "I'm dying": Favre: *For the Record*, p. 124.

"There seems to be an obstruction in his lower intestine": Tim Doherty, "Favre Hospitalized with Stomach Pains," *Hattiesburg (Miss.) American*, August 7, 1990.

Dr. George McGee determined the car accident: Cameron, *Brett Favre: Huck Finn Grows Up*, pp. 110–11.

102   *"Right now I couldn't go out there and play"*: Robert Wilson, "Favre Anxious to Get Going," *Jackson (Miss.) Clarion-Ledger*, August 25, 1990.

"He feels good": Robert Wilson, "Favre Returns to Practice," *Jackson (Miss.) Clarion-Ledger*, August 22, 1990.

103   *Using a run-and-shoot system*: Ron Kaspriske, "Williston, Chipley Will Try to Slow Each Other Down," *Gainesville (Fla.) Sun*, December 2, 1988.

104   *Favre dressed for the game*: John Bjalas, "Favre Opens Season on the Sideline," *Biloxi (Miss.) Sun-Herald*, September 1, 1990.

The Golden Eagles won 12–0 behind two field goals: John Bjalas, "USM Blanks Pesky DSU," *Biloxi (Miss.) Sun-Herald*, September 2, 1990.

105   *"I want to play"*: Chuck Abadie, "Favre Gets OK to Play Saturday," *Hattiesburg (Miss.) American*, September 7, 1990.

108   *"like a damned scarecrow, his uniform hanging all loose around him and stuff"*: Pasquarelli, "Falcons' Search for a Backup QB Leads to a Backwoods Town."

On the first play, Favre dropped back and was drilled: Favre: *For the Record*, p. 125.

109   *"At times," wrote Chuck Abadie*: Abadie, "Heat Was a Big Factor in USM Upset of Bama," *Hattiesburg (Miss.) American*, September 9, 1990.

"This isn't supposed to be happening!": McHale, *10 to 4*, p. 85.

9. Senioritis

111 *"McGwire has the talent to be a great quarterback"*: Samantha Stevenson, "A Large Quarterback Makes a Big Impression," *New York Times,* December 1, 1990.

112 *On one particularly dazzling third-quarter play:* Chuck Abadie, "USM the Better Team, but Key Mistakes Hurt," *Hattiesburg (Miss.) American,* September 16, 1990.

The Bulldogs fought back to take an 18–17 fourth-quarter advantage: Billy Watkins, "Eagles Find Inches Translate into Miles Against Bulldogs," *Jackson (Miss.) Clarion-Ledger,* September 16, 1990.

"I felt real good today": Abadie, "USM the Better Team."

113 *"I remember being intrigued by Brett":* Cameron, *Brett Favre: Huck Finn Grows Up,* pp. 128–29.

114 *During the season, the hottest spot was the End Zone: Favre: For the Record,* p. 117.

115 *"I guess," he said, "I'm a survivor":* John Romano, "Shoulder Injury Won't Allow Nagle to Wing It," *St. Petersburg (Fla.) Times,* February 6, 1991.

"A yard looks like a mile to this attack": John Bialas, "Golden Eagles Facing Fast-Starting Cardinals," *Biloxi (Miss.) Sun-Herald,* September 28, 1990.

more to see *Favre–Nagle than Mississippi State–Louisville:* Tim Doherty, "Favre-Nagle Friendship Blossoms," *Hattiesburg (Miss.) American,* September 28, 1990.

The Golden Eagles won, 25–13: Milton Collins, "Eagles Shuffle Cards," *Student Printz* (University of Southern Mississippi), October 2, 1990.

Neither quarterback did much of anything: Van Arnold, "Walk-on Johnson Gets USM 'Rolling,'" *Hattiesburg (Miss.) American,* September 30, 1990.

116 *Somehow, the Golden Eagles wound up with an 8-3 record:* Tim Doherty, "Golden Eagles Nip War Eagles," *Hattiesburg (Miss.) American,* November 10, 1990.

Then, five days after Hallman and most of his staff departed for Baton Rouge: John W. Cox, and Gregg Bennett, *Rock Solid: Southern Miss Football* (Jackson: University Press of Mississippi, 2004), p. 215.

118 *On the final play of the game:* Tim Peeler, "Remembering the 1990 All-American Bowl," www.gopack.com, December 19, 2008.

As the white-and-red-clad Wolfpack players swarmed: Chet Fussman, "Favre's Rally Falls Just Short," *Birmingham (Ala.) Post-Herald,* December 29, 1990.

"Hell, I got killed," he said of shoddy protection: Cameron, *Brett Favre: Huck Finn Grows Up,* p. 130.

119 *"There's no complete player in this draft":* "Subpar Day for Senior Bowl Quarterbacks," UPI, January 20, 1991.

121 *Favre "probably will be the first quarterback taken":* Allan Malamud, "Notes on a Scorecard," *Los Angeles Times,* April 11, 1991.

hailed him "the best" thrower in the country: David Raffo, "Football Receivers, Tackles Highlight NFL Draft," UPI, April 13, 1991.

the Miami Herald *rated him "the No. 1 QB available":* Scott Fowler, "Erickson, Other QBs Bathed in Questions," *Miami Herald,* April 16, 1991.

Steinberg, finally swayed by Wolf: Rich Cimini, "Jets Weigh Signal-Caller or Defense," *Newsday,* April 17, 1991.

A Hattiesburg-based attorney with a general law practice: Cary Estes, "A Chance Meeting Started It All," *Mississippi Sports Magazine,* December 12, 2012.

122   *In recent days, the Seahawks and Falcons had sent representatives to Mississippi:* Tim Doherty, "Favre Expects to Be First-Round Pick in Draft," *Hattiesburg (Miss.) American,* April 21, 1991.

As most of the Favre attendees hovered around a large television: Robert Wilson, "Favre Goes to Atlanta in 2nd Round," *Jackson (Miss.) Clarion-Ledger,* April 22, 1991.

123   *"Dan McGwire?" Favre yelled:* Tim Isbell, "24 Years Later, Favre's Iconic Draft Photo Still Holds Up," *Biloxi (Miss.) Sun-Herald,* July 16, 2015.

"perceived [by NFL teams] as immature, erratic": Chris Dufresne, "New Look Is Turning NFL Heads," *Los Angeles Times,* April 21, 1991.

During his senior year of high school: Mike Sager, "Todd Marinovich: The Man Who Never Was," *Esquire,* April 23, 2010.

126   *Don Weiss, an NFL official, leaned:* Vito Stellino, "Don Weiss, Pioneer in Shaping the NFL, Dies," *Florida Times-Union,* September 16, 2003.

"I still believe I'm the best quarterback in the draft": Robert Wilson, "Favre Goes to Atlanta in 2nd Round," *Jackson (Miss.) Clarion-Ledger,* April 22, 1991.

10. Hotlanta

127   *Just look through the magazines:* Rob Demovsky, "Favre Honor Will Come Early in the Season," *Madison (Wis.) Capital Times,* April 16, 2008.

Although Jerry Glanville was far from enamored: Rick Reilly, "The Big Black Attack," *Sports Illustrated,* September 17, 1990.

"That Canada stuff, it's just us talking right now": Len Pasquarelli, "CFL Just Talk for Falcons' Pick Favre," *Atlanta Journal-Constitution,* April 24, 1991.

128   *The story ran on May 21:* Pasquarelli, "Falcons Search for a Backup Quarterback Leads to a Backwoods Town."

At long last, on July 17: Len Pasquarelli, "Favre, Falcons Settle on a Deal, but Several Others Still Unsigned," *Atlanta Journal-Constitution,* July 18, 1991.

He placed 70 percent of the money: Brett Favre interview, *Playboy* .

129   *Beginning with the Falcons' debut season:* Michael E. Goodman, *The History of the Atlanta Falcons* (Mankato, Minn.: Creative Education, 2005), p. 4.

"We may not be good": Reilly, "The Big Black Attack."

The team was, in his opinion, "a joke": Mark Kram, "Jerry Glanville's Unbuckled Ego," *Esquire,* October 1990.

Glanville called himself "the dark prince": Ibid.

and issued a challenge to his players: Johnette Howard, "Glanville to the Rescue," *National Sports Daily,* August 2, 1990.

"If the sucker's moving, our goal is to get 11 guys on him": Franz Lidz, "Wise Guy," *Sports Illustrated,* October 30, 1989.

130 *Glanville: "Hey, Mississippi!":* Favre 4 Ever, DVD (Vivendi Entertainment, 2006).

131 *"Throwing a football's something I never had to think about":* Len Pasquarelli, "Favre Figures Wobbling Throws Just a Passing Phase for Rookies," *Atlanta Journal-Constitution,* July 24, 1991.

The headline attached to the Associated Press story: "Chargers' Tolliver Traded to Falcons," Associated Press, August 29, 1991.

Tolliver had been nicknamed "Billy Joe Terrible": Brian Hewitt, "Chargers Misfire from Start to Finish," *Los Angeles Times,* December 4, 1989.

134 *"I was third?" Favre said:* Len Pasquarelli, "Bruce Sits Again; Favre Surprise No. 3," *Atlanta Journal-Constitution,* September 9, 1991.

One of Glanville's favorite quotes—"If you ain't cheatin', you ain't tryin'": Tim Green, *The Dark Side of the Game: My Life in the NFL* (New York: Warner Books, 1996), p. 100.

135 *"I just said, 'The hell with it'":* Cameron, *Brett Favre: Huck Finn Grows Up,* p. 133.

"Hey, I came in and ran out the clock pretty good": Len Pasquarelli, "Falcon Fans Had Braves on Their Minds," *Atlanta Journal-Constitution,* October 28, 1991.

136 *"we gotta have two plane wrecks":* Favre 4 Ever.

138 *"I was hung over":* Ibid.

"I got trapped behind a car wreck": Peter King, "Warmed Up," *Sports Illustrated,* January 27, 1997.

11. Arrival

139 *Yes, Billy Ard—a man who arrived in Green Bay:* Frank Litsky, "Happy Packer," *New York Times,* March 12, 1990.

140 *promptly ended Family Photo Day, an annual fan-favorite event:* Bob Harlan, with Dale Hoffmann, *Green and Golden Moments* (Stevens Point, Wis.: Worzalla Publishing, 2007), pp. 70–71.

141 *At six feet six and 330 pounds, with the quickness:* Rick Telander, "The Big Enchilada," *Sports Illustrated,* April 24, 1989.

143 *"I said I wanted to give him full authority over the football operation":* Harlan, *Green and Golden Moments,* pp. 99–101.

"They had too many athletes whom I hadn't considered: Ron Wolf and Paul Attner, *The Packer Way: Nine Stepping Stones to Building a Winning Organization* (New York: St. Martin's, 1998), p. 31.

145 *"I was real excited":* Timothy W. Smith, "Quarterback Favre Is a Draw in Packer Scheme of Things," *New York Times,* August 10, 1993.

146   *His name was Don Majkowski:* Paul Zimmerman, "The Majik Show," *Sports Illustrated,* December 11, 1989.

      "The transformation from Don Majkowski to Majik Man": Jill Lieber, "The Majik Touch," *Sports Illustrated,* June 11, 1990.

      But it didn't seem to with: Ron Borges, "Don Majkowski and the Packers Hope They'll No Longer Be . . . Missing Majik," *Boston Globe,* August 2, 1991.

147   *"The coldest I've ever played in was 32 degrees":* "Names in the Game," Associated Press, June 8, 1992.

      "I couldn't believe how loose he was for a young guy": Jon Gruden, with Vic Carucci, *Do You Love Football?!: Winning with Heart, Passion, and Not Much Sleep* (New York: HarperCollins, 2003), pp. 122–23.

      To begin with, Favre failed the team-administered physical: Favre: For the Record, p. 132.

148   *He was staying at the Best Western, and that day a young woman:* Favre: For the Record, p. 133.

      The next morning, he arrived at the facility with the scent of alcohol: Ibid., p. 134.

      Favre and some teammates went out for dinner at a Mexican restaurant: Milwaukee Journal Sentinel, *Favre: The Man, the Legend* (Chicago: Triumph Books, 2008), p. 27.

      Favre was able to ease doubts about his maturity: Tom Silverstein, "Green Bay Packers," *Sporting News,* April 13, 1992.

149   *When Favre told the man to get lost, the man charged:* Tom Silverstein, "Altercation in Bar Teaches Packers' Favre a Lesson," *Milwaukee Journal Sentinel,* July 24, 1992.

150   *"Why don't you just pull over and drop your gun?":* Favre: For the Record, p. 138.

151   *He grew up in San Francisco:* Tom FitzGerald, "Legacy of a Native Son," *San Francisco Chronicle,* February 4, 2006.

      At Lincoln High School: Bill Lubinger, "Cleveland Browns' Mike Holmgren Caps a Long Career with Repair Job in Cleveland," *Cleveland Plain Dealer,* January 17, 2010.

152   *Bill Walsh, the 49ers' head coach:* David Harris, *The Genius: How Bill Walsh Reinvented Football and Created an NFL Dynasty* (New York: Random House, 2008), p. 252.

      "The premise was that all the components of the Forty Niners' structure: Ibid., p. 65.

153   *"You could see he had a tremendous arm":* Josh Katzowitz, "Remember When: Brett Favre Completes 1st NFL Pass — to Himself," CBSSports.com, September 13, 2013.

154   *On Green Bay's very first offensive play, Majkowski was intercepted:* Rick Gano, "Packers 21, Chiefs 13," Associated Press, August 8, 1992.

      The Vikings were the far-superior team: Don Pierson, "New-Look Vikings Edge Packers," *Chicago Tribune,* September 7, 1992.

155   *"[Holmgren] said he wanted to experiment":* Fred Goodall, "Buccaneers 31, Packers 3," Associated Press, September 13, 1992.

12. A Packer Emerges

156   *When the Cincinnati Bengals:* Jim Oxley, "Wisconsin Football Countdown: No. 50, Tim Krumrie," *Fansided,* July 28, 2015.

"The computer said I was too short, too slow": Cooper Rollow, "Tim Krumrie May Be a Big-Time Pro Football Player, but . . ." *Chicago Tribune,* January 18, 1989.

"I have seen some very, very tough and aggressive men": Mike Chapman, *Wrestling Tough* (Champaign, Ill.: Human Kinetics, 2005), p. 207.

158   *"We had won our first two games and they were putting:* Jim Armstrong, "No-Fear a Mantra Not a T-shirt Logo," *Denver Post,* January 22, 1998.

"[Brett] barely knew the plays": Jon Gruden, *Do You Love Football?!,* p. 124.

"It's good I'm getting hit like I am: Milwaukee Journal Sentinel, *Favre: The Man, the Legend,* p. 30.

"I was all over the place": Favre: *For the Record,* p. 141.

159   *"it hurts that much," said Sharpe:* Van Arnold, "Mitchell, Momentum Doom Golden Eagles," *Hattiesburg (Miss.) American,* October 22, 1989.

Green Bay was Taylor's fourth pro stop, but he had never caught an NFL: Martin Hendricks, "Taylor Helped Favre Start Off in a Big Way," *Milwaukee Journal Sentinel,* November 8, 2007.

Somehow, the pass slipped between Jones: Bob Baptist, "Jones Not Guilty on Winning TD," *Columbus (Ohio) Dispatch,* September 24, 1992.

160   *"I couldn't bear to look":* Hendricks, "Taylor Helped Favre Start Off."

This was not the staff's way of paying homage to Bart Starr: Gary Mihoces, "Favre Carves Out a Niche," *USA Today,* September 24, 1992.

161   *It was also, briefly, the talk of the league:* Jenny Wang, "Majkowski Better, but Pack Will Start Favre," *Chicago Sun-Times,* September 25, 1992.

"Never in my life did I think": Leonard Shapiro, "The Pack Comes from Favre Back," *Washington Post,* December 23, 1992.

After the throw to Sharpe, Favre sprinted down the field: Favre: *For the Record,* p. 142.

162   *By the time Sunday arrived:* Clay Lambert, "Falcons Can't Stop Favre but Win 24–10," *USA Today,* October 5, 1992.

164   *Lynn, the Bengals' defensive coordinator, compared Favre to John Elway:* Ray Didinger, "Packers' Favre Makes His Move," *Chicago Tribune,* November 15, 1992.

"I wondered, 'Who is this guy?'": Cameron, *Brett Favre: Huck Finn Grows Up,* p. 88.

At halftime Clarence Novotny: Milwaukee Journal Sentinel, *Favre: The Man, the Legend,* p. 35.

165   *The statistics were strong:* Terry Larimer, "Pack Stuns Eagles on Last Play," *Allentown (Penn.) Morning Call,* November 16, 1992.

167   *Three hours before kickoff, thousands of fans:* Shapiro, "The Pack Comes from Favre Back."

"We've got 20 seconds to go": Kevin Isaacson, with Tom Kessenich, *Return to Glory: The Inside Story of the Green Bay Packers* (Iola, Wis.: Krause, 1996), p. 83.

"If there was one game we could have back": Jerry Bonkowski, "Hot Pack Not About to Back Down," *USA Today*, December 22, 1992.

168 "We keep telling ourselves that we had a good year": Mel Antonen, "Packers Pack It In with 27–7 Loss to Vikings," *USA Today*, December 28, 1992.

13. God and the Devil

170 *He even encouraged his sorta girlfriend*: Deanna Favre, *Don't Bet Against Me!*, p. 27.

172 *Without much warning, the NFL offseason*: Peter King, "Trip to Bountiful," *Sports Illustrated*, March 15, 1993.

In Atlanta, Georgia governor Zell Miller: Timothy W. Smith, "2 Teams in New York Want White," *New York Times*, March 16, 1993.

In Philadelphia, a crowd of 2,000 held: Gerald Eskenazi, "Reggie White's Tour Plans Stop on Jets' Pad," *New York Times*, March 4, 1993.

At his core, White was a simple man: Johnette Howard, "Up from the Ashes," *Sports Illustrated*, September 2, 1996.

"I used to tell my mom I'm going to be a pro football player": Rick Gosselin, "Coming In from the Cold," *Dallas Morning News*, September 2, 1993.

173 *("Tougher than nine miles of detour")*: Rich Cimini, "For Gang Green, It's What Coulda Been," *New York Daily News*, January 20, 1997.

"This," White said, "is what I was looking for": Timothy W. Smith, "Packers Land White with $17 Million Deal," *New York Times*, April 7, 1993.

No, it starts in training camp: Cliff Christl, "Tracing the Roots of Players Riding Bikes," www.packers.com, July 23, 2015.

174 *"After years of icy disappointments"*: Gosselin, "Coming In from the Cold."

175 *"A win over the Broncos would change things quickly"*: Jeff Schultz, "Brother, Can You Spare a Healthy Quarterback?" *Atlanta Journal-Constitution*, October 8, 1993.

176 *Before the game, White held a players-only meeting*: Gruden, *Do You Love Football?!*, p. 132.

"Every once in a while he plays young": Don Pierson, "White's 2 Key Sacks Stuff Pack," *Chicago Tribune*, October 11, 1993.

"I got thrown into the toughest offense in the game as a starter at 22": Peter King, "Warmed Up," *Sports Illustrated*, January 27, 1997.

"I want to hug him more than strangle him": Milwaukee Journal Sentinel, *Favre: The Man, the Legend*, p. 36.

177 *"I was so excited I wanted to swap some spit with the guys!"*: Michael Madden, "Favre, Packers Don't Pass Up Opportunity," *Boston Globe*, January 9, 1994.

"Being with Favre was like hanging out with an overdeveloped": Ken Fuson,

"Maybe It's True Favre Has Retired. Maybe," *Des Moines Register,* March 5, 2008.

ever since having 30 inches of his small intestive removed: Ken Hayes, "Top Ten Farting Animals (Including Us)," www.kkcb.com, January 4, 2012.

His gas became the stuff of legend/tragedy: Rupal Christine Gupta, "What's a Fart?" www.kidshealth.org, May 2015.

The Bucs were 3-7 and predictably bad: Dan Bickley, "Packers Drive by Bucs," *Chicago Sun-Times,* November 29, 1993.

178 *"I thought I could run it in":* "Favre Comes Through in Clutch," Associated Press, November 29, 1993.

"*It's like Jerry West, Larry Bird, Michael Jordan":* Rick Gosselin, "Comebacks Still Favre's Calling Card," *Dallas Morning News,* November 30, 1993.

"The field was like concrete": "Chilled Packers Thrilled," Associated Press, December 27, 1993.

180 *He then bumped into Bob Noel, the team's equipment man:* Harlan, *Green and Golden Moments,* p. 135.

14. The Wheels Fall Off

183 *"My opinion," Favre said, "was if you":* "Sports News," Associated Press, September 2, 1994.

"Brett told some reporter that he wasn't going to change: Cameron, *Brett Favre: Huck Finn Grows Up,* p. 154.

184 *He hated sitting, and rightly viewed Brunell as a threat:* Peter King, "Warmed Up . . ." *Sports Illustrated,* January 27, 1997.

186 *"If he'd gotten back in there":* Peter King, "Bitter Pill," *Sports Illustrated,* May 27, 1996.

"He knew I had a separated shoulder": Favre: For the Record, p. 24.

187 *"My headache was gone":* Ibid., p. 25.

"If I saw a teammate who was injured": Ibid.

188 *"I was actually excited about moving up there":* Deanna Favre, *Don't Bet Against Me!,* p. 30.

"I began to realize that Brett was no longer the man I knew": Ibid., pp. 30–31.

192 *"Why?" she asked. "My teeth are fine":* Ibid., p. 31.

193 *"I'd do anything to get it":* Favre: For the Record, p. 18.

"It got to the point," Favre recalled: Ibid., p. 26.

194 *Asked in camp whether he missed the star receiver:* "Training Camp Report," *San Jose (Calif.) Mercury News,* August 13, 1995.

195 *"Opie with a robust arm":* Jon Saraceno, "Pass on the Ordinary," *USA Today,* December 1, 1995.

"the NFL's best quarterback": Jean-Jacques Taylor, "Brett Favre, the League's Hottest Quarterback and MVP, Gives Green Bay . . ." *Dallas Morning News,* January 14, 1996.

T. J. Rubley, the journeyman third-stringer: Paul Rosik, "Remembering Rubley," *Bleacher Report,* May 17, 2009.

Ron Wolf signed Bob Gagliano: Doug Moe, *Favre: His Twenty Greatest Games* (Madison, Wis.: Trails Books, 2008), p. 65.

196   *On Wednesday Favre was still on crutches, and trainers:* Ibid., p. 67.

"There was nothing wrong with the guy from the start": Mike Kiley, "A Feast for Favre," *Chicago Tribune,* November 13, 1995.

Gayle Mariucci, the wife of quarterbacks coach: Deanna Favre, *Don't Bet Against Me!,* p. 32.

197   *"They thought," she recalled, "I was only feeling insecure":* Ibid., p. 34.

The inappropriate weirdness of an NFL lineman: "Referee Turned Autograph Hound Forces Favre to Make the Call," *Los Angeles Times,* November 28, 1995.

When he was told that Andre Rison: "No Star Receiver but Favre Still Shines," Associated Press, December 3, 1995.

"There are some great quarterbacks": Saraceno, "Pass on the Ordinary."

198   *"Right now, Brett Favre is probably the hottest quarterback":* "Packers' Favre Calls 'Em, Wins 'Em Like He Sees Them," *Charlotte (N.C.) Observer,* December 4, 1995.

199   *Afterward, he rightly called the loss a "step ladder":* Rick Cleveland, "Green Bay Learns What Dallas Knows: Ground Game Wins," *Jackson (Miss.) Clarion-Ledger,* January 15, 1996.

15. High and Dry

200   *"Brett Favre was one of the most sought-after people":* Tom Silverstein, "Green Bay Packers," *Sporting News,* February 5, 1996.

"I had about 15 pills left," he recalled: Favre: For the Record, p. 35.

201   *At the conclusion of Brittany's school year:* Deanna Favre, *Don't Bet Against Me!,* p. 367.

202   *"Get his tongue!" Deanna screamed. "Don't let him swallow his tongue!":* Favre: For the Record, pp. 40–41.

"You've just suffered a seizure, Brett": King, "Bitter Pill."

He traveled to Chicago to meet with four league-appointed doctors: Favre: For the Record, p. 43.

203   *The press conference was held on the afternoon:* Arnie Stapleton, "Painkillers Land Favre in Rehab Program," Associated Press, May 14, 1996.

204   *"I'm entering a treatment center":* King, "Bitter Pill."

"Every morning I would get up at 7": Favre: For the Record, p. 51.

205   *Now, hearing things like, "I saw my mom blow her boyfriend's head":* Favre: For the Record, p. 54.

Every time she arrived, Brett proposed: Ibid., p. 58.

"I realize that while I am in this program": Arne Stapleton, "Favre: I'm Going to Beat This Thing," Associated Press, July 17, 1996.

206 *"For the first time in a long time, I began to see"*: Deanna Favre, *Don't Bet Against Me!*, p. 42.

207 *"On summer nights"*: Barry Meisel, "Favre at the Crossroads," *New York Daily News*, January 21, 1997.

"due to his negligence": "Favre Said He's Traumatized by Friend's Death, Brother's Arrest," Associated Press, August 16, 1996.

208 *"Any further punishment would be more punishment"*: Meisel, "Favre at the Crossroads."

An ESPN/Chilton Sports Poll showed him to be: Jeff Richgels, "Marketing Brett Favre," *Madison (Wis.) Capital Times*, November 15, 1996.

209 *The average NFL quarterback's hand measures*: Jonathan Bales, "Exploring QB Hand Size," www.rotoworld.com, April 30, 2014.

211 *Over the final two months of the season*: Dick Schaap, *Green Bay Replay: The Packers' Return to Glory* (New York: Avon Books, 1997), p. 24.

212 *"If anyone wants to play Dallas"*: Ron Green Jr., "Green Bay Fans Want Dallas," *Charlotte (N.C.) Observer*, January 5, 1997.

"I didn't think Dallas could beat us in Green Bay": Favre: For the Record, p. 171.

For two days, the lead story on every local network: Chuck Carlson, *Titletown Again: The Super Bowl Season of the 1996 Green Bay Packers* (Lenexa, Kans.: Addax Publishing, 1997), p. 108.

213 *"Just a typical Sunday evening at home in Green Bay"*: Schaap, *Green Bay Replay*, p. 169.

16. Super Bowl

214 *Only, New England was (yawn) sort of dull*: Bill Parcells and Nunyo Demasio, *Parcells: A Football Life* (New York: Crown Archetype, 2014), p. 266.

215 *At Rooster's Café, a stuffed ribeye was renamed the "Brett Favre Special"!*: Mary Foster, "Packers' Fever Hits Quarterback's Home Town," Associated Press, January 18, 1997.

"ground zero of the football world": Jere Longman, "A Bayou Town Catches Favre Fever," *New York Times*, January 19, 1997.

216 *In another one-on-one session*: Steve Buckley, "Bayou Brett," *Boston Herald*, January 21, 1997.

In the four days before the media tour, the Favres had 52 reporters: Culpepper, "Trip to the Favre Side Seemed a Super Idea."

"There is no private life": Schaap, *Green Bay Replay*, p. 187.

217 *Except for one night where he was reportedly caught out at a strip club*: Michael Felger, "Belichick Must Take a Hard Line," *Boston Herald*, July 16, 2000.

A handful of paparazzi trailed him: George Kimball, "Favre Makes the Rounds," *Boston Herald*, January 20, 1998.

On Thursday he came down with the chills: Michael Silver, "Pay Dirt!" in *Sports Illustrated Presents: The Champions*, February 1997.

219 *At one point, bored by the long wait, Favre reached for his cell phone:* Favre: For the Record, p. 69.

"This is what we've worked for since that first meeting in training camp": Ibid., p. 72.

220 *"Black meant we're changing it":* Milwaukee Journal Sentinel, *Favre: The Man, the Legend,* p. 61.

Rison was now standing across from Otis Smith: William C. Rhoden, "Cornerback, as Always, Is on an Island," *New York Times,* February 2, 2002.

221 *"Pull your head out of your asses":* Silver, "Pay Dirt!"

"I started licking my chops": Schaap, *Green Bay Replay,* p. 212.

222 *"Once I caught the ball":* Ibid., p. 213.

"Even though the Patriots still had some fight left in 'em": Favre: For the Record, p. 78.

"This guy doesn't have any flaws": Thomas George, "Extra! Extra! Redskins Get Howard, Dickerson Dealt," *New York Times,* April 27, 1992.

223 *"Brett, I'm gonna take one of these kicks back":* Silver, "Pay Dirt!"

"It was a dagger that put us away": Jerry Rice, and Randy O. Williams, *50 Years, 50 Moments: The Most Unforgettable Plays in Super Bowl History* (New York: Dey Street Books, 2015), p. 141.

17. Low

225 *As soon as the plane landed:* Don Terry, "Now It's Welcome to Party Town, USA," *New York Times,* January 28, 1997.

226 *In the aftermath of the Super Bowl:* Paul Arnett, "Brunell Better Late Than Never for AFC," *Honolulu (Hawaii) Star-Bulletin,* February 3, 1997.

227 *"But to [Deanna], Brett Favre is the perfect husband and father":* Al Jones, "Stands by Her Man," *Biloxi (Miss.) Sun-Herald,* January 26, 1997.

229 *His life has not been an easy one:* Brad Kessie, "Henegan 'Sorry' for Killing Two Gulfport Neighbors," WLOX.com, February 8, 2008.

In July he inked the largest contract in NFL history: Arnie Stapleton, "MVP Signs Blockbuster Contract," Associated Press, July 25, 1997.

230 *In the years leading up to the Super Bowl:* Barry Horn, "Tyson-Holyfield Rematch Has Makings of a Classic," *Dallas Morning News,* February 5, 1997.

He even earned a spot on the Forbes sports rich list: Michael Lynch, "The Big League Is a Class of Its Own," *Age* (Melbourne, Australia), December 6, 1997.

231 *"I've exorcised one demon":* Dave Goldberg, "Packers 27, Vikings 11," Associated Press, December 2, 1997.

232 *"They wanted me to do more wild things":* Mike Mosedale, "Favre's Karma: Shock Jock Shocked," *City Pages,* May 17, 2005.

"He got what he deserved": "Prankster Pays for Favre Hoax," *Beloit (Wis.) Daily News,* December 5, 1997.

233 *"The quality and amount of sleep athletes get":* Max Hirshkowitz, "Sleep, Athletic Performance, and Recovery," National Sleep Foundation, November 2015.

234 *"Oddsmakers envision another trouncing"*: Jon Saraceno, "Reeves: NFC Will Win Again, but Game Won't Be Blowout," *USA Today,* January 19, 1998.

237 *They ate at George's, a fancy La Jolla restaurant*: Peter King, "A Penny's True Value," SI.com, December 5, 2007.

238 *"Just between you and me, we're going to win the game"*: Michael Silver, "At Last, the Best," in *Sports Illustrated Presents: Super Bowl Champions Denver Broncos 1997,* February 4, 1998.

239 *"No one said it was over on our sideline"*: Favre: For the Record, p. 278.
Beginning when he was seven and growing up in a small house: Terrell Davis, with Adam Schefter, *TD: The Memoirs of Terrell Davis* (New York: HarperCollins, 1998), p. 27.
"I could see nothing clearly": Ibid., pp. 1–2.

240 *"He was lying down out there"*: Silver, "At Last, the Best."

242 *"I didn't give up," he recalled*: Favre: For the Record, p. 281–86
Of the four options, the one Favre trusted: Martin Hendricks, "Receiver Mayes Never Caught On," *Milwaukee Journal Sentinel,* August 30, 2007.

243 *"I know you feel bad and everything"*: James Beckett, *John Elway* (Dallas: Beckett Publications, 1999), p. 66.

18. Something About

244 *On November 13, 1997, six members of the New England Patriots*: Barry Petschesky, "Brett Favre Was the Third Choice for *There's Something About Mary,*" *Deadspin,* November 6, 2014.
Toward the end of the show: "Lane, Bledsoe Settle Stage-Dive Lawsuit," Associated Press, March 20, 1999.
"I can't come and do your movie in Miami": Bernie Augustine, "Brett Favre Was Third Choice for 'There's Something About Mary' Role Behind Drew Bledsoe and Steve Young," *New York Daily News,* November 5, 2014.

245 *"That's the funniest script I've ever read"*: Petschesky, "Brett Favre Was the Third Choice."

246 *(his knee was bothering him)*: Rick Stroud, "Favre, Elway to Skip Game; Young, Bledsoe Will Start," *St. Petersburg (Fla.) Times,* January 30, 1998.
Rex Valenti wound up serving 60 days: "Man Gets 60-day Prison Sentence for Faking Brett Favre Autographs," Associated Press, August 29, 1998.
signed on to have Treat Entertainment sell a six-and-a-half-inch: Tim Doherty, "Favre Figurine Selling Well," *Hattiesburg (Miss.) American,* June 3, 1998.

247 *"He was quieter than he'd been in the past"*: Harlan, *Green and Golden Moments,* p. 192.
"I was even more depressed than I'd been": Deanna Feavre, *Don't Bet Against Me!,* pp. 70–71.

248 *"Brett, I love you to death"*: Mike Mulligan, "Favre's Wife Almost Threw QB for a Loss," *Chicago Sun-Times,* September 26, 1999.

249 *"For the first time in a long time"*: Charles Bricker, "Collins Bares Soul to

Bury Subject for Rest of Week," *Ft. Lauderdale Sun-Sentinel*, January 23, 2001.

"I don't want 15 years to go by": "Favre Boots Booze out of His Life," *New York Post*, April 2, 1999.

250 *"In this job, guys drink beer"*: Mulligan, "Favre's Wife Almost Threw QB for a Loss."

Training camp commenced on: Mike Freeman, "The Best from 1 to 100, and Subject to Debate," *New York Times*, August 1, 1999.

in the Acclaim Sports' NFL Quarterback Club 2000: Daiji Giambalvo, "Super Bowl XXXIV Champion and Top NFL Performers Predicted by Acclaim Sports' NFL Quarterback Club 2000," *Business Wire*, September 10, 1999.

251 *But in an August 23 exhibition game*: "Quarterback Tells of Thumb Injury that 'Ruined' Season," Associated Press, December 26, 1999.

"When Favre extended both thumbs": "Report: Damage to Favre's Right Thumb Is Obvious," Associated Press, November 13, 1999.

252 *The loss was particularly galling*: Donna McWilliam, "Packers, Favre Sinking Fast," *Chicago Sun-Times*, November 15, 1999.

Two days after the Cowboys setback, Brandi Favre: "Brett Favre's Sister Charged with Shoplifting," Associated Press, November 17, 1999.

253 *"Some of their guys were so wide open"*: "Beuerlein Is Just Fine for Panthers," *Orlando (Fla.) Sentinel*, December 13, 1999.

"I'm miffed at myself about it": Scott Fowler, "Packers Coach, Secondary Shoulder Blame After Loss," *Charlotte (N.C.) Observer*, December 13, 1999.

254 *His quarterback rating was 74.7*: Greg Beacham, "Favre Looking for Lost Form," Associated Press, August 19, 2000.

19. Chewed Up

255 *The Gesserts lived in an affluent Milwaukee neighborhood*: Adam Pitluk, "Chmura Friend Pleads Out," *Court TV*, January 17, 2008.

Then, at approximately 3:30 in the morning: David E. Thigpen, "Path of a Falling Star," *Time*, December 31, 2000.

256 *According to the babysitter, who was 17, this is when Chmura*: Todd Richmond, "Packers' Chmura Arrested on Accusation of Sexual Assault," *Racine (Wis.) Journal Times*, April 10, 2000.

The following day, after the teen and her mother: "Chronology of the Chmura Case," Associated Press, October 26, 2000.

Chmura was a vocal supporter of Republican Bob Dole's: Michael O'Keeffe, "Scandal Creates State of Shock in Wisconsin," *New York Daily News*, September 24, 2000.

257 *"He's a selfish guy"*: Chris Havel, "Q&A with Brett Favre," *PackersNews*, April 3, 2006.

258 *Football is a job [now], and it*: Beacham, "Favre Looking for Lost Form."

261 *"Because I like Brett Favre, as a guy and as a quarterback"*: Mitch Albom, "Pack Comes for Dinner — and It's Delicious," *Detroit Free Press*, October 9, 2000.

20. Big Irv

264 *"Irv was everywhere"*: Les Carpenter, "Down-to-Earth Irv Favre Became Big Hit in Green Bay, Just Like Son," *Seattle Times*, January 1, 2004.

266 *Irv was asked to return for the next home game*: Les Carpenter, "Big Irv's Legend Ironclad," *Yahoo Sports*, November 21, 2013.

269 *"He really needed an outlet to pass"*: Rick Alonzo, "Minnesota Vikings' Ryan Longwell on Brett Favre: 'He's the Anti-Superstar,'" *St. Paul (Minn.) Pioneer Press*, September 11, 2009.
"There was no one else around": Ibid.

270 *"It was crushing"*: Ibid.
"Please comfort him and pray for him": Deanna Favre, *Don't Bet Against Me!*, pp. 55–56.
"The news was so shocking that": Ibid., p. 55.

271 *"If you spent 10 minutes with Irvin Favre"*: Thomas Rozwadowski, "Irvin Was a Regular Guy Who 'Enjoyed Life,'" *Green Bay (Wis.) Press-Gazette*, December 23, 2003.

272 *Brett called his mother*: Brett Favre and Bonita Favre, *Favre*, p. 204.
It was Donald Driver, the standout wide receiver: Donald Driver, with Peter Golenbock, *Driven: From Homeless to Hero, My Journeys on and off Lambeau Field* (New York: Crown Archetype, 2013), p. 145.

273 *"By now y'all know what happened with my dad"*: Peter King, "Do You Believe?" *Sports Illustrated*, January 12, 2004.
"I just — I just can't imagine never seeing Dad again": Deanna Favre, *Don't Bet Against Me!*, pp. 56–57.

274 *"Batteries, chicken bones, coins, you name it"*: Damon Hack, "The Black Hole: For Raiders Fans, So Good It's Scary," *New York Times*, January 11, 2003.

276 *"Sometimes in special circumstances"*: "Day After Father's Death, Favre Shreds the Raiders," *New York Times*, December 23, 2003.

21. Heir Apparent

278 *"You are going to finish this season"*: Bob Wolfley, "Favre Ponders Future," *Milwaukee Journal Sentinel*, November 24, 2002.
"The talk gets old and repetitive": Dave Lubach, "Favre's Retirement Talk Boring," *Sheboygan (Wis.) Press*, April 29, 2004.

280 *For the first time since he entered the league*: Joe Menzer, "Favre Is Always Asked When He'll Hang It Up," *Winston-Salem (N.C.) Journal*, September 11, 2004.
"Favre's refusal to retire retirement": Mike Woods, "Favre's Refusal to Retire

Retirement Talk Is Not a Good Sign," *Appleton (Wis.) Post-Crescent,* December 12, 2004.

"I wouldn't do it": Rick Gosselin, "A True Packer Backer," *Dallas Morning News,* August 21, 2004.

For some inexplicable reason: Arnie Stapleton, "Favre's Kindergartner Wants Her Daddy to Quit," Associated Press, October 13, 2004.

281   *"Brett called my cell phone every hour":* Deanna Favre, *Don't Bet Against Me!,* p. 88.

Twelve days later, on October 26, the Favres released: "Wife of Brett Favre Diagnosed with Breast Cancer," Associated Press, October 26, 2004.

"He really studied it": Deanna Favre, *Don't Bet Against Me!,* p. 91.

282   *"I'm gradually cutting it down":* Arnie Stapleton, "Favre Sports Crewcut in Honor of Cancer-Stricken Wife," Associated Press, December 8, 2004.

283   *"what motivation [I] would have to play a 14th season":* Michael Hunt, "A Sad End for Favre," *Edmonton (AB, Canada) Journal,* January 11, 2005.

"I think he's had enough": Andrew Bagnato, "Teammate Said Favre's Finished," *Arizona Republic,* February 2, 2005.

284   *Much of the attention turned to Charlie Frye:* Pete Dougherty, "2005 NFL Draft Preview: Might Frye Be the Guy," *Green Bay (Wis.) Press-Gazette,* April 19, 2005.

285   *"You start questioning everything," he later said:* King, "Do You Believe?"

286   *"I played my whole career with a chip on my shoulder":* Phil Hanrahan, *Life After Favre: A Season of Change with the Green Bay Packers and Their Fans* (New York: Skyhorse Publishing, 2009), p. 114.

Later that day, Rodgers spoke via conference call: Arnie Stapleton, "Packers Pass on Defense, Grab Brett Favre's Heir Apparent," Associated Press, April 23, 2005.

Rodgers scored a 1310 on the SATs: Karen Crouse, "Packers' Rodgers Has Deep Roots in Chico," *New York Times,* January 30, 2011.

287   *The University of Illinois invited him for a visit:* Hanrahan, *Life After Favre,* p. 98.

292   *"It's 2005 and I can't get in touch":* "NFL Star Favre Fears for Family in Storm-Ravaged Mississippi," Agence France Presse (Paris), August 30, 2005.

293   *On the HBO series* Inside the NFL, *analyst Cris Collinsworth:* Pat Yasinskas, "Brett Favre Era Nearing an End?" *Charlotte (N.C.) Observer,* October 3, 2005.

295   *"Do something!" he pleaded:* Don Pierson, "ABC's Madden Said Repeatedly That Fight Appears to Be Gone," *Chicago Tribune,* December 21, 2005.

All told, Favre's 20 touchdown passes: Greg A. Bedard, "The Time Has Arrived for Favre to Walk Away," *Palm Beach Post,* December 24, 2005.

22. McCarthyism

296   *Of all the available coaching candidates:* Rob Reischel, *Mike McCarthy: Nobody's Underdog* (Indianapolis, Ind., Blue River Press, 2012), pp. 18–19.

297 *"How [McCarthy] relates to last year's first-round Packers' draft choice*: Don
     Pierson, "Youth Tapped in Green Bay," *Chicago Tribune*, January 13, 2006.
     On January 26, McCarthy and Thompson made the 100-mile drive: Chris Havel,
     "Packers Make Pitch to Favre," *Green Bay (Wis.) Press-Gazette*, January 28,
     2006.
     Then, in an interview that aired on ESPN three days: Al Jones, "Retirement
     Strong Possibility for Favre," *Biloxi (Miss.) Sun-Herald*, January 30, 2006.
     In mid-February, Bob Harlan told: Mike Vandermause, "Harlan Believes Favre
     Will Be Back," *Green Bay (Wis.) Press-Gazette*, February 19, 2006.
298 *"It's a little bit of a waiting game"*: Jason Wilde, "Favre Wants More Time," *Wis-
     consin State Journal*, March 1, 2006.
     The NFL meetings were held in Lake Buena Vista, Florida: Jason Wilde, "Wait-
     ing Game Wears on Team," *Wisconsin State Journal*, March 27, 2006.
     "No change. I don't know, once again": Joedy McCreary, "Favre Still Unsure if
     He Will Return Next Season," Associated Press, April 8, 2006.
     It was maddening, and when a TRADE BRETT! billboard: Robyn Webb, "Bill-
     board Reading 'Trade Brett' Defaced with Paint," Associated Press, May 15,
     2006.
300 *The Patriots won, 35–0, and a humbled McCarthy*: Jason Wilde, "Rodgers Put in
     Tough Situation," *Wisconsin State Journal*, November 20, 2006.
     "Tell me you wouldn't take him right now," Dave DeLand, "Favre Would Look
     Great in Purple," *St. Cloud (Minn.) Times,* November 12, 2006.
     "How can we tell he's not done with us yet?": Will Leitch, "Oh, Brett, Won't You
     Just Let Us Into Your Heart?" Deadspin.com, December 12, 2006.
301 *Fourteen days after that, he said he was uncertain*: Frank Clines, "The Favre
     Watch Keeps On Ticking and Ticking," *Milwaukee Journal Sentinel*, January
     25, 2007.
     "We have a good nucleus of young players": Al Jones, "Favre to Play in 2007,"
     Biloxi (Miss.) Sun-Herald, February 2, 2007.
     "That was probably chosen over the more candid": Mike Hart, "What Favre
     Should Pass Is the Torch," *Milwaukee Journal Sentinel*, February 8, 2007.
     First, by ripping Thompson in an interview: Tom Silverstein, "Favre Tells TV
     Station Packers Should Have Gotten Randy Moss," *Milwaukee Journal Sentinel*,
     May 12, 2007.
302 *The play was quintessential by-the-seat-of-his-pants Favre*: Rob Demovsky,
     "Favre Uses a Favorite Route to Pass Marino," *Green Bay (Wis.) Press-Gazette*,
     October 1, 2007.
303 *"As I've grown older I've become more of a loner"*: Alan Shipnuck, "Sportsman of
     the Year," *Sports Illustrated*, December 10, 2007.
304 *"He literally eliminated [mistakes] from his game"*: Chris Jenkins, "Brett Favre
     More Careful, Dangerous under Mike McCarthy," Associated Press, January
     18, 2008.
     No, they cited his "perseverance and his passion": Shipnuck, "Sportsman of the
     Year."

305 *"In a nutshell"*: Todd Finkelmeyer, "Favre Doesn't Need to Be Fabulous, Just Smart," *Capital Times (Madison, Wis.)*, January 19, 2008.

306 *"I just didn't throw it outside enough"*: Ohm Youngmisuk, "Is Favre Finished?" *New York Daily News*, January 21, 2008.

    "That's no way for Favre to go out": Barry Wilner, "Favre's Story Needs Better Final Chapter," Associated Press, January 22, 2008.

    "I didn't rise up to the occasion": Ron Schultz, "Favre's Season of Destiny Ends One Game Too Soon," *Capitol Times (Madison, Wis.)*, January 21, 2008.

23. Soap

310 *Later that day, Favre flew home to Mississippi*: Greg Bishop, "Brett Favre," *Sports Illustrated*, July 6, 2015.

    "growing old is just a helpless hurt": Mathew Sekeres and Allan Maki, "To Retire or Not to Retire?" *(Canada) Globe and Mail*, March 8, 2008.

311 *"I would say it's a no-brainer"*: Tony Walter, "Packers to Retire Favre's No. 4," *Green Bay (Wis) Press-Gazette*, March 20, 2008.

    According to Farmer, Cook "had quietly inquired with teams": Sam Farmer, "Favre Retired? Maybe Not," *Los Angeles Times*, April 4, 2008.

    When reached by Sports Illustrated's *website, Favre insisted*: Greg Bedard, "Brett Favre Said He's Still Retired," *Milwaukee Journal Sentinel*, April 4, 2008.

    "It would be hard to pass up": Greg Bedard, "Favre Might Be Willing to Fill In," *Milwaukee Journal Sentinel*, April 9, 2008.

312 *"To me," Murphy said wistfully, "he's made a decision to retire"*: Jason Wilde, "Favre's Final Sendoff Set," *Wisconsin State Journal*, April 18, 2008.

    On May 21, Rodgers arrived, only to look 10 feet away: Colin Fly, "Packers QB Rodgers Said He's Ready for Spotlight Post-Favre," Associated Press, May 22, 2008.

    "I don't feel I need to sell myself to the fans": Lori Nickel, "QB Said Actions Speak for Him," *Milwaukee Journal Sentinel*, July 2, 2008.

314 *On July 8, Thompson, Favre, and Cook spoke via*: Lori Nickel, "No. 4 No More? Favre Asks for Release," *Milwaukee Journal Sentinel*, July 12, 2008.

315 *On July 13, 100 Packers fans held a pro-Favre rally*: "Packers Fans Rally to Support QB Favre," *Florida Times-Union*, July 14, 2008.

    The day after the rally, Favre appeared on Fox News: Don Walker, "Brett Favre Details Past Problems with Packers GM Ted Thompson," *St. Paul (Minn.) Pioneer Press*, July 14, 2008.

    Less than 24 hours later, another pro-Favre rally: David Grace, "Another Day, Another Rally for Favre fans," Associated Press, July 15, 2008.

    On the night of Saturday, July 19, Favre came to Lambeau Field: Lori Nickel, "Favre Mum About Dispute," *Mobile (Ala.) Register*, July 21, 2008.

316 *An exasperated Murphy traveled to Mississippi*: Pete Dougherty and Tom Pelissero, "Favre Considers Offer Not to Play," *Green Bay (Wis.) Press-Gazette*, August 1, 2008.

"I think we have to force it": Tom Silverstein, "Commissioner Gives Packers and Favre a Monday Deadline for Resolution," *Milwaukee Journal Sentinel,* August 2, 2008.

317   *"We agreed to disagree"*: Jason Wilde, "Favre All but Gone," *Wisconsin State Journal,* August 6, 2008.

319   *"I was sure we had Brett Favre"*: "Report: Jon Gruden Thought Brett Favre Would Be a Tampa Bay Buccaneer," *St. Petersburg (Fla.) Times Blogs,* October 1, 2009.

Tannenbaum, head coach Eric Mangini and Brian Schottenheimer, the offensive coordinator: Steve Serby, Steve, *No Substitute for Sundays: Brett Favre and His Year in the Huddle with the New York Jets* (Hoboken, N.J.: Wiley, 2009), p. 12.

"Look, you won't be practicing in Times Square": Ibid., p. 13.

"Mike, he does not like you guys": Ibid., p. 17.

321   *"I have great FUCKING NEWS!"*: Ibid., p. 21.

322   *Within two hours, the two Tannenbaums, accompanied by Dave Szott:* Ibid., p. 26.

At 5:54 a.m., the plane lifted off for Hattiesburg: Rich Cimini and Ohm Youngmisuk, "O Tannenbaum! GM Makes Deal," *New York Daily News,* August 8, 2008.

323   *"Am I boring you?"*: Ibid., pp. 28–29.

324   *"It's a new system for him"*: Ian Begley, "Brett Favre Life of Jets Party in Cleveland," *New York Daily News,* August 8, 2008.

325   *"Just like home," Favre cracked:* Adam Lisberg, "Mayor Bloomberg Introduces Brett Favre at City Hall Press Conference," *New York Daily News,* August 8, 2008.

326   *"You win the Super Bowl"*: Serby, *No Substitute for Sundays,* p. 25.

24. J-E-T-S

328   *On a good day, 2,000 spectators attended practices:* Ibid., pp. 48–49.

The NFL's website broke a sales record by peddling 3,200: Peter Trinkle, "Making the Call: Brett to the Jets Is Good Business," *Gothamist,* August 10, 2008.

"I'll never forget one of the first balls he threw": Favre 4 Ever.

329   *"I heard you're not talking to the media"*: Rich Cimini, "Favre Faces Coles and Subject Is Chad," *New York Daily News,* August 14, 2008.

"There were times in practice I was wondering if": Gary Myers, "Favre, Jets Are Learning to Fly," *New York Daily News,* August 10, 2008.

Favre made his first start: Rob Erickson and Carrie Melago, "Fans on a Tear Four Favre's New $80 Jersey," *New York Daily News,* August 9, 2008.

"I feel like I'm a Jet, I do": Dennis Waszak, "After Solid First Start, Favre Feels Like a Jet," Associated Press, August 17, 2008.

330   *He and Deanna put their 3,000-square-foot:* Patti Zarling, "Brett Favre's House for Sale for $475K," *Green Bay (Wis.) Press-Gazette,* October 2, 2008.

331   *"I think it's disrespectful"*: Simon Evans, "Lights, Camera, Brett vs. Chad," *Montreal Gazette,"* September 7, 2008.

332   *"Take the shackles off . . . let him wing it"*: Steve Serby, "Let Favre Be Favre," *New York Post,* September 7, 2008.
      "I will be alright," he said afterward: Gary Myers, "Brett and His Coach Struggle as Gang Is Not Ready for Prime Time," *New York Daily News,* September 23, 2008.

333   *"He deserved it," Coles said:* Rich Cimini, "Broadway Brett Deep-Sixes Cards," *New York Daily News,* September 29, 2008.

334   *"I don't know where we go from here"*: Ohm Youngmisuk, "Favre Feeling Big Blue Chill," *New York Daily News,* October 1, 2008.

336   *Eric Barton, one of the team's better linebackers, ran over a goose:* Serby, *No Substitute for Sundays,* pp. 110–11.

337   *"The Jets have a solid chance of making the Super Bowl"*: D. J. Slater, "Packers Fans Miss No. 4, Watch Jets with Envy," *Marshfield (Wis.) News,* November 29, 2008.
      After the season, he would learn the cause: Mike Florio, "Report: Favre Played with Undisclosed Shoulder Injury," *Pro Football Talk,* November 14, 2010.

338   *"I don't have all the answers"*: Greg Bell, "Seahawks Upset Jets in Snow, 13-3," Associated Press, December 22. 2008.

339   *"I don't know," he said. "Just knowing my body"*: "Favre Admits Arm Is Bothering Him," *Chicago Tribune,* December 25, 2008.

340   *"Get your hat, boy!"*: Harvey Araton, "Jet Reject Is One Headed to the Playoffs," *New York Times,* December 29, 2008.
      "If he wants to come back and if he can put in: Brian Lewis, "Brett to Have MRI," *New York Post,* December 29, 2008.

25. A Norse God

343   *On June 5, Cook told the Associated Press that Favre:* Dave Campbell, "Favre's Agent Said Quarterback Is Still Retired," Associated Press, June 5, 2009.
      Within 72 hours, ESPN reported that Favre: Lori Nickel, "Report: Favre Has Surgery on Shoulder," *Milwaukee Journal Sentinel,* June 8, 2009.
      He explained that while he and Childress had yet to speak: Rick Alonzo, "Favre's Arm May Be Stronger Than His Desire," *St. Paul (Minn.) Pioneer Press,* June 11, 2009.
      "Let's either get it done": Sam Farmer, "Patience Wearing Thin," *Chicago Tribune,* June 19, 2009.
      On July 20, Childress said he'd: Katie Thompson, "Childress: Favre's Throwing Motion Looks Fine," Associated Press, July 20, 2009.
      "It was the hardest decision I ever made": Jon Krawczynski, "Favre Said No to Comeback with Vikings," *Brattleboro (Vt.) Reformer,* July 28, 2009.

345   *"I can be persistent at times"*: Judd Zulgad, "Remarkably, Favre's Back — Again," *Connecticut Post Online,* August 18, 2009.

"In a sight fitting the moment": Chic Scoggins, "Brett Favre's Arrival," *Minneapolis Star Tribune*, August 23, 2009.

346 *"He talked about the quality team"*: Sean Jensen, "Brett Favre Clears the Air with Speech to Fellow Minnesota Vikings," *St. Paul (Minn.) Pioneer Press*, September 8, 2009.

347 *He played poorly (1 for 4, four yards) and lasted:* Jon Krawczynski, "Favre Welcomed Heartily in Minnesota," *Associated Press*, August 22, 2009.

He went on a few hunting trips with teammates: Jim Souhan, "2008 Sportsperson of the Year: Brett Favre," *Minneapolis Star Tribune*, December 25, 2009.

348 *"You don't find too many players who still love the game"*: Tom Withers, "Favre Has 'a Blast' in Debut as Viking," *Detroit Free Press*, September 14, 2009.

350 *"They were in love with Brett Favre and he dumped"*: Mike Vandermause, "Truths About This Ongoing Packers Soap Opera," *Wausau (Wis.) Daily Herald*, September 30, 2009.

Perhaps a better representation of the mood came from a restaurant: "Burning of Favre Memorabilia Nixed," *St. Paul (Minn.) Pioneer Press*, October 1, 2009.

Aaron Rodgers, Green Bay's quarterback, was asked twice: Sean Jensen, "Aaron Rodgers' Focus Is on Leading Packers, Not on Brett Favre," *St. Paul (Minn.) Pioneer Press*, September 30, 2009.

"Never was motivated for that reason": Chris Jenkins, "Favre Said He's Not Out for Revenge Against Pack," *Associated Press*, October 1, 2009.

"I would want to annihilate Green Bay": "Yes, Brett, Revenge Can Be Sweet," *St. Petersburg (Fla.) Times*, October 5, 2009.

351 *"Favre came out on fire"*: Tom Powers, "Brett Favre's Performance a Hit by Any Measure," *St. Paul (Minn.) Pioneer Press*, October 5, 2009.

352 *"For almost 20 years"*: Nancy Armour, "Wisconsin's Ugliest Divorce Plays Out at Lambeau Field in Favre's Return," *Waterloo (ON) Chronicle*, October 29, 2009.

The local convention and visitor bureau: Tony Walter, "Brett Favre Week Finally At Hand," *Appleton (Wis.) Post-Crescent*, October 26, 2009.

On Tuesday, Schmitt temporarily changed: Paul Srubas, "Flip Flop Friday, Other Ideas Will Welcome Favre, Vikings to Green Bay," *Green Bay (Wis.) Press-Gazette*, October 28, 2009.

The event included an open casket: Ohm Youngmisuk, "Packers Fans Lay Vikings QB Brett Favre to Rest in Mock Funeral as Legend Returns to Green Bay," *New York Daily News*, October 31, 2009.

"If you're a true Packers fan, you want the Packers to win": Pat Borzi, "Mixed Feelings as Favre Returns to Lambeau," *New York Times*, October 29, 2009.

353 *The Vikings stayed at the Paper Valley Inn in Appleton:* Sam Farmer, "Favre's Play Above the Fray," *Chicago Tribune*, November 2, 2009.

"I didn't think it would be a good reception": Interview with NFL Network, "The Franchise," December 2015.

"He wanted us in Lambeau": Greg Jennings, interview with NFL Network, "The Franchise," December 2015.

354   *One-on-one, away from football:* Jim Klobuchar, "The Search for the Real Brad Childress," *MinnPost,* November 9, 2009.

355   *"Brett's mind goes beyond strict execution":* Sage Rosenfels, "Raw Brutality, and Brett Favre's Class," *MMQB* (blog), *Sports Illustrated,* www.mmqb.si.com, August 7, 2013.

356   *He nearly replaced him with Jackson:* Sean Jensen, "Brad Childress, Brett Favre Dispute Has Been Festering for Awhile," *St. Paul (Minn.) Pioneer Press,* December 20, 2009.

      "If [Childress] just manages and doesn't meddle": Sean Jensen, "For Vikings, Trust a Must," *Chicago Sun-Times,* January 14, 2010.

357   *Never much of a pregame trash talker:* Roy Lang III, "Favre Aware of What's at Stake Sunday," *Shreveport (La.) Times,* January 16, 2010.

      "If that doesn't happen": Ralph Vacchiano, "Favre Does It Again!" *New York Daily News,* January 17, 2010.

      The game was ugly: Jess Myers, "Minnesota Vikings Teammates Wowed by Brett Favre's Play," *Fort Worth (Tex.) Star-Telegram,* January 17, 2010.

26. A Saintly Beating

361   *Hargrove later said that after running off the field:* Larry Holder, "Remi Ayodele Fires Back at Anthony Hargrove's Claim Stemming from New Orleans Saints Bounty Scandal," *New Orleans Times-Picayune,* March 3, 2013.

362   *"The football turned seemingly slick":* Jim Souhan, "Curses! Vikings Fumble Away Another Shot at Super Bowl," *Minneapolis Star Tribune,* January 25, 2010.

363   *"Favre was pounded like a gavel, twisted like an Auntie Anne's pretzel":* Gene Wojciechowski, "A Lasting and Painful Memory for Favre," ESPN.com, January 24, 2010.

      One by one, teammates stopped by to pay their respects: Ibid.

365   *On August 16 three veteran Vikings:* Scott Zucker, "Favre Seems Set to Rejoin Vikings," *Manhattan Beach (Calif.) Reporter,* August 17, 2010.

      They spent the night at Favre's house: Brian Murphy, "What Brought Brett Favre Back for a 20th Season? He Missed the Guys," *St. Paul (Minn.) Pioneer Press,* August 17, 2010.

      "I feel as confident as I did this time last year": Brett Martel, "Favre Was Pleased to Come Home for his Comeback," Associated Press, September 9, 2010.

366   *"And it happened multiple times":* A. J. Daulerio, "'Brett Favre Once Sent Me Cock Shots': Not a Love Story," Deadspin.com, August 4, 2010.

367   *"I'm not getting into that":* "Favre Mum on Racy Allegations," *Chicago Sun-Times,* October 8, 2010.

      "I can tell you that obviously, I'm a woman of faith": Kate Magandy, "Deanna Favre: Faith Will Get Me Through This," *Biloxi (Miss.) Sun-Herald,* October 21, 2010.

368   *"This is an exciting move":* "Pats Deal Randy Moss to Minnesota," *Globe and Mail (Canada),* October 5, 2010.

369   *Following a 28–18 loss to the Patriots:* Shalise Manza Young, "Patriots Sideline Favre, Cuff the Vikings Around to Move to 6-1," *Boston Globe,* November 1, 2010.

Favre was recovering from a sprained right: Jon Krawczynski, "Roof Collapse Moves Giants-Vikings Game to Detroit," Associated Press, December 13, 2010.

370   *Eric Sugarman, the Vikings trainer, leaned over the downed:* Bishop, "Brett Favre."

Afterword

372   *Initially, he sat around the house and ate:* Ibid.

On the opening Sunday of the 2011 NFL season: Ibid.

374   *"It's flattering," he said. "But you know there's no way":* Jason M. Breslow, "Brett Favre: 'God Only Knows The Toll' from NFL Concussions," PBS.com, October 26, 2013.

During a 2013 radio interview Favre: "Brett Favre Admits Serious Memory Loss in Interview," CBSNews.com, October 25, 2013.

375   *"The success to date has been awesome":* Steven Davis, "Brett Favre Joins Sqor Board of Directors," SportTechie, June 19, 2013.

376   *A sellout crowd of nearly 53,000 people packed the stadium:* Piet Levy, "Kenny Chesney, Jason Aldean Pack a Punch at Packers Stadium," *Milwaukee Journal Sentinel,* June 21, 2015.

BIBLIOGRAPHY

Beckett, James. *John Elway*. Dallas: Beckett Publications, 1999.

Bowden, Bobby, with Mark Schlabach. *Called to Coach: Reflections on Life, Faith, and Football*. New York: Howard Books, 2010.

Brenner, Richard J. *Deion Sanders & Brett Favre*. Syosset, N.Y.: East End Publishing, 1996.

Brinkley, Douglas. *The Great Deluge: Hurricane Katrina, New Orleans, and the Mississippi Gulf Coast*. New York: William Morrow, 2006.

Brown, Gilbert, and Chris Havel. *A Year of Champions: The 1996 Green Bay Packers*. Green Bay, Wis.: Petasek Promotions, 2006.

Butler, LeRoy, and James J. Keller. *The LeRoy Butler Story: From Wheelchair to the Lambeau Leap*. Neenah, Wis.: JJK Sports Entertainment, 2003.

Butler, LeRoy, with Rob Reischel. *Packers Pride: Green Bay Greats Share Their Favorite Memories*. Chicago: Triumph Books, 2013.

Cameron, Steve. *Brett Favre: Huck Finn Grows Up*. Indianapolis, Ind.: Masters Press, 1997.

Carlson, Chuck. *Titletown Again: The Super Bowl Season of the 1996 Green Bay Packers*. Lenexa, Kans: Addax Publishing, 1997.

Chapman, Mike. *Wrestling Tough*. Champaign, Ill.: Human Kinetics, 2005.

Claerbaut, David. *Bart Starr: When Leadership Mattered*. Lanham, Md.: Taylor Trade, 2004.

Claiborne, J. F. H. *Historical Account of Hancock County and the Sea Board of Mississippi*. New Orleans: Hopkins' Printing Office, 1876.

Cox, John W., and Gregg Bennett. *Rock Solid: Southern Miss Football*. Jackson: University Press of Mississippi, 2004.

Davis, Terrell, with Adam Schefter. *TD: Dreams in Motion; The Memoirs of the Denver Broncos' Terrell Davis*. New York: HarperCollins, 1998.

Driver, Donald, with Peter Golenbock. *Driven: From Homeless to Hero, My Journeys on and off Lambeau Field*. New York: Crown Archetype, 2013.

Dunnavant, Keith. *Montana: The Biography of Football's Joe Cool*. New York: Thomas Dunne, 2015.

Edelstein, Daniel. *The Packer Fan(atic) Handbook.* Oregon, Wis.: Badger Books, 1999.

Ellis, Dan A. *Kiln Kountry: Home of Brett Favre.* Pass Christian, Miss.: self-published, 1998.

Favre, Brett, and Bonita Favre, with Chris Havel. *Favre.* New York: Rugged Land, 2004.

Favre, Brett, with Chris Havel. *Favre: For the Record.* New York: Doubleday, 1997.

Favre, Deanna, with Angela Hunt. *Don't Bet Against Me!: Beating the Odds Against Breast Cancer and in Life.* Carol Stream, Ill.: Tyndale, 2007.

Feldman, Bruce. *The QB: The Making of Modern Quarterbacks.* New York: Crown Archetype, 2014.

Freedman, Lew. *The Packers Experience: A Year-by-Year Chronicle of the Green Bay Packers.* Minneapolis: MVP Books, 2013.

Garcia, Jessie. *My Life with the Green & Gold: Tales from 20 Years of Sportscasting.* Madison: Wisconsin Historical Society Press, 2013.

Glanville, Jerry, and J. David Miller. *Elvis Don't Like Football: The Life and Raucous Times of the NFL's Most Outspoken Coach.* New York: Macmillan, 1990.

Goodman, Michael E. *The History of the Atlanta Falcons.* Mankato, Minn.: Creative Education, 2005.

Green, Tim. *The Dark Side of the Game: My Life in the NFL.* New York: Warner Books, 1996.

Gregg, Forrest, and Andrew O'Toole. *Winning in the Trenches: A Lifetime of Football.* Cincinnati, Ohio: Clerisy Press, 2009.

Gruden, Jon, with Vic Carucci. *Do You Love Football?!: Winning with Heart, Passion, and Not Much Sleep.* New York: HarperCollins, 2003.

Gulbrandsen, Don. *Green Bay Packers: The Complete Illustrated History.* Minneapolis: Voyageur Press, 2011.

Hanrahan, Phil. *Life After Favre: A Season of Change with the Green Bay Packers and Their Fans.* New York: Skyhorse Publishing, 2009.

Hapka, Thomas. *Letters To Brett Favre.* Whitewater, Wis.: Kitter-House Press, 2009.

Harlan, Bob, and Dale Hofmann. *Green and Golden Moments.* Stevens Point, Wis.: Worzalla Publishing, 2007.

Harris, David. *The Genius: How Bill Walsh Reinvented Football and Created an NFL Dynasty.* New York: Random House, 2008.

Heitzmann, Jerry, with Nap L. Cassibry II. *The Favre Family.* Bay St. Louis: Mississippi Coast Historical and Genealogical Society, 1989.

Howard, Joan, and Robert Howard. *Many Faces of Change: Kiln, Mississippi Facts and Sketches and History.* Spartanburg, S.C.: Reprint Company, 1976.

Isaacson, Kevin, with Tom Kessenich. *Return to Glory: The Inside Story of the Green Bay Packers.* Iola, Wis.: Krause, 1996.

Kertscher, Tom. *Brett Favre: A Packer Fan's Tribute.* Nashville, Tenn.: Cumberland House, 2006.

Koestler-Grack, Rachel A. *Football Superstars: Brett Favre.* New York: Checkmark Books, 2008.

Magandy, Kate, ed. *The Brett Favre Story: From the Kiln to Green Bay; the Story of Amer-*

ica's Quarterback as Told by Family, Friends, and the Hometown Sportswriters Who Know Him Best. Biloxi, Miss.: Sun-Herald, 2008.

Maki, Allan. *Football's Greatest Stars.* Buffalo, N.Y.: Firefly Books, 2015.

Mandarich, Tony, as told to Sharon Shaw Elrod. *My Dirty Little Secrets: Steroids, Alcohol & God.* Ann Arbor, Mich.: Modern History Press, 2009.

Maraniss, David. *When Pride Still Mattered: A Life of Vince Lombardi.* New York: Touchstone, 1999.

Marchesani, Laura. *Brett Favre: The All-Time Leader.* New York: Penguin, 2008.

McHale, Mark, with Brett Favre and Tim Stephens. *10 to 4.* Macon, Ga.: Indigo Publishing, 2007.

Milwaukee Journal Sentinel. *Favre: The Man, the Legend.* Chicago: Triumph Books, 2008.

Moe, Doug. *Favre: His Twenty Greatest Games.* Madison, Wis.: Trails Books, 2008.

Parcells, Bill, and Nunyo Demasio. *Parcells: A Football Life.* New York: Crown Archetype, 2014.

Parins, Jerry, with Mike Dauplaise. *Bodyguard to the Packers: Beat Cops, Brett Favre, and Beating Cancer.* Green Bay, Wis.: Titletown Publishing, 2008.

Rand, Jonathan. *300 Pounds of Attitude: The Wildest Stories and Craziest Characters the NFL Has Ever Seen.* New York: Lyons Press, 2007.

Reischel, Rob. *Mike McCarthy: Nobody's Underdog.* Indianapolis, Ind.: Blue River Press, 2012.

Rice, Jerry, and Randy O. Williams. *50 Years, 50 Moments: The Most Unforgettable Plays in Super Bowl History.* New York: Dey Street Books, 2015.

Ruettgers, Ken, with Dave Branon. *The Home Field Advantage: A Dad's Guide to the Power of Role Modeling.* Sisters, Ore.: Multnomah Books, 1995.

Schaap, Dick. *Green Bay Replay: The Packers' Return to Glory.* New York: Avon Books, 1997.

Scharff, Robert G. *Louisiana's Loss, Mississippi's Gain: A History of Hancock County, Mississippi, from the Stone Age to the Space Age.* Lawrenceville, Va.: Brunswick, 1999.

Schnellenberger, Howard, with Ron Smith. *Passing the Torch: Building Winning Football Programs . . . with a Dose of Swagger Along the Way.* Olathe, Kans.: Ascend Books, 2014.

Serby, Steve. *No Substitutes for Sundays: Brett Favre and His Year in the Huddle with the New York Jets.* Hoboken, N.J.: Wiley, 2009.

Shanahan, Mike, with Adam Schefter. *Think Like a Champion: Building Success One Victory at a Time.* New York: HarperBusiness, 1999.

Sports Collectors Digest. *Favre: The Total Package.* Ed. Paul Kennedy. Iola, Wis.: Krause Publications, 2008.

Torinus, John B. *The Packer Legends: An Inside Look.* Neshkoro, Wis.: Laranmark Press, 1982.

Tuaolo, Esera, with John Rosengren. *Alone in the Trenches: My Life As a Gay Man in the NFL.* Naperville, Ill.: Sourcebooks, 2006.

White, Reggie. *In the Trenches: The Autobiography*. Nashville, Tenn.: Thomas Nelson, 1996.

Winkeljohn, Matt. *Tales from the Atlanta Falcons Sideline*. Champaign, Ill.: Sports Publishing, 2005.

Wolf, Ron, and Paul Attner. *The Packer Way: Nine Stepping Stones to Building a Winning Organization*. New York: St. Martin's, 1998.

INDEX